An Introduction to Child Development

An Introduction to
Child Development

second edition

G.C. Davenport

Published by CollinsEducational
An imprint of HarperCollins *Publishers*
77–85 Fulham Palace Road
Hammersmith, London W6 8JB

www.**Collins**Education.com
On-line Support for Schools and Colleges

First edition published 1988 by Unwin Hyman Limited
Reprinted 1989, 1990
Reprinted 1991 and 1992 by CollinsEducational

Second edition first published 1994
20 19 18 17 16 15 14

ISBN-13 978-0-00-322355-2
ISBN-10 0-00-322355-8

A catalogue record for this book is available from the British Library

Edited by Patricia Briggs
Design by Derek Lee
Cover by David John Jones, based on a design by Rhian Nest James
Illustrations by Anna Hancock

You might also like to visit:

www.**fireandwater**.com
Visit the book lover's website

Typeset by Dorchester Typesetting Group Ltd, Dorchester, Dorset
Printed and Bound in Thailand by Imago.

Contents

Acknowledgements

To Jane, for all her encouragement, support and proofreading, and for letting me off my share of the household chores during the writing of this book.

To my parents, Rosa and Dennis, for their love and help in everything I've ever attempted.

To Alison Wadeley, for her patience and diligence in reading and reviewing this book, and for making many suggestions for improvements.

Finally, to countless students who have, over the years, inspired me in so many ways.

The author and publisher would like to thank the following for providing photographs for this book: Albert Bandura (page 109), Martyn Chillmaid (page 180), Martyn Chillmaid and Robert Harding Picture Library (page 187), Colorific (page 126) and Mary Evans Picture Library (pages 69 and 99).

Preface

Notes to the student

The main features of the book
- The text, which contains the essential information.
- A number of exercises designed to see whether you are understanding the work.
- Marginal comments and questions.
- Reviews at the end of each topic.
- Occasional Summary boxes.
- Occasional background readings which illustrate some of the points being made. (You do not have to know what is in these readings for the purposes of the exam.)
- Occasional suggested activities which may help you to apply your knowledge.

I hope you enjoy your study of child psychology. It is a fairly new area for psychological enquiry, yet we have still learned quite a lot about the fascinating world of children.

What the course may require from you
Modern courses in child development are designed so that you will achieve certain aims and objectives. Here is a summary of what you may be expected to achieve during your studies.

1 You'll learn about some of the main ways that psychologists have looked at child development. Not all psychologists have agreed and several have suggested quite different theories to explain various aspects of development. You'll know some of the limitations and strengths of the main theories. Some early ideas have now been changed or rejected. You need to know about a few of them, and about some of the new approaches.

2 You need to understand how psychologists apply their knowledge of how children develop emotionally, intellectually, socially, and behaviourally, at home, in school, in other forms of care, etc. You'll need to know about some of the research on children's development, and whether the research findings are scientifically acceptable.

3 You need to know about the various ways in which psychologists have investigated children's development. They use observations, experiments, interviews, case studies, etc. Each method has its

own uses, advantages, and drawbacks. You will discover what these are.

4 You may need to show that you can use one or two of these techniques of gathering data yourself later on. You may be conducting a piece of original research on some aspect of child development in your own area.

5 You'll learn how to understand and interpret the conclusions from psychological research, how to read graphs, bar charts, pie charts, histograms, and tables, as well as understand written descriptions of research. You'll also be able to present psychological data in the ways described above.

Note to the teacher

Most of the exercises and questions in this text have been used usefully in the classroom. Some may provide opportunities for classroom discussion out of which ideas for coursework may develop. It was never my intention that a teacher would use all (or necessarily any) of the exercises. I hope that some may prove useful.

G. C. Davenport
June 1993

An Introduction to Developmental Psychology

Developmental psychology is a fairly new branch of psychology. It is the scientific study of *how we grow and develop*, from conception until death. It includes trying to understand topics such as emotional development, personality development, the development of intelligence, thinking, communication, and living with others.

Developmental psychology studies the various skills and abilities humans have, including how we acquire them. The first influences upon humans are biological. As humankind has evolved, biology has affected our behaviour in a number of ways.

Great discoveries were being made in biology in Europe during the last century, and some biologists argued that many of our skills, such as intelligence and personality, were genetically inherited in the same way as our sex or the colour of our eyes was inherited. (This became known as the **nature** view.) Others disagreed. They argued that we are the product of all the experiences that we have had as we have grown, we have free will and we can change, and be changed by, our environment. (This is the **nurture** view.)

Cave dwellers
◄

Adaptation

1 What might cave dwellers have done under the following conditions:
   When it got cold at night?
   When they were being chased through the forest by a wild pig?
   When they had been chased to the edge of a lake by a mountain lion?
   When they were hungry?

2 What would a deer do under the same circumstances?

3 Imagine you are in a cave. What do you see around you?

4 Look at your previous answers. What do humans have that other animals do not have?

Review
Adaptation
Human beings are not biologically well adapted to conditions on the earth. Instead they use their intellect to allow them to dominate it.

Background reading – Introduction to developmental psychology

Many people used to believe that children were simply 'little adults' who were useful for doing chores, learning the family trade, and looking after the family's animals, etc. Their idea of childcare was simply 'looking after' the children until they were a few years old. The twentieth century has been called 'the century of the child'. This description reflects the amount of scientific and psychological interest there has been over the last hundred years or so, and particularly since the Second World War, in studying how children develop.

1 The nature–nurture debate

'Normal' humans inherit twenty-three pairs of chromosomes, each probably containing something like 10,000 to 20,000 genes. Our genetic inheritance is a mixture of our parents' genes and is called a **genotype**. A genotype is a sort of blueprint or plan of what we will be like as we grow. Some early philosophers believed that much of our personality, intellect, sex role behaviour, etc., was determined by our genes and couldn't be interfered with. This is quite a frightening thought. It means we have no free will and need not be responsible for our actions.

Nowadays we know that this early view is quite wrong. We don't always achieve the prediction of our genotype anyway. If, for example, our mother had certain diseases, smoked heavily, or had an accident whilst pregnant, or if we are close to starvation, then we may remain undersized, underweight, or have some mental problems. What we actually become is called the **phenotype**.

The 'nature' side of the 'nature–nurture debate' says that our skills are innate, the 'nurture' side says they are socially learned. Do you think that intelligence, personality, and how aggressive people are, is the result of (a) nature, (b) nurture, or (c) both? Could you explain your answer?

We are born with many abilities; for example, certain aspects of our visual system are there right from birth. But much of what we become results from the experiences we have and the people we mix with. Whether our family is strict or easygoing, what our friends are like, the culture we live in, how much money we have, etc., all combine to make each of us what we are. The argument between these two views is called the **nature–nurture debate**.

Background reading – Humankind and evolution

There are about thirty million species of living things on this planet, and human beings are only one of them. We are not particularly attractive compared to some of the other species. We shout and argue and moan. We're quite aggressive, and we're almost the only species that actually makes war on itself. We walk on what should be our hind legs (and suffer frequent back pain in later life as a result!). There are nearly five billion of us, and we seem to be one of the worst-adapted species of living thing on the planet! We can't fly like birds, or even jump very high. We're not very good in water. We can't run as fast or far as many animals, we can't hear as well as a bat, smell as well as a dog, nor see as well as a bird of prey. We have lost most of our body's protective hair covering and have to wear clothes to protect us from the weather. Nature hasn't provided us with any 'tools' like claws or sharp teeth for digging holes, climbing trees, or killing other animals for food. We are not even well equipped to defend ourselves.

The earth has existed for several thousand millions years, there have been some forms of life on the earth for about two-and-a-half-thousand million years but humankind has been around for only about two million years. Yet despite all these limitations, human beings have come to dominate the earth and all its other animals.

Over the course of our evolution, our brains have grown in size and complexity. The human brain is one of the most complex structures in the world. (In fact we have the most complex nervous system of any animal.) This has given us one major advantage over the other animals. We have the ability to *think*, to *look ahead* and to *foresee* the consequences of our actions. Thinking allows us to *organise* our actions and behaviour, and to *invent* machines and tools that do things for us. We can *organise* ourselves and *adapt* our behaviour. We can *change* our environment to suit ourselves, while other animals can only live in theirs. During childhood we acquire the basic ideas and skills which we will need later in life.

2 Maturation

Another biological influence upon us is the rate at which we mature. **Maturation** is the process of physical growth. Maturation starts with conception. All normal foetuses develop at about the same rate. After birth we learn to use our hands, to move our heads, to crawl and walk, etc., according to a particular scale which is more or less the same for most children. It is **genetically determined**. We can only learn to adapt our behaviour when we are **maturationally ready**. For example most babies can stand alone, holding on to furniture, at around six months. They can't walk unaided for another six months. You can try hard to teach a six-month-old to walk, but you won't succeed. They're simply not maturationally ready.

Maturation is the process of physical growth. When does it start and finish?

Human beings do not mature very quickly. For the first few years of life human beings are the most helpless of any species. By a few weeks of age many mammals and birds can fend for themselves. In the West we seem to need 15 years or more! Almost 25 per cent of our entire lives is spent as an immature child. No other animal spends such a long time learning about, and preparing for, adulthood.

When you describe someone as 'immature' you are saying that person is not yet fully grown.

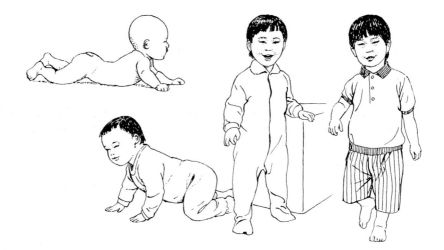

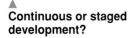
Early maturation

Background reading – Maturation

All people pass through the same stages of maturation in the same order. For example, crawling comes before walking, and we must be fairly experienced at walking before we are able to run very well. However we don't all mature at *exactly* the same rate. Some children might stand at five months, others not until 10 months. If all children mature at *roughly* the same rate, and we all pass through the same stages of development, why aren't all children the same? The answer is that at conception each person's combination of genes is unique. For example some people have genes that contribute to very early motor skills (moving around), while others do not.

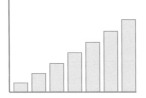
▲
Continuous or staged development?

3 Is development continuous, or does it happen in stages?

There has been some disagreement about how far our genes or our experiences contribute to our development. There has also been disagreement about whether certain of our skills, such as acquiring language, personality, a sense of right and wrong, intelligence, etc., develop through fixed and identifiable stages, or whether they develop continuously, just expanding a little more each day.

If certain skills do develop in stages (and there is plenty of evidence that certain skills do) then the following rules must apply. (We'll take developing language as our example.)

1 Each stage must have a particular kind of behaviour that is not found in previous stages. For example, the first stage in acquiring language can be called the 'babbling' stage. This does not generally occur before four months, and declines as the next stage (learning first words) is mastered.

2 The kind of behaviour (and thinking) that accompanies each stage must be different. For example, as children acquire words they can communicate with those around them. They can ask questions and

state their preferences. They did not have these abilities earlier.

3 All children must go through the stages in the same order and at approximately the same age, for example babbling (four months to one year), using words (one year to 18 months), using simple sentence (18 months onwards). This must be true of children all over the world. It is this combination of mental events (like thought, memory, intelligence, perception, etc.), and actual behaviour (such as speaking, being aggressive, solving problems, etc.) that is the subject-matter of developmental psychology.

Stages or continuous development?

It was suggested earlier that those skills which are linked to maturation could appear in stages, those which are learned need not. Using this argument, which of the following do you imagine might occur in stages?

Becoming sociable, behaving aggressively, behaving appropriately to one's sex, intelligence, language, vision, showing affection, being generous.

Review
Nature–Nurture

We are born with the genetic potential to develop in certain ways. If our environment is stable we will fulfil this potential. Early psychologists were concerned with seeing which skills were genetically inspired and appeared with maturation, and which were socially learned. Those skills which are linked to maturation should appear in stages, those which are learned need not.

4 Developmental psychology

There have always been differences of opinion about important issues in psychology. The next three chapters will examine some children's early experiences, particularly the development of their emotions from soon after birth, and through the early years of life. These chapters will contrast the view that babies and their mothers have a special bond that shouldn't be broken, with the idea that babies are capable of developing a variety of satisfying relationships with a number of different people.

Two other important aspects of individual development will also be covered in these chapters. The first is one of the earliest, most influential and most controversial of views on the origins and development of personality, that of Sigmund Freud. The other looks at how children learn, and how some aspects of their behaviour can be conditioned. The next chapter will look at some of the ways in which these theories may be applied to 'real life', and will examine a major theory of **cognition**, which explains how children think. The theory of cognition challenges both the traditional 'nature' view of intelligence, and also the old idea that children are simply little adults, claiming instead that children use different rules of logic from those used by adults.

The following chapter describes some of the attempts which have been made to understand children's moral development, including, for example, the ways in which school affects children's lives, and the issues concerning 'intelligence', and 'intelligence testing'.

We will then look at what psychologists have learned about the development of language, gender, and aggression.

Terms

There is a series of exercises throughout this book, intended to help and test your understanding. This exercise will be one of the most valuable. Here is a list of the kinds of words you will see in your exam questions. Look up each one in a dictionary and write down what each one means on a sheet of paper. Keep the list of definitions and refer to it each time one of the words appears in a question or exercise.

analyse	argue	cite	compare
contrast	describe	differentiate	discuss
distinguish	evaluate	examine	explain
illustrate	interpret	outline	state
summarise			

Consider the following questions. You should be able to answer them confidently by the end of your course.

1 What do you think the world looks like to a baby?

2 What is the first thing babies recognise?

3 How do babies learn to talk?

4 Why do most children think that things which move are alive?

5 Does our home life determine our behaviour?

6 Does watching violence on TV make us more violent?

7 Why are children from the same family often so different?

8 Why are some children friendly and cheerful, while others are moody and timid?

9 Will severe punishment teach a child not to be naughty?

10 Will children from deprived homes be more likely to become delinquent?

11 Why are we born with some reflexes, such as sucking and grasping?

12 Do dreams mean anything important?

13 Why might some people forget their dentist's appointment?

14 When do children learn about ideas like 'longer' and 'shorter', 'faster' and 'slower', etc.?

15 Do animals have language?

16 Are males the stronger sex?

17 Will children become more intelligent if they are given lots of educational toys?

18 Are childminders good or bad for children?

19 Why might a two-year-old call any four-legged animal a doggy?

20 Do babies need mothers?

Early Views on Emotional Development

In the next three chapters we will be looking at the special bond that develops between infants and the person, or people, who look after them. If you watch parents communicating with their babies you will notice a number of differences in the way they behave, compared to their usual behaviour. They talk more, their voices are lower, there's more repetition of phrases, there's more handling, and they are generally more warm and loving. Babies, in turn, soon learn to recognise the people who take special care of them, and who seem to enjoy being with them. They develop a special emotional relationship which many psychologists have seen as being extremely important to future mental health. That's not to say that everyone sees this early bond as being so important. Humans seem very flexible in the way they develop, and all sorts of early disadvantages can be overcome later. In this section we'll explore the theories and findings concerning emotional development in babies.

Many newborn animals are fairly defenceless and need an adult to look after them. Without an adult to feed the baby, many would die. Predators feed on the young and inexperienced too. Infant animals are often reared for the first weeks and months by one or both of their parents.

So why do parents and babies tend to stay together? Many baby animals appear to be born with an urge to form a special bond with their parents, and their parents have a similar urge to form a bond with them. This two-way bond usually means that the newborn will try to stay close to its parent, and that the adult will feed and protect the infant. Some psychologists argue that humans too have a similar sort of bond. In humans it is called an **attachment bond.**

The first major investigation of this attachment bond was conducted by the influential British child psychiatrist Dr John Bowlby. Bowlby maintained that this bond must be successfully made between human babies and their mothers. It forms the basis for healthy mental development. However not everyone agrees with Bowlby's views.

In this chapter we shall be looking at the following questions.

1 What were John Bowlby's views on attachment and childcare?
2 On what evidence were Bowlby's conclusions based, and was it scientifically acceptable?
3 What impact did his conclusions have on society?
4 What other evidence existed which might not support Bowlby's claims?
5 Is Dr Bowlby right?

What two reasons are given in this paragraph for why some infant animals need parents? Would the same reasons be true of humans? Can you think of any other things that human mothers provide for their babies?

▲
Dr John Bowlby

1 Early Research by John Bowlby

'Maternal instinct' is rather a misleading idea. 'Maternal' refers to the mother providing care and protection. However, males frequently provide this. And 'instinct' implies it is a fixed, reflexive response. Yet some mothers do neglect their babies, and other people can learn to care for them.

From the 1940s, John Bowlby studied how and why babies make attachments. The early theories maintained that the need to make a bond was something that was part of our biological inheritance. The idea that women have maternal instincts to have and care for babies was widely believed. Bowlby collected research findings about children's emotional development, particularly children who had been separated from their mothers. He reasoned that one good way of discovering the importance of forming and keeping a successful attachment would be to study children who hadn't been allowed to form such an attachment, or who had formed one and then had it broken.

Bowlby theorised that if children whose attachments were disrupted did not develop healthy personalities, then this might be evidence that unsuccessful attachments may lead to abnormal personality development. Bowlby also noted evidence from studies of animals who had been deliberately reared without their natural mothers. He became convinced that this early bond was very important for future mental health. The role of the mother is obviously extremely important too. Bowlby claimed that children do need their mothers, or at least a permanent mother substitute, with whom to form an attachment.

Bowlby thought that babies have a biological need, or **instinct**, to form an attachment. They need to get near to their mothers, or to get their mothers to come to them, particularly when they are unhappy, or unsure about something. Babies use such genetically inherited skills as smiling, crying, gazing, grasping, clinging, babbling and crawling, to keep their mothers close. Bowlby believed that this would be a two-way relationship, and that mothers also have a biological need to be near, and to protect, their young.

Bowlby thought that instincts, which are a part of our genetic make-up, must not be frustrated, otherwise normal, healthy mental development could be disrupted. He found several studies conducted during the 1930s and 1940s which had shown that children who had never formed an attachment, or whose attachments were threatened, suffered all kinds of emotional problems later.

Background reading – Attachments

An attachment is an emotional bond which develops between an infant and an adult. A baby who has formed an attachment to an adult will appear to want to be cared for, and stay close to, that adult. By the end of the first year, the infant will not be afraid of that adult, but may appear frightened of other adults. The infant will also become distressed if separated from those adults with whom an attachment has been formed.

Here's a definition: 'Attachment is an affectionate two-way relationship that is formed between an infant and another person.' A respected colleague of Bowlby's, Mary Ainsworth, defined it as: 'An affectional tie or bond that an individual . . . forms between himself and another specific individual.'

Early Ideas

Here is a quote from Bowlby's 1948 book *Maternal Care and Mental Health*:
'Among the most significant developments in psychiatry during the past quarter of a century has been the steady growth of evidence that the quality of parental care which a child received in his earliest years is of vital importance for his future mental health. . . . it is this complex, rich and rewarding relationship with the mother in the early years, varied in countless ways by relations with the father and with siblings, that child psychiatrists and many others believe to underline the development of character and mental health. . . . the evidence is now that the prolonged deprivation of the young child of maternal care may have grave and far-reaching effects on his character and so on the whole of his future life.'

1　How might we see '. . . this complex, rich and rewarding relationship with the mother . . .' in action?

2　Put this sentence in your own words: '. . . prolonged deprivation of the young child of maternal care may have grave and far-reaching effects on his character and so on the whole of his future life.'

3　What sort of 'grave and far-reaching effects' do you think maternal deprivation might have?

Attachments

1　What is meant by the term 'attachment'?

2　Outline Bowlby's main conclusion about the relationship between babies and mothers.

3　What sorts of things do parents do which might encourage the baby to attach to them? (HINT: look back to your answer to Question 1 in the previous exercise.)

4　Why do you imagine mothers might want to attach to their babies?

5　Is attachment the result of genetic factors which we are born with, or do we learn to make attachments, or both? Give reasons for your answer. (HINT: Consider your last two answers.)

Review
Bowlby on attachments

John Bowlby believed that humans have some biological need to have a close, loving bond with their mothers, or a permanent substitute mother. If this bond isn't allowed to form, or is broken, emotional development will be disrupted.

Background reading – Biological needs or instincts

Instincts are unlearned patterns of behaviour that exist in all members of a particular species, and which appear under certain circumstances. We are born with certain instincts which will automatically make us behave in certain ways when particular things happen. If something suddenly frightens us, our instinct to survive prepares our bodies for running away, fighting, etc. These instincts are said to have 'survival value'. Different instincts and reflexes exist in different species, for example, male monkeys have an instinct that triggers threatening behaviour towards other males who challenge them for their mate. Lionesses do the same if some danger threatens their cubs. Male sticklebacks will attack anything that is the same colour as themselves. (Why do you think this might be?)

Bowlby used the case histories of some of his 'patients'. A case study is a detailed study of the background of one individual (or a group whose members have had identical experiences).

Observations, interviews, ratings, test results, school and other reports all go to make up the case history.

Bowlby sees a possible link between maternal separation and disturbed behaviour during adolescence.

2 Bowlby's evidence – babies need their mothers

Bowlby's evidence comes from his own research, other research on children, and animal studies. We will study the first two.

During the 1930s and 1940s, Bowlby worked at a clinic for mentally disturbed adolescents. Between 1936 and 1939 he studied the case histories of 44 of his patients all of whom were known to be thieves and a few of whom had been convicted of theft. Their case notes revealed that 17 of them (39 per cent) had been separated from their mothers for six months or more before they were five years old. Bowlby claimed that this **maternal separation** would have disrupted the children's attachments. He took another 44 adolescents who had emotional problems, but who were not thieves. Only two of them had been separated from their mothers. Bowlby concluded from these observations that maternal deprivation contributes to delinquency.

44 Juvenile Thieves

Bowlby published his conclusions in a scientific paper entitled *44 Juvenile Thieves* in which he states: 'There is a very strong case indeed for believing that prolonged separation of a child from his mother (or mother substitute) during the first five years of life stands foremost among the causes of delinquent character development.'

Comment: Bowlby is saying that separating children from their mothers for some time, during the first five years of the children's lives, makes it more likely that the children will behave like delinquents. His evidence in this study comes from finding almost 40 per cent of a small sample of just 44 thieves had spent some time apart from their mothers during their early childhood. He seems to have overlooked many other variables which could equally well explain their delinquent behaviour, including the reasons for the separation in the first place, and what had happened to the children following the separation.

Causes of delinquency

Let's take an imaginery delinquent who was maternally deprived as a child. Let's look at the reasons for the separation. Imagine that the mother was an alcoholic who wasn't able to care for her son, and that the father looked after him most of the time. Imagine that when the boy was two years old the mother had an accident and had to go into hospital for several months to recover. The father had to get a job to pay hospital fees, transport, etc., so the boy was cared for by a neighbour.

1 Who cared for the child most of the time before he was two years old?

2 Who is the child mostly being separated from?

3 Suggest a possible explanation for any distress the child shows, apart from maternal deprivation.

4 Imagine that this child is a teenager, living in London, during the economic depression before the war. If you can't imagine, find out what it was like, and give possible reasons for why he might become a delinquent.

John Bowlby's *44 Juvenile Thieves* was a biased sample since the subjects were drawn from a target population of juvenile thieves. If we wanted to study the effects of maternal separation, our target population should be 'all those who had been separated', not 'all juvenile thieves'. Children get separated from their mothers for all sorts of reasons, for example, death, long-term hospitalisation, divorce, etc. They don't all become delinquents. Why should short-term deprivation lead to delinquency, when long-term deprivation may not?

John Bowlby's analysis of his case studies revealed that 14 of the 17 juvenile thieves who had been maternally deprived were particularly cold and uncaring about their crimes, their victims, or even themselves. They seemed to feel no shame for what they'd done. They appeared not to have any guilt feelings. They admitted that they almost certainly would continue to steal. They seemed quite detached from normal standards of decency. Bowlby believed that these cold and uncaring youngsters had suffered greatly from losing their mothers' love. They appeared to be incapable of normal emotion. Bowlby described their condition as **affectionless psychopathy**. Only two of the sample of non-thieves showed similar affectionless symptoms.

A sample is a group of people who are going to be studied. A target population is all those who could be studied and from whom the sample will be drawn.

In psychology **affect** generally refers to such human mental events as emotion, mood, feelings, etc. **Psychopath** used to be the general term which described someone who had no moral feelings, no sense of guilt or shame for anything they had done.

---

44 Juvenile Thieves

Outline the main scientific objections to Bowlby's study of juvenile thieves.

Other research on children noted by Bowlby

Bowlby believed that he had found a link between early social experience and later personality problems. He researched the psychological literature to see if he could find any support for this hypothesis. (A hypothesis is a statement for which researchers try to find support.)

Spitz and Wolf

In the 1940s **Rene Spitz** and **Katharine Wolf** had observed 123 babies during the first year of their lives. They were being cared for by their unmarried mothers in a penal institution. When the infants were between six and eight months old their mothers were temporarily moved to another block and the infants were looked after by other people. During the three-month separation each child either did not see the mother at all, or at best saw her once a week. Each baby was

Review
Bowlby's own research

From his own studies of 44 juvenile thieves, Bowlby concluded that being separated from the person with whom one had formed an attachment may lead to retarded emotional development, characterised by a lack of normal feelings. Delinquency would be one symptom of this affectionless psychopathy.

John Bowlby became well known and highly respected for his research on the early mother–child relationship. He collected findings from several other studies.

looked after by the mother of another child, or a woman in the later stages of pregnancy. Spitz and Wolf noted that the babies cried more, they lost their appetites, and they failed to gain weight. The researchers concluded that these reactions were the result of being separated from their mothers. When they were reunited with their mothers their conditions returned to what they had been before the separation.

Do you think these reactions show that each child is missing its mother? Can you think of any other possible explanation for their behaviour?

Comment: Spitz and Wolf showed that there are short-term physical effects of maternal deprivation, despite the nursing they received. But would these effects continue if other adults continued to provide high-quality loving care? We don't know what these babies were like as adults, so we don't know if their separation had any permanent effects. This study doesn't prove that babies need their mothers, but it does show that they become upset and depressed when their routines are disturbed.

Goldfarb

A longitudinal study is a study of a group of people over a period of time – usually months or years. We can see the effects of age or changing situations.

Bowlby also noted the conclusions of a longitudinal study of two groups of 15 orphans by a New York psychologist, **William Goldfarb**, in 1943. The children in each group were matched for sex, age, and the social class background of their parents. Almost all of one group had been fostered from an understaffed orphanage before they were nine months old, and had grown up in a normal family. The other group had all spent at least the first three years in the orphanage before being fostered. Goldfarb visited each child four times. Firstly when they were three years old, then at six, eight, and 12. He measured their intelligence, language skills, social maturity, ability to form relationships, etc. In each case the children adopted early did much better than the children adopted after three years in the orphanage. This was just the kind of evidence Bowlby was after since it showed that those who had a mother – or a mother figure - earliest did best.

Comment: The children may have had quite different intellectual capacities to begin with. Remember Goldfarb matched the two samples for age, sex, and social class background. He didn't match them for intelligence. It isn't possible to test the intelligence of babies. It's quite likely that the children who were adopted earliest were chosen by their new parents because they appeared more lively, more alert, and brighter as babies. If they were brighter as babies they may continue to be bright as they grow up. Also, the children brought up in the orphanage lacked all sorts of stimulation and contact, not just maternal stimulation. For the first nine months they were isolated in cubicles to prevent the spread of any infectious diseases, and so had little human contact. This group lived in almost complete social isolation during the first year of life, and the next two years weren't much better as the nurses didn't have adequate training or the time to spend long with any individual child. This severe lack of contact and stimulation may well have an effect on future development, which has nothing to do with being separated from one's mother.

Spitz

Rene Spitz also studied some children who were raised in poor orphanages in South America. The orphanages were understaffed, and the staff were overworked. They concentrated on the children's physical care and didn't usually have time to spend handling or stimulating the children.

The children were completely indifferent and very unresponsive. They had very little appetite and were undersized and underweight for their age. They appeared unnaturally depressed and passive. Spitz claimed that children who were deprived of adults to form emotional bonds with for just three months would be highly unlikely ever to recover.

Comment: These children were reared in orphanages which provided only physical care. Spitz and Wolf and Bowlby identified the lack of emotional stimulation to be the cause of the children's severe depression. However, the orphanages also failed to provide any other stimulation such as play, games, nature walks, visits, etc. It may be this lack of intellectual stimulation as much as the lack of emotional stimulation that contributed to their depression.

Bowlby also noted the findings of some animal studies. Many newborn animals are fed, protected, and generally cared for by their mothers. Some animals, such as geese and other birds, may be born with an instinct to follow the first thing they see. Bowlby thought that evolution had determined that mothers should look after their offspring.

Hinde and Harlow

Some experiments were conducted by **Robert Hinde** at London Zoo, and by **Harry Harlow** in Wisconsin, USA, which deliberately removed newborn baby monkeys from their mothers and reared them in isolation to see how they coped when reintroduced to the rest of the laboratory-reared monkeys later. Even monkeys isolated for only a few weeks showed odd behaviour, and the longer they were isolated the more disturbed their behaviour appeared. Bowlby claimed that this provided further evidence that babies need their mothers.

Comment: It is always unwise to apply the findings of studies of lower-order animals to human development. We can think and behave in ways that animals cannot. Also, these animals were not simply being maternally deprived. They were being removed from their mothers, and from all social and other experiences. Their behaviour may be influenced by their total isolation, rather than just the separation from their mothers.

Evidence from many other observations, correlational studies, and case studies was reported by Bowlby throughout the 1950s and 1960s. Although he modified some of his earlier claims, Bowlby still maintained that the evidence supports the view that babies need their mothers, or a permanent substitute mother, and that separation during the first five years must be avoided.

During the 1930s and 1940s researchers seemed to be concentrating exclusively on maternal deprivation, as though it was the only kind of deprivation that mattered.

Many baby animals stay close to the first thing they see. This is probably an instinctive reaction. Presumably the first thing they see is likely to be their mother, who will look after them. They have to learn what an adult of their species looks like. This learning is called **imprinting**.

James and Joyce Robertson

Bowlby was impressed by some observations conducted by his colleagues **James and Joyce Robertson** in England between 1948 and 1952, and later during the 1960s. These concerned children, mostly between 18 months and three years old, who went into hospital or residential nurseries, for periods of from a few days to several weeks. The Robertsons were convinced that separating babies from their mothers was harmful. The medical profession disagreed, however, so they obtained a cine camera and made eight filmed observations of children during their separation which could be shown to those involved in caring for children.

Here is a summary of the observations of one separated child.

John (aged 17 months) was put into a fairly typical residential nursery for nine days while his mother had a second child in hospital. His father was at work all day, and there were no relatives near by to look after him. Four of the five other children at the nursery had been there almost all of their lives. They were aged between 15 months and two years and were noisy, demanding, and aggressive. John was a quiet, loving child. He seemed troubled by the noise and fighting going on around him, and tried to get near the nurses for some attention. They had to spend most of their time with the more demanding children, and John was left out. His father visited him in the evening, and John was obviously happy to see him, and wanted to go home with him. On one occasion John fetched his 'outside shoes'. The child continued to try to get some attention from the nurses, and even when he succeeded they soon had to put him down to tend to one of the others. John protested at first, and became angry that he couldn't get attention. After some days John's distress worsened. He started to cry pitifully, for long periods of time.

This distress lasted for several days. The nurses gave John all the attention they could, but it was nowhere near enough. He began to refuse food, and he wouldn't sleep. He had a slight cold, and was sick. With each day that passed John's condition worsened. His cries of distress became huge sobs of despair.

As the separation neared its end, John's behaviour changed again. He stopped trying to get near to the nurses. Instead he would play with whatever toys he could, particularly a large cuddly toy. He began to ignore his father on his nightly visits. John slowly became emotionally detached. When his mother finally came he didn't seem to want to know her. He wouldn't go to her, wouldn't look at her, and resisted her attempts to comfort him. John had started by being loving, and seeking companionship. Over the nine-day separation he had changed to being distressed, despairing, and finally to becoming emotionally detached.

Over the next few months, it was obvious that John had changed. He cried more, had occasional tantrums, and didn't show affection as he used to. One day, when John was six years old, he looked up at his mother and said 'Mummy, why am I so horrible to you?' His early experiences may have had long-term effects.

The Robertsons' research was a series of naturalistic observations. A naturalistic observation is carried out in the subject's natural environment. Although the residential nursery wasn't John's usual environment, it was where he was placed for several days, and so can be regarded as his natural environment for those nine days.

One separated child

1 Why was John separated from his parents?

2 How many children were in the nursery altogether?

3 What was the general level of behaviour like?

4 How did John respond in the first few days?

5 What was John's attitude towards his father's visits in the early days?

6 What changes occurred in John's behaviour after the first few days?

7 How does the passage describe the change in John's emotional state?

8 How would you describe John's behaviour, as the separation came to an end?

9 How did John's behaviour change in the months after the separation?

10 Does this study prove that maternal separation leads to emotional instability? Explain your answer.

After making several such studies, the Robertsons concluded that children who are separated from their mothers pass through the same sequence of behaviour. It starts with **distress**. This gives way to **despair**, and finally becomes **detachment**. Detachment refers to how the children refuse to allow anyone to become involved with them.

Separated children

1 What is meant by 'maternal deprivation'?

2 What name did John Bowlby give to the condition which described someone who appeared to have no emotions and no guilt feelings?

3 Bowlby claimed that we would have developed a need to be near our mothers through evolution because it would have had some 'survival value'. What does 'survival value' mean?

4 Summarise and evaluate Bowlby's evidence from these three studies on children.

Review
Other research on children

John Bowlby's collection of studies of institutionalised children suggested to him that the lack of a mother can have disastrous consequences for healthy mental development. However, all the studies he quoted can be interpreted in other ways.

How convincing is Bowlby's evidence so far?

Bowlby had thought that a useful way to discover the effects of forming attachments was to study children (and animals) who either had not formed them, or who had suffered disrupted attachments. His training as a psychotherapist led him to believe that the mother–child bond is very important in human emotional development. Therefore he would concentrate on finding what happens when the bond isn't able to develop normally.

There are two ways to do this. One is to find older children or adults who are emotionally disturbed in some way, and look back at their early relationships. He did this with his *44 Juvenile Thieves*

A psychotherapist is someone who tries to understand and treat people's mental or behavioural problems.

Bowlby's whole approach starts with
the assumption that babies need
their mothers. He largely ignores
other influences.

study. The other way is to find young children who don't have normal bonding and see what they are like later. This was Goldfarb's and Spitz and Wolf's approach.

There are three possible problems with Bowlby's approach. First, his training led him to believe that the mother–child bond is all important. Nature has given the job of infant bonding (and later childcare) exclusively to women, according to Bowlby. He therefore only looked for evidence which involved children who had been separated from their mothers. He was less interested in children who were equally separated from their fathers or who were being reared by other people.

Second, older people (e.g. the juvenile thieves) may have had all sorts of experiences which pushed them towards emotional disturbance which have nothing to do with their early relationships with their mothers. Bowlby takes the one variable, *being separated from one's mother* and assumes that it is responsible for another variable, *becoming emotionally disturbed*. Thus he ignores all the other possible explanations for the disturbance.

Variables are any aspects of people
or situations which might affect how
someone else thinks or behaves.

Third, finding that people who were deprived of many forms of attention when they were babies have some disturbed behaviour, and assuming that only one of the forms of the early deprivation (from a mother) is important, is highly selective to say the least!

Exercise

1 Name one study that shows that children who make early attachments are better adjusted than those who do not.

2 How far does this study support the claim that deprivation of an early attachment leads to emotional and other disturbances later?

3 Name as many of the types of stimulation that infants might benefit from as you can.

4 Who could provide each of the types of stimulation you have identified?

Background reading

Although we must be cautious in accepting all of the early evidence, there is no doubt that if babies and young children are separated from their special caregivers they may well suffer. Whether they suffer at all, the kind of suffering, and the extent of any suffering will depend on a number of factors.

One of these factors is age of the children. Very young infants who have not formed attachments are less likely to be affected by any separation. Older children who can understand what is happening to them are also less likely to suffer. Another factor would be what happens to the children during the separation. If they are well cared for then any effects should be minimised. Also how securely they are attached to their caregiver will affect how they cope with being cared for by someone else. Finally, if they have been separated previously and know what is likely to happen to them, this may also have some effect.

3 The Impact of John Bowlby's theories

John Bowlby's theories were very popular in the 1950s and 1960s. The World Health Organisation (WHO) quickly supported Bowlby's claims. They described him as 'the wise man of the Western World'. In 1951 a WHO Expert Committee concluded that 'permanent damage to the emotional health of the future generation' could be caused by putting children in day nurseries!

Bowlby's theories also seemed to explain many of the problems that parents and doctors had noticed themselves. What he said about children and mothers seemed to fit the facts. However there may have been political implications. Men were returning home from the war and needed jobs. Women were being encouraged to give up their jobs in favour of the men. Looking after children would make it impossible to do a full-time job.

Several professions concerned with children began to change some of their practices to avoid unnecessary separation of mothers and children. For example, largely as a result of the Robertsons' and Bowlby's claims, many maternity wards started allowing young children to stay with their mothers for longer periods, both before and after the delivery. In some cases sleeping facilities were made available for children to have their naps and still be near their mothers when they woke up. In short- and long-stay children's wards, mothers were encouraged to spend more time with their children. Overnight accommodation was often provided in more serious cases so the mother would be near by if the child woke up. Ward mothers were appointed in some areas. They were usually local women who spent time playing with the children.

Many social workers were taught to regard the separation of a child from its mother as the worst possible solution to the family's problems. Bowlby had claimed that 'a bad home is better than the best institution'. Whatever difficulties stood in the way of the mother and the child staying together, those difficulties must be overcome if at all possible.

Even some aspects of the law were changed to give more rights and benefits to parents. Family allowance benefits, single-parent allowances, housing benefits and so on have all been used, during the last 30 years or so, to support the mother and child. These were other ways of making it possible for mothers to give up their jobs. Many feminists have resented the way that women have been encouraged to stay at home with the children, and discouraged from having a career. They also complain that the mother is automatically blamed if anything goes wrong with the children.

Many influential organisations began to recognise the contribution that Bowlby's theories were making to our understanding of early childhood. His conclusions did seem to fit the facts, although some critics claimed that they were also socially 'convenient'.

Bowlby's influence

Outline some of the influences that Bowlby's work has had on childcare practices during the last 30 years.

Review
Bowlby's influence

Bowlby and his supporters produced theories and explanations that were very influential, particularly amongst those concerned with childcare, such as social workers, nurseries, and the health services. However many saw the implications of his theories being unfair to women.

4 Some studies which challenge Bowlby's views

Bowlby, and others, have consistently pointed to the importance of the early years for normal healthy development. Other researchers, notably **Ann** and **Alan Clarke**, have consistently challenged this view. They do not believe that the early years of life have such great influences on future mental health, and on our behaviour, as Bowlby claimed. There have been some studies of baby animals and humans who have been separated from their parents which do not support John Bowlby's claims. We'll mention some of them here.

The Bulldogs Bank study

The Bulldogs Bank children all had very similar previous experiences and so can be described as a case study.

At the end of the Second World War **Anna Freud** and **Sophie Dann** began a *case study* of six war orphans who, with their mothers, were put into concentration camps in Germany during World War Two. Their mothers died within a year or so, and the infants were looked after by many of the other prisoners in a ward for motherless children in a transit camp. Conditions were very hard, food was scarce, and there were no toys. Forming any secure attachments with an adult would have been impossible as many of the prisoners were moved during their captivity. After the war the infants were moved to several camps, until they were eventually brought to a reception centre in the Lake District in England.

Maternal deprivation means having had a relationship with one's mother, and then losing it. **Maternal privation** means never having formed a relationship at all with one's mother.

On arrival the youngest was about three years old, and the oldest was about three years and 10 months. They had several things in common. For example they had all been *maternally privated* and could not really have known their mothers. They had all arrived at the transit camp before they were a year old. They had always been together, had been moved around a lot, and so were not pleased at being moved again. (After two months in the reception centre they were moved again, to a children's home called Bulldogs Bank.) They were very under-stimulated as they'd never had anyone looking after them for long enough to offer them much stimulation. For example, they couldn't talk very much, and they mostly used a few German and Czech swear words. They didn't know what to do with normal toys, and they destroyed all of the toys they could find, and most of the furniture too! They each adopted one special toy, usually a cuddly toy, which they kept near them and always took to bed with them.

The children didn't seem to have the normal feelings of three- to four-year-olds. They were hostile, aggressive or indifferent towards adults, and destructive towards toys and furniture.

The children were all fairly hostile and aggressive towards adults, or very cold and uninterested in them. They would only turn to an adult if they actually needed something, otherwise they wouldn't take any notice of adults at all. One last thing they had in common was that they were totally devoted to each other. They did everything together and refused to be separated for any reason. For example, if one couldn't go out, none would want to go. If one woke up at night the others would also soon be awake. When one stopped eating, the others would soon stop too. They did everything as a group. There wasn't any single child who was always the leader, each would take the lead in different activities. To put it simply, they appeared to be totally attached to each other.

Although they had different needs it was impossible to treat them as individuals since they were always together as a group. No one child was dominant all the time and they cooperated over nearly everything. Eventually they learned to speak and play like normal children. Gradually they formed emotional relationships with some of the adult members of staff.

They slowly recovered from the early privation, but remained attached to each other. What this study shows is that children can survive without mothers, although we do not know if any of them suffered emotional problems in their later lives.

Constant patient and loving care from their nurses slowly helped these children to behave more reasonably. They formed some emotional relationships, and gradually became more independent. Their early experiences had had a powerful effect, but the children were recovering from them.

The Bulldogs Bank children

1 What kind of mothering do you think the children had during their first few years?

2 How would you describe and explain their behaviour towards each other?

3 What does John Bowlby mean by 'affectionless psychopathy', and what things might cause it?

4 Would the hypothesis 'ignoring the children when they were being disruptive and rewarding them when they were being good' have worked with these children when they first arrived at Bulldogs Bank? Give reasons for your answer.

5 Bowlby said that children who hadn't made attachments to their mothers would suffer later. What alternative hypothesis might the Bulldogs Bank study suggest instead?

Review
The Bulldogs Bank studies

The six war orphans studied by Freud and Dann in the late 1940s were maternally privated, but had made very strong attachments to each other. Since there were no continuous caregivers, and little else to offer stimulation, the babies provided social stimulation for each other.

Studies of children brought up in institutions show they do not automatically develop the symptoms of affectionless psychopathy. What they are like as adolescents and adults largely seems to depend on factors such as whether they had ever formed an attachment, whether they had formed one which had been broken, and how long they were in the institution before being adopted. **Barbara Tizard and Jill Hodges** found that children who spent most of their childhood in an institution could still form loving relationships. We will return to this later.

It is too simple to say that children must form attachments during a sensitive period. Many factors are involved in the likelihood of successful attachments being formed.

Severe deprivation and isolation

Koluchova

In 1972 **Jarmila Koluchova** reported the case of identical twin boys in Czechoslovakia who had suffered severe deprivations. They were born in September 1960. Their mother had died shortly after they were born and their father couldn't really cope. At the age of eleven months they were taken into a children's home where they were found to be normal, healthy children. Their father remarried within

The twins had been cared for, mainly in a nursery, until they were 18 months old. They then returned home to their father and stepmother.

Until they were taken away from their parents at seven years of age, the twins received no love and little care from their parents. They were assessed to be at the same stage of development as a normal three-year-old. (Their stepmother was eventually sent to prison for four years for her neglect of the children.)

With constant patience, stimulation, and enormous loving care, these children did make a good recovery – physically, emotionally, socially, and intellectually.

Review
Severe deprivation

Koluchova studied twin boys who were raised in a children's home for their first 18 months of life where they were found to be normal and well adjusted. Between 18 months and seven years of age they suffered severe deprivation and beatings while living with their father and stepmother. With intensive care, specialist education, and a loving foster home they were able to develop intellectually, socially, and emotionally.

a few months, and the twins returned to their father and stepmother when they were 18 months old. They had two older sisters, and a stepsister and stepbrother. The stepmother was a selfish, unpleasant woman who had no idea about bringing up young children. (Her mother had looked after her children when they were young.) The father was of below average intelligence, and his job on the railways took him away from home quite a lot. The family had recently moved to a city suburb where nobody knew them.

Their stepmother treated them terribly. They were kept in a small unheated room with a sheet of polythene for a bed and very little furniture. They were poorly fed. Sometimes the mother would lock them in the cellar. She would beat them with a wooden kitchen spoon, covering their heads with a mattress in case anyone heard their cries. Their father was also once seen beating them with a rubber hose until they lay unmoving on the ground.

The twins suffered these conditions for five and a half years. When they were finally examined, at the age of seven, they were severely physically and mentally retarded. Their bodies were covered in scar tissue from the beatings. They had severe rickets – a disease of the bones caused by lack of vitamin D. They couldn't stand straight, walk, or run, and their coordination was poor. They hadn't been taught to speak, had no knowledge of eating habits, and were very frightened of people, and of the dark. It was impossible to give them a standard intelligence test as they couldn't understand the instructions, and they weren't familiar with things like pictures on which some tests are based. It was estimated that their IQs would be in the 40s. They were not given standard intelligence tests, but instead their abilities were compared to normal children of their age. Their development was equivalent to that of a three-year-old.

The twins were put in hospital until they were well enough to go to a special school for mentally disadvantaged children. They made good progress at school. When they were more sociable, they were fostered by a particularly kind and loving woman who lived with her sister, who also loved children. She seemed to know exactly what the children needed, and Jarmila Koluchova said, 'There is a happy atmosphere in the whole family, full of mutual understanding.' By the age of 11 the twins' speech was normal for their age. They enjoyed some school subjects, such as reading and playing the piano, and they were both fairly creative. By the age of 15, the twins' IQ scores were normal, and their emotional state had improved greatly. The atmosphere at home was warm and friendly, and although the boys still remembered their early experiences they rarely talked about them, even to their foster mother.

Koluchova's study

1 What is the main advantage of longitudinal studies?

2 Give some examples from the passage of the kinds of thing the twins were deprived of.

3 What evidence is there in the passage that these children improved socially and intellectually?

4 How do Koluchova's findings fit in with Bowlby's theory?

Background reading – The institutionalised child

In the past some orphanages have been so understaffed and under-equipped that the children in them were nearly as isolated as Harlow's monkeys. It wasn't uncommon for a deprived orphanage to have one caregiver for every ten or more children. Contact with the babies was usually little more than changing and bathing them, and propping a feeding-bottle against their pillows at feeding time. The babies spent most of their time in their cribs (without many opportunities to get out and practise motor skills). They had few or no toys to play with, and nothing much to look at. Since the 1940s some studies have been conducted on children who spent their first year or more in these sorts of institution. They show that for the first three to six months, the infants' behaviour is fairly normal – they smile and babble at caregivers, and they cry for attention. During the next six months these normal reactions slowly disappear. They become more rigid in the way they sit and lie. They don't respond to caregivers, and their language fails to appear at the proper time (10–12 months). They look bored by their surroundings and stop trying to get someone to play with them or give them attention. This early behaviour has passed through the three stages described by the Robertsons, from **distress**, through **despair**, to **detachment**.

Another study by the Robertsons

Earlier we mentioned 17-month-old John, who was studied by the **Robertsons** when he spent nine days in a residential nursery. The Robertsons studied several such children, and noticed the same sequence of behaviour in each of them. It started with protest or distress, this gave way to despair, and finally turned into detachment. One reason why John had suffered was because no one would offer to be a substitute for his mother. Thomas was one of four children to whom the Robertsons offered temporary fostering in their own home. He was 28 months, a year older than John, when his mother went into hospital to have another baby. The Robertsons visited Thomas in his own home before his mother went away and took him to visit their home, to let him get to know them. This would reduce the strangeness of the new place when his mother was gone. He was a friendly, outgoing child and was quite comfortable with them.

He settled in with the Robertsons well, although he obviously missed his mother. Every day during separation Thomas received constant, patient, high-quality care from Joyce Robertson, supported by her husband and teenage daughter, Jean. Thomas had brought some favourite things from home, including a photograph of his mother and himself. These things reminded him of his home and his

The Robertsons wanted to show that it is important that young children should not be separated from their mother. If this were inevitable then putting them into residential nurseries or similar places would be very distressing. If they had to be separated then giving the children a temporary foster mother was essential.

mother, and comforted himself. Thomas was pleased when his father visited each night, but understandably upset when his father had to leave. (Thomas wouldn't let anyone else sit in the chair his daddy had sat in, and his father left him his pen 'to look after'.) Thomas had a few problems with food and sleep, and as the separation went into the second week he did cry more for his mother. But Joyce Robertson's patience and reassurance always quietened him.

The Robertsons used a kind of **play therapy** to explain to Thomas what was happening to him, his mother, and his father. They had dolls who they pretended were the people involved. Thomas and the Thomas doll would see daddy going to see mummy in the hospital, and mummy coming out of the hospital where she'd been resting to see Thomas and take him home.

When Thomas's mother finally came he was a bit unsure of her and whether she would be going away again. But this reaction only lasted a few minutes, Thomas was happily and successfully reunited with his mother. In the following months it appeared he had changed a little. He was rather more aggressive and harder to control than he had been before. Separating him from his usual routines may have had some slightly unfortunate effects, despite the care he had received. However there was a new baby in the family and Thomas wouldn't be quite the centre of attention that he had been.

The fostering of Thomas was largely successful. Joyce Robertson's constant care helped Thomas cope with his emotional problems caused by the separation from his mother.

The Robertsons' observations

1 Briefly outline the main differences between the ways John and Thomas were treated.

2 Briefly mention the main differences in the ways John and Thomas responded.

3 What do you think was the point of (a) bringing some toys and a photograph from home, and (b) the play-therapy sessions?

4 What evidence is there in the passage that Thomas's father was trying to help reduce the child's loss?

5 Explain how this study might contrast with Bowlby's theory of the role of the mother in forming attachments.

Review
Temporary fostering

James and Joyce Robertson have shown that taking children into their own home and giving them constant, consistent high-quality care can overcome most problems which a child might have during a short term separation from its parents.

Correlation is a statistical procedure used to see if one variable (e.g. separation from a parent) and another (e.g. delinquency) are linked. A variable is anything which varies in the research situation.

Michael Rutter's correlational studies

Michael Rutter and his colleagues studied one group of nine- to 12-year-olds on the Isle of Wight. A second study was conducted on a group of children of parents who had suffered mental problems in London. He was particularly interested in the causes of anti-social behaviour, such as juvenile delinquency and theft. Rutter found no positive correlation between separation from either parent and high levels of antisocial behaviour. He investigated two other possibilities. One was that the *cause* of the separation may be important. Children of parents who argue and are constantly in conflict will probably feel anxiety and stress. Rutter suspected that there might be a correlation between the amount of stress which children felt, and the likelihood of their becoming involved in antisocial behaviour. The other possibility was that separation from *both* parents, rather than separation from just one parent, might also have something to do with becoming antisocial, since it would mean that the children were being taken away from home, and having their lives disrupted.

Rutter found positive correlations between the amount of stress in a child's background, and the likelihood of the child becoming deviant.

To test the first possibility Rutter used several measures of the quality of family relationships, including questionnaires and clinical interviews. He could divide the sample into 'good' families, 'fair' families, and 'poor' families. Good families had warm, loving, and secure relationships, free from high levels of stress. Rutter found no increase in antisocial behaviour in the children from these homes, or in children from homes described as fair. There was a positive correlation between coming from a poor home where there was separation from one parent. Rutter suggests that it was *not* the separation of the child from one of the parents which correlated well with antisocial behaviour, but rather the *cause* of the separation. As Rutter says, 'The largest differences in antisocial behaviour are associated with the marriage rating and not with separation experiences.' Those children separated because of stress in the home were four times more likely to become delinquent than where the separation was due to illness, i.e. it's not the fact of separation but the unhappiness and stress in the home which lead to it which correlated positively with emotional disturbance. If children from warm, loving homes are maternally deprived, they can recover. (This is true of children who are adopted by other parents.) Ideally what children need is the opportunity to form strong attachments, and a stress-free home life.

A positive correlation is found where two variables seem to occur in proportion to one another so that the more there is of one, the more there is of the other.

Another challenge to one of John Bowlby's assertions was Michael Rutter's finding that separation from either of the parents did not correlate with increased antisocial behaviour, but separation from both parents did lead to a small increase among those families which are insecure to begin with. Perhaps Bowlby's emphasis on maternal separation may have been misplaced. In Rutter's words, 'This difference . . . suggests that the association may not be due to the fact of separation from both parents, but rather to the discord and disturbance which surrounded the separation.'

Rutter tested the possibility that antisocial behaviour could correlate with factors other than maternal deprivation.

Michael Rutter's correlational studies

1 What does 'no positive correlation' mean?

2 What methods did the researchers use to rate the families as good, fair, or poor?

3 Summarise Rutter's conclusions about the possible causes of antisocial behaviour.

Rutter's conclusions are supported by other studies which find a relationship between factors in the home and social development. One found a correlation between factors in the home and the number of times a juvenile appeared in court. Those who got into trouble once often had homes where there had been an outbreak of conflict. When the conflict was settled the children were less likely to offend again. Where the conflict continued the children were likely to get into trouble.

5　So is Bowlby right?

In 1956 John Bowlby was beginning to realise that some of his earlier claims may have been rather too strongly stated. In an article called 'The Effects of Mother–Child Separation' in the *British Journal of Medical Psychology* he said that some of the early work on the effects of separation (e.g. Goldfarb, Spitz, etc.) sometimes tended to exaggerate. Since the 1970s, quite a lot of doubt has been cast on some of Bowlby's views of the mother and her child.

Alan and Ann Clarke have consistently disagreed with the idea that the first few years in a child's life are as important as Bowlby and others claim. Their objections may be summarised in four points.

1 The Clarkes claim that quoting from animal studies is irrelevant to a discussion on human parent–child relationships.
2 Children who haven't had adequate bonding in early life can recover later (e.g. the twins reported by Jarmila Koluchova, the Bulldogs Bank children and many orphanage-reared children who were adopted later in life).
3 Some children have suffered temporary deprivation but show no ill effects later (such as Thomas and many of the children in Michael Rutter's study).
4 Babies don't just need mothers, but can attach to several people (as we shall see in the next chapter).

John Bowlby insisted that (a) the early years are most important for healthy development, and (b) that the mother (or a substitute mother) is crucially important in those years. The Clarkes dispute both these statements. They say 'Early experience . . . is no more than a link in the developmental chain, shaping behaviour less and less powerfully as age increases.'

Review

Long-term consequences of deprivation

Michael Rutter and his colleagues have shown that being separated from one's mother is not necessarily any more likely to have harmful consequences than being separated from one's father. They found no significant positive correlation between the length of maternal separation and the amount of antisocial behaviour, but did find that families which had the highest amounts of stress were also more likely to have children who behaved badly.

> *Evaluation of follow-up studies*

Comment

1 Both animals and humans have been studied in various ways to show either that mothers are essential or that babies can do without them. All the research so far has been used to support either one point of view or the other.

However

1 It is not usual for any study to give such clear-cut results which prove that babies need to attach to their mothers, or that they do not. In quoting research evidence in support of either side we may at best be simplifying its conclusions or, at worst, distorting them to suit our argument.

Comment

2 A major problem with all this research on children's development concerns the methods they use which usually consist of correlations, case studies, surveys, or experiments on animals. All these methods have their weaknesses for establishing the basis of children's emotional development.

3 The case for seeing the mother–child bond as all important, and for wanting to keep mothers and children together at all costs, has been criticised for being politically convenient. During the 1950s it would have suited the government, and men generally, if women had not gone out to work since it would have left more jobs open to men.

However

2 However, there aren't any other methods which can reasonably be used to study children. Observing them, talking to them, interviewing their parents are all widely used.

3 This may be true, but the accusation does not necessarily imply that the theory isn't correct of course. Bowlby does not claim to have invented or discovered the existence of attachment, he has merely pointed out the need for it.

Review
Evaluation of the parent–child relationship

We now know that many of Bowlby's original ideas may not be completely correct. Children and babies may be much more 'flexible' than he believed, and not all difficulties that occurred during their first five years would lead to emotional disturbance or anti-social behaviour. Regardless of 'who is right', without people like John Bowlby, James and Joyce Robertson, Ann and Alan Clarke, and Michael Rutter we would know a lot less about parent–child relationships than we do now.

In any field of enquiry people will put forward ideas that seem to fit the facts. These ideas will attract some support, and some criticism. For as long as John Bowlby's explanations were thought to be convincing his influence was great. He focused attention on the mother–child bond probably more than anyone else before him. When criticisms of any theory and the appearance of alternative explanations outweigh the earlier beliefs, so new insights are gained. While all of Bowlby's claims may not be wholly correct, developmentalists owe him a great deal for inspiring so much debate and research into how children's emotions grow.

Evaluating Bowlby's claims

1 What were the main consequences that Bowlby predicted came from breaking the mother–child bond?

2 Discuss some of the criticisms that have been made of Bowlby's theory.

3

Attachments and Mothering

Earlier we said that an attachment is a special emotional bond that babies make with their particular caregivers. If the attachment bond is broken, however, children don't automatically become delinquents and suffer emotionally. As Michael Rutter suggests, it depends on when and why the separation occurs. Some American research by Yarrow and Goodwin suggests that 5 per cent of three-month-old babies suffer if they are separated from their mothers at any time. But if the break occurs between three and four months, 40 per cent of babies will suffer. By six months 90 per cent suffer, and by nine months all will. Babies seem to form their primary attachments from around four to nine months.

In this chapter we shall be looking at the following questions.

1 How do attachments evolve – what is the role of the child, and what is the role of the parent?
2 How do we know if attachment bonds are being made and who else can the baby attach to?
3 What lessons can we learn from studies of infant–parent bonding?
4 What are the effects of long-term deprivation?

1 How attachments evolve

Many psychologists now believe that human infants are born with some skills which allow them to attract and keep someone's attention. These will be useful for interaction. It may be that the child is born with some instinctive basis for various types of interaction.

Attachments are emotional bonds which occur between babies and those people who are most deeply involved with them. To become involved the people and infant concerned must spend some quality time together, and interact with one another. In order to discover who babies can attach to we must first discover how attachments occur. The old idea that there is some kind of simple instinctive urge that binds mothers and their babies wouldn't be widely accepted now.

Young babies are willing to be sociable with just about anyone who pays them enough attention. After a few months infants are willing and able to let a closer bond develop. For attachments to occur, some of the people who attend to the child – hopefully including the parents – will want to become involved with the child. Over the next few months the infant will grow to trust, and to enjoy the company of, these people, to feel safe and secure with them, and to regard them as a *safe base* from which to explore.

The child's role in forming attachments

Some animals follow the first thing they see. They must have some instinct which tells them that this 'thing' will look after them and feed them. In the wild the first thing these baby animals will see will be their parents who will look after them. Following their parent around obviously has some *survival value*.

Humans rely much less on instincts than most animals do, as we have great capacities to learn and adapt our behaviour. We slowly learn whom we enjoy being with, and maybe whom we can trust. To do this, human babies must be capable of being *sociable*. A great deal of research has been conducted recently, including some ingenious experiments and some detailed observations, on how babies appear to enjoy interacting with other people. Some of the conclusions are summarised here.

Human babies seem to enjoy company. They will give a social smile (i.e. not just wind!) within a few days of birth, and will start to imitate their mother's facial expressions after just a week or so. They have reasonably good hearing and will turn their heads towards sounds. (Our senses of sight and hearing are closely linked, right from birth.) Babies seem to have an innate preference for looking at things like the human face, and hearing the human voice too.

Ahrens

Over 30 years ago **Ahrens** found that one-month-old babies will smile at a picture of human eyes in an otherwise blank space. Over the next few months more details such as a nose and mouth are required to make a baby smile, and by five months the picture has to be three dimensional. A smiling baby is likely to encourage the mother to smile and talk to the child.

Close bonds may develop between the baby and certain people. These people may then become a *safe base* from which the child can explore.

Innate means inborn, hereditary, something which is genetically transmitted and exists right from birth (or the potential for it does).

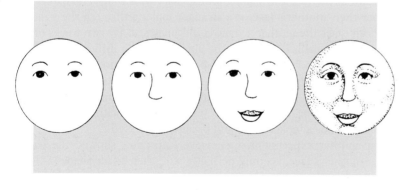

◀
Ahrens's face shapes

Ahrens and Fantz conducted controlled experiments. Scientists use controlled experiments to measure whether changes in one variable (called the **independent variable**) cause changes in another variable (called the **dependent variable**).

Fantz

Over 20 years ago **Robert Fantz** designed some apparatus called a *looking chamber*, which allowed babies to be shown particular things, while their reactions could be recorded. He showed various pictures to babies from a few days old, and he measured the amount of time they looked at each one. He found that they preferred to look at round objects, especially those which were most like a face.

Fantz's face shapes ▶

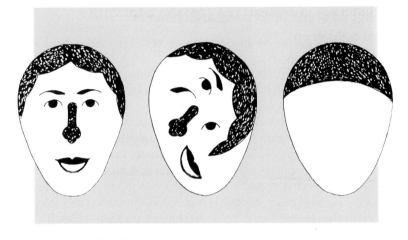

Early psychologists claimed that babies have certain kinds of preferences for the things they look at and listen to. The things they seem to enjoy most are 'human'. Now we think the preference is more for interesting symmetrical objects rather than human-face shapes particularly.

Condon and Sander

William Condon and **Lewis Sander** played tape recordings of various sounds, including human speech, to babies from just a few hours old. The babies heard someone speaking American, another speaking Chinese, someone making vowel sounds, and a regular tapping sound. In addition to these tapes they also heard a live adult speaker. The babies reactions as they heard the sounds were filmed. By two days old, these American babies started to move their arms and bodies in time with the speech, while not appearing very concerned with the tapping or vowel sounds. This research suggests that humans may be genetically programmed for responding to human speech.

Carpenter

Genevieve Carpenter took a sample of babies between one and eight weeks old, and put them in some apparatus that had a viewing window at the top, and a small loudspeaker next to it. The babies saw either their mother's face or a stranger looking through the window. In both cases the mother's voice could be heard. By two weeks of age many of the babies seemed to be able to tell the difference between their mother and a stranger, and preferred their mother. The babies turned away when they saw their mother's face in this strange apparatus, although they appeared to be interested in their mother's voice. When the mother's face was presented with the stranger's voice the babies looked away and became distressed.

In another experiment, Genevieve Carpenter showed the babies their mother's face, keeping perfectly still, then a face shape (a flesh-coloured kitchen collander with three knobs on it to resemble facial features), and finally a shop dummy face. The babies were vaguely interested in the collander and the shop dummy. But when they saw their mother's unmoving face they looked away. Carpenter's experiments suggest that by just a few weeks of age many babies:
(a) can recognise their mother's face,
(b) can recognise their mother's voice,
(c) expect the face and voice to go together, and
(d) expect the face to have movement.

A Summary of Genevieve Carpenter's findings

First experiment

	Mother's face and voice	Mother's face, no voice	Stranger's face and voice	Mother's face, stranger's voice
2-week-old baby's reaction	Happy	Unhappy	Happy	Unhappy

Second experiment

	Mother's unmoving face	Abstract face shape	Shop dummy face
Baby's reaction	Restless	Vague interest	Vague interest

Condon and Sander, and Genevieve Carpenter, have suggested that human babies are born with very clear preferences for 'human' things. Name the main IVs and DVs in these experiments.

Psychological experiments

1 What are controlled experiments?

2 What is a hypothesis?

3 Draw up a table like the one below and fill in the gaps.

	Hypothesis	IV	DV
Fantz's faces			
Carpenter's first experiment			
Carpenter's second experiment			

For the first few months this **sociability** is only directed towards adults. It used to be thought that children only started taking notice of other children when they were about three or four years old. We now know that even babies of 10- to 12-months old will copy and smile at another baby. Given the choice they would probably prefer an adult, or even a toy, but if neither are available, another baby will do.

The sociable newborn baby

1 Write a paragraph summarising the evidence so far that supports the view that human babies are genetically programmed to interact socially. Refer to the research of Fantz, Condon and Sander, and Carpenter in your answer.

2 What effect is the baby's willingness to be sociable likely to have on its mother? What might it make her want to do?

3 Suggest how the skills discussed in the paragraph you wrote might contribute to survival value?

4 What advice would you give a new mother about talking to her baby?

Review
The sociable infant

Human infants appear to be genetically programmed to become aware of, and respond to, people around them. They appear to have genetically inherited preferences for things which are human, such as voices and faces.

Next time there's a discussion between two people on television, and you can see them both, turn the volume right down. Try to work out who's talking, whether the other agrees, whether and how they butt in and so on.

How do we know if an infant is being sociable?

Watch two friends talking. When Lee talks to Mick he moves his hands and arms to emphasise the point he's making. Sometimes his voice grows louder or softer, sometimes it goes up in pitch. Mick looks at Lee, sometimes nodding his agreement. He remains quiet until it's his turn to speak. If he wants to butt in he'll raise his hands, and his voice. When it's time to go, or to talk to someone else, Lee will let Mick know. Babies and their mothers do much the same sorts of thing.

Trevarthen and Richards
Colwyn Trevarthen and **Martin Richards** filmed a sample of five babies for an hour each week for the first six months of their lives. Sometimes the babies were in their cots with toys hanging in front of them, and sometimes they were with their mothers. Their behaviour was quite different in each situation. They explored and played with the toys, but they held a sort of **conversation** with their mothers. From around two months of age they would open their mouths when their mothers spoke to them, but remained silent, as though they were preparing to reply. A few months later the babies and their mothers took turns in their conversations. When the mothers stopped speaking the babies would make little sounds. This encouraged the mothers to speak again, and again they would wait their turn before answering. This highly elaborate activity seems to show that even very young babies are ready, willing and able to communicate with their caregivers. The babies weren't communicating in order to make their mothers do anything, such as feed or change them. They appeared to be doing it just for the fun of it. The communication was mutually enjoyable. Moving one's face and body in time with what is going on around us is called **interactional synchrony**. Condon and Sander's sample of babies from just a few hours old showed interactional synchrony with the human speech they heard.

Stern
Daniel Stern is an American professor of child psychiatry who has spent many years studying parent–child interaction. Although he agrees that there is an instinctive basis to attachment formation, he

▲
Interactional synchrony

thinks too much is sometimes made of it. He believes that children develop an idea of who they are and what they can do fairly soon after birth through social interaction. He found that, by three months of age, babies use the same face-to-face type behaviour as two adults. The babies look for their mother. As she approaches they look away for a moment. Then they look again and hold eye contact. Then they break it. They will smile and move their heads in time to what is being said. If the mother is talking and they want to butt in they do the same thing as adults do, they raise their hands, heads (and their voices!). They are extremely good at regulating the amount of contact they have. They will let the mother know when they want company, which one of them they want to talk, and when they want to rest. Stern maintains that all this behaviour is purely for fun, for mutual enjoyment, and for sharing each other's experiences.

People move their heads, hands, arms, and body position to emphasise what they are saying. When they're listening they are more at ease. Babies respond in this way in their 'conversations' too. It's called interactional synchrony.

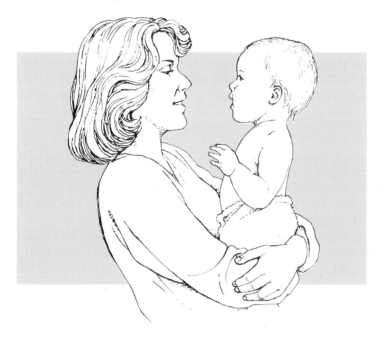

Do you wave your hands around when you're talking, to emphasise your point? How does the person you're talking to look when you're talking? And how does this change when you stop and it's their turn?

Harriet Rheingold and **Judith Adams** suggest that both care-givers and infants enjoy their conversations. Babies will often stop crying and look around when they hear a human voice.

Not everyone agrees with those researchers who believe that the infant is able to start off, and contribute to, 'conversation-like' exchanges with their caregivers. Some researchers believe that babies are born with a few primitive reflexes, and that maturation and learning will be necessary before children are capable of any of the communication skills described by Colwyn Trevarthen, Daniel Stern and others. People like **Kenneth Kaye** argue that whenever an infant behaves in a way that appears to have some social meaning – such as a smile communicating happiness to be with someone – then adults

Babies are said to be quite skilled at regulating the amount of contact they have. How might we observe this?

interpret it as though it actually did have this meaning, and treat their babies accordingly. Crying may be a reflexive response to pain or hunger. A parent will interpret the cry, and will respond as though the child actually was trying to ask for food. Kaye does not believe that tiny babies are capable of many of the social exchanges described earlier.

Not everyone agrees that babies are so sociable. We may misinterpret their sounds and movements as signs of sociability.

The sociable behaviour of the infant

1   When does turn taking in conversations begin, according to researchers such as Trevarthen and Richards?

2   What is meant by interactional synchrony?

3   Why are babies sociable, according to Daniel Stern?

Review
Preparing for an attachment

Very young babies respond to social signals like smiling, and can take turns in their communication. They seem to enjoy these interactions. Critics of this view say that we exaggerate infants' social skills by choosing to interpret their behaviour in that way.

The mother's role in forming attachments

Since most infants don't begin to talk until 10–12 months of age, they must use other signals for communicating their needs. Such signals may include smiling, eye contact, gazing, reaching, grasping, and (from about six months), babbling. All these abilities are genetically inherited. Adults who are sensitive to these signals may become more deeply involved with their children. One of the most powerful signals an infant has is crying. Crying is usually the last resort for the child, when all other attempts to attract attention have failed. Babies don't usually just start to cry unless there's something wrong. Babies probably don't enjoy crying. Given the choice they'd probably rather smile. Wouldn't you?

So what can parents do about reducing babies' crying? **Silvia Bell** and **Mary Ainsworth** conducted a naturalistic observation study of 26 mothers and babies in their own homes for four hours at a time, once every three weeks for the first year of the babies' lives. Some parents tend to their babies as soon as they begin to cry. Others wait a short time to see if they will quieten on their own. Some parents even leave their babies for several minutes, believing that they will learn that all they have to do to attract attention is cry. The researchers wanted to see if there were any differences between the mothers' responses to their babies' crying, and the amount of time each baby cried. The mothers who responded most quickly and were most attentive to their babies' needs had babies who cried least. The babies were most likely to cry when they were left alone.

If babies are capable of social communication, or if they simply make demands to have their needs met, they will need some means of attracting their caregivers' attention. Crying is a powerful signal.

During the first year of life babies learn other ways of attracting attention and so don't need to use crying so much, particularly if their mothers have responded sensitively before. As Mary Ainsworth says, 'An infant whose mother has responded to his cries promptly in the past should develop both trust in her responsiveness and confidence in his increased ability to control what happens to him.'

Mary Ainsworth uses the term *the sensitive mother* to refer to one who is quick to respond to her baby's needs. Babies should feel loved and secure which should help them become more independent later. The opposite of this may also be true, babies who are not sensitively dealt with may tend to become more demanding and clinging.

Sensitive mothers respond quickly when their baby cries. Babies who are being attended to are least likely to cry.

Background reading – Crying

On average, infants spend about six to seven per cent of their time crying (although it seems like more!). Healthy babies have several different sorts of crying.

There's the 'I'm hungry, feed me' cry. It starts with a quiet whimper and becomes louder if food doesn't appear. Then there's the 'I'm absolutely furious about . . .' cry. It is louder and more piercing, and harder to quieten. And there's the 'I'm in pain, something really hurts' cry. It starts as a long scream, a pause for breath, and another long scream, and so on. A mother will soon learn the difference between them, and what to do for each. There's another noise that babies of just a month or so may learn to use. It's the 'There's nothing wrong with me, I'm a bit fed up, come and play with me' noise, and isn't a real cry.

Crying babies

A young mother enters the kitchen. She looks exhausted and flops in a chair by the phone. She dials the number of her best friend from the garage where she used to work.

'Hi Cathy, it's Jan. Just thought I'd give you a ring to let you know how it's going.'

'Great Jan, how's young Peter?'

'He's fine, he's getting quite fat now, but the doctor says he's about right for six months old. I am slightly worried though. He seems to cry quite a lot. I asked Mum and she said that me and my sister used to, it's nothing to worry about. So long as I keep to the routine of feeding him, and putting him down afterwards every four hours he'll learn what to expect and won't be any more trouble. The problem is, he hasn't quite got the hang of it yet.'

1 If you were Cathy, what would you like to say to your friend?

2 Could you think of any explanation for why Jan and her sister cried a lot when they were young?

3 Describe one piece of research on mothering of young babies. Say what method was used and describe the sample. What were the findings, and what do they tell us about young babies?

Review
The sensitive mother

Mothers who put their babies' needs first, and who respond quickly to their needs, have babies who cry less, and who may become the most content and confident children.

How important are very early experiences?

Klaus and Kennel

Marshall Klaus and **John Kennel** conducted an experiment on contact comfort between mothers and babies in the mid-1970s. They hypothesised that a mother's sensitivity towards her baby may be affected by the amount of contact she had with it immediately after birth. They managed to find 28 expectant mothers who could comprise a control and an experimental group.

The control group underwent the normal routine – seeing their babies briefly after delivery, then six to 12 hours after the usual tests and rest. They had feeding sessions for half an hour with their babies every four hours.

A control group is one whose behaviour is constant. It is the group with whom the experimental group is compared.

Background reading – What helps a mother be sensitive to her baby?

Here are some possible suggestions.

Support from her partner and family, and sharing childminding. Sensitive mothers could offer lots of contact comfort to their babies.

Mary Ainsworth believes that from around one year old human babies will have learned who their safe bases are. She says that we have an instinct to attach, which is followed by an instinct to explore. Sensitive mothers will help babies become independent.

Klaus and Kennel observed two groups of new mothers, one of which underwent the normal hospital routines while the other was allowed an extra 15 hours' contact with their babies. This is a controlled experiment.

The experimental group had more contact. Within three hours of birth they had an extra hour's contact. Then they had an extra five hours a day contact with their babies compared to the control group. Altogether the extended contact group had 15 hours' extra time with their babies, compared to the controls.

One month later Klaus and Kennel interviewed the 28 mothers and filmed them with their babies (including a feeding session). The extended contact group seemed much closer to their babies generally and held them much closer during feeding. Eleven months later Klaus and Kennel conducted a follow-up study. The extended contact mothers still cuddled and soothed their babies more than the controls, and were more likely to say they'd missed their babies when returning home. Their infants too seemed more mature and sociable than the normal routine group. They were also physically bigger and stronger. Five of the pairs in each group were studied again at two years, this time focusing on the language used. The differences were still evident. The mothers in the extended contact group used longer sentences, more adjectives, and gave fewer commands.

Klaus and Kennel claimed to have found support for their hypothesis that extended contact between mothers and babies after birth strengthens their relationship later, i.e. that the dependent variable changes as the independent variable changes.

Klaus and Kennel's experiment

1 What independent variables (IVs) are being controlled here?

2 What is the size of the sample?

3 Why was a control group used here?

4 What measures of the dependent variable (DV) were taken when the babies were a year old? And at two?

5 Summarise the conclusions of this research in your own words

There has been a great deal of criticism of this experiment, and not everyone accepts its findings. Some of the interpretations were accused of being exaggerated. Similar experiments have been conducted, under strictly controlled conditions, and have found no great differences between extended and non-extended contact groups. What we can conclude is that, while extended contact just after birth may not necessarily have any long-term benefits, it is unlikely to do any harm!

Mothering

1 Why do babies cry?

2 What advice would you give to a new mother about her baby's crying?

3 What does *socially learned* mean?

4 Describe *interactional synchrony*?

5 What did the following researchers conclude:
   William Condon and Lewis Sander
   Colwyn Trevarthen and Martin Richards
   Genevieve Carpenter
   Daniel Stern
   Mary Ainsworth and Silvia Bell
   Marshall Klaus and John Kennel

6 Are six-month-old human babies helpless and passive? Give reasons for your answer.

7 What is naturalistic observation? How have psychologists used observation to study mother–child interaction?

2 How do we know if attachment has occurred?

By around eight months babies could have become firmly attached to their primary caregivers. There are said to be two ways of telling if a baby is attached to someone. First a baby is said to be attached to someone if the baby is not afraid of that person, but is afraid of strangers. Secondly, a baby is said to be attached to someone if being away from that person causes the baby to become upset. These two conditions are called **stranger fear** and **separation distress**.

Stranger fear
For the first three months of their lives, babies will smile at strangers; by four months this begins to turn to a stare; and by six months they often freeze if approached by a stranger. This fear gradually disappears as the child becomes more independent. Whether a baby shows stranger fear depends on three factors: firstly, whether someone to whom the baby is attached is near by, second, where the baby is, and third, how the stranger behaves.

▲ **Stranger fear**

If the baby is being held by its mother, for example, it will show little fear if a stranger approaches. If it is on its own in a familiar place it will show fear. If it is with its mother in a strange place it will show fear. If it is alone in a strange place (particularly the open air) it will show less stranger fear, and may even allow itself to be picked up by a stranger. If the stranger approaches slowly, and talks and acts in a quiet, friendly way, the baby will show less fear. If the stranger approaches more quickly and gets too close, tries to pick the baby up, or talks too loudly, the baby will show fear.

The pattern of stranger fear

1 Under what conditions is a baby least likely to show stranger fear?

2 Under what conditions is a baby most likely to show stranger fear?

3 If you want to speak to a mother who is carrying a 12-month-old baby, what is the best way to approach her?

A baby is said to be attached to an adult if it shows no fear of them, while showing fear of others. What survival value might stranger fear have?

The most obvious explanation for why a baby shows a fear of strangers is that the baby is afraid that either it or its mother is going to be taken away by the stranger. Babies only show fear of adults they do not know. For some reason they do not show fear of unknown children. Perhaps this is because they haven't much idea of what a child is until they are older. Babies develop stranger fear towards other children during their second year.

Separation distress

Babies are also said to be attached if they show distress when absent from their main caregivers. What are the three stages of separation distress that the Robertsons identified?

From around 12 months a firmly attached baby will be upset when it is away from the person it is attached to. The baby will resist anyone else who tries to offer comfort. If the separation continues for some days, the baby may go through the three stages identified by James and Joyce Robertson.

Making multiple attachments

Being able to measure whether babies have made any attachment also allows us to identify the people to whom they are attached. Bowlby claimed that babies have some biological need to attach to their mothers, or at least to a permanent substitute. In 1964 **Rudi Schaffer** and **Peggy Emerson** reported on their most important ethological study of 60 Glasgow children from birth to 18 months. They interviewed the mothers once a month and asked them about who their babies smiled at, who they responded to, who caused them separation distress and so on. They found that many of the infants were attaching to several people. Where several adults took an interest in a baby, that baby could attach to them all.

Ethology is the study of behaviour in its natural context. Ethologists often use naturalistic observation.

Having multiple attachments means being attached to more than one person.

Background reading – The explanations for separation distress

There are a few possible explanations for separation distress.

Association learning

If an infant has been separated from its mother (or caregiver) before, and been hungry, wet or lonely during the separation, it may associate those unpleasant feelings with the absence. When the mother is absent again, the baby might think it is about to become hungry, wet, or lonely again. Any future absence will remind the baby of these feelings and it will become distressed.

If this explanation were correct, however, then babies would show the same amount of distress wherever they happened to be when the separation occurred. So John would have been as upset if he had stayed at home while his mother was in hospital as he was in the nursery for nine days. This probably isn't true. Babies tend not to show as much separation distress if they are at home when their mother is away as they do when in strange surroundings. Association learning can't be the whole answer.

Instinct

Another possibility is that we have an instinct which tells us that we must be near a caregiver. This instinct declines during the second year. If the baby is separated this instinct is disrupted, and the baby automatically becomes upset. But why then do infants of 10 months or so quite happily crawl away from their mothers to play in a different room?

Schemas

A third possibility is that, by about 12 months, children are developing the appropriate schemas for 'caregivers in places'. A schema is an idea of what something is, and how to deal with it. So the one-year-old baby may have a schema for 'mother in sitting room' and 'mother in kitchen'. That knowledge will allow the baby to feel secure in the living room while its mother is in the kitchen, and vice versa. If she then goes somewhere that the baby does not have a schema for, it may become upset.

Schaffer and Emerson

Schaffer and Emerson's sample went through four stages. For the first six weeks the children had no particular preferences about who they were with. Between six weeks and six months they became increasingly sociable with anyone. By seven months they wanted to be near their main caregiver and started to be wary of strangers. This marks the beginning of the first attachment. Within a month or so of this first attachment they started to attach to other people. Schaffer and Emerson found that each attachment was much the same in quality. The infants responded in the same way to each attached adult. They seemed to use different adults for different things. If they were frightened they generally preferred their mother; if they wanted to play they usually preferred their father. Babies who are attached to several adults can be just as deeply attached to each. As Rudi Schaffer says, 'being attached to several people does not imply a shallower feeling towards each one, for an infant's capacity for attachment is not like a cake that has to be shared out. Love, even in babies, has no limits.' Nowadays most families don't have lots of adults around with time on their hands to spend with the baby. If they did, no doubt we would see many more examples of multiple attachment.

John Bowlby's research and conclusions were well known when Schaffer and Emerson undertook this research. Their conclusions did not entirely support Bowlby's.

For attachment bonding, the implications seems to be 'it's the quality, not the quantity, that counts'.

Review
Multiple attachments

Schaffer and Emerson's classic study of bond formation shows that babies are capable of forming more than one close attachment, and that the mother's role is not as important as some people had believed. This means that childminding could be successfully shared between several people.

These findings contradicted Bowlby's theory in several ways.

First, Bowlby claimed that there would be a hierarchy of attachments, with mother being at the top. However, 20 of the 60 Glasgow babies were not attached to their mothers, but to someone else altogether. In some families it was the father or another relative, while in others it was a neighbour.

Second, infants don't have any one person to whom they must attach. Rudi Schaffer continues, 'There is, we must conclude, nothing to indicate any biological need for an exclusive primary bond.' Attachments could be made to several people.

By seven months, 17 (29 per cent) of the sample had attached to two people. By 10 months, 36 (60 per cent) had more than one attachment. By 18 months, over 50 (87 per cent) had more than one attachment and 25 (30 per cent) had three, four, or five attachments. In Schaffer's words, 'There is . . . nothing to suggest that mothering can't be shared by several people.'

Third, these attachments weren't different in any way. The infant behaved in much the same way with each person it was attached to. Schaffer and Emerson conclude that attachments are most likely to be formed with those people who are most sensitive to the baby's needs (they call this **sensitive responsiveness**). They do not necessarily attach to those people who spend most time with them.

Background reading – Theories of attachment

There are a number of psychological theories which try to explain aspects of development. They range from those which claim attachments are instinctive to those which say they are socially learned.

Biological or instinctive theory: This says that the baby has an instinct to bond with the person who feeds and cares for it.

Behaviourist theory: Behaviourist psychologists reject the role of instinct. They say that our behaviour is the result of what we have learned in the past. The baby learns who looks after it, and wants to be near that person.

Cognitive theory: Cognition refers to mental events like thinking, remembering, reasoning and so on. Cognitive psychologists believe that children develop schemas (ideas) through interaction with the environment when they are intellectually mature enough. Babies will attach to those people who help them to develop positive schemas about security, enjoyment, care, etc.

Sensitive responsiveness theory: This is Schaffer and Emerson's explanation for who babies attach to. It has something in common with cognitive theory. Babies form attachments with those who are aware of the babies' social needs and interact with them, rather than those who largely ignore them, except when they're crying.

Communication theory: This is similar to Schaffer and Emerson's explanation. Children don't like being alone and so develop communication skills in order to keep adults near them.

Which of these theories do you think comes nearest to the truth? Or perhaps you have one of your own?

Making attachments

1 What sort of things would you do if you wanted a baby to become attached to you?

2 How do we know who babies are attached to?

3 What advice would you give a new mother who wanted to return to work a year after having a baby?

4 What is the difference between an ethological study and an experiment?

5 Describe one study of parent–child interaction that was not conducted in a laboratory. Name the technique used, and the findings made.

Is the attachment process the same everywhere?

The research mentioned so far is from Europe and America. It seems that different patterns of bonding occur in different parts of the world.

An example of early bonding was noted by Mary Ainsworth. She conducted a study of some Ugandan mothers and children of the Ganda tribe. (Uganda is a country in central Africa.) She found that the children showed separation anxiety by five to six months. Ugandan children and mothers spend more time close to each other, right from birth. They have more skin-to-skin contact too. Some research in some poorer countries has shown that mothers are less likely to neglect their babies if they have lots of skin-to-skin contact. Ganda children sleep with their mothers, and are breast fed, until they are about two years old. They go everywhere with their mothers, who carry them in a cotton sling. Being separated would be very unusual, so they show more anxiety when it happens.

An alternative kind of mothering is found in the kibbutz. In Israel about 4 per cent of the population live in large agricultural communes called kibbutzim. There are farms, some light industry, and some shops and offices in each kibbutz. They try to be self-sufficient, growing and making enough to keep everyone fully employed. There are about 250 kibbutzim altogether in Israel. Everything should be shared equally between all the people who live in the kibbutz. Everyone works and receives the same wage and a share in the profits. Everyone should be regarded as equal in all respects. There should be no discrimination.

This has important implications for childminding. In order to return to work and start contributing again, the mothers of newborn babies only stay with them for a few weeks. During this time intense bonding behaviour usually occurs (lots of cuddling, talking, playing, handling, etc.). The mother starts to go back to work, just for an hour or two a day. A trained children's nurse, called a metapelet, looks after the baby. Gradually the mother increases the number of hours she works and the metapelet is increasing her time with the baby.

▲ **Skin-to-skin contact**

Mary Ainsworth conducted a cross-cultural study. She compared mother–child interaction in one culture with that in another. If any particular aspect of development is the same in every culture it is almost certainly the result of genetic inheritance (nature). If it differs across different cultures, it probably results from socialisation (nurture).

By the end of the first year the mother has returned to full-time work and the child is living in the Children's House with all the other youngsters. These children spend an hour or so in the evenings with their parents before returning to sleep in the Children's House. The children stay more closely attached to their parents, who spend just an hour or two each day with them, than they do with the metapelets who are with them all day. The parents have not abandoned their children in any sense, but they leave the routine of child-minding to other people.

In the kibbutz, babies form multiple attachments with their mothers, their nurses, and possibly even with each other.

The reason why the kibbutz system works for many children is that it is possible for them to make multiple attachments. Many will start to attach to the metapelet. The very high intensity and quality of the love between the parents and their children ensures that the children feel wanted and secure. Part of the reason why the children in the studies quoted by Bowlby suffered while their mothers were away may have been because the alternative care was inadequate. In the kibbutz the children spend many days away from their parents, and the substitute care is good.

Attachments and other family members

Bowlby claimed that a baby makes one central attachment to one main caregiver. Although that caregiver doesn't have to be the baby's natural mother, in most cases it would be. However, we now have lots of evidence that babies can make multiple attachments, including attachments with different family members and other people.

Bowlby thought that there would be a hierarchy of attachments, with one main caregiver being at the top, and all other attachments being inferior to that one.

In **Schaffer** and **Emerson's** Glasgow study, about half of the sample of 60 children had also made attachments to their fathers or other family members within two months of making their first attachment. Each attachment can be of equal strength and equal value to the child.

It seems that much of the evidence today does not support Bowlby's view that babies make one central attachment to one main caregiver. It appears they can make several attachments, each of which is of equal value. They may make their first attachment with their mother, but soon other attachments can be made.

Ten years later **Barry Lester** and his colleagues found that the babies that Schaffer and Emerson studied had all made strong attachments with their mothers by the time they were nine months old, but had also attached to their fathers by 12 months.

Daniel Stern has shown that babies can signal their needs to their parents and help to regulate the type and amount of contact that they received. This suggests that babies are quite aware of their own needs and soon learn how to express them. In the late 1970s **Michael Lamb** went further. He had noticed how babies use different caregivers for different activities. Babies appeared to prefer their mother's company if they were distressed. They would respond to their mother's soft soothing voice and gentle cuddles. However, they seemed to prefer their fathers for rather more adventurous activities. Fathers are often more playful with their babies, where mothers are often more nurturant. Fathers offer rough-and-tumble type activities. They can also be gentle with their infants, and the infants can form strong emotional ties with them. These three things – tenderness, emotional warmth, and more physical activities - might help

It is important to note that 'attachment' is not an absolute relationship that a baby either has or doesn't have. Different babies will form different strength attachments with their mother and with other family members.

babies use the father as a safe base from which to explore the world.

Siblings are probably very important to young children. They often spend more time with one another than with their parents. Children with brothers and sisters are more likely to have to learn to compete and to share than single children. Schaffer and Emerson also found that younger children are quite likely to form attachments with their older siblings in much the same way as they do with their parents. Siblings imitate each other, compete with each other, and protect each other. They learn about love and rivalry, trust and aggression, and many other emotions from these early relationships with other family members.

Cross-cultural data

1 Does the bonding behaviour reported from the kibbutz confirm or challenge John Bowlby's explanations? Explain your answer.

2 Does it confirm or challenge the findings of Rudi Schaffer and Peggy Emerson? Give reasons for your answer.

3 What are the advantages to psychologists of using findings from cross-cultural research? What does it allow them to show which they may not be able to show otherwise?

4 What do you imagine might be the problems with comparing data from our society and that from cross-cultural research?

5 Discuss one cross-cultural study of mothering.

Review
Does the same attachment behaviour happen everywhere?

Children everywhere seem to want to form attachments to those people who are most deeply involved with them. The age at which attachment starts varies according to the kind of experiences the child has. Even where childminding is not mostly done by the parents, such as in the kibbutz, babies may still attach to their parents.

3 Lessons from attachment studies

From what we've seen so far we can draw some conclusions. We know that children need parenting. Parenting includes providing for children's physical needs for food, comfort, and rest. It includes providing children with emotional security and a sense of trust. And it includes providing social stimulation through play, games, explanations, and social experiences such as going to the shops or the park.

Also, we now know that babies as young as seven or eight months are capable of making more than one attachment. There are obviously differences between individual children, but the usual pattern is:

up to 3–4 months	Babies generally don't mind who is with them.
3–5 months	They start to decide who they feel safe with.
6–7 months	They express their preferences clearly – stranger fear begins. All this time they are attaching to their caregivers.
6–18 months	They start forming multiple attachments if other adults are available and willing.

Further, the success and intensity of the attachment does not depend on the *amount* of stimulation the baby receives, but on the *quality* of

Babies are most likely to make attachments with those people who offer them high-quality, meaningful care and affection. Those people who enjoy the child are more likely to be responded to than those who only take care of it.

it. Infants may form attachments with those people who are deeply involved in playing with them for just an hour a day, and not form attachments to others who care for them physically but who don't play with them. This quality in relationships is achieved through play, cuddles (contact comfort), individual attention, exchange games (e.g. 'conversation'), and generally enjoying one another's company. It will provide children with a sense of trust, security, and the knowledge that it has a safe base from which to explore.

Lessons from attachment studies

1 Name three things that parenting provides for children.

2 What advice would you give to parents who wanted to know how to be certain of making a strong attachment with their baby?

3 Do parents make attachments *to* their children, or *with* them? Explain your answer.

4 If 'Love, even in babies, has no limits' (Schaffer), what implications does this have for sharing childcare?

Attachment in older children

In the early years attachment is an emotional bond from which babies derive feelings of trust. By three or four the child looks for stimulation, as well as care and protection. By the school years the children are becoming more independent and confident, so that they can share their interests and affection among friends. During the teenage years the needs for attachment can include members of the opposite sex.

From around two years of age, well-attached children will be increasingly independent and willing to explore any new environment. They are inquisitive and enthusiastic. By this time they have developed enough language and thinking to enable them to experiment with their world to see what happens. They are able to learn for themselves. New situations and people may cause temporary shyness, so that some children will seek the security of the safe base (usually just behind their parents!). Less well-attached children are less adventurous and less independent and will want to stay nearer to their parents. Two- and three-year-olds maintain their close attachments to mothers, fathers, and other significant people in their lives. During the pre-school period (three to five years old) they become steadily less clinging. Peer groups (almost always of the same sex) are becoming important, and children start to attach to their peers. Peer groups continue to be important until the children reach adolescence and begin to prefer the company of single members of the opposite sex to the company of several members of their own! Boyfriends and girlfriends become attached to each other and will use each other for emotional security and social stimulation.

Other attachments

1 Define the term attachment.

2 Apart from our parents, who else might we form an attachment with?

3 When do the two measures of attachment start to decline?

4 What do infants below one year of age need from an attachment?

5 What do three-year-olds need from an attachment?

When attachment fails

We have mentioned some of the problems with insecure attachment. When it fails completely children suffer terribly. For example child abuse is sometimes the result of a failed attachment. The circumstances under which attachments are least likely to be made include those where the problem lies with the baby (the first two points below), and those where the parents are responsible (the rest).

Problems with disabled babies: In 1974 and 1975 **Selma Fraiberg** studied some blind babies and their mothers. Blind babies aren't able to join in exchange games, imitating their mother's expressions, smiling back when smiled at and so on. They obviously can't recognise their mother's face and smile when they see her, as sighted babies can. They were more likely to be rejected by their mother for being unresponsive. For example, when the mother of a blind baby enters the room the baby freezes so that it can listen very hard. Some of the mothers interpreted this as the baby not welcoming her. Selma Fraiberg developed a programme for teaching parents how to cope with blind babies. For example, the programme advises parents how to read their babies' signals, to talk to the babies as they approach them, and to put toys that make a sound near the babies so that they will touch them and so forth.

Problems with difficult babies: Some babies simply are difficult to love sometimes. They may be hyperactive, often irritable, or unresponsive. Some adults find it difficult to attach to babies who cry during play sessions. (In America they have a special test to diagnose difficult children.) We will return to the issue of temperament later.

Some adults simply do not make good parents, particularly if they were abused or unloved themselves as children.

Unplanned babies: Children who are the result of unplanned or unwanted pregnancies are sometimes more at risk.

Unaware parents: Some parents are inflexible and insist on a certain routine rather than letting the child decide when it's hungry or tired.

Problems with the situation: Children in environments such as large families, or with parents who aren't close to each other, or where the housing itself, or the income of the family, is inadequate are also often at risk.

The more of these factors there are, the less likely it becomes that the child will be able to make firm attachments.

Review
Changing needs for attachment

Children need parenting. This is best provided by people who enjoy being with children and stimulating them. Dependence on caregivers declines as children are able to explore and communicate. Children who are securely attached are likely to feel more confident to investigate and experiment with their new world.

If attachment fails

1 What differences would you expect to see between the behaviour of an insecurely attached child and a securely attached child?

2 Review the reasons for a child and its parents not forming a secure attachment.

4 The effects of long-term deprivation

Short-term separation often produces separation distress in young children, as described by Rene Spitz and by the Robertsons. There is disagreement about whether these problems persist. In 1975 J. W. B. Douglas (Director of the National Survey on Health and Development) found that children who had been in hospital (and therefore separated) when they were young were more likely to become delinquent when they were adolescents. This directly supports Bowlby's theory. The Clarkes reanalysed his data and found that the reason why many of the children went to hospital in the first place was because of problems of disadvantage in their homes. Many were from poor families, often having a poor diet. Many lived in cramped, overcrowded and inadequate homes. They often played on the street in dirty and dangerous areas. This social deprivation was usually the reason why the children had to go into hospital, and therefore may also contribute as much to their delinquency as any maternal deprivation they suffered. Michael Rutter came to much the same conclusion in his studies of adolescents.

The effects of short-term deprivation on children will largely depend on their age and previous experience. If the children aren't firmly attached they will not feel the pain of separation so much. The long-term effects of separation are harder to judge since they depend on so many more things.

While reviewing the case against some of John Bowlby's early ideas, we mentioned some orphanage studies which have shown that children can overcome the lack of an early attachment without suffering affectionless psychopathy. Children raised in orphanages behave like any other children for the first few months of life. From around six months their behaviour starts to change. They begin to lose interest in just about everything. William Goldfarb and Spitz and Wolf found that children who stayed in under-stimulating orphanages did not develop normal social or intellectual abilities. However, these children were not just maternally deprived, but were deprived of all sorts of stimulation.

Deprivation of parenting will almost certainly have unfortunate consequences if nothing is done to help make up for the deprivation. We mentioned Barbara Tizard and Jill Hodges's conclusions that children who were adopted quite late could, with patience and understanding on the part of their new parents, form loving relationships and enjoy a perfectly normal adulthood. The identical twin boys studied by Jarmila Koluchova seemed to have made an excellent recovery, and the war orphans studied by Anna Freud and Sophie Dann made good progress during the course of their study.

Long-term effects of deprivation

What sort of advice do you think someone adopting a child who has spent some time in an orphanage ought to be given concerning parenting the child?

Can children from deprived environments recover later?

Michael Rutter found many of the adolescent children he studied had recovered from their early deprivation. Wayne Dennis suggests that, if the child is below the age of two when the deprivation ends, then a full recovery is possible. He studied a number of children who had been adopted from a deprived orphanage at various ages. Those adopted after the age of two never fully recovered intellectually.

Background reading – Why is maternal and social deprivation so harmful?

Here are the main hypotheses:

The maternal deprivation hypothesis: This was first advanced by people like John Bowlby and Rene Spitz. They say that children need warm, loving relationships with their mother (or a permanent substitute). But Rudi Schaffer and Peggy Emerson have shown that babies from about eight months old can have many attachments, not just one with their mother.

The stimulus deprivation hypothesis: Children need different kinds of stimulation for them to become responsive to their environment. Children raised in unstimulating environments had little to look at or play with. There were no dependable people to show them how to respond socially. There were few toys to manipulate (to learn hand-to-eye coordination and practise handling skills). There were few opportunities to move around (to develop motor coordination and exploration skills). Altogether there was little opportunity for social, emotional, intellectual, or cognitive development.

The social stimulation hypothesis: Some investigators now believe that children need to have their social signals responded to. They use signals like crying and babbling to attract human attention. If this signalling fails, they become apathetic, and eventually give up trying. **Sally Provence** and **Rose Lipton** studied a sample of children in an institution. The children had toys to play with, could see and hear other infants, but had little contact with adults, i.e. they were socially deprived, not deprived of stimulation. They became emotionally, socially, and intellectually retarded.

The reason why social stimulation is so important is probably because the stimulation depends on the infants' own behaviour. When children cry, babble or smile, people will interact with them, i.e. they start the interaction. This may give them some feeling of control over their environment. They become more sociable as they learn to use their social signals when they want to attract other people's attention. The children in the institution wouldn't have their signals responded to, so after a time they would stop signalling, as it clearly didn't work. They may develop a sense of learned helplessness. This may explain why some deprived children are withdrawn and apathetic. NB Only the first hypothesis refers to mothers at all. In all the others, reference is made to either adults or situations.

Review
Failed attachments

Attachments can fail for a number of reasons which could originate with the children or with the parents. The effects are emotional disturbance which might affect other aspects of development. Children can recover from failed attachment if there is adequate, high-quality, continuous care available.

Other research on children in their normal homes also supports the case for social stimulation. Mentally retarded children from poverty-stricken homes are unlikely to have parents who are able or willing to provide the kinds of stimulation they need, and the children don't recover. Those in more affluent homes with better educated parents are more likely to recover.

No one can say for sure that the effects of prolonged early social deprivation are completely permanent or completely reversible. The children in Koluchova's study seemed to recover intellectually and socially, but it is harder to measure emotional development.

Can deprived children recover later?

Write an essay to answer the question: To what extent does the available evidence support or challenge the view that the effects of long-term deprivation are irreversible?

The Family and other Caregivers

In the last two chapters we have discussed the nature of attachments. We have defined an attachment as the close, emotional bond that develops between a baby and some of the people who care for it. We said that an attachment develops from when the baby is around five to seven months old. We suggested that children who are strongly attached feel more confident, and may become more competent, knowing that there is someone who will support them when things are going well, and care for them when things go wrong. There are many other benefits in having strong attachments too. Inevitably not all children are going to have strong, uninterrupted attachments.

In this chapter we will be looking at some of the major issues that can affect a young child's life. These include:

1 the family, including different types of parenting;
2 some problems associated with divorce;
3 the effects of care outside the home;
4 the possibilities for successful fostering and adoption.

1 The family and the parent

The vast majority of people in the West will be born into a family, will be reared by it, and will eventually marry and form a new one of their own. Various people have tried to analyse the *functions* of the family, and have concluded that the family reproduces the children, looks after them physically and emotionally, teaches them those things which they must know in order to become useful members of their society, and provides them with a status. **Robert LeVine** studied families from several cultures and concluded that they all fulfilled the following functions which can be described as the objectives or goals of parenting:

A function is a purpose or intended use.

The three goals of parenting, and how we achieve them in the West

1 To survive   Parents provide food, warm clothes,
                             and shelter. They nurse children
                             when they are sick, and comfort

Becoming a parent usually means taking on certain responsibilities. These include keeping the child physically safe and secure, and passing on useful knowledge.

2 To learn the norms and values of our culture

them when they are unhappy. Parents socialise their children into understanding about right and wrong, good and bad, and what norms (appropriate behaviour), and values (appropriate attitudes, beliefs, etc.) are acceptable in their culture.

3 To become economically independent

Parents teach their children some of the skills they will need to know in order to survive economically. Some parents may pass on the skills of their trade, others may teach their children about business.

Other people may also be involved in socialising children, of course. In our society teachers, medical staff, social work agencies, the churches, job training and opportunity agencies, and others may also be involved in the functions mentioned above. In other societies the responsibilities fall entirely on the parents. Parents are almost always more involved with a younger child, and the other people may start to become involved as the child gets older.

The arrival of a child usually marks some major changes in the parents' behaviour. These changes can affect the parents' attitudes and behaviour towards each other, towards friends and relations, and towards any other children they have. Mothers in particular often become more caring and come to devote most of their time to the infant.

The baby's needs have to come first, and this can mean a change in the way other family members feel. Older children may start to feel neglected. Their relationship with their parents may become weaker if they think their parents are rejecting them in favour of the new baby. Fathers who are less involved with the new baby may feel left out, and some mothers will be too tired or busy to tend to normal family routines.

Can you think of any other stresses that having a new baby might place on a family?

A baby can be an expensive addition to the family, particularly if one of the parents gives up work to spend time with it. Social engagements may have to be limited if babysitters have to be paid. Having less money, not seeing friends so often, and having to put someone else's needs first all the time, can place great strains on family life. Just about all of the research in **parenting** shows that the months and years following the birth of a child can be stressful for all concerned, and some families seem unable to cope. If the parents are older and more mature, financially and socially secure, and want, and plan for, a baby then the stress is least likely to be damaging to the family. Where the parents are younger, possibly unmarried, and the pregnancy is unplanned, the stress is likely to be greatest.

Conception and births outside marriage

(England and Wales)

	1979	1989
Conceptions outside marriage as a percentage of all conceptions	26%	42%
Of those conceptions the percentage that led to Births outside marriage	37%	53%
Births inside marriage which were conceived outside	23%	10%
Abortions	40%	37%
	100%	100%

1 What is the difference between conceptions and births?

2 Give two reasons why a conception may not lead to a birth.

3 Describe the change in the percentage of conceptions that took place outside marriage between 1979 and 1989.

4 What kind of problems might be faced by young parents when their baby arrives?

Review
The new baby

Where parents have planned for a new baby it can be a source of great joy to them. Caring for a helpless infant may bring couples closer together. However, babies can also be a source of great stress, especially where couples haven't realised the demands babies can make, or where they don't feel that they are able, or want, to cope with these demands.

The effects of early experiences on the child

Research in child development shows that the ways in which parents behave towards their children can have a very great effect on much of a child's development. We can identify three aspects of the parents' behaviour which will have major effects on their children. The first can be described as general *warmth and love* towards the children. For children of a few months of age onwards, parental warmth takes the form of attachment behaviour. The second consideration is the actual **child-rearing style** used. Some parents are strict about their children's behaviour, and may punish them quite severely. Some may be highly permissive in what they allow their children to do. Some will be tolerant of some things and not others, while others will be inconsistent, and punish their children, apologising to them later. The third factor is the extent to which the parents *accept the children* for what they are, without imposing unrealistic expectations on what they should achieve. We will summarise each in turn.

Child-rearing style refers to the general approach taken by the caregivers towards the child.

Warmth in the parent

Unfortunately not all children are wanted and planned. Those who are wanted and planned have parents who are ready and willing to offer them the warmth and love they need. It is more difficult for a mother or father to feel the same way towards an unplanned baby. Some children may simply be difficult to love. Hyperactive babies, ones who will not settle to a regular pattern of feeding and sleeping, babies who are uncooperative, and even handicapped babies may all be difficult to love.

We know that parents and children should build strong attachments during the first few years. John Bowlby had claimed scientific evidence to support his view that the early relationship between mother and baby is extremely important for the child to be able to build a sense of confidence and trust. He believed that babies have a hierarchy of preferences, with mother (or substitute mother) at the top, and other family and non-family members further down. Babies and mothers will form a bond which must not be broken. If it is broken, usually because mother and baby are separated, then emotional development will be interrupted, and the child may have problems rebuilding relationships later. Other researchers have suggested that Bowlby's view of parenting is too limited. For example, **Colwyn Trevarthen** and **Martin Richards** believe that babies are much more flexible in the range of social relationships they can enjoy, and they do not need a single, dominant attachment. Nor will separation from any one person necessarily be devastating if good alternative provisions are made for the infant.

Children of parents who are unable to show warmth and love, and children who were unplanned, tend to be insecurely attached, which can lead to lower levels of curiosity and independence. They may be more selfish and less sociable, have a lower opinion of themselves and their worth, and tend to have a high fear of punishment and parental disapproval. They may constantly seek approval before acting on any decision they have made.

Successful parents must show warmth towards their children. By warmth we mean that children enjoy being close to their parents, and enjoy doing things with their parents. The children of warm, loving parents will probably feel that they can confide in their parents too.

Child-rearing style

There's a lot more to bringing up children than just forming attachment bonds, and helping the children to learn about trust. Parents vary in their attitudes towards how their children should behave, and they may use different sorts of child-rearing style. A number of studies of child-rearing styles have shown the effect that parents can have on their children's long-term behaviour. **Mary Ainsworth**, a colleague of John Bowlby's, has shown that sensitive mothering, which puts the infant first, seems to be more successful in producing contented babies. Others have noted correlations between sensitive mothers and more independent, sociable, curious children too. Parents who are either too restrictive and domineering, or too easygoing and inconsistent, may encourage their children to develop a rather distorted view of the world.

Parents who use reasoned explanations, who use discipline in a warm and caring way, and who restrict any excessive aggression in their children, seem to be encouraging their children's maturity in several areas of development.

We will discuss two of the best-known studies on the effects of child-rearing styles and children's social behaviour in the chapter on aggression. Briefly, they conclude that **permissive** parents allowed their children to do almost anything they wanted to. Their children become highly aggressive. **Punitive** or **authoritarian** parents disciplined and punished their children a great deal. Their children learn that aggression was an appropriate way to achieve what they wanted although they were used to having other people decide what they should and should not do. A **democratic** or **authoritative** group of parents used a degree of discipline and restricted their children's aggression, without excessive punishment. Their children were more in control of themselves, and were more advanced in other skills too. They were also the least aggressive of the three groups.

Acceptance of the child as an individual

Parents should accept their children's worth. The children's opinions and ideas should be taken seriously and discussed, so that they build up confidence in their ability to make contributions to decisions. Children's ideas should not be overlooked or rejected, just because they are children's ideas. Parents who accept their children 'as they are' do not make unreasonable demands on their behaviour, nor do they set them unreasonable targets to achieve. Rather, they support and encourage their children in whatever direction (within reason) their abilities lie.

Parents who accept their children's attitudes and ideas, who listen to them and show an interest in what they think and do, are more likely to have children who are more willing to join in, more confident, and more able to be independent.

Relationships within the family

Apart from how parents treat their children, how the children see their own position in the family is also important. The oldest child may feel more responsible, and more important, or may be 'left in charge', or told to 'look after' the younger ones. The youngest child may feel inferior, or that his or her wishes and requests are swamped by those of older brothers or sisters. Or the youngest child may have to fight more to establish a distinct place in the family.

The sex of the child will also be important. One study of the effects of birth order on children suggested that first borns have slightly stronger consciences, are more curious and interested in new things, show more responsibility, and are less aggressive. If the next child is the same sex, and less than two years younger, he or she would be very similar to the first born. Where the next child was three or four years younger the older child tended to be more aggressive. This may have been because when the new baby arrived the older child may have felt threatened by all the attention that the new baby received. The older child may have become more noisy and aggressive in order to gain more attention.

Girls who had brothers rather than sisters tended to be more aggressive too. They had clearer ideas about what they wanted out of life, and were more determined to achieve their goals. They were slightly more intelligent than girls who had sisters too. Girls with older brothers were more tomboyish, and boys with older sisters were less aggressive and less curious.

▲
Older and younger children

Learning from our parents

1 Name three goals of parenting, according to Robert LeVine.

2 Name some of the changes that may happen to a couple's life when their first baby is born.

3 Name some of the consequences of an unsuccessful attachment.

4 Here is an extract from Diana Baumrind's description of the authoritative parent. 'The authoritative parent . . . attempts to direct the child's activities, but in a rational . . . manner. She encourages verbal "give and take", and shares with the child the reasoning behind her policy. . . . She balances her own special rights as an adult [against] the child's individual interest.'
Rewrite this extract in your own words.

5 Here is an extract from Diana Baumrind's description of the permissive parent. 'The permissive parents attempt to behave in a nonpunitive, acceptant, and affirmative manner towards the child's impulses, desires, and actions. She consults with him about policy decisions, and gives explanations for family rules. She makes few demands . . . [and] presents herself as a resource for him to use as he wishes, not as an active agent responsible for altering . . . his behaviour.'
Rewrite this extract in your own words.

Review
Parental influences

Children acquire many of their attitudes and behaviour from their parents. Parents who are warm, accepting, and authoritative in their dealings with their children, may be more able to achieve the three goals of successful parenting: survival, independence, and socialisation.

2 Children and divorce

Divorce is increasingly common in many Western societies. Some social groups are more at risk than others from divorce. This can have serious consequences for children.

Many children spend all or part of their lives away from one of their parents. In America it is estimated that about half of all marriages are likely to end in divorce, and almost half of all children are likely to spend some part of their lives in a single-parent family. In Britain and most of Europe divorce rates have been increasing over the last few years. About a quarter of all new marriages in Britain are likely to end in divorce. Some couples are more at risk than others. The latest statistics show that the highest rate of divorce is among people who have been married between eight and 10 years. About 12 per cent of all brides in Britain are under 20 years of age on their wedding day, and, of these, about three-quarters are pregnant. Teenage marriages have a very high risk of ending in divorce.

Psychologists have been interested in the effects that divorce is likely to have on the children. Freud argued that the absence of a father during a son's personality development would have disastrous consequences for the child's personality, as we shall see in the next chapter. A girl would suffer less because she still has her mother. Other psychologists say that children learn by observing and imitating their parents, if one parent is absent, then the child will be missing an important source of information about how a member of that sex behaves. The extent of these effects will depend on the age and level of understanding of the child, and should change between the short term and the long term.

Mavis Hetherington has reviewed most of the research on the effects of divorce on children. She claims that just about all children will show some short-term distress. For a year or so after the divorce, children may feel angry, guilty, afraid, and depressed. She calls this the **crisis phase**. Younger children may even see themselves as partly responsible and this can add to their distress. Their behaviour

Conducting research into the effects of divorce is very difficult. Who do we talk to? What should we ask? How should we phrase a question?

may change as a result of these feelings. Many children become more disobedient and more difficult to handle, while the parent who has custody may become more intolerant, bad tempered, and more inclined to use punishment. This may increase the child's anxieties, and lead to more unsettled behaviour. These effects will obviously depend on how close the child was to the parent it has lost, and how close the remaining parent was to the spouse. Emotional, social, and cognitive development can all be upset by the loss of a parent. Usually the mother has custody of the children and some research has shown that boys who were close to their fathers may suffer more than girls who were, and tend to remain, close to their mothers.

> Cognitive development refers to the child's increasing understanding.

The effects also depend on the reasons for the separation in the first place. As Michael Rutter and others have shown, conflict and distress in the home can have much worse effects on a child than simply losing a parent. Even many years after the divorce children may still feel bitter, although studies in America suggest that they do not seem to bear any grudges against either parent. After the **crisis phase** comes the **adjustment phase** as the child becomes used to life in a one-parent family, or life in a family with a new parent if the parent who had custody remarries.

> The effect that divorce will have depends on factors like how old the child is, how close the child was to the absent parent, and the levels of tension, stress and conflict in the home already.

Divorce

Here are some quotes from some children whose parents were divorced.

Sarah – (aged 10)
'I live with my Mum now, but Dad is here quite a lot too. They don't argue any more . . . and he buys me presents. He has another wife now, but I don't call her Mummy. They tried to explain what was happening when they got divorced. . . . Having parents who are divorced is okay . . . they're friends.'

Michael – (aged 7)
'I had to go to court . . . the people asked me questions about what I thought. It went on a long time, and Mum and Dad never spoke. It was cold and I cried. I only see Dad sometimes now. He comes for my birthday and I cry when he leaves. . . . I wish Dad still lived here but I don't think he likes us any more. He doesn't talk to me much, even when we go out.'

Andrew – (aged 14)
'No one really cares at school, loads of kids have parents who are divorced. I remember being frightened when they shouted. They probably thought we couldn't hear. We knew exactly what was going on, but they wouldn't talk to us. I hated him for going at first, but we got used to it.'

1 Summarise the differences in the way these children are coping with their parents' separation.

2 Do children always suffer when their parents divorce? Explain your answer.

3 Children can often understand a lot more than adults think they can. What evidence is there for this in the quotes above?

4 Children should never be allowed to feel guilty or responsible for their parents' divorce. Is there any evidence that any of these children do?

Review
Divorce

Statistically, the most usual length for a marriage that ended in divorce in the last few years has been between eight and 10 years. Any children in these families are likely to be young enough to be quite badly affected by the experience. They may feel resentful, angry, afraid, and may even feel partly to blame. However, as Rutter says, a couple whose marriage is full of conflict and bitterness may be better apart. Staying together for the sake of the children is not necessarily thought to be a good policy by most psychologists now, as the children may be hurt more by the conflict between their parents than they would by their separating.

5 How do you think parents who are planning to divorce could minimise the effects the divorce will have on the children?

Such statistics as we have suggest that divorce may well have long-term effects on the children. The children of divorced parents are more likely to leave school at 16 and leave home, owing to friction, than children in conventional families. They are also more likely to be married or cohabiting, and to have had children, by the time they are 20 years old.

However, the extent of these effects depends on what happens in the children's family after the divorce. For example, the effects are more likely to occur if the parent with whom the children stay remarries.

Long-term effects of divorce

Likelihood that children from divorced families, compared to those from intact families, will . . .

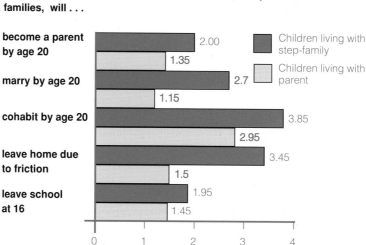

(adapted from: Family Policy Studies Centre, *Bulletin*, December 1991)

---

1 From the table above how much more likely is (a) a child from a lone parent family, and (b) a child from a step-parent family to become a parent by 20 years old, compared to a child from an intact family?

2 How much more likely are they to leave home because of friction?

3 What method do you think has been used to provide this table: experiments, case studies, observations or correlations?

4 Do you think that these effects are caused by the divorce or the remarriage? Explain your answer.

3 Care outside the home

Child rearing is a fairly full-time occupation. Bowlby claimed that it was a job which women were naturally equipped to do. Over the years many women have realised that there could be more to being a woman and a mother than just looking after children. Feminists and the women's liberation movements have condemned Bowlby's insistence that a woman's place is in the home with her children.

Because of the pattern of unemployment in Britain many women now go out to work while their husbands stay at home. It's too early yet to say what effects this pattern of childcare might have on the children. Michael Lamb found that fathers could provide soothing care as well as physical stimulation, so we shouldn't expect children looked after by their fathers to suffer any ill effects.

Apart from being reared full time by one or both parents, there are a number of alternative means of bringing up children. These range from those which give the caregiver a couple of hours a week away from the child, to those which give several hours a day. Some are more successful at recognising and meeting the child's needs. Some children will have a parent, or both parents, who aren't able to manage their children's lives because of some temporary difficulty such as illness, a problem with housing, or a problem with the courts. In such situations, the children may have to be taken into care by the Local Authority.

Do you agree with John Bowlby that women are naturally equipped to be mothers, and to look after the children? Or could men who stay at home bring up the children quite satisfactorily?

Childminding

Childminders are usually women with children of their own who take other children into their homes for a few hours during the day. This form of childcare could be of benefit to all concerned. It allows the mothers to keep their jobs, or whatever engagements they have, the minders to earn money, and the children to have another adult to attach to, interact with, and learn from. A child might go to the same childminder for several years and the childminder could be another continuous presence in the child's life.

Childminders should be registered with the local Social Services department who should inspect their premises and see that the facilities available for the children (toilets, heating, ventilation, play area, protection against infectious disease, and so on) are adequate. The child's physical needs and comforts are accounted for. Unfortunately there aren't similar regulations about the child's emotional needs.

In *Minder, Mother, and Child*, **Betty Mayall** and **Patricia Petrie** report the findings of their study of 39 registered childminders in four rather depressed inner city areas in London. Mayall and Petrie believed that the minders they studied were among the best available in the four boroughs. They said, 'We saw no minders living in bad housing conditions, and . . . their accommodation was (mostly) clean and well kept.' Most of them had experience of working with

Alternative forms of childcare are available – at a cost – in most areas for children whose parents do not look after them all of the time.

Apart from being brought up at home, some children spend time with a childminder, at playgroup, at nursery school, or at a day nursery. Did you or any of your friends have any of these forms of childcare? What sorts of thing did you do?

Mayall and Petrie conducted naturalistic observations of the minders and children, and interviewed the minders.

Childminders are usually married women who look after someone else's child alongside their own.

children, and most were trained. 'Nearly a third of them had had some work experience relevant to childminding [and] more than two thirds had contact with a special social worker who devoted himself or herself to childminder support or training.'

Mayall and Petrie took 27 of the children, and observed their interaction with their minders, and with their mothers. They were interested to see what kind of activities the children were involved in at the minders, and whether these activities encouraged cooperation, whether the children were being stimulated, and whether they appeared to be happy. Mayall and Petrie also interviewed the minders to discover what they thought their role was, and the children's mothers to find out what the children were like at home.

A study of childminders in the inner city

1　What research method did Mayall and Petrie use in their study?

2　What measures of the independent variable are being taken (i.e. what exactly were they interested to see)?

3　How could their findings be checked?

Mayall and Petrie's conclusions paint a fairly depressing picture. It seemed that an opportunity for the children to have an enjoyable and stimulating experience was not being taken.

Mayall and Petrie found that the minders were not attempting to act as substitute mothers, neither were they offering the children the chance to form any kinds of **attachment**. Many of the children looked almost **detached**. They seemed to have little real interest in what was going on, and weren't offered any kind of involvement with the minder. Many of the children studied didn't seek stimulation or company. Others were noisier, but there wasn't very much for them to do, and they were there really just to fill in time. They weren't benefiting much at all. To sum up, Mayall and Petrie found unstimulated children being looked after by childminders who didn't offer them the chance to become very involved. They said, 'The children spent a low level, under-stimulated day in unchanging, often cramped, surroundings.' Many did not receive the love and attention they needed. Some had experienced frequent changes of minder, and most of their mothers were not satisfied with the standard of care offered.

In the early 1970s a group of people interested in childcare for the under fives came together under the leadership of Professor Jerome Bruner to investigate the state of various aspects of childcare in Britain, and to spread such information as already existed as widely as possible. It was called the **Oxford Preschool Research Group**, and reported on such topics as playgroups, nursery schools, childminding, and day nurseries.

As a part of the Oxford Preschool Project, run by the Oxford Preschool Research Group, **Brigit Bryant, Miriam Harris**, and **Dee Newton** studied some childminders in a fairly affluent part of Oxfordshire. They sampled 165 minders randomly from the list of registered childminders, although only 66 were minding a child at the time of the research. Between them they were looking after 98 children, so most of the minders were caring for one child who was not their own. The researchers used a questionnaire, an interview, and observations as the main data collection methods. The observations were modelled on those conducted by Mayall and Petrie so that direct comparisons could be made. Bryant, Harris, and Newton found none of the problems of shortage of toys and play materials, or cramped conditions that Mayall and Petrie had found.

Most of the minders Bryant, Harris and Newton studied were reasonably well off, and 'housing conditions seemed . . . to be very good, particularly in comparison with inner city minders'. Houses were warm, and all but one had a garden, and a nearby park in which the children could play safely. Like those minders Mayall and Petrie had studied, this sample also put their own families' needs first. Shopping, cleaning, cooking, and looking after their own children came before stimulating the minded children. About three-quarters of the children's days were spent at the minders' homes while the minders did their chores. Consequently few of the minders found much time for playing with the children, or offering them any specific stimulation.

Bryant, Harris, and Newton conducted observations of the children, both at home and while with the minders. They also interviewed the mothers and the minders. They found that few minders wanted the mothers to do anything other than drop the children off, then leave. They felt it was their job to look after the children. They did not see any great need to form any kind of a relationship with them, and since they were fairly busy people they didn't have very much time to spend with each child.

Overall, the researchers were able to divide their sample up into three groups of children. Twenty-nine per cent of the children (who were seen both at home and with the minders) were described as being in the 'lively' group, while 26 per cent were described as being in the 'quiet' group. They didn't seem to be involved in anything except repetitive, solitary play, both at home and at the minders.

Bryant, Harris, and Newton found that childminding seems to work well enough for those children who are happy at home, and who do find stimulation at the minders. It is tolerable for other children, who are content to fill in time until they can go home. The opportunities that minding could offer were lost for these children. Those children who are not stimulated at home were unlikely to be stimulated by the minder.

Background reading – A description of a 'typical' minder

She is 'married, in her early thirties, with three, or possibly four [of her own] children, and, quite likely, a foster child too. Some of her children are already at school. She has lived in the same area for most of her life, and has parents, brothers, or sisters living near by. She left school at 16 and went more or less straight out to work until her marriage or the arrival of her first baby, after which she stayed at home, or perhaps worked part time. At some point she may have worked with children.

'She has married a man who is in skilled or semi-skilled work, and they are still living together. She feels little stress at being a mother and housewife, and is strongly convinced that she should stay at home with her children at least until they start school. Indeed she may be rather unsympathetic towards mothers who leave their young children and go out to work.' (Bryant, Harris, and Newton).

Children who are unstimulated at home are unlikely to find stimulation with a minder. The third group was the largest group, made up of 45 per cent of the sample. These children were usually unnaturally quiet and good while at the minders but were also quite happy at home. These children could have benefited from childminding, but were not doing so. Overall, almost three-quarters of these children were happy and lively at home, but less than a third were lively at the minders.

Better-off parents may employ a full-time nanny to look after their children. She could form an attachment with the children in her care, and provide a rich source of stimulation. This works well if the nanny stays for some years, but the child can become upset if the bond is broken when she leaves.

Childminding

1 Write a brief paragraph under the heading, 'The main benefits of childminding could be . . .'.

2 If you have a child that you want to be minded, what steps do you think you should take, in the first instance, to find a minder?

3 Having found one, how might you want to settle the child in? (HINT: What did the Robertsons do before having Thomas stay with them?)

4 If attachment doesn't depend on the quantity of time spent with the child, what does it depend on? Briefly explain your answer.

Review
Childminding

While we know that children can make multiple attachments, and that they can benefit from having a variety of adults and children around them, the major studies of childminding show that children are not benefiting in the ways that they could. The reason for this is not so much lack of knowledge, but more a lack of resources. Parents are unlikely to want to pay enough to a minder to allow her to devote herself to a few children. Most minders take in someone else's children while remaining mainly concerned with their own family's needs.

Playgroups

Playgroups are not usually run by qualified professionals, but rather by groups of mothers. They may hire a local hall, such as a club hut, school, or church hall for a few mornings each week. (Some charitable bodies even run Playbuses to serve families in poor or outlying districts where facilities aren't always available.)

Nursery schools

Nursery schools are run by some Local Education Authorities which employ professionally trained teachers, and sometimes qualified children's nurses, to staff them. Parents and other helpers are also often invited to become involved. Most nursery classes offer preschool children wider opportunities to play and wider social experiences than they might have at home.

Kathy Sylva, **Carolyn Roy**, and **Marjorie Painter** conducted a study of nursery schools as part of the Oxford Preschool Research Project. They made detailed observations of children's activities in the schools, and assessed the contribution of nursery school experiences to the children's development. In *Childwatching at Playgroup*

Evaluation of follow-up studies

Criticisms	Advantages
1 The source of information, i.e. the memories of the adopted or fostered person, and their parents, may not be valid or reliable.	1 There is no better alternative. It is not possible to conduct controlled experiments on the variables 'being fostered or adopted' and adult 'emotional responses' in humans.
2 They rely on the researcher observing and conducting tests to judge how well adjusted the people are. Observations may be partial, and tests may be invalid.	2 Judgements based on observations and test results are used throughout psychology. Results gained here are no more likely to be mistaken than results gathered in other areas.
3 Such studies usually rely on seeking correlations.	3 Correlations may not show cause, but do give an indication of a relationship.

Adoption

Fostering may be a solution for those children who need short-term care in a family or those whose parents haven't signed the release forms for the children to be adopted. Most psychologists agree that the best solution for children who are not to be brought up by their natural mothers is full adoption. Clearly we would like the child to become deeply attached to its new parents. Whether or not this happens depends on things like how deeply the child had been attached to the natural mother. If the child is a few years old, and was deeply attached, then the loss will be deeply felt. The new parent may have great problems in convincing the child that he or she will be loved and cared for. A child whose trust has been badly broken once is unlikely to give it very easily again. The new parents must be very willing to offer enormous patience, stability, consistency, and security. A child's age and maturity will also influence the level of emotional stability and whether, or how, this will be affected. Before babies have learned a strong attachment (before six or seven months of age), a successful substitution should be quite possible. At the other end of the age range, older children may find it easier to understand what is happening to them, and may settle into a new home more easily. An American study by Alfred Kadushin found that children of up to 12 years of age have been adopted satisfactorily, and made good, loving relationships.

If we can't measure someone's emotional state with any accuracy, how will we know whether being adopted has provoked any effect? For example, can we say that a little girl's occasional bad moods are the result of her adoption? Is she unapproachable because she misses her real mother? Can you think of any reason why someone might be in a bad mood? Does it have to be anything to do with their parents?

Despite these difficulties, careful observations, interviews with parents, and reports from school are the only techniques that can be used to investigate the effects of substitute parenting. As it is impossible to conduct controlled experiments, researchers must either use follow-up studies or find children who are being offered for adoption or fostering and monitor their progress.

Fostering and adoption

1 Think of some reasons why children might be fostered.

2 Think of some reasons why children can't stay with their natural parents, and so are offered for adoption.

3 Here is an advert from a local paper.

The Astonville Courier   Wednesday 19th August

WANTED

A very special family.

Nick is 13 years old and needs someone to look up to.

He's stayed with two families before, but didn't really settle in.

Nick is quiet and plays on his own quite a lot. He is quite shy, and takes time to get to know. We believe the effort would be greatly rewarded. Nick can show a great deal of affection. If you'd like to find out more about Nick, or about becoming a foster parent, please ring Emily Pankhurst on Astonville 393456.

---

4 What evidence is there in this advert to suggest that Nick may have some emotional problems?

5 What sort of (a) behaviour and (b) emotional problems might Emily Pankhurst warn anyone replying to this advert to look out for?

6 Imagine your Director of Social Services has asked you to conduct a study into the success rate of adoptions in your area. Write a brief report setting out how you intend to investigate it.

Barbara Tizard, Judith Rees and **Jill Hodges** conducted a follow-up study of 65 children from deprived families, who had been put into residential nurseries before they were six months old. They hadn't formed strong attachments, and they didn't have the opportunity to form any in the nursery. There were plenty of toys and games and other stimulating materials in the nursery, but the nurses rarely stayed long and were not encouraged to become too involved with the children. Apart from being fairly noisy, rather afraid of strange adults, and very clinging, the children seemed to be coping fairly well in their nursery.

Between two and three years of age some were adopted, some were returned to their natural mothers (many of the mothers weren't married and hadn't been able to cope previously), and some remained in the nursery (because their mothers couldn't be found to sign the necessary forms for the babies to be adopted).

Background reading – Can older children benefit from adoption?

During the 1950s and 1960s a number of children from Dr Barnardo's Homes and other orphanages were adopted at three, four, five years of age, and even older. They made great demands on their new parents, many of whom couldn't cope with the treatment they received from the children, and some of the children had to be returned to the orphanages. Some of the children seemed unwilling to make an attachment so it was assumed that children above one or two years old couldn't be adopted. Bowlby's work was quoted to support this.

There is a more likely explanation why these adoptions failed. Many of the adopting parents weren't well enough informed about what to expect. Many thought they were adopting a normal child who was no longer a baby. Many social workers themselves weren't trained to be aware of the likely problems. The adopting parents and the children weren't given enough time to get to know each other. The adoptions failed through a lack of information and preparation, not through the child's inability to make another attachment to its new parents.

The early years of our lives are important, but not as important as used to be believed. Ann and Alan Clarke have reviewed a great deal of evidence to show that children are capable of adapting to major upheavals in their lives. We also now know that late adoptions can be successful.

The problems of measuring success

1 Try answering these questions about yourself:
When did you first have a best friend? Did you often argue with him/her? Did you join in with the other children at school? Were you popular at school? Do you like being alone sometimes? Did you often get nervous and anxious? Have you had many girlfriends/boyfriends, or do you prefer permanent relationships? Do you have a bad temper? Did you cry very often?

2 When answering questions like these, can we be sure that you have understood what the questions mean? (How often is 'very often'?) Can we take your word that you have remembered everything correctly? Or that you've told the truth? Even if we ask your parents to give their opinions of what you're like, will we have an accurate picture of your emotional state?

Here's a brief extract from a case study of a 19-year-old who was adopted. It was written after naturalistic observation and interviews.

'Sharon is usually calm and in control of her feelings. She is rarely aggressive or self-centred, and is popular among her wide circle of friends. She expresses her feelings well, and is absolutely truthful. She occasionally

Review
Adoption

Barbara Tizard and her colleagues have shown that adoption can be a very satisfactory solution. Younger children who have no parents may be offered for adoption. Very young children can attach to their new parents with the minimum of fuss. Older children, who had already formed attachments, may have greater problems. Adoption is still the best solution for parentless children, as all the alternatives seem unable to provide the essential elements of parenthood, warmth, consistency, accepting the children for who they are, and using a sensible, reasonable system of acceptable and unacceptable behaviour.

Environmental factors appear even more important for emotional, social, and cognitive development than biological ones. Barbara Tizard and her colleagues have shown that full adoption seems to be the best alternative for children who aren't able to stay with their natural mothers and fathers in a well-equipped home.

The success of the adoption seems to depend on factors such as how far the new parents are prepared to go to show the child that they will love and support it, and that the child is special to those parents.

has bad moods, and becomes depressed. At these times she is quiet and unapproachable.'

3 How scientifically acceptable are such observations?

_____

Barbara Tizard and her colleagues followed up these three groups, and a control group of babies (who had not been in an institution and were being brought up 'normally'). The four groups were all studied at two years old, then at four and a half, and then at eight years of age.

At two years old the nursery children were all fairly similar. They were largely unattached. They were quite different from the controls, who were more secure and independent.

By four and a half years old some differences between the nursery groups were emerging. Those who had been adopted formed attachments with their new parents, but made great demands on them. They had almost caught up with the controls intellectually, but their emotional behaviour was not as advanced. They were still rather shy and weren't very adventurous. They would cling to their parents, and still showed stranger fear. The next most mature group at four and a half years old were those who'd stayed in the orphanage. They received some stimulation, both from toys and from humans. They were often noisy and boisterous. Some weak attachments had been made. The least well developed intellectually were those who had been returned to their mothers. Their families still lived in rather deprived conditions and the children lacked two of the main things they seem to need for healthy psychological development: people who enjoy interacting with them, and things to play with and manipulate.

By eight years old the adopted group was still the most advanced group (after the controls). They had developed strong relationships but were still rather restless and timid. They didn't make friends as easily as the controls, and they were still rather clinging towards their new parents. The lack of an early attachment was still being felt. They weren't able to concentrate on schoolwork for very long either. Those returned to their mothers and those who had stayed in the orphanage were not as well developed in their social relationships or intellectual abilities.

Evidence from this and other studies suggests that children can overcome even the most deprived early experiences. Adoption into a family that desperately wants a child, and which is capable of providing the kind of care the child needs, is the best solution for a child from a deprived background. John Bowlby claimed that children need their mothers, and that even a bad home is likely to be better than a good institution. Tizard's study does not support this claim. The children who were returned to their mothers did not develop as well as many of the others who were adopted.

Follow-up studies

1 What was Triseliotis's sample size?

2 Summarise the conclusions from John Triseliotis's follow-up study.

3 Why did Barbara Tizard and her colleagues use a control group in their study?

4 Why did they follow up the four groups several times over the next few years?

5 Briefly describe the development of each of these four groups.

6 Bowlby had claimed that it is best for a child to be brought up by his or her natural mother. The study by Barbara Tizard and her colleagues casts doubt on that claim. For example, if the caregiver has a strong motivation to be with the child, can provide stimulation, and can show due love and affection, then this can be a positive alternative for the child, providing the important factors for his or her healthy development. Summarise the evidence for this statement.

Residential nurseries

Apart from minding, nannying, and other temporary forms of child-care, there are some more permanent ways of looking after children for short periods. Residential nurseries were available in some areas for very young children awaiting adoption, or entry into an orphanage. Some children were also admitted for a period of a few days or weeks, while their parents weren't able to look after them. If the children's mothers had to go into hospital, for example, and no one else was able to take care of them, they may have been placed in a residential nursery. The Robertsons made detailed observations of the progress of several children who were temporarily placed in residential nurseries. Some children would have survived the experience, some might even have benefited from it. The likelihood is that most would have suffered. This was certainly James and Joyce Robertson's conclusion. Factors which would influence the children's experiences include how long the children stay in the nursery, the kind of care available for them while there, and the amount and type of stimulation available.

We have said that children from between approximately six months and five years old need to form an attachment bond with their main caregivers. Bowlby had warned about the terrible consequences of breaking this bond. He warned that a separation of just a fortnight could have permanent ill effects. Even separations of just a few days can have serious short-term effects, such as poor sleeping, increased temper tantrums, wanting to be carried rather than walking, increased stranger fear, being over-affectionate and clinging. James and Joyce Robertson's pioneering work in the 1950s and 1960s showed that this experience could be very upsetting for children who were temporarily placed in residential nurseries. Despite fierce hostility from some members of the medical and childcare professions, the Robertsons' warnings have now largely been accepted, and every effort is made for young children who have to be temporarily separated from their parents to be fostered.

Residential nurseries are not widely available now, and children are much less likely to be separated from their parents than was the case 20 years ago.

The type of care available will also have some effect. Many institutions used to employ systems of group care, where a small number of nurses simply looked after a group of children. Inevitably the noisier, more demanding children were likely to attract the most attention. Children who had been in the nursery for a long time would have learned that they must make their demands loudly and insistently if they were to attract the nurses' attention. Children who were placed in the institution temporarily may have been unable to compete. They may have felt left out, and may have felt their isolation even more.

In many child care institutions now, the system of group care has been replaced with a system of individual care. Each child is assigned one, two, or three particular nurses who are to act as temporary *attachment objects*. The children may come to feel that their nurses are special to them. James and Joyce Robertson's work has shown that many of the problems that young children in brief separation face are caused not necessarily by the separation itself but by what happens to the child while separated. Being given one special person to form some kind of attachment with may help the child overcome some of the problems of breaking the bond with the usual caregiver.

Having a few special people to attach to will not solve all the child's problems, of course. The child is still separated from permanent caregivers, and will feel that loss. Three other factors must be mentioned which may affect the child.

First the child's age is an important variable. For children below six months, who haven't yet formed a strong attachment, the effects of separation are unlikely to be very harmful. Children over four or five years old can have the cause for the separation explained to them, although they may not see why they can't stay at home while their mother is away. Children between six months and three or four years old are likely to feel the loss most deeply.

A second factor is the willingness and ability of the children's nurses to provide constant love, warmth, comfort, soothing explanations, and reassurance. This isn't always easy, since nursing staff often work very long hours, doing very tiring work.

A third factor is the availability and use of intellectually stimulating toys and games. Young minds need to be occupied, and something which challenges children's imagination and intellect may take their mind off the separation, and make the time seem to pass more quickly.

A criticism that has been levelled at some of the early work on the effects of separation is that it overlooked a key variable, i.e. what happened to the child during the separation. As the Robertsons showed, the detachment suffered by some of the children they studied wasn't wholly the result of the loss of their mother, but rather the lack of any permanent substitute.

Review
Residential nurseries

Residential nurseries may be used by children who are awaiting adoption or moving permanently into an orphanage. The Robertsons found that systems of group care were not at all helpful for some of the young children they studied during the 1950s and 1960s. Children in residential care need intellectual and social stimulation as well as warm, consistent, and loving substitute mothering.

Residential nurseries

1 Why might a child have been put into a residential nursery in the 1960s?

2 What is meant by a system of 'group care', and how does it differ from individual care?

Temperament and Personality

Parents often compare notes about what their babies are like and the progress they are making. Some boast that their baby has always been good, rarely cries and seems very alert and interested. Others complain that their child often cries and doesn't seem very settled. It seems that, right from birth, there are quite noticeable differences between babies, and this would suggest that these differences are largely the result of genetic inheritance.

Some babies are easy to handle. Their moods don't swing much and their reactions are fairly predictable. They aren't over-active or under-responsive. Other babies are more difficult. Their moods change quickly and their behaviour is unpredictable. They do not adapt to change and they seem unsettled. These differences in temperament often last well into childhood. As children gain more experience of the world, their understanding combines with their temperament to produce their personality.

If temperament were simply the consequence of genetic inheritance then it would be fairly stable and consistent. This isn't wholly true. A baby often responds differently with different caregivers. It may be rather more difficult when cared for by one person, and rather easier if cared for by another.

The problem here is that most of the evidence for what babies are like comes from interviews with mothers and observations of them and their babies. Such methods aren't always valid or reliable.

There is some psychological evidence which does show that temperament may be influenced by social experiences. Mary Ainsworth shows how a mother who responds quickly and sensitively to her baby's crying tends to have a more contented baby. Barbara Tizard and her colleagues noted how babies who had been adopted from an orphanage changed their responses too.

For the rest of this chapter we will review Sigmund Freud's contribution to our understanding of personality development. His was one of the first complete theories, and one of the most influential.

Freud spent most of his life constructing **case studies** on his patients, and developing explanations why their personalities changed. Psychological theories which attempt to explain how people change are generally called **psychodynamic** theories. Freud's was one of the first of these. His particular explanations are usually known as **psychoanalysis**.

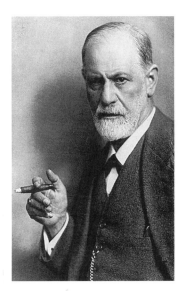

Sigmund Freud

Research is said to be valid if it really does investigate what it claims to be investigating. We cannot be entirely sure that mothers will remember precisely or report truthfully what their children were like. And reliable means that the observations would always lead to the same conclusions on other occasions.

Review

Temperament may best be thought of as a way of describing how babies are generally likely to respond to stimulation. It is probably a process that changes as the child has new experiences.

Freud was interested in physiology and neurology. Physiology is the branch of biology that studies what animal cells, tissues, and organs do, and what they are made of. Neurology is the branch of medicine concerned with studying the nervous system.

Here are some suggestions for activities that you may find useful during this section of the course. Collect any articles or newspaper reports, or something similar, on anything involving people with personality or behaviour problems. Make notes from any television programmes you see on mental health. Keep a diary of any dreams you have during the next week.

Here we have a picture of a number of patients with particular illnesses which don't appear to have any conscious, physical cause. Can you think of any other possible explanation for their illness? HINT: There's a clue in the first sentence of this comment.

Do these findings about hypnotism fit in with your answer to the last question? Do they offer any further explanations? Where do these patients' illnesses seem to come from? HINT: Look at the last HINT. It has something to do with the causes of the symptoms.

In this chapter we shall be looking at the following areas.
1 The origins of Freud's theory, and the methods he developed to investigate it.
2 What Freud discovered about the unconscious.
3 The structure of human personality.
4 The stages of personality development.
5 Some evaluation of Freud's approach and explanations.

1 The background to psychoanalysis

One of the earliest and best-known explanations for personality development comes from Sigmund Freud (1856–1939).

While studying medicine at the University of Vienna towards the end of the last century, Sigmund Freud had become particularly interested in human anatomy, and intended to do research in human physiology and neurology when he graduated.

Freud had attended some neurology lectures on patients with severe headaches, temporarily paralysed limbs, temporary blindness, and similar symptoms. These are typical of particular disorders of the nerves and muscles. But the surgeons couldn't find anything wrong with these particular patients' nerves or muscles. Freud, and a colleague, Dr **Josef Breuer**, had some patients with similar problems for which they could find no organic cause. (NB: Organic refers to the organs of the body.)

While still puzzling over the possible causes of their symptoms, Freud heard about some work being conducted on hypnosis in Paris by **Jean Martin Charcot**. Professor Charcot was using hypnotism to show that patients could be made to feel they had certain symptoms such as numbness, paralysis, etc. When they were brought out of the hypnotic state they couldn't remember anything about the trance they'd been in, and they had the symptoms that Charcot had told them they would have. Freud wanted to know if hypnosis could work the other way round, i.e. could patients with such symptoms be hypnotised into believing that their symptoms had disappeared?

Freud believed there must be some relationship between the mind and the body. In 1885 he went to Paris to study hypnosis with Charcot. During the four months he was there he became fascinated by the **unconscious mind**. He returned to his patients, determined to develop techniques, like hypnosis, for exploring the unconscious mind.

The unconscious mind

A five-year-old boy named Ounkar was taken to the dentist for his usual check-up. He had been eating lots of sweets recently, and the dentist told his mother he would have to give the child's teeth a bit of a scrape. Ounkar didn't like the sound of this. He didn't enjoy the scrape either. Ounkar said the dentist had hurt his mouth. When he got home his mother told him he would have to stop eating so

Sigmund Freud – A biography

Sigmund Freud was born in May 1856, in Frieberg, now Pribor in the Czech Republic. Freud's father was a rather unsuccessful wool merchant. When Sigmund was three, the family moved, first to Leipzig in Germany, and then to Vienna, the capital of Austria, in the hope that business might be better there. Vienna was dominated by the Roman Catholic religion, and Jews were discriminated against. The Freud family was Jewish, and this was to have important consequences for Sigmund Freud later.

Freud's parents encouraged him to be independent and he was always studying. He started school a year earlier than was usual, and did well there. At 17 he entered the medical school of Vienna University. He didn't particularly want to be a doctor, although he knew he could make a living at it if necessary. His real ambition was to do scientific research. He went to as many science lectures as he could. (This is why it took him eight years to finish his degree!) He finally obtained his MD (Doctor of Medicine) in 1881 and started work at a large hospital in Vienna.

In June 1882, he became engaged to Martha, with whom he was passionately in love. Neither of them had any money, and their four-year engagement was rather stormy. Freud borrowed money from his close friend, Dr Josef Breuer, and even pawned his watch to find enough money to live. He took several jobs at the hospital, and learned as much as he could about the areas he studied. He had to give up the research he was doing and concentrate on earning more money, specialising in neurological and physiological cases. His private patients were mostly poor Jewish people. He worked and saved for four years. By September 1886 he had enough money to marry his beloved Martha.

Freud became interested in the mind, and for almost 50 years he investigated the origins of personality. He developed a theory which was to have lasting effects on psychology in Europe and America (although it had little impact in Russia, China, Africa, and Asia). He wrote several books on psychology. The first, published in 1895, was called *Studies in Hysteria* which he wrote with Breuer. By the 1930s his work was being translated into different European languages, and hospitals were opening psychiatric departments based on using Freudian psychoanalysis.

Freud lived and worked in Vienna almost all of his life. When it finally became obvious in 1938 that the Jews would be further persecuted by the Nazis, the Freud family came to Britain where Sigmund spent the last year of his life working on his final book. He died in September 1939 at the age of 83.

---

many sweets and then the dentist wouldn't have to scrape his teeth.

Ounkar soon forgot his mother's warning, however. Six months later, on the morning of the day of his next check-up. Ounkar was violently sick and had to stay in bed with an upset stomach.

1 Ounkar was genuinely sick and complained of a poorly tummy. He didn't have any particular illness, and he was fine by teatime. Can you think of any explanations for this mystery illness?

2 Would it be possible to check any of your explanations?

Do you think that there are any illnesses which might be caused by mental events which may be unconscious? Do you know of an example? Check with other people to see if you can find other examples.

If researchers discover some symptom of a disorder that is unknown to science, they give it a name. Bowlby did this when he discovered the condition affectionless psychopathy. Freud described

Freud concluded that the causes of hysteria lay in the unconscious, and wished to find ways of investigating it. Can you think of any ideas? We've already mentioned something which could help. HINT   Remember Freud's visit to Paris?

Review
The origin of Freud's theory

Freud had some patients with problems for which there was no organic cause. He called them symptoms of hysteria. The patients had no conscious knowledge of the cause of their hysteria, so Freud thought the cause must lie in their unconscious. Freud thought the unconscious has a powerful influence on us. He believed it contains deep forces which make us behave in all sorts of ways. He wanted to investigate his patients' unconscious minds.

Freud made detailed observations of some of his patient's behaviour. Science is very concerned with making observations, and making educated guesses based on them. All scientific investigations must involve observation.

the type of mental disorders his patients suffered as *hysteria*. Nowadays we use terms like 'hysterical neurosis' to describe some of the symptoms Freud observed. The term 'hysteria' had been used for hundreds of years, usually to describe odd female behaviour. (The term literally means wandering uterus!) Can you think of any illnesses that are named after the person who first researched them?

As a doctor, Freud could look into someone's throat, or stomach, or chest, but how was he to look into their unconscious minds? Freud was a dedicated scientist and realised that he would have to develop scientific techniques for finding out what was going on in the unconscious.

Freud's background

1 Approximately when did Freud start work as a doctor? Was it the middle of the last century, during the second half of the last century, or in the first half of this century?

2 What do neurologists and physiologists study?

3 What does the term 'organic' refer to?

4 Why did Freud become interested in hysteria?

5 Name three symptoms of hysteria.

6 Where did Freud think these symptoms came from?

7 Write a paragraph beginning 'Freud believed the unconscious mind. . .'.

Techniques for studying the unconscious

Freud thought the human mind was a bit like an iceberg. The tip which can be seen – or understood – is the **conscious** part. The **unconscious** part is much larger, and is hidden from view. He developed a number of techniques for investigating the unconscious part. Most resulted from his **clinical interviews** with his patients. He started with hypnosis which he had tried to learn from Charcot. However not everyone can be hypnotised, and unfortunately Freud was not always a very successful hypnotist. Hypnosis sometimes gave contradictory results and Freud soon gave it up, saying it was temperamental. Instead he made some deductions from his observations of some of his patients.

Freud asked some of his patients to talk freely about their earliest memories, and how they felt about the people in their lives. If they seemed to run out of things to say Freud would give them key words, like 'happiness', 'love' or 'fear'. When Freud asked them direct questions their replies were often fairly predictable, but when they were just talking freely they occasionally said things that were more revealing. Freud thought they seemed to give some clues about what was going on in their unconscious. Several patients mentioned being very frightened of some things. It was as though they were off their guard when talking freely, and able to say things which they may not have said otherwise. Freud asked more of his patients to talk freely, and he began to try to piece together their backgrounds. This technique is called **free association** and became a major tool for investigating the unconscious.

One of the earliest, and probably best known of psychoanalytic case studies was conducted by Josef Breuer on a patient referred to as Anna O. (Her real name was Bertha Pappenheim and she went on to become a well-respected social relief worker.) When she was a young woman, she suffered a number of symptoms, including temporary paralysis of her limbs and multiple personalities. Breuer began Anna's free association treatment when she was 21. Anna O was a very stubborn, determined woman, and she insisted that talking about her problems made her feel better. She invented the term **talking cure** to describe the effects the therapy had on her.

One of Anna O's problems was paralysis of an arm. Breuer thought he had found the cause in something that had upset her a great deal when she was younger. Anna had been looking after her father, who was very ill in bed. She worked very hard and was very tired. While sitting in the old man's sick room waiting for the doctor, she imagined she saw a large, black snake slithering towards her sleeping father. This frightened her very much. She tried to stand up and go to her father, but her right arm, which was draped around the back of the chair, just wouldn't move. Breuer concluded that this combination of wanting to protect her father and the fact that her arm wouldn't move, explained Anna's paralysis. She had buried the fear and the guilt she felt about being unable to protect her father in her unconscious, and this somehow caused her paralysis. As Anna began to realise what the things she described meant, so her condition improved.

Freud and Breuer developed a technique called free association which could encourage their patients to reveal their deepest feelings.

Anna O, a case study in hysteria

1 Name some of Anna O's symptoms.

2 What did Breuer conclude was causing her symptoms?

3 Do you think that Breuer cured her? Explain your answer.

During a free association session, one of Freud's patients started to tell him about a dream he'd had. Freud had thought that dreams might be another way of the unconscious breaking through into the conscious world, as when we are asleep we are relaxed. So Freud analysed his patients' dreams. He came to the conclusion that during our daily lives there are so many rules and restrictions governing what we can and can't do that we can never be truly free. While we sleep many of these restrictions are cast aside and our innermost

Freud thought that dreams revealed what was going on in the unconscious. Do you have any recurring dreams? Can you remember what you dreamed last night? We all have a few dreams each night, but we usually forget them quite quickly. Why do you think we dream? Do you think that what we dream is always what we wish would happen?

thoughts and wishes can be revealed. Freud believed that dreams reveal what we really want. He said that dreams show our **concealed wish fulfilment**.

▶
A therapy session

Freud had a great interest in ancient civilisations and some of his ideas about the mind appear to have been influenced by it. He was fascinated by archaeology, and, when he could afford to, he bought objects that had been discovered by archaeologists. Although his consulting room and treatment room were small, they were full of his treasures.

It seemed to Freud that, while we are awake and alert, a kind of guardian or censor watches over us, making sure we don't come into contact with anything too upsetting. While we sleep, however, our censor is rather off guard as little can upset our conscious mind while we are asleep. The parts of the dream that can be remembered may provide a skilled psychoanalyst with the clues as to what the dreams really mean. Dreams are a 'window on the unconscious' which, with skilful interpretation, can be understood as signs from the unconscious. Freud described **dream analysis** as 'the royal road' to the unconscious.

Apart from dream analysis Freud also noticed that people sometimes say something which comes out all wrong. They are called **slips of the tongue**. Freud thought that what we actually said was often what we meant. Freud analysed any slips of the tongue his patients made (which later became known as Freudian slips). He concluded that these slips of the tongue were also a sign that our guard was down and the unconscious was breaking through.

Slips of the tongue may also be the unconscious breaking through into consciousness. Have you ever meant to say something, but when you spoke it came out all wrong? Do you think you really meant what you actually said?

Freud used a number of other methods to investigate his patients' unconscious minds. For example he examined occasions when people seem to forget things on purpose, without being aware of what they are doing. He studied their sense of humour to see if there were any clues there about what they thought. Freud used clinical interviews and the techniques of psychoanalysis to develop case studies of his hysterical patients. His case studies relied very much on his own observations and interpretations of what his patients said and did. They weren't just the usual medical case notes that doctors make.

Freud slowly developed his theory of psychoanalysis based on many of the case studies he had conducted over the years, and on the folklore, myths, and taboos of some other cultures which he had studied to see if they contained any familiar themes.

A patient's dream

A man was suffering from depression which he said was because he was bored at work. During psychoanalysis he said that he had dreamed about running through a vast desert, on his own. In his dreams, he felt very happy although he knew he had a long way to go. He was looking forward to the journey, and waved and shouted greetings to groups of people as he passed them. In his dream the people looked like animals, some were tied to stakes, others were in cages. In a previous session he had stumbled over his wife's name. Her name was Lesley, but he had distinctly said 'Left me'. They had been unhappily married for over 20 years, and had only stayed together because of their children.

1 What might a psychoanalyst think the man meant when he said he was enjoying running through a desert on his own?

2 What might the psychoanalyst make of the people looking like animals who were either tied up, or in cages?

3 How might this dream confirm the man's previous slip of the tongue?

4 Comment on Freud's claim that dream analysis was 'the royal road' to the unconscious.

Review
How to study the unconscious mind

Freud developed the techniques of free association, dream analysis, and analysing slips of the tongue for investigating the unconscious. He had tried to use hypnosis, but wasn't successful. He used clinical interviews to build up case studies of each patient.

The unconscious mind

1 Name three of the main methods which Freud used to investigate the unconscious?

2 What is science?

3 What are clinical interviews used for?

4 What are case studies?

Write a paragraph beginning 'Freud wanted to investigate the unconscious. To do this he had to develop some. . . .'

A child's dream

Read this extract from a therapy session.

Analyst: What was your dream about?

Martin: I don't know.

Analyst: But you said it frightened you.

Martin: It did.

Analyst: Can you tell me anything about it?

Martin: I fell over playing and came home.

Analyst: Is that why you were frightened?

Martin: Mummy made it better and kissed me and made it feel warm. Then daddy came in.

Analyst: Does mummy usually kiss you better when you're hurt?

Martin: Daddy says big boys don't need kissing better.

1 How might the therapist interpret Martin's statement that he didn't know what his dream was about?

2 What do you think the therapist might make of Martin's feelings about his mother, and his father?

2 Instincts and the unconscious

Freud derived his ideas about a force for life, and a competing force for death from ancient myths. The concept of the libido still exists in psychology, and in many other people's minds. Do you know anyone who is always rushing about, who seems bursting with energy? Freud would say they have a strong libido. Libido can be a useful concept in describing some behaviour, but some psychologists reject it. They say our behaviour is the result of observing, imitating, and learning from others. They say that to talk of instincts ruling our lives is wrong. What do you think? Is our behaviour the result of our instincts? Or is it the result of learning while growing up? Or both?

After his return from studying with Charcot in Paris in 1886, Freud began to believe that there were certain instinctive forces that rule much of our behaviour. By **instinct** he meant an irresistible biological urge. For over 30 years Freud investigated these instinctive urges. By 1920 he had settled for the existence of two main instincts, one concerned with love and life, the other concerned with death. Many of Freud's ideas were based on ancient Greek mythology which told of Eros, the god of love, and Thanatos, the god of death.

All scientists know that all activity needs some kind of energy to maintain it, e.g. cars won't run without petrol, computers won't work without electricity, and your body gets the energy it needs from food. But where does the energy to fuel these instinctive urges come from? Freud thought there were a number of sources of mental energy.

The force for life is mostly maintained by the energy which Freud called **libido**. The libido is to do with the amount of energy we put into life and being whichever sex we are. It is a positive force for survival, reproduction, and well-being. It provides the energy that we need to deal with the tensions that build up when we are frustrated. Opposing this force for good is the force for bad, which Freud calls the **death instinct** or **death wish**. The death instinct is to do with how we deal with aggression, danger, denial, anger, guilt, temptation and so on. It is to do with negative, unpleasant emotions. It pushes us towards the state when all our tensions will be relieved, i.e. death.

Much of our personalities will be the result of a competition between these two forces. Some people will have stronger libidos, and will be a force for good in the world. Others have dominant death instincts, and will be generally harmful, and even self-destructive.

Describing libido and death instinct

Here is a list of words which describe aspects of human personality. Have two lists, one headed LIBIDO and one headed DEATH INSTINCT and put the appropriate words in each list. Use a dictionary if necessary.

Brutal, energetic, generous, aggressive, sadistic, sporting, unemotional, hardworking, cooperative, autocratic, withdrawn, intuitive, domineering, purposeful, authoritarian, caring, suicidal, thoughtful, aloof, enthusiastic, quick-tempered, helpful, quarrelsome.

Instincts in the unconscious

1 What do you know about the sample of patients from which Freud drew his data? Answer in terms of:

(a) Representativeness – What did all of Freud's patients have in common?

(b) Were they a typical cross-section of people of that time? Yes/No

2 Where do the libido and death wish come from?

3 Which do you think should be the stronger of the two?

4 What is the (very important) missing word in this sentence: 'Libido and death instincts will always be in _____, and the stronger will determine our personality.'

5 What would the world be like if everyone had a very powerful death wish?

6 What would it be like if everyone's libido were much stronger?

Review
The unconscious mind

Freud knew that we are born with a number of reflexes: for example, sucking. These are instincts, i.e. behaviour which doesn't have to be learned. He began to believe that we are born with other instincts too. After many years' research he concluded there are two important instincts which will determine the way our personalities develop. They will always be in competition, and the stronger will determine our personality. One is a force for good, which Freud called the libido. The other is a force for evil, which Freud called the death wish.

Background reading – The two instinctive urges

The Libido   The force for life takes its energy from the libido. The libido is the main source of our sexual energy which is concentrated on things like survival, worthwhile achievements, love, kindness, and on all the ways in which humans can find expression and fulfilment.

Everyone has a libido. It makes us behave in many ways which relieve pressure that would otherwise build up. When the libido is frustrated, emotional problems will occur.

The death instinct or death wish   This was the basis of Freud's theory of aggression. He said the origins of human aggression are instinctive, not learned. Death wish is destructive and makes some people want to dominate others. It makes us want to put ourselves in dangerous situations, and even want to harm those people we hate. (The first people we hate will be our own parents when they start to refuse to let us have things we want!) Freud believed we must transfer these feelings from our parents on to things like toys or furniture. (Children often take out their anger or frustrations on toys and furniture.) If the death wish is not released when the frustrations build up, then Freud believed that some personality problems will almost certainly occur later in life. In Freud's later writings he seemed less convinced about the existence of the death wish.

So, according to Freud's psychoanalytic approach, these two instincts are responsible for much of our personality later. Much of our behaviour is directed towards gratifying these basic instinctive urges. The ways in which we gratify these urges change as we grow.

3 The structure of personality

Freud's analysis of his patients' problems led him to view the personality as consisting of three related elements. The first is primitive, illogical, and totally demanding. Freud calls it the **id**. This gives rise to the second part of the personality, which is a more realistic awareness of

Is your libido strong or weak? Complete this sentence in your head: 'The libido and death instincts are. . . .'

oneself and one's world, and is called the **ego**. These two give rise to the third part, which concerns moral feelings, and is called the **superego**.

The id

The id exists right from birth and is the most basic, primitive part of the personality. It can be thought of as being the true unconscious. Id is mainly concerned with things which ensure that a person survives, and with those things which give it pleasure, such as food, comfort, and avoiding pain. Id demands that its needs be satisfied by the other instincts immediately and at all costs. Freud said the id operates on the **pleasure principle** which means that the child is only interested in things which give it pleasure. The id is irrational and isn't in touch with the real world.

The ego

For the first year of life the id dominates a child's personality and behaviour. Between one and two years of age children start to use language and begin to learn that they must ask for things. Id is still making demands about what it wants, but parents stop giving in to the child's demands and id will become frustrated.

Frustration of instinctive urges could be dangerous. Children have to become more realistic and realise that making demands which aren't met is a waste of energy. The id is still demanding satisfaction, so the second aspect of personality, the ego, appears. The ego is in touch with the real world. It is rational and logical. It consists of all that we know, our memories, how we solve problems, how we regard things and so on. It allows the child to realise that talking, explaining, planning, negotiating, asking, etc., will be more effective in satisfying the id's demands. It relies more on the **reality principle**.

The superego

By the age of about three we have a child whose unconscious id makes selfish demands for things which will give it pleasure. Ego is trying to satisfy id's demands. For example, the id might demand the satisfaction of food. The ego will know that this demand can be met by taking some food. But taking food without asking our parents may be wrong in some homes, and may result in pain (being smacked).

So we need a third part of personality which will help us know what is right and not right for us, and what we may and may not do. This is the role of the superego. The superego makes sure the ego does not use unacceptable means to satisfy the id's demands. It is a sort of censor. It consists of two parts, our **conscience** and our **ego ideal**. Our conscience gives us feelings of right and wrong. The ego ideal tells us what is good and what we should be like. In other

The irrational id is present from birth. Freud thought that some people would continue to have a dominant id throughout their lives. What kind of personalities do you think they'd have? Find some words that might describe someone with a strong id. Here are a few to start you off: ruthless, determined, inconsiderate, cheating.

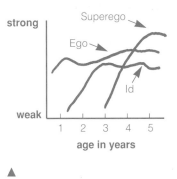

▲
Id, Ego and Superego

The ego and superego try to find reasonable ways of satisfying the id's demands. Briefly describe what you think would be the characteristics of someone with a weak superego. Now describe an adult whose superego is very strong.

words, conscience is about *should not*, and ego ideal is about *should*. The superego relies on the **morality principle**. Ego's job now is to satisfy id, without upsetting superego.

A mature personality will be the result of continuing clashes and compromises between these three parts of personality. Sometimes the id will make demands which the ego can't find acceptable ways of satisfying, and the superego will suffer. We feel guilty. Sometimes ego will be dominated by superego, when we refuse to follow our impulses into doing something we know to be wrong. The ego has the most difficult task, trying to satisfy both id and superego. Not everyone will have egos which can cope and they are more likely to develop an abnormal personality.

Guilt and the superego

An experiment was conducted on a sample of five children in each of the following age groups: four and five, six and seven, and eight and nine. The researcher wanted to see if those with strong superegos behaved differently from those with weak superegos. One by one they were put in a room with some very expensive looking dolls, a train set, a ball, and other toys. They were told that the researcher's favourite plant (a large Swiss cheese plant in the corner of the room) was sick, and they agreed to watch it for her, in case it wilted. The experimenter left, explaining that she would be next door, in the kitchen.

Some children soon forgot the plant and started playing with the toys. Others lasted several minutes, but eventually took their eyes off the plant. If the child ignored the plant for more than one minute the experimenter would release a wire which made the 'trick' plant wilt. She quickly entered the room to confront the child, and record its reactions to the wilted plant, and to its broken promise. Some of the children felt guilty and apologetic. Others tried to defend themselves by telling lies, and didn't seem to feel guilty at all.

1 What sample size is being tested here?

2 What is the hypothesis of this experiment?

3 Why did the experimenter time how long it took each child to stop looking at the plant?

4 How would those children with strong superegos react to their broken promises?

Parts of personality

1 What is the difference between the id and the ego?

2 How does Freud explain aggression in children?

3 Write a paragraph beginning 'According to Freud there are three forces which shape our personality. Their roles are. . .'

Review
The id, the ego, and the superego

We have three parts to our personalities. The id says, 'I must be satisfied now.' The ego says, 'I'll work out how to satisfy you.' The superego says, 'You can't do or have it at all; it's wrong.' The id is irrational and is based on the pleasure principle. The ego is more realistic, and is based on the reality principle. The superego is less concerned with rationality or reality, and more concerned with moral judgements and censorship. It is based on the morality principle.

4 The stages of development through which we acquire our personality

Babies' lips and tongues are covered in sense receptor cells. Babies of just a few hours old can tell the difference between salt and sugar on their tongues, and they know which they like and don't like! Can you think of any other possible reasons why babies put things in their mouths?

Freud thought the personality would be influenced by the part of the body that was particularly sensitive at the time. These sensitive parts are called erogenous zones. If these sensitive parts received too little, or too much stimulation, then normal personality development will be disrupted, and the personality may become fixated.

Review
Development of personality through stages

As children grow up, different parts of their bodies become especially sensitive – first, the mouth, then the anus, then the genitals. Libido will seek expression through these erogenous zones. If too many painful experiences occur, the child's personality will become fixated in the stage the child is in at the time.

Before discussing Freud's four main stages of personality development we need to say something about why they occur. Babies put everything they can into their mouths. A baby's mouth is very sensitive and babies get some pleasure or satisfaction from this. Freud thought that different part of our bodies become particularly sensitive as we grow. Freud called these areas **erogenous zones**. Freud thought the libido would concentrate its energy on these erogenous zones. Each zone would represent a stage of personality development.

Many of Freud's explanations involve the idea of psychic energy. He imagined that people are born with a certain amount of energy which is gradually used up as we develop. Id, ego, and superego all need a certain amount of energy. Whenever someone faces a particular crisis, or does something which causes strong guilt or anxiety feelings, this will use up even more energy. For example if a baby's demands to be fed aren't being met quickly when it is less than a year old, then a certain amount of energy will be used up to cope with this. Equally, if the baby is constantly being encouraged to eat, this too will need to be dealt with. Some energy has to be used up as the child grows, to deal with the feelings of anger or frustration felt at the time.

In the next stage if, for example, a child faces a problem with potty training this will require more energy to be used up, or as Freud called it, energy is **fixated** on the problem. A parent might be too strict in insisting the child always uses the potty, and may be angry or punish any 'accidents'. Or a parent may not encourage the child to use the potty, and the child continues to relieve itself whenever it wants to. The more problems the child faces the more energy the child will have to use up to deal with them. Each of us will have fixated different amounts of energy at different stages in our development, as we faced different problems. An adult's personality will be determined by the different amounts of energy used to cope with the various fixations that person has encountered.

If someone faces a great many problems during development that person may not have sufficient energy left to go any further. In this case the personality will stop developing at the last problem that was met. Being fixated means that the person will continue to seek pleasure or satisfaction through the erogenous zone which gave that person pleasure or satisfaction when the fixation occurred. Children with some fixation in the oral stage, for example, will be very concerned with their mouths. They may talk a lot, eat a lot, chew their pencils at school, and suck their thumbs. Fixation might cause personality problems later which may have to be dealt with by psychoanalytic therapy.

Erogenous zones

Write a paragraph on the role of the erogenous zones in Freudian theory. It could begin, 'According to Freud we have some basic instinctive urges. . . .'

Background reading – The erogenous zones

According to Freud the first erogenous zone is the mouth. After a year or two, satisfaction results from being able to control the bowels, and the anus becomes the source of the child's satisfaction. From his patients' case studies, Freud concluded that children of just three and four years of age appear to have some kind of sexual feelings. Freud called these feelings pre-genital sexuality. For boys, the phallus becomes the next source of satisfaction after the anus. Real genital sexuality occurs between puberty and adolescence. The stages of personality development in traditional psychoanalysis reflect these erogenous zones. They are the oral stage, the anal stage, the phallic stage, and the genital stage.

The oral stage – from birth to 1 year

This is the first stage of personality development. At this age pleasure is gained through the mouth (even where food is not involved). Freud thought we were born with a feeding instinct, which must be satisfied. No doubt Freud had observed his own and other children putting everything they could into their mouths. Freud said the baby is only aware of its own needs, and will only do those things which give it pleasure or satisfaction. The oral stage is dominated by the pleasure principle.

According to Freud, the libido needs a certain amount of oral satisfaction. Too little or too much satisfaction may lead to the infant becoming arrested or fixated in this stage. This may result in **oral dependency**. Children who have had too little stimulation will become pessimistic, unable to develop personal relationships, aggressive, often depressed, and will see other people only as objects to satisfy them. They will be selfish, uncaring, and untrusting. More recently it has been suggested that too little oral stimulation also produces people who are sarcastic, who smoke, drink, eat sweets, and talk too much! Too much stimulation means that people will be easily taken in (fooled), and will have a high opinion of themselves. They will be excitable and over enthusiastic about things. They will also be rather dependent on other people and unable to make decisions and take responsibility for themselves. The right amount of stimulation results in someone who is fairly optimistic and cheerful, and who enjoys other people's company.

Review
The oral stage

Freud said the oral stage is the first stage of personality development and exists for the first year to two years of life. Freud believed we have an instinct to take pleasure from feeding and so the first erogenous zone is the mouth. Fixation can occur because of either too much or too little oral stimulation, i.e. too little oral stimulation produces an aggressive, depressed, and pessimistic personality. Too much stimulation produces an over-optimistic, over-dependent, and over-excitable personality.

The oral stage

1 What is the function of the libido in the oral stage?

2 What does fixated mean?

3 How does the id become satisfied in the first stage of development according to Freud?

4 What did Freud mean by 'oral dependent'? How might such dependency develop?

The anal stage – from 1 to 2 years

Freud never intended us to think that one stage disappears as another appears. He said, 'One may appear in addition to another, they may overlap one another, they may be present alongside of one another.' In the anal stage, the child's behaviour is still dominated by the pleasure principle. Now satisfaction will be gained from controlling the bowels.

Bowel control is to do with giving and not giving faeces, i.e. the products of one's own body. The id is demanding immediate satisfaction (i.e. children must relieve themselves as soon as they need to), while parents are trying to train them to control themselves. Some personality problems might occur if this conflict isn't resolved. The ego, which is more logical than the id, appears now, in order to help solve this problem.

If the id wins the struggle the child will be slow to potty train and the child's personality may become fixated. This can lead to two types of adult personality. Firstly, there are those who had great pleasure from getting rid of their faeces (the *anal expulsive* personality). They will be over generous, probably very untidy, will agree with whatever anyone says, etc. Secondly, there are those who were forced to give away their faeces (the *anal retentive* personality). They may become over-possessive, obsessive about things such as tidiness, punctuality, and cleanliness. They may be sadistic and generally miserable.

Between the ages of one and two children start to learn to talk. They begin to realise that they are not the only thing in the world. The id's demands to be satisfied are beginning to fail. Parents will not let their two-year-olds do everything they want to do. We need the rational ego to help satisfy the demands of the id.

Write a paragraph beginning, 'According to psychoanalysis, someone fixated in the oral stage will . . .'

Do you know how old you were when you were potty trained? See if you can find out whether you potty trained easily, or were you reluctant to train? If you have children, how easy were they to train?

Note, there is virtually no evidence for these claims. People with the personality characteristics described here may or may not have been harshly or over indulgently potty trained or fed too little or too much when they were younger.

Review
The anal stage

The anal stage follows the oral stage. The child still derives pleasure from the mouth. During the anal stage the child starts to learn to control the trunk and legs and the anus becomes a source of pleasure. Fixation here can be caused by very strict, or very easy-going potty training.

The anal stage

1 What is the child in the anal stage able to do (which it couldn't do before), that will allow it to be potty trained?

2 What is the id's main function?

3 How is the ego different from the id?

4 Why does the ego appear?

5 Describe someone supposedly fixated in the anal stage.

6 Write a description of the role of the anal stage in Freudian psychoanalysis.

The phallic stage – from 2 to 6 years

This is probably the most important stage in the child's personality development, according to Freud. Until now children's personalities have been developing as a result of the strengths of their libido, death instincts, id, and ego. During the phallic stage children will be socialised into learning what is right and wrong, what they should and shouldn't do, and they learn the different ways in which boys and girls are expected to behave.

Freud suggests that children from around three years of age start to have actual (pregenital) sexual feelings about their (opposite sex) parents. The basis for this is quite unconscious. In this stage children are starting to develop an interest in their own, and their parents' genitals and will experience some kind of sexual feelings. Children often play with their genitals. Unconsciously, boys will start to regard their mothers (who first fed them and formed an attachment with them) as love objects. Girls will unconsciously want their fathers, as they are big and strong and manly, and are associated with pleasurable genital feelings.

Freud called this idea of wanting to have some kind of sexual contact with the opposite sex parent **the Oedipus Complex** and said that it can cause **Oedipal conflict**.

At the same time as unconsciously wanting one parent, each child will, Freud argued, feel jealous of the other parent. For example, a boy wants his mother, but can't have her because his father, whom he loves, already has her. The son begins to hate his father, and is afraid that his father will punish him, even castrate him, for his feelings. He starts to feel guilty about his feelings and afraid of the possible consequences.

These feelings are negative and dangerous and must be dealt with. Freud claimed that all these feelings are unconscious, as is the way

There has been some argument over the idea of unconscious feelings. One side claims that if the feelings are unconscious we could not feel them, while the other says that it is the cause of these feelings which the child is not aware of.

Background reading – The Oedipus Complex

Throughout his life Freud had been fascinated by ancient history. He knew many of the legends from ancient Egypt, Rome and Greece. One Greek story, written by Sophocles, told of Oedipus, the king of Thebes. Oedipus unwittingly killed his father, Laius, and married a woman called Jocasta, who turned out to be his own mother. When he realised what he had done, he blinded himself. Another legend told of a woman called Electra. Her father, Agamemnon, was murdered by her mother's lover. Electra urged her brother to kill her mother for revenge.

Freud's ideas for the Oedipus (and Electra) conflict also came from his self-analysis after his own father had died. He spent half an hour at the end of each day in self-analysis for most of his life, and could remember the feelings of warmth and tenderness that he had for his own mother. His feelings about his father had been very mixed. Although he loved his father, he could remember being afraid of him. His father had been rather strict. His mother would look after him, and he loved her for it. He believed he had been jealous of his father for having so much of his mother's attention.

the child is going to deal with them. The boy is very frightened by the idea of castration. He may even develop a castration complex. He begins to be like his father, to act like him, to talk like him, and to think like him. Unconsciously the boy hopes that the father won't be angry with someone who is so much like himself.

This unconscious process of taking on the characteristics of someone else is called **identification**, and it helps explain how boys develop their ideas about what men should be like. If the father is dominant and aggressive, the child will have greater castration anxiety and will identify more strongly with his father. This will reduce his fears, but will make him think that boys should be aggressive. Children also develop their ideas about right and wrong (their superego) from identification. We will return to this when we study moral development later.

A case study of identification – Little Hans
Probably the best known of Freud's case studies is that of 'little Hans'. Hans's father was a musician and an admirer of Freud, and also worked in Vienna. Hans was born in 1903, and his father soon started to write to Freud to inform him of his son's progress. Freud would reply, interpreting the boy's personality development according to psychoanalytic theory. When the boy was four he developed a phobia of horses.

The streets were full of horses in those days. (The family lived opposite a coaching inn, where horses and carriages came and left all the time.) The boy became terrified of going outside. He said he thought the horses might fall over, they might make a noise, or they could bite him. It seemed that Hans was more afraid of some horses than others. He was particularly afraid of big carthorses pulling heavy loads, like horse-drawn buses. (He'd seen a horse which was pulling a bus fall over when he was younger.)

There are several possible explanations for Hans's phobia. You might think that being frightened by seeing a large horse falling over could cause a fear of horses. He also had a younger sister called Hanna, and he could have been jealous of her for taking so much of his mother's attention away from him. He could have been pretending to be afraid in order to have more of his mother's attention. Freud was convinced that it was more complex. As he was four years old, Hans would have been in the phallic stage, and would have been experiencing all sorts of feelings about his mother and his father. Freud thought that the phobia was something to do with the child's identification with his father during his phallic stage. Hans was very fond of his mother, and enjoyed spending time with her. Freud and Hans's father concluded that Hans was afraid of his father and was transferring his fear of his father on to horses. He was afraid that his father would become angry with him for wanting his mother. His father might castrate him for his feelings.

Hans and his father spent a long time talking about the child's feelings. His father used the free association technique. Gradually Hans's phobia disappeared. Freud claimed that this was because he had sorted out his libido's problems.

Write a paragraph beginning, 'According to Freud, the Oedipus Complex is . . .' Mention the process of identification.

A phobia is a strong, and often quite illogical, fear of such things as spiders, snakes, heights, etc. It results in feelings of anxiety. Do you have any phobias? Ask your friends if they have any. Many people do.

Little Hans

1 Outline Freud's explanation for Hans's phobia.

2 Suggest some other possible explanations for the boy's fear of horses.

3 What does free association involve?

4 Outline the main limitations of this method for psychology?

5 How convincing is this case study for Freud's theory?

The Electra Complex

Freud paid relatively little attention to explaining girls' personality development, and his preoccupation with the phallus is evidence of this. His ideas seem ridiculous now. No one would take them very seriously. He said that girls realise that they have no penis, and that they must have been castrated (by their mothers), who are also castrated. Girls start to hate their mother for that, and for possessing their father. They turn to their fathers for love, and unconsciously hope that this might get their penis back. Girls may develop *penis envy* and imagine that taking (possibly their father as) a male lover, and having a male baby, will give them a penis of their own.

At the same time, girls fear losing their mother's love, and so identify with her, taking on her sex roles and moral standards. The fear of loss of love isn't as powerful a reason for identification as fear of castration, so a girl may not identify as strongly with her mother as a boy does with his father. She may not have such a strong sexual identity or superego as the boy, and may overcome her penis envy by concentrating on, for example, child rearing or having a career.

This explanation has been so severely attacked (particularly by female psychoanalysts) that few people would promote it now. Freud might have argued that a female psychoanalyst is only working to overcome her penis envy!

As we have seen, the superego appears during this stage, alongside the id and ego. It is concerned with moral and ethical feelings. The irrational id is making demands to be satisfied, for example, sexual feelings about the opposite-sex parent. The rational ego is trying to find ways of satisfying the id, while also trying to discourage its more illogical demands. Now the superego begins to act as a judge between what we should and should not want and do. The superego develops as the child is punished for some things, and rewarded for others. Things which we know are good and will be rewarded by our parents become our ego ideal.

Freud's idea that all three-year-old girls are familiar with male sexual organs wouldn't necessarily be accepted now. Many families do not have such sexual liberation! Presumably Freud would claim that a girl without a father or brother will have problems with her identification, since, if she doesn't know about male sexual organs, she presumably can't be too envious. If she isn't envious then she has less need to identify with her mother.

Some boys are very like their fathers, and some girls are very like their mothers. How would you explain this, apart from using Freudian theory? Give some examples in your answer.

The role of the superego

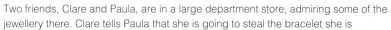
Two friends, Clare and Paula, are in a large department store, admiring some of the jewellery there. Clare tells Paula that she is going to steal the bracelet she is

Review
The phallic stage

Between the ages of three and six, boys' and girls' personalities begin to differ. Boys and girls have pregenital feelings for their opposite-sex parent. This makes them feel rather resentful of their same-sex parent, and this leads to feelings of guilt. They resolve these problems by identifying with the same-sex parent. If children don't pass through this stage successfully, they may have all sorts of problems with members of both sexes later.

admiring. She persuades her friend to steal something too. Paula is reluctant, but doesn't want to draw attention to them, so she agrees. Later that day she feels terribly upset about what she's done, and the next morning she posts the jewellery back to the shop anonymously. Clare proudly wears her bracelet to school and isn't at all worried about how she got hold of it.

How might a psychoanalyst explain the differences in Paula and Clare's behaviour.

Fixation in the phallic stage leads people to become unreasonable, and to think a lot of themselves, to be obsessed by power, particularly in relationships, and to become dominant and uncaring, big-headed and exhibitionist. They may have great pride, and even great courage. They may also have sexual problems.

The superego

During a 30-minute therapy session a 27-year-old man made the following collection of remarks. Read them and answer the questions at the end.

'I've always felt that other people don't get on with things. They seem to get sidetracked so easily. I think if you're going to do something, just get on and do it, and worry about the consequences later.'

'I never feel comfortable if I'm a passenger in someone's car. People just don't drive safely anymore. I always want to say, "For goodness sake let me drive".'

'I hate people who pretend to be modest. I think you've got to make as much of your chances as you can in this world.'

'I believe a man should be master in his own house. I would never marry anyone who wanted to tell me what to do. I don't really want a wife; you can't trust people.'

'It's about time the police got tougher on troublemakers like strikers and students. There are far too many scroungers these days.'

'No, I don't think I've ever been nervous of anything.'

'Yes, I do wish I was in the government. I could do a lot better than all of that lot. They're too soft and stupid.'

1 What is this method of investigation called?

2 Describe a major drawback with it as a means of gathering psychological data.

3 Psychologists from different theoretical backgrounds (which we will study later) would explain remarks such as these in different ways. How might a psychoanalyst interpret such statements?

4 Describe briefly the role of the superego in the development of personality, according to psychoanalytic theory.

The phallic stage

1 Outline what is happening during the phallic stage.

2 Freud said that boys and girls start to have 'pregenital sex drives'. What does he say this make them want to do?

3 Describe the functions of the superego.

4 What did Freud mean by identification?

The latency period – from 6 to 11 years

This isn't a stage of development, because personality doesn't change very much during it. It is a time of consolidation, of sorting relationships out, of overcoming the Oedipus Complex, and channelling the libido's energy elsewhere. Children are going to school, which absorbs most of their energies. They are socialising with (same sex) peers, and directing their energies into sport and games. They concentrate on learning the roles which will be expected of them later. The genitals are still the main erogenous zone, but children stop associating them with sexual feelings. They try to have nothing to do with sex (including members of the opposite sex).

Solving the Oedipus Complex and completing the latency period may be a stressful time for both sexes, and many children don't come through it successfully. When they are adults they may be rather afraid of members of the opposite sex, and uncomfortable with them.

Review
The latency period

Between around six to 11 nothing much is happening to the personality. This is more a time for becoming used to people, activities, and situations, and for preparing for the next major step forward, the genital stage.

The genital stage – from 11 years onwards

Two very important physiological changes are occurring during the teenage years. Firstly, the hormone levels alter as people mature, and secondly, the sex organs are maturing in shape and are functioning. If children have successfully resolved the Oedipus Complex and sorted their feelings out, the result of these two body changes is that children start taking an interest in the opposite sex. It's a sort of *sexual attachment*. They have crushes on film stars, their teachers, or even each other. At around puberty children begin to change from being interested in friends of the same sex to members of the opposite sex.

This is a healthy and normal development, according to Freud, but not all societies were very open or approving of sexual relations between unmarried people. This was very true in the later nineteenth century of (Roman Catholic) Vienna where most of Freud's patients lived. The libido may want some sexual experience, but society forbids it. This can lead to all sorts of frustrations. If fixation occurs in this stage, the adult will find difficulties in relating to the opposite sex. They may be shy and immature.

During the genital stage, from about puberty, we are starting to develop an interest in relationships. Can you remember having any fantasies about meeting film and pop stars when you were aged 11?

Genital maturity

Anthony is a quiet, reserved man. He doesn't make friends easily because he talks a lot, and is rather shallow. He smokes a pipe almost constantly. He is a very generous person – some people accuse him of trying to buy friends. He can be very sarcastic at times, and can have a cruel sense of humour. He is particularly shy with women and blushes easily. His mother and father are both loving and kind, and he always had a good relationship with them.

Anthony is rather lonely, and begins a course of therapy with a psychoanalyst.

1 What kind of diagnosis do you think the therapist might reach, based on the evidence in the passage? (HINT: Think about fixation.)

2 Can you think of any other explanation?

3 What is the main function of the genital stage?

4 How does the libido seek satisfaction at the beginning of this stage, and how does this change?

5 What personality characteristics will be produced by fixation in this stage?

A summary of Freud's stages of psychosexual development

If you've been collecting cuttings or notes on cases on TV, do you think psychoanalysis could make a contribution to explaining any of them?

Stage and Age (approx)	Erogenous Zone	Main Characteristics	Tasks to Achieve
Oral 0–1	Mouth	Main source of pleasure is the mouth, lips, tongue, etc. Biting, licking, swallowing etc. The main concern is with immediate gratification of urges so id dominates.	Satisfactory feeding (weaning)
Anal 1–2	Anus	Controlling and not controlling the bowels and bladder. The ego starts to control id.	Potty and toilet training
Phallic 2–6	Phallus	Some pleasure is gained from playing with the genitals. This pleasure is associated with the opposite-sex parent leading to the Oedipus and Electra Complexes. Id demands, ego tries to satisfy id, and superego tries to impose moral choices.	Successful solution to Oedipal and Electral conflicts
Latency 6-11	None	Oedipus and Electra identification with same-sex parent, and loss of interest in opposite sex. Id, ego, and superego continue to compete.	None

Genital 11 onwards	Genitals	Increasing concern with adult ways of experiencing sexual pleasure.	Good relationships with members of both sexes.

Review

The genital stage of development

Once the genital period has begun human beings should reach genital maturity and most of our personality development will centre around members of the opposite sex. Libido will seek sexual expression.

Some suggested activities

1 Write down some examples of behaviour that you could look for in junior school children which might indicate fixation in any of the early stages. Say which stage the fixation would be in.

2 Construct a questionnaire which might be used to investigate whether a patient is fixated in any of the stages given above.

3 Write an essay describing how children's personalities develop, according to Freud's psychoanalytic approach.

When conflicts occur – defence mechanisms

As we pass through the phallic and genital stages, the three parts of personality will occasionally come into conflict. The irrational id will make demands that the ego and superego will resist. This conflict between the pleasure principle and the reality and morality principles will produce anxiety. Too much anxiety causes neuroses.

Background reading – What happens when conflict occurs

Thirteen-year-old Fiona is babysitting her one-year-old sister Angela while their parents are out. Fiona has a couple of friends round, and they are listening to music. Angela has been crying all evening, and Fiona has tried everything she can, but still her sister cries. Fiona wants to be with her friends, and she's becoming annoyed by her sister's crying. She wants to scream 'What's the matter, what do you want?' (Impulses from her id want her to shut Angela up in any way she can.) She goes to the crying child and picks her up to soothe her. (Fiona's ego is encouraging her to find a logical way of settling her sister.) Angela quietens for a while, and Fiona goes back to her friends. Soon the crying starts again, and Fiona wishes she could lock the baby in a soundproof room, but she knows it is not the baby's fault. (Her superego is contributing a moral element.) Hopefully their parents will return soon and Fiona's responsibility will end. Her patience is being stretched. Sometimes this conflict is just too much to bear and produces real anxiety.

Anxiety

Anxiety is an unpleasant emotional state which involves feelings of unhappiness, uneasiness, dread, fear, or apprehension. It may include worry about not knowing something which appears to be important.

Can you remember feeling very anxious about something? What did you do about it? Did it worry you for a few minutes, a few hours, or a few days? Make two lists of the sorts of thing that make you 'very anxious', and 'a bit anxious'. You could compare your list with a close friend and see how similar or different you are.

Review
Conflict in the personality

If the various instincts and parts of personality can't settle on a way of resolving the demands made on them then the personality will not develop normally. We have a number of defence mechanisms to limit the damage that might be done. They are quite normal and quite unconscious.

Freud said people have a large number of unconscious defence mechanisms which help us reduce anxiety. Defence mechanisms are mental processes which are automatically triggered when anxiety occurs. There are many defence mechanisms. Here are a few of the main ones:

Repression
Occasionally we have experiences that could set off unpleasant thoughts and memories. These thoughts and memories might make us feel guilty or frightened, anxious or worried. Such negative emotions could interfere with our ego's functioning. Repression is an unconscious defence mechanism that our ego directs to protect us from becoming aware of such emotions. According to Freud, the Oedipus Complex is the result of feelings that cause anxiety. Such feelings may need to be repressed.

Projection
Although repression serves to stop us from becoming aware of such potentially harmful emotions, it may not always succeed. We might become conscious of other unpleasant thoughts and feelings. Projection is a defence mechanism by which we deny that we have these thoughts and feelings, and instead we project them on to someone else. If we believe that someone else has those feelings, then that should make us feel better. The possible problem here is that if we constantly project our feelings on to others we may begin to lose touch with what we do feel.

Displacement
Sometimes we might have inappropriate thoughts, feelings, or attitudes towards another person or an object. Loving a doll is all very well for a child, but the same feelings in an adult would be inappropriate to say the least! Displacement is a defence mechanism whereby we transfer these feelings to something or someone so that the feelings are more acceptable, for example to our partner or child.

Sublimation
Sublimation is a special form of displacement. Freud had been influenced by the evolutionary biologist Charles Darwin. Darwin wrote about instinctive forces that direct much animal behaviour. Humans have a libido which channels primitive instinctive urges such as hate,

love, and self-preservation. Sometimes these emotions are directed on to something inappropriate. Hating someone who has been unfair to us may make us feel aggression. Aggression is undesirable so we may channel it into sporting activity.

Rationalisation

Sometimes we do, say, think, or feel things that aren't acceptable. They may not appear to be rational and may confuse us and anyone else observing us. Freud thought that these things display what we are really like, and that we actually do mean to do, say, think, and feel them. Rationalisation is a defence mechanism that allows us to explain our behaviour both to ourselves and to others who might ask us, 'What did you do that for?' If we can explain our actions so that they seem to make some sense, then we won't feel so bad about them. For example, if you do badly in a psychology exam you may rationalise it by saying, 'I didn't get the chance to do much revision.' The truth may be that you had the opportunity to revise but chose to do something else instead.

Defence mechanisms

Can you think of an occasion when – you now realise – one of these defence mechanisms may have helped you? Write a brief story of someone (real or imaginary) who used one or more of these defence mechanisms, and identify which mechanism is being used.

Answer these questions from memory.

1 Name three examples of defence mechanisms and say what each of them does.

2 Where do defence mechanisms come from?

3 What causes a defence mechanism to be set off?

Write a paragraph on why we have defence mechanisms.

5 The strengths and weaknesses of psychoanalytic theory

Freud believed that his research was a major scientific breakthrough in understanding how the human mind works, and how to treat it when things go wrong. And it's only fair to say that many other people believed this too. Freud believed the techniques he used were scientifically acceptable, and led to scientifically acceptable conclusions.

The only certain way we can assess the value of a scientific explanation is to see if it stands up to thorough testing. Freud's theories have probably been examined more thoroughly than any others in the history of psychology, although not so much during the last 20 years or more. The problem for psychoanalysis is that many of its ideas cannot be experimentally tested. Various attempts have been made to

Science is a means for examining how some variables relate to others, what leads to what, and even what causes something else.

test some of Freud's specific ideas, although now few psychologists would support some of Freud's more extreme claims about infantile sexuality and aggression.

Some experiments on aspects of Freud's theories

Here are some of the studies which have tried to demonstrate the validity of some of Freud's concepts and claims. Read through them and you'll see just how difficult it is to test these claims.

Yarrow (1954)

One consequence of oral fixation might be thumb sucking. Yarrow studied 66 children and found that those who had spent the shortest time being fed during their first six months of life sucked their thumbs the most later.

Problems with this study: mothers couldn't be expected to remember exactly how long they had allowed their babies to stay at the breast, and many would try to give what sounded like the most acceptable answer. Also Yarrow only asked about thumb sucking, but what about all the other things children could put in their mouths for oral gratification?

Daston (1956)

Freud claimed that people who had great fear of being attacked all the time (caused by a strong id overcoming a weak ego) hadn't sorted out their identification with their same-sex parent, and would have repressed homosexual feelings. Daston mixed words relating to homosexuality among 'neutral' words, and showed them to a sample of such people, and also to a control group of ordinary people. The subjects saw the words for a fraction of a second (using a machine called a tachisto-scope). Those with the worries about being attacked did react more to the stimulus words, and Daston claimed this as proof of Freud's claim.

Problems with this study: if they were repressing these feelings then they should surely have shown less response to them, not more.

Skodel (1957)

Some Freudians have claimed that men who are fixated in the oral stage will have oral dependency characteristics. They will have an unnatural interest in women with large breasts, and will want to be mothered by such women. A carefully conducted experiment studied 169 male subjects' body-shape preferences, and how dependent on others they were, as measured by a Thematic Apperception Test (TAT). The results seemed to point to the opposite of what was predicted! Men who were rather weak and seemed to have greater oral dependency characteristics seemed to respond more to small breasts.

Problems with this study: the TAT is a series of drawings of people in various situations. They can be interpreted in a number of ways. Each subject is asked to say what he thinks is going on in the picture, to tell a story about it. The scorer tries to see if the stories have any under-lying theme. If so, the theme is supposed to reveal what's going on deep in the subject's unconscious. It is a subjectively scored test, i.e. the scorers decide for themselves whether they think there is any theme emerging. Although three judges were used, it could still be coincidence.

Kline (1968)

According to Freud, excessively strict toilet training would result in fixation in the anal stage, leading to obstinacy, meanness, and orderliness. Kline sampled a group of 46 students and investigated correlations between meanness (as measured by questionnaires), and a part of a test which concentrated on measuring anal eroticism. There was a moderate correlation, and Kline believed that this supported Freudian theory.

Problems with this study: both tests used leave a great deal to be desired. Many of the questions seeking to discover such personality characteristics as 'over concern with cleanliness' seem pretty stupid. For example, one question asked, 'When eating out, do you wonder what the kitchens are like?' What is this supposed to tell us about the personality of the respondent? A second question was, 'Do you regard the keeping of household dogs as unhygienic?' Even if the answer is yes to both questions, does that show us anything about anal fixation? And, in any case, Freud never imagined that anal (or any other) fixation was particularly common among normal people.

General criticisms of experimental studies of Freudian theory

1 Studies like these seem to be the result of the following type of approach: A researcher makes an assumption about what Freud said, for example on the consequences of fixation. The researcher then carries out a study, the results of which support this prediction and, the researcher claims, support psychoanalytic theory. Many other hypotheses, however, could equally well have explained the findings.

2 Psychoanalysis seems to have an answer for everything and can never be proved wrong. Even Skodel's findings, which found the opposite of what was predicted, can still be made to fit Freudian theory (i.e. oral-dependent men prefer large breasts). They know their feelings are wrong, and this makes them anxious, so the preference for small breasts is simply reaction formation! How can we evaluate something which seems to have an answer for everything?

Reaction formation is a defence mechanism whereby people exaggerate the opposite of what they really feel.

3 The statistics used in these studies are generally simple correlations, and correlation cannot prove cause.

4 The research isn't usually repeated, so we can't know whether the conclusions are reliable.

5 Only those studies whose findings are significant are likely to be published. It's quite possible that very many studies are conducted which don't yield the results which would support Freud's explanations. These simply aren't published.

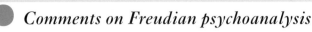

Comments on Freudian psychoanalysis

The attractions of Freudian theory

1 Freudian psychoanalysis has stimulated a great amount of research. Whether they were trying to find evidence to support or destroy psychoanalysis, it is probable that psychologists know a lot more because of Freud than they would otherwise have done.

2 It provides an explanation for the relationship between childhood experiences and later personality characteristics. Parents could acquire a better understanding of their children's feelings and problems by being aware of Freud's work.

3 It is an ages and stages theory (i.e. it links physiological maturation – age – with psychological changes – stages of development). Many human abilities appear to occur in a sequence. Perhaps personality development does too. Knowing a child's age would allow us to say what is going on in its personality development.

Some criticisms of Freud's theory

1 Stimulating other research doesn't, of course, mean that psychoanalysis itself is right. An influential school of thought (which we shall examine shortly), called behaviourism, rejects psychoanalysis as unscientific and totally worthless.

2 Freud's 'evidence' for his explanation of how children's personalities grow does not come from experiments or any scientifically acceptable means of data collection. It doesn't even come from observing normal children. It comes from the dreams and spoken memory of a relatively small number of people who mostly lived in Vienna, who had some personality problems.

3 There is no evidence for the existence of the stages of development as Freud described them, and the theory is not predictive. To be of any use psychological theories must attempt to allow prediction of future events. Such evidence as there is in Freud's work is retrospective (i.e. it looks back, and therefore explains what's happening now in terms of what has already happened).

4 It shows the important role of caregivers in development. Children don't just grow up quite independent of others. They respond to the things which are close and important to them. As we saw in the sections on attachment formation, Freud is right to emphasise the bond between the parent and the child.

5 Freud offers a number of useful concepts, like the id, ego, and superego, and defence mechanisms, which do seem to explain some familiar aspects of children's behaviour. And identification has been widely used to explain much of children's early behaviour.

6 Freud offered an explanation for sexuality and aggression in early childhood.

4 Freud's view of the child is that it is rather helpless and passive. The child must try to resolve the Oedipal conflict that it will have and has to do this by identification. Children are far more active in their own socialisation than Freud suggests.

5 There is no evidence to support the existence of such personality dimensions as the id, ego, and superego, or the libido itself. There is no evidence to prove that anything like the unconscious exists either. Without the unconscious Freud's theory lacks any credibility at all.

6 There is no evidence that all four- and five-year-olds know the biological differences between the sexes, and nor is there any evidence for the Oedipus Complex. Freud makes much use of the process of identification with the same-sex adult. This may occur for a number of reasons that have nothing to do with sexual feelings towards the other parent.

Review
Evaluation of Freudian psychoanalysis

It is impossible to test Freud's claims experimentally. There are, however, a great many aspects of the human condition that can't be tested experimentally either. He spent a lifetime producing a radically new and different theory. Some of his earlier claims about aspects of infantile sexuality were, he admitted, rather overstated. However, he has provided a new and revolutionary view of the development of personality and uses of therapy. Some of Freud's techniques are still widely used, and some of his insights, for example in the area of defence mechanisms, are still highly regarded. Many would agree that without Freud's contribution to psychology our understanding of human development would be much poorer today.

Evaluation

Explain what Freud claimed for each of these features of personality development:

1 The mouth and anus.

2 The Oedipus Complex, castration complex, and penis envy.

3 The unconscious id, the conscious ego, and the moral superego.

4 The repression of unpleasant feelings into the unconscious.

5 Dreams convey our real wishes, and are a way of seeing into the unconscious.

Summary of Freudian psychoanalytic theory

We are born with

two instinctive urges (libido and death wish), which provide psychic energy.

These urges are gratified by

three parts of personality (id, ego, and superego);

through

four stages of development (oral, anal, phallic, genital);

which reflect the

four erogenous zones (mouth, anus, phallus, and genitals).

Painful experiences may cause conflict between the three parts of personality. Conflict causes anxiety that might threaten our development. It can be dealt with by defence mechanisms. Once repressed, some memory stays in the unconscious and may disrupt the personality, and appear later as a symptom of neurosis (hysteria). It must be dealt with by the therapeutic psychoanalytic techniques of free association, dream analysis, analysing slips of the tongue, etc.

Acquiring Behaviour – Conditioning and Social Learning Theory

Freud claimed that children's personalities are partly formed through the process of **identification** with their parents. He believed that deep instinctive urges direct much of our behaviour. A radically different view for explaining how we learn has been developing, notably in America, for the last 50 years. This approach believes that psychology ought to be much more scientific, and should study people's actual behaviour, rather than the supposed instinctive causes of it. This is known as the behaviourist approach, and has had a very strong influence on the way that psychologists view how children learn, as well as on treatments and therapies for children with problem behaviour.

Humans have a greater capacity to learn, and to act on the results of that learning, than any other animal on earth. What do you think might be the first thing a baby learns? What do you imagine was the hardest thing you ever learned? What made learning it so difficult?

Background reading – Learning and behaviour

When psychologists study animals and humans, they often observe and measure their behaviour. Behaviour is simply what a person or animal does. Learning is a mental process that can't be observed. Much of our behaviour is the result of having learned what to do, but other things affect it as well. For example, really wanting to do something may affect how we do it. If you really want to learn to play the guitar you'll work hard at your lessons, and you may learn to play better than someone else who isn't all that bothered about learning to play.

A subject's behaviour is all that can be measured. We can only assume that changes in it are the result of learning, but they may not always be. They may be no more than changes in the person's (or animal's) willingness or ability to cooperate.

Although we can't know whether single-cell organisms are capable of learning, we do know that such low-level organisms as the flatworm are capable of some learning. For years it was assumed that most animals, particularly the lower-order ones, relied exclusively on instinct. We now believe that most species have some learning ability, i.e. they can adapt their behaviour to new circumstances after some previous experiences. Circus animals can be trained to do all sorts of things which they wouldn't normally do. As we shall see, pigeons have even been taught to play a kind of table tennis.

Higher-order animals, such as humans, can learn many different kinds of things. The reasons for this are threefold. First, humans can take in, process, and store a vast amount of information in their heads. Second, they can organise the information which is being taken in, and that which is to be learned, so that it can be understood and used most easily. And third, human beings can use language to communicate with and teach each other. As each of these skills develops during childhood, so children become more able to learn.

What is learning?

Learning is a term that we're all familiar with. Most of us learn something every day. Some things are easier to learn than others. It doesn't take much to learn who has the latest number one record in the pop charts. It takes rather more effort to learn to drive a car. Everyone will find some things easier to learn than others, and the kinds of things that we learn helps to make each of us so different. Babies have a lot to learn, and start doing it from a very early age.

Learning has been defined as 'a relatively permanent change in behaviour that occurs as the result of prior experience'. For example, a young girl who has already had an unpleasant experience at the dentist may do her best to avoid going to the dentist again in the future.

However, not all behaviour is the result of previous experience. The very first words you spoke, knowing what you meant by them, and the very first steps you took, were not the result of previous experience. As you practised your walking you were learning to walk, until eventually you could walk without bumping into anything, or falling over. So we may behave in all sorts of ways. Some of them may be practised until they are learned.

Perhaps the simplest form of learning is **associative learning**, i.e. the organism makes a simple association between something it becomes aware of (a **stimulus**), and some reaction it must make (a **response**). For example, you learned to put your coat on (a learned response) when it started to rain (a stimulus in the environment) when you probably weren't much over two years old. Other learning is much more complex, however. You couldn't learn about attachment in babies, or how to play netball, by simple association.

Some psychologists see the process of learning as a gradual, continuous adaptation to our environment. They argue that every day some new experience alters the way we think about our world. Others, like Piaget, whom we will study shortly, believe that the way children think (and therefore the way they learn) occurs in quite distinct stages, each stage marked off from the one before, and the one which will follow.

In this chapter we will examine three theories which may help to explain some of children's learning. They are:

1 classical conditioning,

2 operant conditioning, and

3 social learning theory.

The first two originated nearly a century ago and were mostly tested using animals as subjects, although they both now have some very important uses for humans. Social learning theory was developed during the last 30 years or so.

Make a list of some of the things a child does, which don't appear to have been learned consciously at all. How would you explain how children acquire these skills?

In your own words, explain what learning is.

Review
What is learning?

If a young boy usually behaves in a particular way (e.g. waits for a parent to button his coat), then has some experience (e.g. playing at doing up buttons) which leads him to behave in a consistently different way (e.g. to button his own coat), then we might say that he has learned from the experience. Young children learn by repeating actions (like throwing a rattle), by making associations between things, people, and places, and by observing and copying others.

When the term 'classical' is applied to a theory it usually means one of two things: either that the theory was the original which set the standards for those which followed, or that it is rather old-fashioned and probably wrong. (The first meaning applies here.) Conditioning is a process by which some learning takes place under certain conditions.

Ivan Pavlov

1 Classical conditioning

The founder of classical conditioning was **Ivan Pavlov**. While doing some research on the digestive system in dogs, Pavlov noticed that some of his older experimental dogs had learned to associate a particular **stimulus** with a particular **response**. He noticed that they started to salivate just as one of his assistants entered the laboratory with their food. Salivation is a **reflex** and is the normal response to food. But were the dogs salivating to the food, or to the sight or sound of the assistants? Pavlov imagined that the dogs had associated the sound of the assistants' footsteps, or the sight of the assistant (the stimulus) with the expectation of food in their mouths, and that this knowledge set off their salivation reflex (the response). The younger dogs didn't salivate. Pavlov concluded that they hadn't learned to associate the assistants with the food they brought.

What evidence does this paragraph contain that a careful observer like Pavlov could use to suggest that the dogs' salivation was caused by the assistants rather than the food?

Pavlov decided to investigate how well dogs could learn associations. He set up an experiment in which the dogs' food was presented immediately after a particular sound was made. The two stimuli were being **paired**. Each **pairing** is called a **trial**. Pavlov used bells, buzzers and a metronome as stimuli in different experiments with different dogs. He constructed some apparatus which measured the amount of salivation in the dogs' mouths, and the amount of digestive juices in their stomachs. This was the response: after just a few trials, the dogs started to salivate when they heard the sound, and before the food was presented. The animals had learned an association between a noise and some food, and that learning set off the physiological reaction of salivating.

You may have noticed that there are two stimuli here. The food, which you might expect to make a dog salivate, and the artificial sounds, which Pavlov controlled. Pavlov suggested that there are also two responses. The reflexive salivation caused by the food, and the learned salivation caused by the sound. He called the food an **unconditional stimulus** (US), and the salivation it produced was called an **unconditional response** (UR). Animals generally don't have much control over their reflexes. Pavlov proved that they can be set off by quite artificial means. He called these artificial means (such as the bell, and each of the other sounds in the various experiments) a **conditional stimulus** (CS), and salivating to them was called a **conditional response** (CR). NB: The response is always the animal's salivation. The difference lies in what causes the salivation.

Pavlov taught some laboratory dogs to salivate when they heard a particular sound. How do family pet dogs behave when they hear the rattle of their lead, or someone saying 'walkies'? Why do they behave in this way?

The food and the salivation are unconditional because they will occur under all natural, normal circumstances. They do not require any special conditions to exist before the stimulus will set off the response. A bell will trigger salivation on condition that it has been paired with some food in the past. The salivation to the bell is therefore conditional upon the bell having been associated with food.

To elicit something means to make something happen which wouldn't normally occur. In Pavlov's experiments a reflex is being elicited by a sound.

▶

Pavlov's dogs

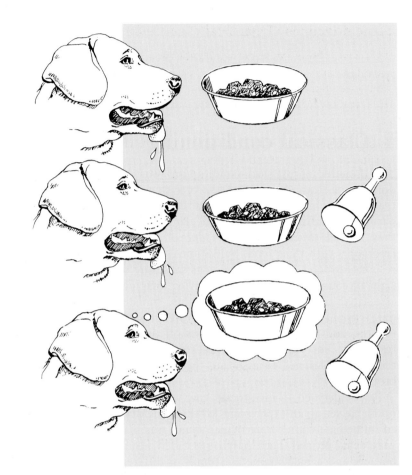

Background reading – Ivan Pavlov's biography

Ivan Petrovich Pavlov was born in 1849 in a small village in Russia. His father was the village priest, who sent his son to the nearby church school. Here he took an interest in biology, and eventually went to St Petersburg University where he studied animal physiology. He went on to study medicine, and took a medical degree. After further studies in Germany he returned to Russia and became a researcher and assistant in a physiological laboratory. At the age of 41 he became the head of a laboratory specialising in physiological research. When he was 50 he began to study how certain reflexes (such as salivation) could be triggered by things which were associated with food. Four years later he was awarded one of the first Nobel prizes in medicine.

At this time many psychologists were studying sensations and experiences, dreams and memory, and all kinds of things which went on in the mind. Ivan Pavlov was a dedicated Russian scientist who had little time for such things. He believed that science should be concerned with observing and measuring things, and finding out what caused things to happen. The mind couldn't be studied scientifically, so psychology was of no interest to him. He even threatened to dismiss any members of his staff who used psychological rather than biological explanations!

He continued his research into classical conditioning for 30 years, until his death in 1936.

Some principles of classical conditioning

As a very thorough scientist, Pavlov was careful to measure and record everything he found. He extended the experiments to see what else could be discovered. Here is a brief summary of some of the features of classical conditioning that he discovered:

The Learning Curve: This is shown on a graph and represents the amount of salivation by the number of trials. (Remember a trial is a pairing of the US and the UR.) The number of trials is placed on the horizontal axis while the amount of salivation is placed on the vertical axis.

Stimulus Generalisation: Pavlov conditioned his dogs to salivate to different sounds. An animal conditioned to salivate to a bell tuned to the musical note 'middle C' would also salivate to bells with different notes without any further conditioning. However, as the sounds became less like the one the animal was conditioned to respond to (a bell producing middle C), so the amount of salivation decreased.

Discrimination: This literally means being able to tell the difference between one thing and another. As Pavlov's dogs learned that other buzzers or bells did not mean that food was about to appear, so they learned to discriminate between those that did and those that didn't, and they only salivated when they heard the bell or buzzer that had been used to condition them.

Extinction: This means that the response stops (is **extinguished**). It happens when the animal hears the sound (the CS), but isn't given any food (the US). After a few trials the CR (salivation) will cease. The animal is learning not to respond when it hears the bell. Pavlov plotted this on an **extinction curve**.

Spontaneous Recovery: This sometimes happens after a learned response has been extinguished. Every now and again, for no apparent reason, the animal will give the response. For example, the dog will salivate when it hears the bell. Clearly it hasn't completely learned not to expect food. The CR hasn't been fully extinguished. After a time this spontaneous recovery will disappear, and the response will be extinguished again.

▲ **Conditioning**

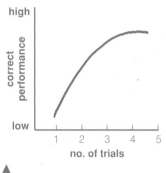

▲ **Learning curve**

▲ **An extinction curve**

Some features of classical conditioning

Here are the names of the five principles of classical conditioning described above:
(1) the learning curve, (2) generalisation, (3) discrimination, (4) extinction, (5) spontaneous recovery.
Here are some definitions of the principles of classical conditioning:
(a) When feeding is stopped the response gradually disappears.
(b) A line on a graph to show an animal's progress in developing responses to conditioned stimuli.
(c) A response to a given stimulus may also occur to a different, but similar, stimulus.

(d) Occasionally a response which the animal has learned not to give will recur for no obvious reason.

Fit each definition to one of the principles by putting the correct letter next to its number: (1) (2) (3) (4) (5).

An experiment on conditioning

Two psychologists wanted to see whether very young babies can be conditioned. They observed that infants of just a day or two old will begin to make sucking motions when they see a nipple. They sounded a tone immediately before some two- and three-day-old infants were breast fed. After a very few trials the infants started to make sucking motions when they heard the tone.

1 How old were the infants used in this experiment?

2 What is meant by a 'trial' in this passage?

3 Does this experiment suggest that very young babies can be classically conditioned or not?

4 Many reflexes can be classically conditioned. Apart from sucking, what else might be conditioned in children below the age of one?

2 Operant conditioning

The key feature of operant conditioning is that the subject behaves in some way which is followed by some 'reward'. The subject may associate its behaviour with the reward, and so learn to repeat it. The behaviour the animal learns is called an operation or an **operant**. If your dog fetches the stick you have thrown, you reward the dog in some way. Its operant behaviour (fetching the stick) comes first, and your behaviour (giving a reward) is a response to it. It may also be a reinforcer for the animal. In classical conditioning the experimenter's stimulus comes before the animal's response (Pavlov's bell rang before the dog salivated). Also, in classical conditioning, only behaviour which is mainly automatic (like reflexes) is conditioned. In operant conditioning just about any behaviour can be conditioned.

In classical conditioning the person doing the teaching does something which triggers some reflex in the animal. In operant conditioning the animal must do something first, for which it will then be rewarded. To obtain another reward it will have to do the same thing again.

Early research on operant conditioning

Early this century **E. L. Thorndike** put cats (and later other animals) in various puzzle boxes which he had made. Outside the box he placed some food. In order to escape and reach the food they had to perform some act, such as pulling some string, or pressing a treadle. After some time in the box, and usually by chance, the animals managed to pull the string or press the treadle and escape. The next day they were put back into the puzzle box, and Thorndike timed how long it would be before they escaped again, having performed the operations of pulling some string, pressing a treadle, etc. After a few trials, they were able to escape immediately.

In classical conditioning the researcher does something to elicit some behaviour from the subject. In operant conditioning the subject 'emits' a response without its being elicited. What does 'emit' mean?

Thorndike's experiment

1 How long does it take the animal to escape the first time it is put in the box?

2 About how long does it take by the sixth trial?

3 Summarise the conclusions of this graph in our own words.

Thorndike assumed that the animals learned the association between a stimulus (for example pulling the string) and a response (escaping and reaching the food) because escaping and eating gave them pleasure. Presumably being in the box was unpleasant. Thorndike used several species of animal in various puzzle boxes, and most eventually learned the appropriate operant. Thorndike summarised these conclusions in his 'Law of Effect', which he first proposed in 1904. It states that a response will follow a stimulus if it is associated in the animal's mind with 'a satisfying state of affairs'.

So: being put in a box,
   (a STIMULUS)
   will emit

                    pulling strings,
                    (a RESPONSE)
                    if associated with

                              escape and food
                              (SATISFACTION)

Having established this **stimulus–response (S–R)** association, Thorndike then extinguished it, i.e. stopped giving the reward (freedom and food), although the animal had given the right response (pulling the string). After a few more attempts at string pulling the animal stopped. Thorndike believed this was because the animal stopped receiving pleasure. As it had learned to respond, so it now learned not to.

Thorndike stated that animals will learn to emit a response if giving this response results in something pleasant or satisfying happening to them.

The 'Law of Effect'

In your own words, describe how Thorndike's 'Law of Effect' explains his experimental cat's behaviour.

One of the most influential psychologists this century must be **B. F. Skinner**. During the middle part of this century he developed Thorndike's 'Law of Effect'. He was unhappy about Thorndike's ideas of pleasure and satisfaction. He thought they would be extremely hard to measure in humans, so how can anyone really know what cats experience as pleasure? Thorndike's law wasn't nearly scientific enough for Skinner.

B. F. Skinner

B. F. Skinner insisted that psychological research must be scientific, and therefore only those things which could be studied scientifically were worth bothering with.

A Skinner Box

Skinner used some apparatus called a Skinner box, which was similar to Thorndike's puzzle box, to study the way rats and similar animals learn. Inside the box was a lever and a food tray. Pressing the lever released a food pellet into the tray. Like Thorndike's animals, Skinner's rats soon learned to press the lever. Skinner found that a number of things, apart from food or escape, would act as rewards, and not all animals would respond in the same way to what Thorndike saw as pleasure-giving. (A well-fed rat is less likely than a starving rat to regard food as pleasure.)

Skinner used the term **reinforcer** to apply to anything which would make the animal (or human) repeat the response. In many societies on earth money is a powerful reinforcer! Skinner found discomfort might act as a reinforcer. If giving a response caused pain to stop, this was quickly learned (and slowly forgotten).

Background reading – B. F. Skinner's biography

Burrhus Frederic Skinner was born in America in 1904, and he became interested in biology. Only when studying it at university did he take an interest in the writings of people like Ivan Pavlov. Whilst Pavlov always regarded himself as a biologist specialising in physiology, because he was using animals, Skinner started to think about applying some of the principles of conditioning to human behaviour. He graduated from Harvard University in 1931 with a doctorate in psychology. He spent a few years researching, before starting to teach and write about what he thought were the principles of learning, and the way psychology should study them. While Pavlov had little time for psychology, thinking it too unscientific, Skinner devoted all his work, and most of his life, to making psychology scientifically acceptable.

B. F. Skinner died in 1990.

The nature of reinforcement

The main purpose of reinforcement is to shape, and then maintain, particular behaviour, so a reinforcer can be anything which leads to some behaviour being repeated. The reinforcer may please us personally. If you want money and are paid for doing something well, you will have a good reason for wanting to do it well again. We may also do something because we know that it will please other people. The reinforcer here may be the satisfaction of having done something for someone else. This kind of reinforcer probably only applies to humans.

Skinner identified **positive** and **negative** reinforcers. Positive reinforcers may be **primary** (i.e. the reinforcer is a naturally occurring phenomenon like food or sleep which directly satisfies some physical need) or **secondary** (i.e. things we have learned can be worth having, such as money). Secondary reinforcers may be exchanged for primary reinforcers. Reinforcement can also be **negative**. It's not just 'nice things' which will make us behave in certain ways. Stopping or avoiding unpleasant things can also be strong reinforcers. If the school bully demands a child's lunch money, and pulls the child's hair until the money is handed over, then the child will give the money in order to escape from the pain. In the future the child may try very hard to avoid the school bully. Negative reinforcement has been demonstrated on some animals.

One final method of changing some behaviour is by using **punishment**. Punishment involves causing some kind of physical or mental distress by either giving some unpleasant stimulus (like a smack), or withholding a pleasant one (like not being allowed to go out for a week). If we know that we will be punished severely for doing something, we are less likely to do it (or more careful not to be caught!).

Operant learning theorists are critical of the use of punishment, saying that all it does is reduce one undesirable response, while not replacing it by reinforcing a desirable one. They believe that using

If some act is followed by a reinforcer it is likely to be repeated. Reinforcers can be positive or negative. Give some examples of things which you would find positively or negatively reinforcing.

How would negative reinforcement explain the behaviour of the child whose hair was pulled?

Can you work out what the CS and CR are in avoidance learning?

Background reading – Negative reinforcement

Here are the steps in negative reinforcement.
(a) An animal is being subjected to continuous pain. For example, a rat is receiving a mild electric shock through the floor of its cage.
(b) Pressing a bar in the cage will turn the electricity off.
(c) The animal presses the bar (by accident probably) and the shock stops.
(d) After a short period the electricity is turned on again.
(e) The animal quickly learns to press the bar (and who can blame it!).

This form of negative reinforcement is called escape learning. A more complicated extension of escape learning is avoidance learning, the steps of which are as follows.
(a) A buzzer is sounded immediately before the electricity is turned on.
(b) The animal learns to associate the buzzer with the pain.
(c) The animal becomes very anxious and will soon learn to press the bar to avoid the pain.

reinforcement to increase some desirable behaviour will be more effective than using punishment to decrease some undesirable behaviour.

Schedules of reinforcement

Skinner experimented with reinforcers. He stopped reinforcing the animals every time they gave correct responses. Instead they were given reinforcement every other time, or every third time. He reinforced some every few minutes rather than every few times they gave a correct response. Skinner taught a pigeon to peck a coloured disc when a particular light came on when it only received reinforcement once in one thousand pecks. The animal seems to know that it will receive a reinforcement sometime, and continues to give the correct response until the reinforcer occurs. There are five possible ways of reinforcing. They are called **schedules of reinforcement**.

The five major schedules of reinforcement are:

(a) **Continuous:** where the desired behaviour is reinforced every time it occurs.

(b) **Fixed Ratio:** such as when every fifth, tenth, twelfth, or any other such regular correct response is reinforced.

(c) **Variable Ratio:** where the number of necessary correct responses is constantly altered.

(d) **Fixed Interval:** reinforcement made once every fixed number of minutes, so long as there has been at least one correct response during that time.

(e) **Variable Interval:** where the time between reinforcements is varied.

Although animals are quickest to condition using continuous reinforcement, Skinner found that switching to one of the others made the response harder to extinguish. If the animal isn't led to expect a reinforcement after every correct response, it will give many correct responses before stopping.

It isn't necessary to reinforce an animal every time it gives the correct response. Using one of the other schedules of reinforcement makes the response less likely to extinguish quickly. Why would circus elephant trainers switch to one of the other schedules as soon as their animals were trained to perform some trick?

An experiment on animal learning

Stage One: A rat was conditioned to expect some food powder when it pressed a lever in its cage. After a few hours a red lamp was switched on outside the cage. It stayed on for a few minutes and then was turned off. The rat had to press the lever five times while the light was on. It was eventually conditioned to pressing the lever when the red light was on. Occasionally a green light came on, and the animal pressed her bar. As the rat wasn't given food, it soon stopped pressing the bar when the green light came on. The rat's feeding sessions were thus controlled by the amount of time the red light was on, and the rat learned that pressing the lever when the red light was on was the way to receive food.

1 Define the term reinforcement, as used by learning theorists.

2 What do psychologists call the kind of reinforcer that was first given to the rat in Stage One of the experiment described above.

3 What operant response did the rat have to give to receive this reinforcer?

4 What schedule of reinforcement was used originally, and how was this changed a few hours after starting Stage One?

5 What feature of conditioning is demonstrated when the animal wasn't given food when the green light was on?

Stage Two: After several days the routine was changed. Food appeared in the food tray at mealtimes, to keep the animal alive, regardless of whether the lever was pressed, or any light was on. At first the rat continued to press the lever, although it eventually stopped. Every now and again the rat would leap at the lever and press it furiously, often when the red light was first switched on, but the rat would stop after a few seconds.

6 What two features of conditioning are shown in Stage Two?

Stage Three: After a few more days the routine was changed again. The red light would come on and two seconds later a loud whistle was blown. The rat rushed around and tried to climb the bars of its cage. During this frenzied behaviour the animal fell on to the lever, which stopped the whistle. It took some minutes before the animal's behaviour was 'normal'. Some time later the red light and whistle routine happened again. After a few trials the rat would leap at the lever as soon as the red light came on.

7 What kind of learning is being demonstrated in Stage Three?

8 What is the difference between punishment and negative reinforcement?

❛ *Comments on conditioning*

Good point

1 **The** major contribution of Pavlov, Thorndike and Skinner is not so much what they discovered – much of it had been known for years – but that they applied strict laboratory and scientific techniques to testing behaviour, and found that they worked.

2 Classical and operant theories are clearly described and their principles are not difficult to understand. Reinforcement and extinction, for example, are widely used and understood. Such principles offer clear guidelines for childrearing.

Criticism

1 Experiments conducted on animals under strict laboratory control can't really be generalised to all of human learning. There are many factors in a child's real life which affect the way he or she will behave. Many of these could not be tested in a laboratory.

2 The principles are just too simple to explain all learning. When children experiment with plasticine, sand, water, building blocks, Lego, jigsaw puzzles, etc., they may do so for fun, for enjoyment or for the challenge. They don't necessarily do so because they've been reinforced in any way.

Review
Operant conditioning

Thorndike, Skinner, and others have shown that many aspects of human behaviour, apart from reflexes, can also be conditioned. Any behaviour which is reinforced, they believe, is likely to be repeated. Behaviour which is not reinforced will extinguish. The reinforcement needn't be continuous. The expectation of receiving some reinforcer will be enough to keep a child behaving in some appropriate way for quite long periods. However, not all learning can be explained by reinforcement.

3 Conditioning theory is practical and avoids references to mental events such as libido, morality, guilt, etc., which cannot be observed, measured, or proved to exist. Behaviour is observable, and so are many of its causes.

3 Fun, enjoyment, challenge, etc., are 'mental events' and are not observable reinforcers. Behaviour may be observable, its causes are likely to be more complex than can be explained by the principles of conditioning. In any case, Skinner explains why existing behaviour becomes repeated, he doesn't adequately explain where new behaviour comes from.

Pavlov's, Thorndike's, and Skinner's work has been applied specifically to two aspects of childhood which we shall examine later. These are the way some aspects of problem behaviour can be shaped to become more acceptable, and are the techniques and principles of programmed learning that were quite widely used in many secondary schools some years ago.

Now answer the following questions

1 What is the main difference between classical and operant conditioning?

2 What was Thorndike trying to discover with his puzzle box?

3 According to Thorndike, what acted as rewards for his experimental animals?

4 What exactly does Skinner mean by 'reinforcer'?

5 What is the main consequence of reinforcement?

6 What is the difference between primary and secondary reinforcement?

7 How might a parent use positive reinforcement for teaching table manners to a child?

3 Social learning theory

Social learning theorists accept that children learn a great deal from reinforcement and punishment, but they claim that children also learn by observing and imitating. If children see that someone's behaviour leads to something pleasant happening, they are likely to try and copy it. For example, a young child can't reach the biscuit jar in the kitchen, but then he sees an older child pull up a chair to stand on to reach the jar. The young child may imitate that behaviour so that he too can have a biscuit.

Social learning is often called **observational learning**. A child will not simply observe and then copy someone. Some people will be more important to a child than others, and these people's behaviour is more likely to be copied. The child will **model** aspects of his or her behaviour on these important people. Reinforcement isn't necessary for observational learning, although it may be important that the correct behaviour is reinforced if performance is to improve. For example, if standing on the chair results in having a biscuit, then the child has a good reason for improving the ability to climb on chairs. If the child doesn't receive a reward then there's no incentive to improve.

Each child will observe and copy different aspects of behaviour of different people. Also each child will be reinforced and punished for different sorts of things too. Different parents use different kinds of punishments and rewards, and some parents are more severe or generous than others. If personality is affected by its environment, then each child's personality will inevitably be quite different.

Albert Bandura is a social psychologist who has conducted many studies of who children are most likely to model and imitate. He believes that much of our behaviour and personality is learned, i.e. it is the result of our nurture.

With various colleagues, Bandura has conducted numerous experiments during the last 25 years to see the ways in which children model themselves on adults. Here is one example:

Three groups of nursery school children were chosen to watch a short film with three different endings. Each child would see an adult model attacking an inflatable plastic doll (called a **Bobo doll**). He hit it with a mallet, threw it on the floor, sat on it, punched it, kicked it across the room and threw balls at it. At the same time the adult shouted at the doll saying such things as 'bang, bang, bang', and 'Sockeroo'.

Social learning theorists add observational learning and modelling to reinforcement as explanations of how children learn.

▲
Albert Bandura

◄
A Bobo doll

In one of the films, someone came in and gave the adult some sweets for such a good performance. In another, the children saw the model being told off and smacked for his aggression. The third group didn't see any reward or punishment.

After watching this performance, the children were given a chance to play with the Bobo doll, and some of the objects (like the mallet) that the adult had used to hit it. Their behaviour was recorded. Those who had seen the aggressive model being rewarded, and those who hadn't seen any consequences were equally aggressive towards the doll (on average they each committed over two and a half aggressive acts). The group who had seen the adult being punished were much less likely to be aggressive (one and a half aggressive acts).

In general, Bandura and his colleagues found that the aggressive model influenced the behaviour of the children in two ways. First it taught them new ways of being aggressive, and second it increased the number of times the children were aggressive in many ways, not just in relation to their toys.

However, several criticisms have been made of such experiments. For example the experiment is rather artificial because in real life people are rarely rewarded for behaving aggressively. Rather, in real life aggression against people is likely to be discouraged or punished. The children may not have been familiar with Bobo dolls, and may have believed that hitting and kicking them was the appropriate thing to do with them. If so, they weren't necessarily being aggressive in their treatment of the doll, they may simply have been imitating appropriate behaviour.

Most influential models will be those who seem to have higher status, those who are loving towards the children and those who are similar to the children.

As we said earlier, some models are more likely to be imitated than others. Bandura said that if children are to learn by observation, they must study a model quite closely, and some models are more worth looking at than others. The models who have the most influence will be people who are warm and loving towards children, or people who have more power, influence, or competence, and people who are similar to the children (same sex, etc.). Some of these will be more important at some ages than others.

Bandura's findings have important implications for childminding. If parents or teachers are not seen as warm, powerful and competent, for example, their influence over children will be weakened. Other

Background reading – Why is Observational Learning so widely used?

Bandura claims that most of what children learn is the result of observation and modelling. The reasons for this are as follows.

1 Learning by observing someone else achieve a good result is a lot more efficient than learning by trial and error, or waiting until a reinforcement is given.

2 Many abilities that children master could probably never be learned by simple trial and error. Learning to use a language is probably the best example. Listening to someone, and then incorporating their words or grammar into correct speech, is largely the result of observational learning.

role models, such as fictional TV characters or pop stars, may have influences on children of which the parents may disapprove.

Comments on social learning theory

Good points

1 Bandura accepts that biological factors can affect learning and personality development, but he emphasises the importance of situational variables.

2 Social learning theorists show that particular role models (people likely to be copied) can make learning more efficient.

3 The theory explains why some people are more influential than others over what children learn, and how their personalities grow.

4 Social learning theorists see a child's personality being the result of it modelling its ideas as well as its behaviour on various adults.

5 It emphasises how social forces act on the child, making it behave or think in one way or another.

6 It explains how children learn.

Critical points

1 Some psychologists claim that our genes determine certain characteristics, such as gender behaviour or aggression.

2 Children are all different and even if they see the same role model they may interpret its behaviour in quite different ways.

3 Children don't automatically copy the behaviour of people who may appear to be influential. Their behaviour may be the result of trial and error, misunderstanding, or have no apparent cause at all.

4 If true then children's personalities would be constantly changing, depending on whom they were modelling at the time. This view isn't widely shared by psychologists.

5 It pays little regard to what the child makes of all these influences. Many psychologists claim that children are rather more actively involved in their own learning. (Bandura has modified the original theory to take account of this.)

6 It doesn't describe what children are capable of learning at different ages.

Review
Social learning theory

Albert Bandura has shown that children can learn from observing and modelling. This is a very efficient way of learning how to do complicated things. The people who are most likely to be copied are those who are powerful, competent, kind to the child, or are rewarded for behaving in some way.

Social learning theory

Some psychologists arranged for four samples of five- to seven-year-olds to hear and see an adult model. One group heard and saw an adult being charitable and saying that it was good to donate things to poor children. The adult then gave some valuables to charity. A second group heard the adult talking generously, but then didn't give anything away. The third group heard the adult saying it was alright to be greedy, asking why he should give his money to anyone else. The adult then refused to donate. The fourth group heard the greedy adult talking, but then saw him being generous.

The children were each then given some tokens which could be changed into sweets, and asked if they would like to donate some of them to needy children. Here is a histogram displaying the results.

Children's behaviour after being exposed to different kinds of model

charitable behaviour			
selfish behaviour			
model preached charity and behaved charitably	model preached charity but behaved selfishly	model preached selfishness and behaved selfishly	model preached selfishness but behaved charitably

1 Which experimental groups resulted in the most generous behaviour and which the least generous?

2 What factor seems to be the most influential in determining these children's levels of generosity?

3 Are these findings consistent with social learning theory? Explain your answer.

4 Children of parents who smoke are much more likely to smoke themselves. True or false?

5 According to Bandura, why do children model themselves on some people rather than others?

Changing Problem Behaviour

Is it normal for a child to wet the bed occasionally? Is it normal for a child to tell a lie? Is it normal for a boy to fight another boy, or for a girl to call another girl names sometimes? Your answer to each of these questions is probably, 'It depends on the circumstances.' It would be very convenient to think that people were either normal or not normal. Of course this simply isn't true. Most people have done something in their lives that others might describe as very odd indeed. As we grow our behaviour changes. Behaviour in a three-year-old that was seen as unfortunate, an accident, or only to be expected, might be regarded as a problem in a six-year-old.

For various reasons not all children will grow up to behave in the ways that we might describe as normal or well adjusted. For example, temporary or permanent separation of children from their parents can result in emotional difficulties; conflict and stress in the home can lead to anxiety; parents who model aggression tend to have aggressive children; and an unstimulating environment can lead to retarded mental development. Children may suffer from intellectual, emotional, personality, or social problems. Such problems may gradually disappear on their own, may stay throughout childhood, or may become worse until the children must receive some kind of treatment.

Nearly all children have minor problems at some time. For example, they may be overactive, have temper tantrums, constantly seek attention, tell lies, talk too much, act aggressively and destructively, sleep badly, be disobedient, refuse food, and so on. Most grow out of these difficulties. But some problems can persist, or become more serious. Children who are extremely shy, or very aggressive, who have severe temper tantrums, or continue bed-wetting, may create difficulties for themselves, for their parents, teachers, and others. Something like 15–20 per cent of children have some problem which will need special help at some time. Therapy may be the best answer for children with severe problems. The type of therapy given depends very much on how the therapist sees the cause of the problem.

Even problem children are a lot more like normal children than they are unlike them. For example, a child who has reading difficulties may be quite as good at other tasks as other children. Even quite severely mentally retarded children may have been fairly normal

Most children display some minor problem behaviour. For most of them it will be temporary, and treatable.

babies, and have learned their attachments and so on in much the same way as normal children.

Some widely used therapies have developed out of some of the principles of classical and operant conditioning, and Sigmund Freud's psychoanalytic theory. Classical conditioning has given rise to a number of techniques, generally referred to as **behaviour therapy**, for use in the treatment of certain kinds of phobias and other fears. Skinner's work has been developed into rather different kinds of treatments, called **behaviour modification**, which can be applied to all sorts of learned behaviour. Freud's ideas have led to **play therapy** for use with some children.

Background reading – Childhood problems

The causes of many of the problems that children suffer can be divided into three categories. (a) Some babies arc born with problems caused by genetic abnormalities. Down's Syndrome, for example, is caused by there being an extra 21st chromosome, so the baby inherits 47 chromosomes instead of the usual 46. (b) Something that happens to the mother during pregnancy, such as an accident, or catching some infectious disease, can also lead to abnormal development, and problems for the child later. (c) Other problems are caused by factors during childhood (such as having some kinds of disease), or by upbringing.

Psychologists are concerned with investigating problems caused by factors in children's upbringing, while medical researchers are concerned with the other problems.

Most traditional approaches see the cause of children's problems coming from within the children themselves, and they seek a 'cure' to each particular problem. For example, Freud argued that children must resolve the problems that arise during the Oedipal Complex if their personalities were to develop normally. Others believe that many of the problems that children suffer may be caused by difficulties in the home, school, or even society itself. For example, R. D. Laing has written a number of books on the origins of mental problems. Laing argues that many families force children to obey petty rules which may be of little benefit to the child. Some parents may use a great deal of physical punishment to control a child's behaviour. According to Laing it is often the family, not the child, which needs therapy.

Here we will review:
1 classical conditioning's behaviour therapy;
2 operant conditioning's behaviour modification;
3 Freudian psychotherapy.

1 Behaviour therapy

In Chapter Six we saw how classical conditioning had been developed by Pavlov, leading to the establishment of certain principles of learning such as generalisation discrimination, and extinction. Pavlov found that he could teach an animal to associate a neutral stimulus such as a buzzer or bell with a stimulus such as food that normally produced a reflexive response such as salivation. Pavlov was able to elicit the reflex by just giving the neutral stimulus – ringing the bell elicited the salivation.

People are able to learn many more associations than animals are, and we do not always need actual, physical rewards. Just knowing that we are succeeding may be a sufficient reward for adults and older children. People who know they have a problem may see getting better as a reinforcer. Here are brief descriptions of some therapeutic techniques which have been developed out of classical conditioning. Before describing them, it is important to stress that, if any therapy is to succeed, the most important factor is the cooperation of the child.

Classical conditioning showed how associations between various kinds of stimulus and response could be learned. Pavlov developed some 'principles of learning' from his studies of classical conditioning. What do these 'principles of learning' mean: Generalisation, discrimination, extinction, spontaneous recovery?

Systematic Desensitisation

'Systematic' means in an ordered way, and 'desensitisation' means becoming less sensitive towards something. This technique can be used with adults and older children.

Systematic desensitisation gradually replaces the phobic reaction with relaxation.

A child who has had or imagined some unpleasant experience at school may develop a phobia about going to school. This will be a real problem since not attending school is illegal. The first stage in successful therapy is for the therapist to establish exactly what tolerance the child has to school. For example, a schoolboy may be able to talk about school, watch TV programmes featuring school, but cannot bear to go past or into his own school. This is the starting point for therapy.

The next thing to establish is exactly what is to be achieved through therapy. For example, we need the child to attend school regularly and benefit from school in the usual ways. This is the end point of therapy. Having decided where to begin and where to end systematic desensitisation may now begin.

The child is taken near to his school and helped to get used to being there. Some rewards such as praise, attention, sweets or promises of treats may be used. Or the child may simply be helped to relax. When he can cope with this he will be encouraged, with the therapist, to approach the school gates. All the time, relaxing and reassuring messages will be given. Slowly the child will be helped to approach the school, until finally the end point is reached. This may have taken several hours, days, or even weeks.

Implosion therapy

The sufferer is made to face the thing which causes the anxiety without either relaxation or being gently exposed to it. The panic reactions will eventually subside, and the response should extinguish. The greatest of care will be necessary in using this technique with children.

Implosion therapy rapidly replaces the phobic reaction.

Aversion Therapy

Some punishment is given for undesired behaviour. It is not widely used by child psychologists! The idea is to weaken the association the person has made between a 'bad' response, such as taking illegal drugs, solvent abuse, and so on, and an inappropriate emotion, such as pleasure. The person is faced with the thing that gives pleasure at the same time as something unpleasant is happening.

Aversion therapy replaces a pleasant response with an unpleasant one.

With children a mild form of aversion therapy has been used to 'treat' bedwetting. The child sleeps on a special sheet that can detect any sign of wetness. As soon as the child starts to urinate the sheet sets off a mildly unpleasant buzzer which should wake the child quite quickly. The child should soon learn that not waking voluntarily when the bladder is sending messages that it needs relief will result in being rudely woken.

❝ *Evaluation of behaviour therapy*

Good points	Criticisms
1 Pavlov showed how associations between various kinds of stimulus and some reflexive response could be learned.	1 Learning associations between neutral stimuli and reflexive behaviour does not explain how or why the majority of our behaviour occurs.
2 Pavlov's detailed scientific investigation led to the establishment of some therapies for dealing with people who have phobic reactions to certain objects or events.	2 The therapies therefore will only apply to a limited range of problems, such as phobias.
3 The therapies can be effective.	3 The therapies can be expensive since they may take a long time. With some disorders, such as acute anorexia nervosa, the time isn't available.

Review
Behaviour therapy

Classical conditioning has been used to treat a variety of adult and children's disorders, notably things which produce anxiety or fear such as phobias. It is often used in conjunction with other therapies too, particularly for learning which has been strengthened over many years.

❜

2 Behaviour shaping and behaviour modification

Skinner's ideas about learning and behaviour were discussed in Chapter Six. They were developed out of E. L. Thorndike's 'Law of Effect' which stated that if something pleasant or satisfying followed some act, then that act was likely to be repeated. All sorts of things can satisfy or please people. Almost every day parents and teachers use smiles, nods, encouragement, rewards, and attention to reinforce good behaviour in children. Punishments are also used to *shape* children's behaviour.

Skinner's techniques involve **behaviour shaping**, and **behaviour modification**. Their principles are not difficult to understand, and put into practice. Behaviour shaping involves deciding what behaviour we want to teach to a child or animal, and gradually building up

We all use operant conditioning techniques to teach our pets and children how to behave. Many children use conditioning to 'train' their parents too. Can you think how?

to it. Again, the child's cooperation will be one of the most important factors in the likelihood of success.

Behaviour shaping

Behaviour shaping simply means changing someone else's behaviour until it resembles the kind of behaviour we want. We might look disgusted, or ignore someone who has behaved badly, or we may punish them in some way. We hope that showing them our displeasure will stop them from behaving badly. Or we may smile and say something which means 'well done' to someone who has acted in a way that we approve of, hoping that this will encourage repetition of the behaviour. We all use these reinforcers every day to shape the behaviour of people around us. Skinner developed a version of this which is called **behaviour shaping by successive approximations**.

Using behaviour shaping by successive approximations Skinner taught pigeons to play a version of ping-pong. Two pigeons are reinforced for standing in the right places on a model ping-pong table. When this behaviour is conditioned, reinforcement will only be given if they allow a ball to hit a part of their bodies while they are standing in the right place. When this is conditioned, reinforcement will only be given if they hit the ball with the upper part of their bodies. Later, reinforcement will only occur if they hit the ball with their heads, and later their beaks must be used to hit the ball if they are to obtain a reinforcement. Finally they will have to move towards the ball, and hit it in the right direction with their beaks, in order to be reinforced.

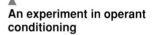
An experiment in operant conditioning

Can you see why Skinner calls his approach 'behaviour shaping by successive approximations'?

Behaviour modification

Behaviour modification attempts to extinguish problem behaviour in favour of normal behaviour. It is not concerned with the causes of problem behaviour, only with the actual behaviour itself. Here is a summary of the procedure, using the example of a five-year-old who hardly ever stops talking.

In order to modify some aspect of behaviour, three things are necessary. First, we must define precisely the behaviour that needs to be reduced, for example, amount of talking, talking when eating, talking when in the car, talking in the shops, etc. Second, we must identify and define each aspect of behaviour that is to be increased, for example, being quiet for a few moments. (As these last two statements are opposites, any change in one of them is bound to produce a change in the other.) The child's cooperation is essential here. Third, we must identify what is reinforcing the problem behaviour, for example, the pleasure of being the centre of attention. And we must then try to change it, either by ignoring or punishing the undesired response, at the same time as reinforcing appropriate behaviour, for example, ignoring the child when the child is talking. Eventually the child should be quiet for a few moments. We should then pay attention after such a silence. When the child realises that it is necessary to be quiet in order to get a response, the child should learn to talk less. It should be possible to get the child to lengthen the silences by withholding the reinforcer until there have been longer periods of silence.

This procedure must be applied consistently by all the adults from whom the child seeks attention; for example, parents and teachers must all be willing and able to join in with the therapy. Frequent checks must be made to measure the length of time for which the child is talking. These will be compared to the length of time the child was talking before the treatment started. Only in this way will we know if the treatment is working.

Another possible type of treatment is modelling therapy, and is based on the Social Learning (or Observational Learning) theory developed by **Albert Bandura** and his colleagues. The child is shown examples of people behaving in the desired way, and sees them being rewarded for doing so. People who are behaving in an unacceptable way are seen being punished for doing so. So our talkative child will be shown (perhaps a film of) someone being praised and given sweets for keeping quiet, and someone being told off and not be given any sweets for talking too much.

Of course there'll always be some children (and adults too) who just do not seem to respond to this kind of treatment. For example the child here may continue to chatter away despite being ignored by the teachers and parents. The child may not even notice this treatment, or the treatment might even lead to more talking!

Here are some examples of behaviour to be decreased: shouting, being destructive, being greedy, bed-wetting, being disobedient. What should replace them?

An example of behaviour modification

A four-year-old boy named Jasvir spent most of his time at playgroup sitting down. The adults tried to encourage him to move around, but without success. A psychologist suggested that having so much adult interest shown in him was reinforcing Jasvir's behaviour. The adults were instructed to ignore him completely when he was sitting down, and speak to him when he was standing. He was observed for 30 minutes each day and the number of minutes spent sitting or standing was noted. Here is an extract of the record which was kept of his behaviour.

	Unacceptable Behaviour (Sitting)	Acceptable Behaviour (Standing)
Day 1	23	7
Day 5	24	6
Day 9	19	11
Day 15	14	16
Day 21	11	19
Day 30	5	25

1 What explanation does the psychologist suggest for Jasvir's behaviour?

2 What recommendation does the psychologist make?

3 Why is it necessary to keep a record of Jasvir's behaviour each day?

4 Does the extract of the record shown here support or contradict the psychologist's suggestion?

6 *Comments on behaviour modification*

Advantages

1 The technique is not difficult to understand, and fairly easy to teach to parents, teachers, and others involved in dealing with problem children.

2 Several kinds of problem behaviour have been successfully treated by behaviour modification.

3 Behaviour modification can be successful in changing problem behaviour.

4 Behaviourists remove the reinforcer that is maintaining the problem behaviour.

Disadvantages

1 It is extremely time-consuming and demands almost the full attention of the parent or teacher. The temptations to give up are enormous, particularly if the child's behaviour worsens in the beginning.

2 It is unlikely that all human behaviour has been learned. If some behaviour is the result of biological forces it may not respond to operant conditioning.

3 Behaviour modification treats problem behaviour. It does not attempt to find or treat the cause of that behaviour.

4 Much of children's learning seems to occur without the need for any observable reinforcer. For example, some may be the result of simple trial and error.

Review
Behaviour shaping and behaviour modification

Skinner developed his ideas about behaviour modification out of his studies of the effects of operant conditioning on shaping behaviour. This view maintains that since all behaviour is learned, problem behaviour must be the result of the unfortunate pairing of a response with a reinforcer. To correct the behaviour it is necessary to find that reinforcer and remove it. Then the problem behaviour will extinguish. At the same time good behaviour must be reinforced.

3 Freud and psychotherapy

Play therapy has been developed from Freudian views of personality development. The main terms we use here were explained in Chapter Five so look back if there's a term you don't understand.

Freud said that if something which is making us anxious can't be removed we will unconsciously use some **defence mechanisms** to protect ourselves from it. Perhaps we might bury it in our unconscious. If the anxiety remains unsettled it may appear later as some **neurosis** needing to be dealt with by psychoanalytic therapy. Some series of problems during our childhood may have caused our personality to have become arrested or fixated in one of the stages of development. This will limit the extent to which any future development can occur. The cause of this fixation must be found and removed by **psychotherapy**, so that development can quickly catch up, and become normal.

Psychotherapy generally means using just about any (legal) technique that either makes patients actually better, or at least think they feel better. It can be applied to any mental, emotional, or behavioural disorder. Psychoanalysis specifically uses the techniques developed by Freud to investigate and interpret the unconscious mind.

Freud's therapy was to use the techniques of psychoanalysis to explore the unconscious. Eventually, he believed, he would find the memory of some incident which probably occurred during one of the stages of personality development. It would probably have produced a great deal of anxiety at the time. This could have caused the **libido** to become fixated. Encouraging the patient to face whatever caused the anxiety will help the patient to overcome it, and the hysterical symptoms should disappear as the libido is freed.

> Freud believed we have very many defence mechanisms which are unconscious, and perfectly normal ways of dealing with anxieties. If the anxiety is too great it can lead to repression.

> What is a neurosis?

> Freudian psychoanalysis was intended to free anxieties which had become repressed in the unconscious.

Starting analysis

If a patient said something about her or his past which an analyst thought was interesting, the analyst might ask a question. Write down five questions that Freud might have asked a patient during treatment, giving the reasons for the questions.

Psychotherapy and children

Psychoanalysis is much more than a theory of development, it is a therapeutic technique for curing problems. For adults it uses the techniques of analysing their dreams, slips of the tongue, and free talk. These techniques do not work with children.

Play therapy

Since the usual psychoanalytic techniques weren't suitable for studying children, another technique had to be found. Freud himself never really investigated this, but other psychoanalysts, starting with Freud's own daughter Anna (who followed her father into psycho-analysis) did. (With Sophie Dann she studied six war orphans at the Bulldogs Bank, which was described in Chapter Two.) Psychoana-lysts believe that children express all their concealed emotions through play, just as adults are supposed to through dreams, so play therapy would involve letting children be themselves.

Play becomes a window through which the skilled analyst can see into the child's unconscious. Having seen the child's problem being acted out through play, the therapist tries to help the child to see it too – to make the unconscious conscious to the child. As Freud said, 'where the id was, let the ego be'. The id is the primitive uncon-scious, which is the source of energy for all our instincts. The ego is rational and logical.

There are several versions of play therapy, but they can be loosely grouped according to their main purpose. These are for diagnosis and for treatment.

Play Therapy for Diagnosis

The child is invited into a playroom full of toys, and encouraged to play with whatever she wants for as long as she wants, and how she wants. The therapist encourages the child, but doesn't suggest to her what she should do. This is called **non-directive therapy**. The therapist doesn't question her but lets her become herself. A good therapist responds to anything which the child says or does which shows that she is becoming aware of her true self by expressing her feelings. (NB: different play therapists go to different lengths to encourage self-expression. Some are less non-directive than others.)

> Why wouldn't analysing children's mistakes in speech be much of a guide to their unconscious?
>
> Children spend a lot of their time playing. Play is often used by children for expressing their emotions, as well as for developing other skills.

> Diagnosis is the process of categorising various symptoms as belonging to various diseases and putting someone with particular symptoms into the appropriate category of disease.

◄ A therapy playroom

Background reading – An application of Freud's techniques

One of Freud's last students in Vienna was Bruno Bettelheim. He was put into a concentration camp by the Nazis and there he saw many horrific things. He felt afterwards that he had needed all his knowledge of psychoanalysis in order to survive. When he was released he went to America where he was appointed the head of a school for very severely disturbed children. He used Freudian techniques of allowing free expression, and letting children feel that no one was trying to trap them, and that adults could be trusted. About four in every five children who went to the Orthogenic School (orthogenic means getting straight, right from the beginning) were able to leave and go on to lead normal lives. However, even this totally child-centred version of psychoanalysis couldn't cure all the children.

Psychoanalysts have developed a number of versions of play therapy to deal with particular children's problem.

Play Therapy as treatment

Children are encouraged to play out their frustrations and tensions in the playroom. According to psychoanalytic theory, normal, healthy children use play activities to help them sort out their understanding of things which are going on around them. For example, through play they can *relive* experiences which they weren't able to understand fully when they first had them. Some emotions may be too painful to be dealt with all at once. Through play, children can *regress* to some earlier time, and go through the events again, both in their imagination, and in the play activity. They use real or imaginary objects to *symbolise* the real world, and playing with them is like 'playing through' whatever is really going on. Negative feelings can be *displaced* on to dolls or imaginary people, and any emotions which the children still can't deal with can be successfully *sublimated* through play.

Joyce Robertson used a version of play therapy with the children she and James Robertson looked after, including Thomas, a 28-month-old child whom they fostered for 10 days while his mother was having a second child. Joyce Robertson used some simple props to show Thomas what was happening to his mother, and to him. She enacted the scene using three dolls, representing the mother, the father, and Thomas. Mummy was in hospital, where she was resting. Daddy visited her and came to see Thomas. Soon mummy would be all rested and would come to see Thomas. Mummy gave daddy a kiss for Thomas, and Thomas would send a kiss back to mummy. Thomas wanted Joyce Robertson to play this game several times, and it may well have helped him understand what was happening.

An example of play therapy

Virginia Axline is an American play therapist who reported on a six-year-old boy called Dibs whom she had studied in 1964. Her book, describing her therapy, is called, *Dibs: In Search of Self*. It provides an excellent illustration of one technique of play therapy.

Dibs was a five-year-old American child who was attending elementary school. His teachers found him rather mystifying. They couldn't really decide whether Dibs was backward or not. He didn't seem to be able to do many of the things that the other children could, and this gave the impression that he was mentally retarded. Then sometimes he would do something that suggested that he was really quite intelligent. He had never been particularly friendly with his teachers, although they had tried to establish a good relationship with him. He was a rather lonely child, and tended to shy away from all the other children and the teacher. As Axline said, 'If he thought anyone was watching him, he quickly withdrew into his shell.'

One very obvious problem was that Dibs never seemed to want to go home after school. He 'backed into a corner of the room and crouched there, head down, arms folded tightly'. He had 'always behaved this way when it was time to go home'. When Dibs's teacher went across to him, to encourage him to get ready to go home, he screamed and fought not to go. He tried to scratch and bite with all his strength. Something about home obviously upset him very greatly.

In the play therapy sessions Virginia Axline allowed Dibs to explore the playroom slowly. She used a non-directive technique, so didn't interfere with Dibs's exploration in any way. She didn't make any suggestions or comments about his activity unless he invited her to contribute. Even then she merely confirmed what he had already said. She didn't show surprise, approval, or disapproval at anything he did. As Axline said, 'I wanted him to learn that he was a person of many parts, with his ups and downs, his loves and hates, his fears and courage, his infantile desires, and his more mature interests.'

▲
Not joining in

◀
Play therapy

There was a sandbox and a number of toy cars and trucks in the playroom. He would play with them in many inventive games. There was a doll's house and a number of dolls too. Dibs gave the mother doll long walks around the park, watching the birds, flowers, trees, and even the water in the lake. The sister doll was taken out of the doll's house. He said, 'The sister is going away to school. They have packed the bags and sent her away from home and she goes far away all by herself.'

The father doll was often treated quite differently from the rest. It didn't go out of the house to the park. 'He didn't want to be bothered.' A soldier doll, possibly representing the father, was repeatedly buried in the sandbox. Dibs took the boy doll from its room in the doll's house, after the father doll had unlocked the little boy's room. Dibs moved the boy doll outside the house, although he didn't take the doll far away. Dibs broke down and cried that he was sometimes locked in his room. It emerged that the child's father wasn't very tolerant of Dibs, and Dibs was sometimes locked in his room. This upset him very greatly. After some time spent in play therapy Dibs seemed more in control of himself and his emotions. It seemed as though he had worked through all his feelings of hate and despair, of loneliness and sadness. Virginia Axline claimed that he understood his feelings better, having been allowed to express them, especially to himself, and was more in control of himself. He could understand, control, and cope with his feelings. His attitudes and behaviour slowly improved, as did those of his family.

Play therapy

1 Virginia Axline used non-directive therapy. What does this mean?

2 Think of an emotional problem a child might have. What kind of play materials might be useful to have around?

3 What do you think Axline means by 'his infantile desires'?

❛ *Comments on play therapy*

Psychoanalysts believe that:

1 Causes of problems can be found in the frustration of instinctive urges in the unconscious mind.

2 These problems can be successfully treated by play therapy helping the child to understand the problem that is causing the anxiety.

Criticisms of play therapy

1 It isn't possible to test ideas about repressed anxiety causing childhood problems.

2 The therapy cannot be measured for success, as any number of factors, such as the personality of the analyst or the fact that an adult is giving individual attention to the child, could have brought about the same behaviour.

3 Once a child has understood what is causing his or her problem behaviour, the behaviour will disappear. The child has been successfully 'cured'.

4 Children use play in many ways, which helps their personalities develop.

3 What exactly is 'success' when we are talking about a child's problems? It cannot be defined (or measured) precisely.

4 Play therapy could only work with those children who are young enough to play with toys.

Therapy

1 Identify three problems in childhood that may affect personality development.

2 Where do childhood problems come from, according to Freud?

3 Why do play therapists use non-participant observation?

4 Do you think a very destructive, aggressive child could be treated by play therapy?

5 How were the six war orphans at the Bulldogs Bank 'treated'?

Write a short 'essay' summarising the usefulness and limitations of play therapy.

Review
Psychoanalytic therapy

Freud's techniques for investigating the unconscious turned out to be useful tools for diagnosis and treatment of personality disorders in adults. Many psychoanalysts throughout Europe and America still use free association a great deal in their treatments. With children, the main psychoanalytic technique is play therapy. This involves watching the children, and encouraging them to play out their problems. Once the problems are in the open, they may be dealt with. However, it isn't certain that any change in the children's behaviour that does occur is the result of the therapy.

Jean Piaget's Theory of Cognitive Development

Jean Piaget

As we have seen, B. F. Skinner has explained some of the principles of learning. We can apply these principles to a number of areas of psychology, notably when dealing with problem behaviour in children. Skinner's contribution to psychology has been vast. In our ordinary daily lives we all know that some things are easier to learn than others. We often say that those people who seem to be able to learn things quickly are more intelligent than other people. It isn't always clear what this means, however. Some people seem very 'intelligent', and yet have trouble with the simple things of life!

In this chapter we will be looking at a very different way of understanding how children acquire knowledge about their world. **Jean Piaget** developed a theory of *how* children learn about things. He believed that it would be more useful to study the ways in which children *take in* and *use* information, rather than *how much* knowledge or intelligence they are supposed to have.

In this chapter we will be examining the main features of Piaget's theory. However we start with how it came about.

1 We see the background to his theory.
2 Then we examine his biological view of behaviour.
3 We describe Piaget's belief that cognition is the result of adaptation.
4 We will examine the stages Piaget proposes for intellectual development during childhood.

Jean Piaget probably conducted and stimulated more research into how thinking develops in children than anyone else. He disagreed with those who saw intelligence comprising one or a number of fixed characteristics that could be measured. Unlike most biologists and psychologists earlier this century Piaget did not believe that intelligence was fixed at birth so saw little point in trying to measure it. Instead he researched into how **logical thinking** develops in children, and suggested a way of understanding how children acquire and use information from their environment. Piaget's basic idea is that our senses take in information about things around us, our brains process and store this information, and our behaviour changes as a result of it. This process is called **cognition**.

1 The background to Piaget's theory

Piaget's biological background led him to believe that every animal's genetic make-up prepares it to live and behave in certain ways. For example, fish inherit gills which allow them to breathe under water. They can't live out of water. Most birds need to be able to fly, so nature has provided them with wings. Giraffes have long necks which allow them to reach the new shoots which grow at the tops of bushes. The older leaves further down are eaten by the smaller animals. Anteaters have long snouts with longer, sticky tongues which they can flick into anthills. Moles eat worms and spend much of their day burrowing. Their front paws are well adapted to digging. Each of these animal species can only survive in the environment in which nature intended it to survive. A polar bear wouldn't survive in the desert, and there aren't any zebra at the North Pole! But one animal manages to 'cheat'. Humans have learned to adapt. Answer the following questions and you'll see how.

How do humans cheat?

1 How do polar bears cope with their freezing climate? How do Eskimos cope with it?
2 If we can't get a giraffe to clean the bedroom windows what can we do?
3 If we need to dig the Channel Tunnel must we recruit an army of moles? If not, why not?
4 If we want to explore the sea bed shall we train dolphins to go down, and tell us all about it when they surface? How else could we find out?

Piaget's pioneering work into the way children take in and use information (cognitive development), has had enormous impact on our understanding of children's mental development.

Review
Piaget's approach

Jean Piaget was a biologist and zoologist working in Switzerland earlier this century. He believed that biological principles and research might reveal much about some aspects of mental, cognitive development. He had noticed that children don't use the same rules of logic for solving problems as adults do. Their thinking was consistently different. Piaget decided to find out why.

Background reading – Jean Piaget's biography

Piaget was born in Neuchâtel, Switzerland on 9 August 1896. He was a brilliant scholar, particularly in science subjects. Before he was 10 he had made a detailed study of birds, fossils, and mechanics, and had his first article published on the subject of sea shells at the age of 11. He had published 20 scientific papers on molluscs (snails, oysters, limpets, etc.) before he was 21.

Piaget also read articles and books on religion, psychology, sociology, and philosophy throughout his adolescence. He studied biology at Neuchâtel University, and graduated in 1916 at the age of 20. Two years later he had written a most detailed study of the mollusc, for which he received his PhD, and had written a semi-autobiographical novel at the same time. He wasn't particularly interested in children at this stage.

He started to become interested in psychology in 1919 and worked in psychological clinics and laboratories in Zurich and Paris. At first he was interested in Freudian psychoanalysis and thought that biology might help explain aspects of psychological development. While studying clinical psychology at the Sorbonne (a famous university in Paris) in 1920 Piaget helped in the standardisation of intelligence test procedures at Alfred Binet's laboratory in Paris. Piaget wasn't very interested in intelligence tests, and standardising a test was very repetitive and boring. However Piaget started to notice that five-year-old children seemed to give the same wrong answers to particular questions. It seemed to Piaget that the children weren't just guessing. They were using rules of logic to solve their problems. These rules were not the same as the ones that adults use. In other words Piaget started to believe that children are not just 'little adults' in the way they think, and that there might be stages in the development of the intellect, just as Freud had claimed there were stages in personality development.

Piaget had learned the clinical method of talking to patients, asking them questions, and observing their behaviour. He used this method to study the children who were doing the tests. He asked them questions like, 'Why does it rain?' Obviously the children weren't going to know the answer, so what would they say instead? He asked a sample of children from each age group between three and 12 to see if their answers had anything in common.

It soon became clear that children below the age of about seven years use different principles to base their judgements on, compared to older children. For example, they appear to think that all things have life, and therefore have feelings. A child may well say 'naughty table', if he's just walked into it and hurt himself. His mother might console him with 'David smack naughty table'. Piaget called this idea that everything has consciousness **animism**.

Piaget was also studying some children who had mental problems, at a hospital in Paris. They couldn't answer his questions, so he had to find another way for them to express their ideas and abilities. He gave them materials like clay to manipulate. The kinds of things they did with it gave him the idea that the way they think and behave also changes with age. Piaget wrote down some of his findings, hoping that

others would take up his research, while he returned to studying pond life! However Piaget was offered the job of Director of a famous Institute for research on children in Geneva, Switzerland, which he took in 1921 at the age of 25. He intended to spend about five years researching in psychology. He was studying children's language development, reasoning, and moral development, as well as intelligence as such, and publishing some of his preliminary findings. To Piaget's surprise several well-known psychologists started to regard him as an authority on child development.

Piaget had married Valentine Chatenay in 1923 and they had their first daughter, Jacqueline, in 1925. With his wife's help he began to investigate how Jacqueline's thought processes developed. This continued with the birth of their second daughter, Lucienne, in 1927, and their son, Laurent, in 1931. Piaget kept detailed diaries on the development of each of his children's cognitive development.

Piaget spent 50 years studying children, and has had enormous influence on the way people now regard how children think. Read this list of the positions Piaget held, and you'll see what his influence was during the middle part of the twentieth century.

He was the Director of the International Bureau for Education between 1929 and 1967, Director of the Institute for Educational Sciences at the University of Geneva from 1933 to 1971, Professor of Psychology and Sociology at the University of Lausanne from 1938 to 1951, Professor of Sociology at the University of Geneva from 1939 to 1952, Professor of Experimental Psychology, University of Geneva from 1940 to 1971, Professor of Developmental Psychology at the Sorbonne from 1952 to 1963. He died in 1980.

Piaget applied the same principles of adaptation to human cognitive development.

If we want to study the development of any human skill a good starting point is birth. Piaget noted that human infants are born with a few **reflexes** which allow us to survive the first few months and years of life. A reflex is any action which is triggered by some particular stimulus. If dust blows near your eye you will blink. If you feel very cold you will shiver. If you touch something extremely hot you will withdraw your hand. The individual cannot control these reflexes, they are therefore **involuntary** responses to particular stimuli. These reflexes are the result of our first **mental structures**.

Breathing, crying, smiling, and looking are all behaviour that children have at birth. Breathing is the constant response to needing air, crying may be a reflexive response to being upset or in pain. Smiling starts as a reflexive response to some activity in a child's brain. Looking may be a response to hearing something of immediate importance. We tend to think of reflexes as set, fixed patterns of behaviour over which we have very little control. They are also very fast since the brain is not informed until after the response has begun. It is this speed of response which lets us drop a very hot object before it has time to burn us badly. Almost all reflexes seem to have one thing in

Jean Piaget applied the biological principle of adaptation to human mental development. He thought that there would be biological structures in our brains which would represent our knowledge. The first structures represent the reflexes which humans have at birth. Can you name any of the reflexes which we are born with?

Background reading – some human infant reflexes

Babies have many (possibly 50) reflexes, but the extent to which they show their reflexes varies a great deal.

Two of the earliest reflexes to occur are breathing and crying. (Fairly obvious survival value here!) Crying may help the newborn infant to breathe in during the first moments of life. Later babies will use crying to tell their caregivers that they are not entirely happy. Crying is not a way of preparing for talking, except it might help in exercising the voice muscles. When infants are a little older, crying is used when all else they can do to attract attention has failed. Crying stops being reflexive when children start to use it deliberately.

Smiling takes much longer to establish than crying. During the first fortnight babies smile during sleep, but not much when they're awake. Either way they are probably not always smiling to show pleasure at anything going on around them. Smiling is often simply the result of some brain activity stimulating various facial muscles. At some time between six weeks and three months, babies will start to use smiling to show pleasure. By the third month the smile, like deliberate crying (both of which are being used to attract attention), stops being reflexive and starts being social.

The looking reflex begins right at birth. As soon as babies open their eyes, their visual systems are sufficiently well developed to allow them to see. For example, babies are able to follow and focus upon an object within minutes of birth. No learning is necessary.

During the first few days babies usually show the doll's eye reflex: i.e. if you turn a baby's head round when the eyes are open, the eyes tend to turn rather more slowly. By the end of the second week this reflex will have disappeared.

Other reflexes include sucking, which is clearly an essential reflex for feeding. Babies can move their lips to the correct shape, and use their lungs to suck. A reflex which is sometimes used by doctors to check normal development is called the Moro Reflex. This occurs when a baby's head is supported with one hand and the body with another, then lowering the first hand will result in the baby's head falling because it is too great a weight to be supported by the baby's neck muscles. When the head falls, the baby raises both hands upwards, cries, and stiffens shoulders. Another reflex concerns a baby's hands. When the baby's fist is clenched, a touch on the back of the hand results in the hand's opening. If the open palm is touched with a finger, the finger will be grasped.

common – some survival value – that is, in some way, they help us to protect ourselves.

Three things might happen to a reflex. It may stay for life (e.g. breathing), it may disappear altogether (e.g. touching the hand makes it open or close), or it may be modified into some other piece of learned behaviour (e.g. the grasping reflex becomes the deliberate use of the hand for picking things up, etc).

Reflexes

1 What is a reflex?

2 Name three reflexes that exist during infancy, but not during adulthood.

3 Why are we born with some reflexes?

2　Invariant functions and variant structures

Reflexes are the first schemas. Thinking develops within a few months. Piaget claimed that human thinking develops in a fixed sequence of stages. Remember that Skinner would disagree. He would argue that development is a continuous process.

Just as birds can fly, and fish can swim, human beings have the ability to think as part of their genetic inheritance. According to Piaget, thinking develops in the same way, and through the same sequence of stages, in all humans. It starts off in babies as very simple mental structures called **schemas**. The first schemas are for reflexes. Thinking is only really concerned with the information which is picked up through babies' senses, and with learning to control their movements. For the first few years thinking is mostly concerned with children's own needs and wants. Young children's thinking is quite illogical, and they can't see things from anyone else's point of view. By around the age of seven, children start to think about their own actions and the consequences for other people. As children reach puberty they start to develop logic and reasoning, and start to think what things ought to be like. According to Piaget this sequence is 'fixed' and all children will go through it in the same order. It isn't possible to skip a stage. Piaget describes the sequence as **invariant**; it cannot vary.

As we develop cognition from our experiences, and everyone has different experiences, so everyone will have different levels of cognition. Do you have any areas of well-developed cognition?

Every individual has had different experiences. We've mixed with different people in different places, at different times. Even identical twins can't have had exactly the same experiences. Because we each learn through our experiences we must all know different things, and know similar things in different ways. Each person's cognition is the result of countless ideas, or mental structures in their heads, and must be **variant**. There are two sorts of these **variant mental structures**. These are called **schemas** and **operations**.

Schemas are ideas and plans we have for dealing with things. Operations refers to the way we can combine schemas and modify our ideas, mental states, thoughts and so on. What schemas are being combined in the activity of riding a bike?

Schemas are mental representations or ideas about what things are and how we deal with them. In the West, we have schemas for eating with a knife and fork, crossing the road, and buying things in shops. We don't all have schemas for eating with chopsticks, swimming, or being a shop assistant. As soon as babies develop a schema they will apply it to all things. For example, babies soon find that they can grasp some things in their hands. They will now try to grasp everything. By trial and error they will find that this isn't possible. So the grasping schema will gradually be refined into schemas for graspable objects and non-graspable objects. Later on infants will develop schemas about playing games, speaking, passing exams, driving a car, and so on.

The second type of mental structures are called **operations**. They allow us to combine schemas in an orderly, sensible, logical way, for example, the schema for gazing will be combined with the schema for reaching, and the schema for grasping in order to pick up a rattle. As children grow, and their experiences broaden, so they will be able to handle increasingly difficult operations. Operations take place in the imagination. They allow older children to imagine what might happen if something else were to occur.

Schemas and operations occur as we interact with other people and things in our environment, that is, they are mostly learned.

Review
Functions and structures

All human beings are born with a few reflexes which may help them to survive, and then use their senses to help them to adapt to their environment. The way in which we are able to adapt goes through an invariant sequence. We all have different experiences and so all have different kinds of cognition. The mental structures which make up our cognition are variant. Piaget believed that cognition isn't something which can be measured as it is totally individual.

3 Learning as a process of adapting to the environment

Piaget believed that intelligence was all about making appropriate **adaptations** to things around us quickly and efficiently. By adaptation he meant a way of taking in, processing, and using new information in an appropriate way. If a five-year-old girl wants to design and build an office block from Lego bricks, she must know which pieces to pick up. She must look at the Lego bricks in front of her, and realise what she needs to do first. This process of taking in the main elements of the situation is called **assimilation**. She chooses the various pieces and puts them together in an appropriate way. Some bricks fit together in the way she thought they should. This makes her knowledge about how Lego fits together even more certain. However some bricks do not seem to fit together as she thought they would. She'll have to modify some of her schemas about building with Lego. Piaget called this process of extending and modifying schemas **accommodation**.

In order to adapt her way of thinking about what she is building, the child must **organise** her experiences in some way. For example she may recognise that she is running out of Lego bricks. She will combine this experience with the knowledge that there aren't any more bricks, and switch to building something which needs fewer bricks. Without some **mental organisation** we would find it difficult to learn from our experiences. This mental organisation obviously involves intelligence, memory, etc. Fortunately much of our early mental organisation is automatic. Babies seem able to combine

We must take in and understand (assimilate) any new information which applies to a schema we have, then we must modify or extend (accommodate) the existing schema with the new information. How would this process apply to playing the guitar?

Organisation is the general principle that all living things seem to have of making what seems like the most sensible use of whatever knowledge, skills, or functions they possess.

certain schemas and behaviour to achieve particular ends without ever having been taught what to do.

For example, a nine-month-old boy sees a favourite toy, recognises it, decides he wants it, crawls to it, reaches for it, grasps it, takes it away with him, plays with it, etc. There must always be a balance between assimilation and accommodation. The child mustn't take in more than he can practise, use, and come to understand. The child needs to do these things to fully accommodate the new information. Too much stimulation produces confusion because the existing information hasn't been accommodated before new information is being added. Piaget calls this balance **equilibrium**.

> There must always be a balance between information which is being assimilated, and the accommodation that is already occurring. This balance is called equilibrium. If children try to take too much information in all at once they will become more confused than they were to begin with. Has this ever happened to you?

Background reading – *An example of adaptive behaviour*

A child learns that if he pulls the cork out of a bottle he can drink the contents. He has assimilated the schema 'pulling at the top of a bottle to open it'. He will now apply that schema to all bottles, including screw-top ones. He will eventually realise that his earlier schema doesn't work and that it only applies to certain bottles. Accommodation is this 'finding out and modifying existing schemas' process. Clearly it is a very active business. The child must explore, discover, experiment. The first schemas consist of a small number of actions and perceptions. Later the child is able to let one thing (e.g. a word) stand for another thing. He doesn't need to be so active any more but can think more. For example, an infant must turn a box round in his hands in order to see what it looks like from the other side. A 10-year-old can imagine what it looks like, without touching it, and could probably even draw what it looks like.

Piaget's Model of Cognition
▶

Review
Adaptation

Piaget sees intelligence as adaptation. Having met some unfamiliar event, object, or experience, for example, we try to understand it in terms of our existing schemas. When we assimilate this new experience our cognitive mental processes try to fit it in with the most appropriate schemas. The new perception may modify existing schemas, or cause other schemas to join together. This new set of schemas will then be applied to the next situation.

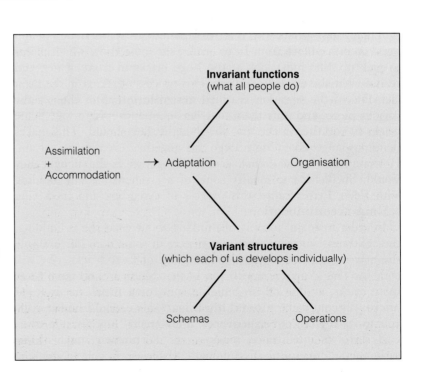

The structure of cognition

1 Explain in your own words what Piaget meant by the terms schemas and operations.

2 What did Piaget mean by assimilation, accommodation, and equilibrium?

3 What is adaptation?

4 Piaget's stages of intellectual development

1 The sensory motor stage – from 0 to 2 years

Piaget observed several very young babies, particularly his own three children, very closely indeed. Much of what he regards as the functions or purposes of the sensory motor stage are the results of these naturalistic observations and interpretations. Piaget claimed that most of the first schemas during an infant's first few weeks of life are to do with movement. Much of a baby's behaviour is **reflexive**. Some particular stimulus appears, such as something touching the baby's face, and the reflexive response is that the baby's head will turn towards the thing which is touching it. This reflexive schema provides a solution to this experience. After the first few weeks of life the baby will learn to use some muscles and limbs for movement, and will begin to understand some information received through the senses. Piaget calls these first ideas which babies develop about how to deal with their world **action schemas**. The baby is totally **egocentric** and unable to take anyone else's needs or interests into account.

Babies start to learn about objects and what they can be made to do. They are assimilating and accommodating lots of information about themselves, their world, and the people in their world. They begin to understand how one thing can cause another, and begin to acquire some simple ideas of time and space.

Even babies of less than a year old can show some intelligent behaviour. For example, imagine that a ten-month-old girl sees, and wants, her rattle. Suppose the rattle is resting on a cushion. The infant will reach for the cushion, and pull it towards her, until it is close enough for her to grasp the rattle. She has used the cushion as a tool to reach what she wants. Quite a large amount of *intelligent behaviour* is to do with inventing and using tools.

Infants build up a *mental picture* of the objects around them based on their knowledge of what they can do with them, for example, sucking them, shaking them, throwing them, etc. By about eight months of age babies become more interested in the objects for their own sake. They feel them, study them, and try to do other things with them. A great deal of babies' experience is concerned with

According to Piaget, egocentric refers to the way in which children's thinking is dominated by their own ideas. Children 'centre' on their own actions, their bodies, their knowledge. They can't take other aspects of a situation, or other people's ideas, into account.

objects. It doesn't matter too much what the object is: what's more important is that they should be able to explore it, to see what it does, and what they can do with it. Existing **action schemas** have to be expanded to take account of these new assimilated experiences.

Piaget studied babies' reactions to objects they could see, and then ones that were hidden from them. For example, a five-month-old boy may be looking at his rattle. The rattle is slowly covered by a cushion. Although the infant has seen the cushion, he seems to lose all interest in the rattle. Piaget concluded that the infant behaves as though he believed that an object which is out of sight no longer exists. By eight to 12 months old babies continue to look for the hidden object. Piaget concludes that they must now have learned that an object is still there, even though it can't be seen. Piaget called this ability **object permanence**.

Piaget's view of object permanence has been challenged by other researchers. For example, **Tom Bower** has spent many years studying the visual abilities of babies and young children. In several ingenious experiments he has shown that one- to four-month-old infants have some idea of object permanence. The skill may even be innate. Bower knew that infants learn a great deal by simply looking, and that they can see quite well right from birth.

He showed infants an attractive toy placed on a table in front of them. The toy could be hidden from the infants' view by a screen sliding in front of it. The toy could be left there, or removed before the screen slid away again. If the babies had knowledge of object permanence they would expect the toy still to be there when the screen was removed. When they saw it again they would continue to look at it. The older ones might even smile. If the toy had been removed they would show surprise. They would be expecting to see something

Background reading – An experiment to demonstrate object permanence

Two researchers named Mundy-Castle and Anglin sat a sample of four-month-old infants in front of some apparatus consisting of two 'portholes', A and B. An object travelled in an ellipse in a clockwise direction so that it entered porthole A at the bottom and moved towards the top, and entered porthole B at the top and moved towards the bottom. For the rest of the time it was hidden behind the screen.

The researchers watched the infants' eyes. After a few revolutions they started to 'follow' the object round the ellipse, anticipating where it would appear next. These four-month-old infants seem to have object permanence.

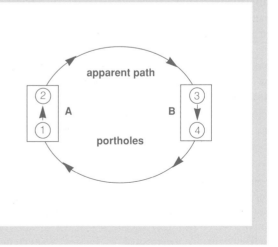

that wasn't there. Most of these one- to four-month-old infants were surprised when the screen slid back and the toy was missing. Bower claims that they must have object permanence several months before Piaget believed they had any schemas for it. Bower believes that several perceptual skills may be innate, as we shall see shortly.

The sensory motor stage

1 Name and describe the first of Piaget's stages of intellectual development.

2 What is meant by 'object permanence'?

3 At what age did Piaget believe object permanance was achieved?

4 Outline one piece of research into the existence of object permanence in young babies. Identify the age of the babies studied, and the apparatus used.

---

2 The pre-operations stage – from 2 to 7 years

Earlier we defined Piaget's use of the word *operations* as meaning combining schemas in an orderly, sensible, logical way. In this second stage of cognitive development children's thought processes are developing, but are far from logical (in the adult sense). The thinking of two- to seven-year-olds is **pre-operational**.

Piaget used the clinical interview technique with several hundred children to discover any similarities in the way they think. He was always looking for average or typical modes of thinking (and has been criticised for having no interest in children whose thinking was different from the average). The clinical interview consisted of asking children questions (in language that they could understand), and interpreting their answer. Towards the end of this stage Piaget did use some formal experiments. The main features he identified in this stage were **symbolisation, egocentrism, animism**, and **moral realism**.

Symbolisation

The first feature of the pre-operational stage is **symbolisation**, whereby we allow something to stand for, or symbolise, something else. Anything which we allow to stand for something else can be a symbol. A red traffic light is a symbol which means stop. The thumbs-up sign is a symbol standing for agreement. Words are symbols too. During this stage a child's vocabulary of words will be expanding. As such symbols expand they allow the child's imagination to expand as well. This is best seen in children's play.

Symbolisation

Think of some play activities for which knowing words like house, sun, mummy, car, tree, dog, etc., will help children of two years of age to use their imagination.

Review
Sensory motor stage

For the first couple of years children are developing basic egocentric schemas which allow them to practise and master sensory and motor skills. They achieve object permanence during their first year, so must be able to tell the difference between themselves and other people and things around them.

Symbolisation is the ability to think in ideas, and use words to express those ideas. It stimulates the child's imagination.

Piaget's mountains

Hughes' doll experiment

Egocentrism

All pre-operational children are usually **egocentric** in the way they think. They can only see things from their own point of view, and imagine that theirs is the only point of view that anyone could hold.

Piaget had three model mountains, made of papier-mâché. Each mountain was a different shape and colour, and each had different things on the top. One had a cross, like a church, one had a hut, and one was covered in snow. The child sat with the three mountains in front of her, and a doll was placed behind the first. The child was asked, 'What can the doll see?' The child was shown a number of pictures of the mountains from various viewpoints, including the one the doll could actually 'see', and what the child could see from where she sat. The doll was moved in front of the second, and then the third mountain. Again the child was asked which of the pictures represented what the doll could 'see'. Children up to about seven years old usually chose the picture representing what they could see from where they were looking. Only later do children learn to imagine that they are looking from the doll's viewpoint. Seeing things from a different perspective can only happen when children can stop centring on themselves (being egocentric), and can imagine something else to be the centre of attention. This ability is called **decentring**.

Not everyone agrees with Piaget's claims that children need to be over seven before they can decentre. In the mid-1970s, Martin Hughes constructed a game with a policeman doll and a boy doll. Each doll could be moved to various positions around two walls which joined in the middle to form a cross. The idea was to involve children in the game, and draw on their previous experience. Each child was asked questions like 'Can the policeman see the child if we put him here?' or 'put the boy where the policeman can't see him'. Most children will have had some experience of 'hiding' so this game should appeal more than asking them to make guesses about a doll looking at three model mountains. Very few of the children made many mistakes, and Hughes would explain to them where they went wrong if any did. Piaget didn't give the children many opportunities to ask questions, or to explain where they were going wrong. Hughes's conclusions were quite surprising. Almost all of his samples of three- and four-year-olds could imagine themselves in the place of the policeman, and of the boy doll. Hughes introduced more dolls, and more walls. The children still gave the correct answers. Hughes has shown that children of three and four could decentre and show reversibility.

Animism

The third feature of the pre-operational stage which Piaget identified is **animism**. Animism is the belief that everything that exists has some kind of consciousness. A car which won't start will be described as being 'tired' or 'ill'. A high mountain will be thought of as 'old'. A child who has hurt himself colliding with a chair will happily smack the 'naughty' chair. Animism can also be explained by the fact that children's thinking is still egocentric. Since children can't see things from anyone else's point of view, so they will assume that everyone, and everything, will be like themselves. Since they have emotions and can feel pain and pleasure, so they believe that everything else can too.

Moral realism

The fourth feature which dominates the way children think in the pre-operational stage is the way they view moral issues. This too can be explained by egocentric thought. **Moral realism** is children's belief that their way of thinking about what is right and wrong will be shared by everyone else. Being egocentric they can only focus on one aspect of a situation at any one time. They develop a respect for rules and insist that they must be obeyed at all times. They can't take anything else, like motives, into account.

To discover how children of various ages regard rules, Piaget played marbles with them. He asked them questions like 'What are the rules of this game?' 'Where do these rules come from?' 'What would happen if I did . . . (something which would break the rules as explained by the children?)', 'Must everyone obey these rules?', 'Could anyone change the rules?', etc.

The pre-operational stage

1 What is the name of the method of investigation which Piaget used to investigate children's ideas about rules?

2 What do you think might be the advantages and disadvantages of this method of collecting information on the way children think?

3 Summarise the main differences in the ways that sensory motor and pre-operational children think.

4 What did Piaget mean by egocentrism? Describe one of Piaget's demonstrations of egocentrism.

3 The concrete operations stage – from 7 to 11 years

Thinking is becoming operational. This means it is becoming more rational and adult-like. This takes from around seven years of age to well into the teenage years. Piaget divides this period into two stages which he calls the stage of **concrete operations** and the stage of **formal operations**. During the concrete operations stage children can think 'logically' if they can manipulate the object that they are thinking about. In the formal operations stage they can manipulate their thoughts, and don't need the real object.

During the concrete operations stage, egocentric thought declines. So does the belief in animism. Piaget claimed that until the beginning of the concrete operations stage children's ideas about objects

Review
The pre-operational stage

Thinking in the pre-operational stage is egocentric, illogical, and dominated by animism and moral realism. It will gradually become more logical and less egocentric as the child learns to symbolise.

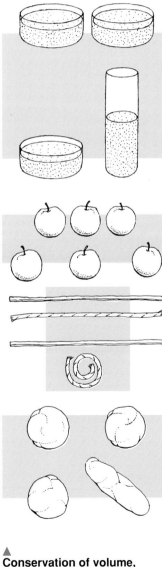

▲ **Conservation of volume, number, length and mass**

are dominated by how those objects appear. Something which looks heavy will be thought of as being heavy. So a balloon which is fully inflated will be described as being very much heavier than one which is only half the size because it's only half inflated. According to Piaget children gradually learn, sometime after their seventh birthday, that objects are not always what they appear to be. This skill is called **conservation**. Children learn to conserve things like number, weight, volume, mass, length, etc.

Conservation

To conserve means to be able to think about several features of an object at the same time. Pre-operational children can only think about one or two features of an object at a time (this is called **centration**). Children need to learn that not all of the features of an object change just because one of them does. Younger children think that things are what they look like. Different kinds of objects can alter their appearance in different ways. Children learn to conserve each of these changes.

Conservation of volume: The child adjusts the amount of liquid in two identical containers (e.g. tall thin vases) until they hold the same. One of them is chosen and its contents are poured into a differently shaped container, e.g. a short, wide jug. A child who cannot conserve volume will claim that the tall thin vase now contains more liquid than the shorter jug. It 'looks more' when its surface is further up the container.

Conservation of number: The child is shown two rows of apples and agrees that they contain the same number. The apples in one row are then spread out, and the child is asked if either of the two rows now contains more apples. A child who cannot conserve number will say that the 'spread out' row must contain more apples.

Conservation of length: A child is shown a stick and a piece of string of equal length. The string is then curled and the child is asked if the stick and the string are still the same length. A child who cannot conserve length will say that the stick is now longer than the string.

Conservation of mass: The child agrees that two balls of clay contain the same amount of clay. One of the balls is then rolled into a sausage shape and the child is asked whether they both still contain the same amount of clay. A child who cannot conserve mass will say that the sausage shape must contain more clay than the other ball because it looks as though it contains more.

Conservation of area: Two identical sheets of cardboard have wooden blocks placed on them in identical positions. The child agrees that both sheets of cardboard have the same area left uncovered. One of the sets of blocks is then scattered around the cardboard and the child is asked if they still have the same area left uncovered. The scattered blocks seem to cover more area to the child who cannot conserve area.

An experiment by McGarrigle and Donaldson

Not everyone agrees that children cannot conserve until they are seven or older. McGarrigle and Donaldson changed the context of one of Piaget's conservation experiments so as to involve the child more. They sampled four- and five-year-olds, asking them to watch a glove puppet (called naughty teddy) spreading out one row of sweets while not moving a second row. The children had agreed that there were the same number of sweets in each row before teddy started being naughty. They knew that there were still the same number afterwards. Many of the children may have seen 'naughty teddy' as a game in which they could become involved, and something they could understand. When an adult had moved one of the rows they said that something had changed. But this may have been *because* it was an adult who moved one of the rows. A child's experience of adults is that they are always changing things! Few were fooled by the glove puppet.

In response to a number of studies such as these, Piaget did accept that children as young as five could start the concrete operations stage.

◄
Naughty teddy

Children are usually more familiar with some objects than with others, and these are likely to be the things they conserve first. For example children become aware of numbers from quite a young age. They learn to count and do simple arithmetic almost as soon as they start school. They usually need real (concrete) objects to count. A six-year-old's teacher might well ask what happens 'when we take three apples away from five apples?' By around the age of seven many children will have learned to conserve number. They no longer need the actual apples to count. They will probably know that the row containing the apples which have been spread out still has the same number of apples as the other. By nine or 10 years of age most children should have learned enough about weight to be able to conserve it, and by 11 or 12 years of age most children will understand volume. Children become more logical, according to Piaget, between the ages of seven and 12, but only if they have the real object near to them, to look at or to touch.

An extension of conservation is reversibility. This is the knowledge that things would be returned to normal if we reversed the steps we took to conserve.

Review Concrete operations stage

Children in the early years of the concrete operations stage can solve mental problems, as long as they have real objects to check what they are doing. During this stage children learn conservation and reversibility and become more able to see things from other points of view.

Reversibility

The ability to go back through a process or sequence of events is known as **reversibility**. Having learned to conserve, children will slowly realise that if the procedure in the conservation exercise were to be reversed, things would be as they were to begin with. For example, in the conservation of volume experiment, using the different-shaped water containers, a child who is capable of **reversibility** knows that there would still be the same amount of liquid if the contents of the small jug were poured back into tall jar.

According to Piaget the concrete-operational child's thinking is becoming logical and is using mathematical principles. It is characterised by conservation, reversibility, and decentring (seeing things from other people's viewpoints).

Conservation

1 What does Piaget mean by conservation?

2 Outline one experiment which Piaget used to demonstrate conservation.

3 Explain what is meant by decentring?

4 Piaget claims that there are differences in ways of thinking between children in the pre-operational stage, and the stage of concrete operations. Summarise the differences which Piaget noted.

4 The formal operations stage – from 11 to 16 years onwards

From around puberty the ways in which many children think change again. They become more adult-like, and can rely more on ideas rather than needing to manipulate real objects. Most children learn how to work some things out in their heads, without having to see the real objects. As we saw, a seven-year-old will learn addition and

Background reading – One of Piaget's tests for formal operational thinking

Someone old enough to have reached the formal operations stage is shown a number of weights which can be hooked on to the end of a piece of string to make a pendulum. The youngster is allowed to choose the length of the string, the weight to be attached, and the height at which the weight is to be released. She or he has to work out which of these three factors, or which combination of them, determines how quickly the pendulum swings. The way to do

this is to alter one of the variables (weight, length, or height), while keeping the other two constant, and see if the alteration has any effect. Children in the pre-operational or concrete-operational stages will randomly alter the variables and find it difficult to solve the problem. Someone who uses formal operational thought will soon realise that the length of the string is the determining factor – the shorter the string, the faster the pendulum swings.

subtraction by counting numbers of apples, sweets, or blocks of wood, etc. By 12 years of age most children can do some mental arithmetic. Teenagers start to think about moral and philosophical issues too.

Piaget argued that the changeover from concrete to formal operations takes several years to become fully established. But do all people reach this last stage? Some recent research shows that quite a number of adults never do. Correlations have been found among some adults between the variables 'low scores on IQ tests', and 'not appearing to think in formal operational ways'. There are also cross-cultural differences. In some societies children are not reared to use the same rules of what we in the West think of as formal logic.

Comments on Piaget's theory

Piaget devoted most of his life to making us aware of the cognitive development of children, rejecting totally the previous belief that children are merely little adults. Many people believe that his theory is the most comprehensive and detailed analysis of the way children think that exists to date. He has shown that children are naturally curious and willing learners who need stimulation. Like any good theory, Piaget's has stimulated an enormous amount of research, and inevitably some questions and criticisms will be raised. Here are some of the main ones.

Criticism

1 Piaget claimed that children spend the first 10 years or so not able to use the rules of logic which most adults are supposed to use. (You might think that Piaget, as someone who was considering scientific issues while still a child himself, would have had a more optimistic view of children's ability to think logically and abstractly!)

2 Piaget suggested that logical thought develops from around puberty. Several studies have shown that many adolescents and adults are not capable of logical thought.

Comment

1 Countless hours of careful research led Piaget to this conclusion. He may have regarded himself as an exception to the general rule.

2 Piaget was attempting to find the main stages of development that most people pass through, and the ages at which they occur.

3 Piaget was probably mistaken about the timing of when children can first do certain things (such as conservation). Researchers, such as Jerome Bruner, have shown that five- and six-year-old children can be taught to conserve if they are encouraged to think things through for themselves.

3 Piaget did accept this criticism, and modified his views about the ages at which the different kinds of thinking occurred. He had thought that children's mental abilities changed at particular ages, that is, 2, 7, and 11. These seemed to fit the ages of the children he had observed and tested who were capable of understanding the various games and tests he used.

4 Peter Bryant has shown that many of Piaget's tests were too complicated for many of the children to understand. Bryant simplified some of Piaget's experiments and found that children under five were capable of logical thought when they knew what was being asked of them.

4 Piaget simply gave children particular objects and asked them to answer specific questions. This may not have been the most sophisticated research, but it was among the first on the subject of children's cognitive development.

5 Piaget's main method for finding out about children was the clinical interview. This can be rather vague and open to the interpretation of the interviewer.

5 Piaget was aware of the problems of 'leading' the child, but children still say and do things for many reasons, particularly when a strange person is watching them and asking them questions.

6 Some researchers, such as the behaviourists, suggest that development does not occur in stages but is gradual and continuous.

6 A number of other aspects of maturation, such as motor skills (crawling, walking, running), and language (babbling, single words, and sentences) do appear to occur in stages. Cognition might too.

7 Piaget did not make clear what makes one stage end and another begin. (This criticism is also levelled against Freud's theory.) Presumably children are constantly adapting to new information – assimilating and accommodating it. Why should there be particular stages?

7 Piaget maintained that there are distinct stages, each stage following on from the previous one. They partly reflected the child's state of maturation. Different skills would develop in each stage.

8   Piaget is said to put too much emphasis on the role of the intellect in development and thus overlook the effects of the child's emotions and motivations, personality, etc.

8   This isn't entirely fair. Piaget often makes reference to the whole child. But Piaget was a biologist primarily concerned with exploring the maturation and functioning of mental structures.

9   Some of Piaget's terms such as 'equilibrium', 'schema', 'accommodation', etc. are criticised for being rather general.

9   Piaget needed general terms which could apply to how human thinking is organised, since thinking is so abstract and varied.

10   There is no firm evidence that Piaget's concepts, no matter how loosely or accurately defined, actually exist. Piaget observed children's behaviour, and made assumptions about the organisation of mental functioning, which he then named.

10   Most scientific enquiry involves scientists making educated guesses about the existence of things, which they then try to prove. It is necessary to give them a name in order to discuss them with others.

11   Piaget was always looking for what the average or typical child could do and so ignored the great variations in the ways individual children think.

11   While he was aware of individual differences he didn't consider that trying to understand them would help his general theory.

12   Piaget concentrated on children's interactions with their environment, mostly when they were alone. Latest evidence suggests that children's social development with others has a great deal to do with their cognitive development.

12   Piaget offered the first radical alternative view of how children's thinking develops. His early ideas are bound to be refined and improved greatly.

Conclusion

Research in cognitive development in the years since Piaget's death in 1980 has not confirmed some of his ideas about stages of development. **Olivera Petrovich** has asked children questions and found that they can decentre and are capable of reversibility when the issues are explained to them. Piaget's methodology, his stories and his experiments were probably too difficult for younger children to understand.

Despite all of the criticisms we have mentioned, Piaget's contribution to our understanding of children's cognitive development has been enormous. Psychologists have been retesting and confirming many of his ideas for years. Valid criticisms have been made, but it is not doubted that Piaget – through his intellect, energy and enthusiasm – led us to a deeper understanding today of the way children think. One final criticism suggests that there is another stage, after the stage of formal operations, which Piaget didn't identify. It describes the highest level of thinking. In this stage, thinking is abstract and highly sophisticated. Only the greatest thinkers reach this stage. Some who did might include Einstein, Freud and, of course, Piaget himself!

Review
Evaluation of Piaget's theory

Piaget's research was a major breakthrough in the way we understand children's thinking, and his ideas have dominated cognitive psychology for nearly 50 years. Many other psychologists have confirmed his conclusions, but others still have challenged them. His ideas have stimulated a massive amount of further research, all of which increases our knowledge of children's development.

Evaluation of Piaget's contribution

1 Describe the main methods which Piaget used in his research.

2 What is a 'stage theory' of development?

3 Outline two criticisms that have been made of the way Piaget conducted his research.

4 Describe and evaluate four criticisms that have been made of Piaget's explanations of cognitive development.

Children's Moral Development

An important part of the **socialisation process** is learning what is right and wrong. Each society has rules and laws governing what is right and wrong, or good and bad. In Europe, for example, we accept that one man may be married to one woman at any one time. In some Arab countries some women may have several husbands, and some men may have several wives. People in all societies can only live at peace with each other because they agree to live by their society's rules.

Socialisation is simply the name of the process by which we learn those things that we must know in order to fit in with the rest of the people in our society. We must learn to speak the language, learn the customs and habits of our society, and learn about the acceptable ways in which we must think and behave.

Moral development

How do you think a person knows about right and wrong? Here are some possible sources of knowledge: instinct, inner knowledge, God, upbringing, commonsense.

1 Are there any other sources of knowledge that you think could be included in this list?

2 What percentage of our knowledge of right and wrong would you imagine comes from each of the items in the list?

People probably acquire some sense of morality during their childhood. Some people will have very strong ideas about proper behaviour, others will be less concerned about doing and saying the right thing. For example those delinquents whom John Bowlby described as suffering from *affectionless psychopathy* had very little concern for moral or decent behaviour. The process by which children acquire their sense of morality has been explained in quite different ways. Freudians see it as the result of identifying with a parent in order to resolve some of the conflict that children feel during the *Oedipus Complex*. Behaviourists see children as little adults who will learn appropriate behaviour by a combination of *reinforcement*, *imitation* and *punishment*. Cognitive psychologists see moral judgements developing as children's cognitive skills develop generally. The result of our moral development is that we acquire a **conscience**.

All societies have developed rules about right and wrong. Many of the rules have been made into laws which all the people should obey. Can you think of any rules which we agree to obey, but which aren't legally required.

A conscience is a set of moral principles that we each develop. We usually try to live by these principles. In the past some people believed that the conscience was the voice of God, but now many psychologists see it as something we each acquire as we are socialised.

Review
Moral development

Psychologists have concentrated on different aspects of how children develop ideas about right and wrong. Freud concentrates on the origin of moral feelings, Piaget and Kohlberg explain moral reasoning, and behaviourists explain moral behaviour.

Conscience

1 Define the term 'morality'.

2 What is meant by 'conscience'?

3 Where do our 'consciences' come from?

Just because we have a conscience, we don't always live by it, especially if the rewards for not doing so are great, or the risk of being caught is slim! In psychology we are interested in questions like, 'Where do children's ideas about morality come from?', 'When and how do children learn about moral ideas?' or 'What kind of moral thinking are children capable of at different ages?'

In this chapter we will be examining these different explanations, by considering the following areas.

1 Freud's psychodynamic explanation.
2 Piaget's cognitive explanation.
3 Kohlberg's development of Piaget's views.
4 The main behaviourist theories.
5 The role of peers in moral development.

1 Freud's psychoanalytic theory of moral development

Sigmund Freud once said that one of the hardest tasks facing parents was the moral development of their children. Freud attempted to explain the growth of personality, and was interested in how children felt about right and wrong. Freud claimed that the personality mainly consists of three unconscious parts, the id, the ego, and the superego. For the first year or two the primitive, unconscious id dominates. It makes demands which must be met. In a child's unconscious the ego tries to modify some of id's demands and find rational ways of meeting them.

During the phallic stage of development children begin to have unconscious, incestuous feelings about their opposite-sex parent. These feelings will make the child feel aggressive towards the same-sex parent. For example the boy may see his father as a rival. He will have unconscious feelings of hostility towards his rival. He may be afraid that his father will punish him for his feelings, or that his father may even castrate him. Hostility towards someone the child loves, and the fear of punishment, will produce feelings of guilt and anxiety. Freud suggested that the superego would be an unconscious force which would help us to set our own standards of acceptable feelings and behaviour. The superego is involved with overcoming these feelings by making the boy identify with his father. If the child loves his father, and is deeply attached, the tensions caused by his feelings will be stronger, so the need to identify will be even stronger. Also, if the father is very dominant, very demanding, and seems threatening to the boy, he will feel a stronger urge to identify.

By **identification** Freud meant the process by which a child is seen to 'take on' the attitudes and ideas of its parent, to become like the parent, so that their personalities are supposed to become similar. When a child identifies with its parent it's as though the child becomes like (a smaller version of) its parent. This smaller version of the parent is represented by the child's superego. The child's ideas about its parent's standards of 'good' behaviour become a part of the child's **ego ideal**. What the parent seems to think is 'bad' behaviour becomes a part of the child's **conscience**. If the child does anything 'wrong', which it knows would hurt its parent, it would be, in effect, hurting itself.

Girls identify with their mothers more than boys do with their fathers. The girl knows that she can't be hurt in the same way as the boy, since she already appears to have been castrated, and so her fear of her mother may not be as strong. However she is afraid that her mother may stop loving her, and so identifies with her.

Freud saw these identifications occurring to resolve what he called the Oedipus Complex for boys, and the Electra Complex for girls. (A 'complex' is a group or collection of, in this case, unconscious feelings, desires, ideas, wishes, etc.) They draw the child towards its opposite-sex parent, and make it want to eliminate the same-sex parent. If the tensions and conflicts that these unconscious urges produce are not resolved satisfactorily, the child may develop some neurotic disorders later.

The superego is described as having two parts. One is a sort of 'conscience'. It punishes us when we do wrong by making us feel guilty and uncomfortable. The other part contains the ideal moral code that we think we ought to live by, which Freud called the 'ego ideal'.

According to Freud, during the phallic stage children are unconsciously drawn towards their opposite-sex parent, and feel hostile towards their same-sex parent. This produces unpleasant feelings. How does Freud explain how these feelings are resolved?

Background reading – People's attitudes towards right and wrong

In a survey conducted in 1970 for the Independent Television Authority, a sample of adults were asked, 'How do you think a person knows what is right and what is wrong?' Here is a summary of their answers:

Conscience, inner self, or God   43%
Upbringing   28%
Commonsense   16%
Instinct   13%

It seems that many people think that upbringing and conscience are quite separate. Many psychologists claim that conscience is the result of upbringing.

Evaluating Freudian psychoanalysis

Try to remember as much of the evaluation of Freud's theory in general as you can. Make two lists, one headed 'contributions', and the other called 'criticisms' and see how many points you can remember.

Review
Freud's explanation of moral development

Children in the phallic stage identify with their same-sex parent, to overcome their Oedipal conflict. Through identification they accept their parents' views of right and wrong.

Psychoanalytic explanation of moral development

1 According to Freud the family will have an enormous influence on a child's moral development. Write a paragraph explaining the role of the superego and identification in Freud's theory of moral development.

2 Freud explains how children acquire their moral feelings. What other aspects of morality are there, apart from feelings?

⁶ Comments on Freud's ideas

Before reading the evaluation of Freud's ideas on moral development you should look back to the evaluation of Freud's general theory at the end of Chapter Five.

Contribution

1 Freud offered one of the first, and most complete explanations for the development of moral feelings in children. It was central to his whole theory, and claimed that one of the three parts of personality, the superego, developed to guide children's moral behaviour.

2 Freud's theory suggests that children of three and four years old would be more likely to imitate the moral attitudes and behaviour of the parent with whom they are identifying than anyone else.

3 According to Freud, children learn their moral norms and values from their same-sex parent.

4 Freud claimed that children would have resolved their Oedipal problems by the age of six or seven, and would be morally mature by then.

Criticism

1 Other studies of moral development do not show much support for any of Freud's ideas. For example, the claim that boys have stronger superegos than girls, and therefore are less likely to behave badly than girls, seems to be the opposite of the truth!

2 Children do not usually start to understand and imitate the feelings of one parent more than the other until they are older than the three or four years that Freud suggested.

3 If so, how could boys being raised by their mothers in one-parent families learn their moral code? Yet they do.

4 There's little evidence for this either! Children eight, nine, and ten years old can still have all sorts of confused moral feelings, for example about their family.

Other psychoanalysts do not agree with Freud's explanations of moral development, and Freud himself modified his own ideas several times.

2 Piaget's view of moral development in children

Freud sees the child as a rather helpless and passive receiver of other people's views. For Freud, boys acquire moral feelings in a desperate attempt to protect themselves against their fears about what their fathers might do to them. He believes that girls are supposed to identify with their mothers who have already punished them by castration. Piaget sees children as being much more actively involved in their own learning about the world than Freud did. Since cognition develops through the four invariant stages which we studied in Chapter Eight, moral reasoning should follow a similar course.

Piaget used a number of techniques to investigate how children think about rules, honesty and truthfulness, right and wrong (justice), motives, and punishment. For example, he played some games with children to investigate their thinking on rules. He told children stories which could be interpreted in different ways, to see if they could understand about intentions. He observed the way they played and he conducted experiments, to see how their thinking on moral issues changed. Here are some examples.

Piaget's cognitive view sees the child as an active partner in the child's own cognitive development. The child will apply the same rules to learning about moral issues as to learning about many other issues.

Piaget's main stages

Here are the names of the main stages in Piaget's cognitive theory. You have to fill in the gaps.

Name	Age	Main features
Sensory motor		
Pre-operational		
Concrete operations		
Formal operations		

Children's views on rules

Piaget played games of marbles with many Swiss children. Young children usually invent their own rules when playing marbles, so Piaget asked them about where the rules came from, and whether they could be broken or changed. He played marbles with children of various ages who were in each of the stages of development he had identified. He found that their thinking on rules tied in with their general stage of cognitive development.

Two- to three-year-old **pre-operational** children used no rules at all, but played with the marbles in any way they wanted to at the time. (This is an example of **egocentric** behaviour.) By four or five years of age they were starting to imitate each other's games, although they were still largely egocentric. When they were taught some of the rules of marbles they followed them without question, as

▶
Piaget playing marbles

though the rules were absolute laws and couldn't be broken or changed at all. The children seemed to accept that rules are made by authority figures such as adults, and they must not be broken at any cost. If they are broken, punishment will be immediate and severe. This did not stop individual children changing, amending, and breaking the rules for their own advantage, while trying to resist any-one else's attempts to change them!

Children in the stage of **concrete operations** still obey the rules, but not quite so slavishly as they had before. They accepted that rules were there for the players' benefit, and could be changed, as long as the change was fair to everyone. (Children can now **decentre**.)

Egocentrism and decentring

1 Explain what the terms egocentrism and decentring mean, according to Piaget. (Look them up if you have to.)

2 Name three games that young children play which demonstrate their egocentrism.

3 Name three games that operational children play, which demonstrate that they are able to decentre.

4 Write a few sentences summarising the way that pre-operational and concrete-operational children regard rules.

Piaget's research into honesty and truthfulness

To investigate children's attitudes towards lying, cheating, stealing, and similar wicked behaviour, Piaget developed a new method of investigation – the storytelling technique. For example, he would tell children of various ages two stories. One concerned a child who deliberately told a lie which had minor consequences. The other told of a child who accidentally said something which wasn't true, which had a major consequence. For example:

Story A: A little boy says that his dog is as big as a horse, and the postman won't come to their house because he knows he will be eaten alive.

Story B: A little boy tells his father that their dog has just run off down the street. He waits until his father is ready to go out and search for the animal before saying that it hasn't really run off at all, but has been taken for a walk by his mother.

In the first story, the untruth is so silly that no adult would begin to take it seriously. In the second story there is a deliberate lie. Pre-operational children here are judging how wicked something is by how big a lie it is. They judged the child in Story A to be more wicked than the child in Story B because what he said was obviously a long way from the truth. What the child in Story B told his father could have been true.

Piaget found that pre-operational children can't take account of someone's intentions either. Here are two more stories:

Story A: A little girl stole a loaf of bread from a shop to give to her friend who was very poor and was starving.

Story B: A little girl stole one cake from a shop, not because she was hungry, but just because she fancied a cake.

In the first story the dishonest act was committed for a good reason. In the second it was committed for a selfish reason. However a loaf of bread is larger than one cake, and pre-operational children judge by appearances. Being egocentric they can't understand intentions. Many claimed the child in Story A was more wicked than the child in Story B.

By the time children acquire operational thought they are able to take other things into account when making judgements. They could see that deliberate lying is worse than exaggerations or accidentally telling an untruth. They can see that consequences of an act aren't the only things to judge by, but intentions must also be understood.

More examples of the kind of stories that Piaget told

Story A: A boy called John is in his room, when he is called to dinner. He enters the dining room, but doesn't know that there is a tray with 15 cups on it, just behind the door. The door knocks the tray over and all the cups are broken.

Story B: A little boy called Henry decided to have some jam one day when his mother was out. He climbed on to a chair to try to reach for the jam jar which was in a high cupboard. While stretching up he knocked over a cup, which fell to the floor and smashed.

1 Which would you say was the naughtier child?

2 Why?

3 Would a pre-operational child say John or Henry was the more wicked?

4 What do pre-operational children base their judgements about right and wrong on?

Until children reach four or five years of age they are in the **pre-moral stage.** This is when children have little understanding of rules, and much of their behaviour is the result of the search for enjoyment, experience and the fear of punishment.

Between five or six and about ten years of age, children's thinking about rules changes. They now regard authority figures such as God, parents, the police, the government or the headmistress as having power over many aspects of their lives. Such authority figures make rules that must not be broken. If they are broken then punishment must follow and will be severe. This is known as the stage of **heteronomous morality** (or moral realism).

Heteronomous means imposed from the outside.

By around puberty, children are beginning to decentre and can take several features of an event into account at the same time. They no longer judge solely by consequences. They now take intentions and motivations into account. Rules are regarded as social agreements that can be negotiated and changed. Since children can now think more for themselves, and don't rely on outside authorities to direct their behaviour, this is called the state of **autonomous morality** (or the stage of moral relativism).

Autonomous means imposed from within.

6 *Comments on Piaget's theory*

Piaget's work is still regarded as a revolutionary step forward in the way we understand how children think. Many attempts have been made by other researchers in Europe and America to test and refine Piaget's ideas and methods. There does seem to be considerable evidence that children's moral reasoning does change with age, and distinct stages of development do seem to exist. However Piaget's methods have been criticised, and if the method isn't totally acceptable, the data it gathers may not be wholly acceptable either. This is particularly true for younger children. Many may not really have understood Piaget's stories, and what children say in response to a story told by a strange adult may not be really what they think.

Piaget claimed	However
1 Heteronomous stage children cannot take other people's intentions into account.	1 Piaget told children stories and asked for their responses. He did not investigate whether the children understood the point about intentions that the stories made. If all they understood was that one child broke 15 cups and another broke one cup then it's not surprising that they thought that the first child was more wicked than the second. Recent research has shown that even three-year-olds can take someone's intentions into account when making judgements, if the intentions are explained to them.
2 Heteronomous stage children have absolute respect for rules.	2 There's more than one sort of rule, and even three-year-olds respond differently to them. They think a child who breaks moral rules such as not hitting, spitting, scratching, stealing, etc., should be punished. On the other hand they think a child who breaks social rules such as not staying at playschool, or not eating all of a meal when he or she hasn't specifically been told to, is not nearly as wicked. The respect for moral rules occurs in younger children than Piaget imagined, and the respect for social rules is much more open to negotiation than Piaget claimed.

One of the criticisms we made of Piaget's cognitive theory in general was that his methods weren't as precise as they could have been. They led to some claims being made about what children can and cannot do which were rather pessimistic. Latest research on moral development shows that children can take other motives into account, when they understand what those motives are, and they do not see all rules as being equally important. Despite these criticisms, we still owe a great deal to Jean Piaget. His pioneering work has led to much more realistic ways of understanding children's moral development.

Piaget and morality

1 Outline Piaget's explanation of how children view rules.

2 How do children's ideas about people's intentions change, according to Piaget,

Review
Piaget's explanation of moral development

Before the age of five, children do not think much about what makes something right or wrong. The first stage of development of moral thinking is heteronomous and is dominated by rules imposed by some authority figures from outside the child. After about 10, children's moral reasoning is autonomous – they can think about moral issues for themselves.

and why does this change occur? (HINT: What can older children do that younger ones can't?)

3 What does Piaget mean by heteronomous morality and autonomous morality?

4 At what age does the change from one to the other generally occur according to Piaget?

---

3 Kohlberg's cognitive theory of moral development

A dilemma is a problem which has two or more solutions, each of which is somehow 'wrong'.

Lawrence Kohlberg asked some children and adults to respond to a series of stories about people facing **moral dilemmas**. In each story the subject could choose to support the moral rights of some authority, or could support some deserving individual whose needs were fair and just, and weren't being met. After hearing each story the listener was invited to say what should happen to overcome the difficulty. This meant they had to make a choice between either obeying a law or rule or someone in authority, or taking some action that conflicts with these rules. In probably the best known of Kohlberg's moral dilemmas, someone chooses one of the alternatives, and the listeners are asked about what should happen. Here is a summary of it:

> A woman was very near to death from a particular form of cancer. There was a type of radium that a chemist in the same town had recently discovered which might save her. The drug had cost a great deal of money to make, but the chemist was charging ten times as much as it cost for just a small amount of it. The sick woman's husband borrowed all the money he could to buy the drug, but it only came to half of what the chemist wanted. He told the chemist that his wife was dying and asked him if he could have the drug cheaper, or even have the drug now and pay the rest of the money later. The chemist refused, saying, 'I discovered the drug, and I'm going to make money from it.' The man was desperate, and later on he broke into the shop and stole the drug.

Kohlberg asked 'Should he have stolen the drug?' Some of the sample said that theft is wrong and the thief must be severely punished. Others said that the man shouldn't be punished very severely as he was trying to save his wife. Kohlberg was not particularly interested in the actual answers, but rather how each person explained or justified her or his answer. Kohlberg asked them questions like, 'Should the husband be punished for stealing the drug?', 'Did the chemist have the right to refuse to sell it to the man?', 'Should the police arrest the chemist for murder if the woman died?', 'Should the chemist be punished more if the woman who died had been a very important person?', etc.

Kohlberg's thief

Background reading – Lawrence Kohlberg's view

Since the late 1950s Lawrence Kohlberg of Harvard University has extended and refined Piaget's views. He agrees that moral develop- ment is one aspect of general cognitive devel- opment, and develops in stages, just as Piaget claimed that the rest of cognition does.

Storytelling

Like Piaget, Kohlberg is using the storytelling technique to investigate the way children and adults think.

1 What did Kohlberg's stories ask the listeners to choose between?

2 Why may storytelling not reveal what the subjects really think?

Kohlberg identified about thirty aspects of moral thought which develop through three distinct levels of moral reasoning. Each level contains two stages. Everyone passes through them in the same order, but not everyone achieves all the stages.

In the first level, the **level of pre-conventional morality**, children respond to rules which they see as being imposed by authority figures such as parents or teachers. Rules must be obeyed simply to avoid punishment or to obtain some personal reward or benefit. If you asked a girl at the beginning of this level why she should eat all her food she might say that it was because she'd be punished if she didn't. Anyone in the level of pre-conventional morality would not be concerned with why the husband in Kohlberg's dilemma stole, they would only be concerned with the consequences of the theft. Their thinking would follow these lines: the husband stole, stealing is wrong, what he stole was important therefore he must be severely punished. Later in the first level children behave in the way they do because they expect some personal reward. Now the girl eats all her food so that her parents will be pleased with her. In one survey Kohlberg found a substantial number of 10-year-olds were still thinking in ways typical of the first level of moral reasoning.

At the second level, the level of **conventional morality**, children try to obey the rules laid down by others in order to be praised or recognised for being good, being nice, being friendly, etc. They start to be able to take other people's intentions into account. Everyone who reaches the second level of moral reasoning would either say that the husband should not be punished, because he was trying to save his wife, or that he should be punished, because the chemist needs to be protected from people like him. Judgements seem to be made on the basis of what most people would think. Later, people at this level start becoming concerned with society being kept in good

The level of pre-conventional morality is generally associated with young children, but some older people may occasionally behave in such a way. Can you think of an example, either real or made up?

In the stage of conventional morality people start to accept that people must not be judged only by their behaviour, but also by their intentions. They may also become concerned with the smooth running of society.

In the last stage people develop individual principles of acceptable and unacceptable behaviour, both for themselves and for others. Not everyone reaches this stage.

order. Anyone who steals should be punished because they upset the order of society in which most people do not steal.

Not everyone reaches the third level, the level of **post-conventional morality**. It involves each person deciding just what is right and wrong for themselves as individuals, and always trying to live by their own rules. People who had reached the third level said that other factors ought to be considered, such as why the chemist was unwilling to sell the drug, and that the government should make such drugs available to everyone who needs them. Thinking is more concerned with justice and injustice, changing bad rules, comparisons with other society's ideas, etc. The last stage is only reached by a few. They have developed an individual set of principles, beliefs, and codes of ethics which they apply to other people's behaviour, according to that individual's particular situation. They have firm ideas about equality and inequality, freedom, individual rights and responsibilities, etc.

A Summary of Kohlberg's levels of moral reasoning

Kohlberg suggests that there are three levels of moral reasoning, each having two stages.

Level 1 The level of pre-conventional morality

Stage 1   Children are only concerned with the outcome of some behaviour. They aren't able to take motives into account. They are mainly concerned with avoiding punishment.

Stage 2   Children judge things in terms of what gives pleasure to them or their favourite people, toys, pets, etc.

Level 2 The level of conventional morality

Stage 3   People at this stage are very concerned with trying to win approval from others.

Stage 4   They will insist that there are rules which must not be disobeyed. If these rules are broken, then punishment will certainly follow. Children's ideas about guilt usually start during this stage.

Level 3 The level of post-conventional morality

Stage 5   People at this stage start to become aware of the interests of the wider community, and of the individual. They may start to see that the community's needs may sometimes be of greater importance than an individual's needs.

Stage 6   This is the level of the deepest moral principles and conscience. Some deeply religious or philosophical people, and people who think deeply about events, such as some politicians, may use these principles. Relatively few people reach this stage.

According to Kohlberg, people pass through these stages in the order shown. For example, it wouldn't be possible for someone to show much consistent understanding of the wider community's needs (Level 3, Stage 5), before being very concerned with his or her own (Level 1, Stage 1). However, even people who have shown that they can think in the more advanced ways may occasionally revert back to the type of thinking typical of some earlier stage.

The opposite also seems occasionally to be true. Children who think at a certain stage are sometimes able to understand, and be persuaded by, the kind of thinking typical of someone who is one, or even two stages, above them. This is usually only specific to with one issue. They do not apply the principles to their wider thinking until they have passed through the stages outlined.

Comments on Kohlberg's approach

Kohlberg's stages of moral development do seem to reflect changes in children's cognitive development. However a number of criticisms have been made.

Criticism

1 Kohlberg has examined how children make moral decisions, and how they justify them. This doesn't explain actually how they behave in the real world when faced with a moral dilemma of their own. Their behaviour varies, according to how they see the particular situation they are in at the time. Certain behaviour would be acceptable in one situation and not in another.

2 Other research suggests that there may be some differences in the ways that boys and girls see moral issues. If we acquire our consciences through socialisation, and if there are any differences in the way we socialise boys and girls, then it is not surprising that one sex's reactions to moral issues will be different from the other's. Perhaps a fuller theory of moral development will need to explain any differences between the sexes.

Comment

1 Kohlberg is interested in the way children make and justify their moral judgements. Their explanations may not always reflect what they would do in real life, but Kohlberg was not primarily interested in their behaviour, but in their powers of reasoning. Kohlberg claims that storytelling is an acceptable means of investigating moral reasoning.

2 Whenever we begin some research we try to operationalise and limit the key variables. Kohlberg concentrated his research on boys in order to obtain an overall impression. Initially he asked boys aged 10, 13, and 16 to respond to his dilemmas. When the research on boys had provided a model for moral development, then research on girls could begin. Other people are comparing girls' and boys' moral reasoning.

3 Some psychologists claim that Kohlberg underestimated the ways in which young children see moral issues. This was partly because of the methods he used. They relied heavily on the children's understanding of language, and their ability to communicate their ideas in words. The children may not always have understood the stories, and may not have been able to express their ideas in words.

4 Social learning theorists have shown that children will often imitate the behaviour of certain models in certain situations. If so, then moral behaviour cannot pass through the stages of cognitive development outlined by Piaget or Kohlberg. A theory which explains the growth of moral thinking may be more valuable if it also explains children's moral behaviour.

3 There are very few ways in which children's moral development can be assessed. Facing them with real problems in real life would be unethical. Telling them stories may be the next best thing, in which case the stories have to be sufficiently detailed for the dilemma to be made clear. The boys tested were aged between 10 and 16. Their language should have been sufficient for them to express their ideas.

4 Children will behave in certain ways, imitating important models, under certain conditions. Reinforcement and modelling are indeed strong influences. This doesn't mean that children's moral reasoning does not pass through identifiable stages, however, since younger children's statements and their behaviour do not always match!

Review
Kohlberg's theory of moral development

Kohlberg extended Piaget's two stages of moral thinking into six stages, in three levels. First-level children will reason in ways designed to bring them pleasure and avoid punishment. During the level of conventional morality the children's reasoning makes them do things which bring them praise and satisfaction. Many people never really leave this stage. Those who do leave it pass into the level of post-conventional morality. They see and do things for the general good of the wider community, and are concerned more with wider social justice. Kohlberg does not tie his stages of development to particular ages in quite such a rigid way as Piaget did. He accepted that people would reach the stages at different ages.

Kohlberg's theory of moral development

1 What is a moral dilemma?

2 Outline Kohlberg's three levels of moral reasoning.

3 Discuss some of the criticisms that have been levelled against Kohlberg's theory of moral development.

4 Evaluate one method used to study children's moral development.

5 What is meant by a stage theory of moral development?

Fit these six words together so that they make three pairs – Freud, Piaget, Behaviourists, reasoning, feelings, behaviour.

4 Behaviourist theories of moral behaviour

While Freud emphasises how children learn to adopt their parents' moral feelings, and Piaget and Kohlberg show how children apply their own rules to making moral judgements, behaviourists empha-sise the role of the parents as trainers of behaviour. Behaviourists claim that all behaviour is a result of reinforcement, possibly modified by punishment, although modelling has also been shown to be effective.

The effects of reinforcement

As we saw in Chapter Six, the effect of reinforcement is to increase the likelihood that certain behaviour will occur again. All parents, teachers and animal trainers use reinforcement to teach particular behaviour. The first stage is to decide exactly what we want the child to do. For example, we may want her to be generous and caring towards others. Every time the child acts in a thoughtful or consider-ate way she is praised and encouraged. Eventually it shouldn't be nec-essary to reinforce the child continually as she will eventually learn to reinforce herself. When children know that they have performed some-thing to their own satisfaction, that in itself should become a reward.

Reinforcement

How might a parent teach a child to help look after a younger brother or sister? Identify the reinforcers used, and say what schedules of reinforcement might be employed.

The effects of punishment

We would all agree that rewarding good behaviour is likely to

Background reading – When is punishment most likely to be effective?

Most research shows that punishment can be effective for developing morally acceptable behaviour if certain factors apply, for example, if the wicked act is punished just before or just after it occurs! That is, a child who is about to do something which he or she knows is wicked will probably have some feelings of anxiety about doing it. This anxiety will be reduced after the wicked act has occurred. If the child is punished while this anxiety is at its height, he or she should learn a strong association between the anxiety involved in being wicked, and the anxiety of being punished. This is an example of classical conditioning. Any plans to be wicked in the future should remind the child of the anxiety, and hopefully stop him or her from wanting to behave badly.

Children should never be punished more severely than is necessary to stop them behaving badly again. Severe punishment may well stop some behaviour from occurring again, but it will make the child afraid of the person who gives the severe punishment. The child will try to avoid that person. This is simply avoidance learning. This will reduce the influence the pun-ishing adult had over the child, which is pre-cisely the opposite result from the one intended.

Parents and teachers must be consistent in what they punish children for. A child who sees that the bad behaviour has upset a loved one, and might stop that person loving the child, is less likely to be wicked again.

After about the age of three years, children should be able to understand simple explanations. Explaining why the child is being punished can strengthen the effectiveness of the punishment.

encourage more good behaviour. But will punishment act as a deterrent, and decrease bad behaviour? According to behaviourists, at the very best, punishment will discourage someone from doing something. It doesn't show a wrongdoer what to do, only what not to do. Also, if bad behaviour goes unreinforced, it is likely to extinguish by itself. Behaviourists do not favour the use of punishment.

Punishment

Why do behaviourists generally reject the use of punishment for modifying bad behaviour?

Review
Behaviourists' views of moral development

Children's responses to moral decisions depend on their previous experience of similar situations. If influential models have been seen behaving in some way, the child is likely to behave in a similar way.

The effects of modelling

Albert Bandura's **social learning theory** emphasises the way children learn by observing and modelling their ideas and behaviour on important people they see around them. Mothers and fathers will be especially important to the young child. Unlike Piaget and Kohlberg, Bandura doesn't see moral development occurring in any particular sequence. Instead children behave in the ways in which they've seen others behave, particularly if those others are important to the child, or if they have been rewarded for behaving in that way previously. For example, if children observe their parents behaving in generous ways, they are more likely to behave in a generous way themselves.

Comments on behaviourist views of moral development

Good points

1 Behaviourists see learning moral behaviour in the same way as they explain learning any other behaviour, largely as a consequence of reinforcement. If good behaviour is reinforced it is likely to be repeated.

2 Punishment isn't generally necessary, or effective to extinguish bad behaviour.

Criticisms

1 Human learning and human behaviour is much more complex than animal behaviour, and requires more than simple reinforcement to explain it. Children may still behave badly, even when they have previously been reinforced for behaving well.

2 Punishment can be an effective deterrent if it is given in a sensitive, caring way.

3 Children also learn by observing and modelling the behaviour of important models they see around them.

3 Imitating an important model's behaviour isn't to be confused with learning their attitudes to moral issues. Young children are egocentric and may have little idea of the effects of what they are doing.

Moral behaviour varies according to the situation a child is in. A child who is generally truthful and honest may cheat and lie in some circumstances, and a generally wicked child may sometimes behave like a saint. Their behaviour does not change just because their thinking may be passing through different stages. Instead it depends on factors like how the child sees the situation, whether the child has previously been rewarded or punished in similar situations, and whether the child has seen other, influential models behaving in some way.

Behaviourist explanation of moral development

1 Summarise the three factors which are likely to influence a child's moral behaviour, according to behaviourist psychologists.

2 Put a tick in the appropriate columns here:

MAJOR THEORIES OF MORAL DEVELOPMENT

	Stage theory	Continuous development
Freud		
Piaget		
Kohlberg		
Behaviourism		

5 Peers and moral development

Peers are people who share the same status, who interact often, who have similar attitudes, beliefs and behaviour, and who often share the same aims. They can be important role models to children, particularly when at school. Being a member of a gang or group may be very important to children and some will go to almost any lengths to stay in the gang.

Between six and 12 years of age, children tend to become increasingly conformist, particularly if the leadership is older and more competent. They probably need the recognition of their peers which

All peer groups develop norms of the type of behaviour that is typical of that group's members. Anyone who doesn't support these norms won't last long in that group.

conforming to the group's norms and values would encourage. If no one else in the group appears to be deviating from its norms, any one individual may find it difficult to deviate.

Children learn much through observation and modelling. However it would be quite a mistake to think that all children blindly imitate all of the behaviour of others. Nor do they necessarily obey the wishes of their gang leader if that means doing something the child knows to be wrong. Most children are not mindless slaves who simply follow their gang leaders, nor are they the constant victims of bullying for rejecting the leader.

The Development of Play

10

As children in Western countries, most of us played with toys and games. We had dolls and construction sets, swings and skipping ropes, footballs and plasticine. We painted and drew, played hide and seek, and tried to solve puzzles. We've been in teams, and amazed our friends with the tricks we've learned. However, not all children have enjoyed these experiences. Not all families have the money to buy toys and games, and many children do not attend well-equipped schools. In some countries children are expected to work as soon as they are old enough, while in others there are different types of play activities. For example, children in America are encouraged to be individualistic and competitive while children in parts of the old Soviet Union are encouraged to work and play as a team, not as individuals.

In this chapter we will be looking at:

1 what play is, and why children spend so much time and effort on it;
2 how play changes during childhood, and whether boys and girls play in the same ways;
3 what play means to children who have some emotional or behavioural problems;
4 Piaget's explanation for the functions of play;
5 peers, friends and play.

Think of some answers to these questions before going any further. What is play, and why do children play? What kinds of play activities might help a child develop, and in what ways? How might playgroup and nursery school benefit a child?

1 What is play?

Let's try to define play. Adults might say that play is something we do for fun which shouldn't be taken too seriously. Children often take it very seriously. They may concentrate on something for quite long periods, and practise it over and over. For example learning to roller skate may take a great deal of time and effort, yet children do it for fun. When parents tell their children to go out and play they usually mean 'go and pass some time in a pleasant way'. But the ways in which children play may have important consequences for other aspects of their development. For example, skipping and chasing each other may be fun, but they are also activities which help build concentration and healthy muscles. One dictionary says that play

Think of some examples which illustrate how the ways in which children play may have important consequences for other aspects of their development.

means to *move around in a lively manner*. Another says play includes activities with *no other goal than enjoyment*. Others say play is activity which has *no serious point to it*. Psychologists would not totally agree with these definitions.

Why do children play?

Our ideas about why children play have changed quite a lot during this century. There are at least three views of what play is for. The first was the old-fashioned and non-psychological view that play was just a way of passing time for babies and young children until they were old enough to work. Second, Piaget offers the view that play contributes to cognition. Third, learning and social learning theorists say that play is for learning and practising those skills that we will need as adults. Freud suggests a fourth possibility, that play may help children to overcome potential problems, for example, some Oedipal conflict.

Play almost certainly caters for all of these things. As we shall see, some play activities do merely pass time in a fairly pleasant way, some activities do encourage cognition, while others allow us to practise adult skills.

Children's pastimes

Sue and John are studying GCSE psychology. As part of their project on changing fashions in children's pastimes they make a list of the toys and games they used to enjoy. Make four lists with these headings:

Developing muscles and coordination	Developing cognition	Developing cooperation	Passing time

Sort their pastimes into the most appropriate list(s).

Reading books and comics, playing football, Cowboys and Indians, skipping, Brownies, building things with blocks, jigsaws, races, playing with a doll's house, playing cars in the sandpit, riding a scooter, lying in bed, puzzle books, adventure playground activities, marbles, board games like draughts and chess, train set, rounders, children's crossword puzzles, hide and seek, making model aeroplanes, watching TV, dressing-up games, hopscotch, watching adventure films at the cinema, table tennis and snooker, riding a bike or tricycle, colouring books.

Imagine a group of children playing hopscotch. Is it possible to say whether they are passing time, developing social skills, or developing cognitive skills? Or could they be doing all three?

Mammals are animals who have a spine, who suckle their young, who have hair (rather than feathers or scales, etc.), who breathe using a diaphragm, etc.

Children, and many other young mammals, spend much of their time playing. One reason for this is that they learn a great deal through play. Social learning theorists like Albert Bandura say that children will observe and imitate adults and build what they observe into their play. A child who does something adult-like is likely to be reinforced. Children certainly have a lot to learn about their world. There are three categories of things to learn during childhood.

First, children must learn how to deal with *things*. Infants will manipulate just about anything they can get their hands on. If they can't touch an object they will stare at it. As they grow older they will experiment with larger objects such as building blocks, and materials which can be used for something, like water, playdough (the modern equivalent of clay or plasticine), or sand. Most teenagers enjoy the challenge of investigating things, solving puzzles, and practising skills like swimming. As well as learning what to do, children must also learn what they must not manipulate. Young children should be discouraged from investigating sharp knives and boxes of matches!

Second, children must learn how to deal with *people*. Children learn about who they can rely on from their caregivers. They may continue to show fear of strangers until they are a few years old. Children don't take very much notice of other children until they are three years of age, or older. Until then they play mostly on their own. If there's nothing else to play with, a baby will touch and explore another baby. A two-year-old infant is more likely to ignore other children unless they are in the infant's way, or are trying to take one of the toys the infant is playing with. Then they'd be aggressive. After about three years old children who are aggressive or spiteful may find that other children do not want to play with them. Those who are more willing to share their toys will be more popular. Older children learn to cooperate in team games and learn about loyalty and competition.

Third, children must learn about themselves. From around the age of seven children are becoming more aware of themselves, and the effects they can have on things around them. We all learn something about what we are like from the ways that other people treat us. If lots of people want to be friends with us it might be because we are pleasant to be with. Friendly behaviour will be reinforced: unfriendly behaviour should be extinguished. As children play roles in games, they learn about how other people see them, and this influences their ideas about themselves. When there are disagreements, children have to learn to compromise, and this may alter what they think they are like.

Review
What is play?

Play allows children to practise the skills they will need as adults. They must find out about dealing with things, how to deal with people and who and what they are themselves.

What each child must learn

1 Name some games or pastimes that you would associate with a child of (a) 12 months, (b) 3 years, (c) 8 years, (d) 14 years.

2 Which of the following groups of people will be important to a child of (a) 12 months, (b) 8 years, (c) 14 years: Parents, teachers, friends?

---

2 How play changes as we grow

According to some psychologists, infants and toddlers are totally egocentric. A child will only play games with her or his parents as long as the game pleases the child. When children become bored they will turn their attention to something else, regardless of the other players. Children up to about two years of age are in a stage of **solitary play**.

From around two or three years of age children start to take some notice of each other. They sometimes try to join in another child's game, while trying to stop another child joining in their own. Even two children are playing the same game and sitting right next to each other would not usually be playing together. For example, two girls might be playing nurses, each with her own doll. They may be playing right next to each other, but each is playing her own game quite separate from the other. This is an example of **parallel play**. Parallel play begins as an extension of *solitary play.*

During the next year children engaged in parallel play become increasingly aware of each other. They occasionally touch or take each other's toys. They occasionally invade each other's space, or might bump into each other. They begin to communicate with each other. The communication will usually include talking. One child may explain its game to the other. Slowly the other may be drawn in. This is called **associative play**.

Eventually most children start to adopt **cooperative play** and begin to share their games, although solitary, parallel, and associative play do not disappear altogether. Some children seem less willing or able to join in and cooperate with others, and they will continue their solitary-type play, sometimes even for years to come. All children may prefer to play on their own sometimes. Cooperative children may take on roles, copying TV characters perhaps. They will use simple props, like furniture or bits of wood or metal, imagine themselves to be something else, and invent a whole, complicated drama around themselves. The game can last for several days. Some games can involve aggression, often against an imaginary enemy.

Solitary and parallel play
▶

> ## *Four stages in young children's play activities*
>
> | Age | Type of play | Main features |
> |---|---|---|
> | 0–2 | Solitary play | Toddlers live in a very private world. They play with things in all kinds of inventive ways, exploring and trying things out. |
> | 2–3 | Parallel play | Although aware of each other's existence, children aren't able to cooperate for very long since each is still thinking egocentrically. They will play alongside, but not with each other. |
> | 3+ | Associative play | The awareness of the other child is increased as they start to communicate. |
> | 3+ | Cooperative play | As children start to be able to take other people's wishes and needs into account so they start to become more sociable. They gradually learn that cooperation can lead to new and interesting things to do and games to play. They start to be able to make 'best friends' out of people who live near and have similar interests, although they can also fall out just as quickly! |

Peers, friends and play

Pre-school children

During solitary and parallel play children may be near others, but generally do not take much notice of them. From around two and a half to three years of age many children are associating and later cooperating with others. Children of two to three years old don't really have 'friendships' apart from with siblings. Such relationships as they do have are often random and brief. A 'best friend to play with' one day might be 'just someone to play with', or even 'someone not to play with', the next.

At around three to four years old individual children start to make special 'friendships' with other children. These relationships are often quite intense and the children are fiercely loyal and faithful to each other. However this special friendship might only last a few days. Each child may form another intense relationship with a different child for a few more days and so on. Other children are more wary and less likely to want to form such relationships. Those children who are emotionally withdrawn, for example, may be less able to benefit from these relationships.

Review
Differences in play

During the first two years children are finding out about things, people and themselves largely through play. Their play is solitary, becomes parallel and associative around three years of age, and they learn to share and cooperate after three. Boys tend to play with the noisier, more adventurous toys, girls are generally quieter, preferring more 'domestic'-type play.

Piaget claimed that children in the pre-operational stage do not think logically and cannot conserve 'friendship'. They are egocentric and use their friends to do what they want.

Freud claimed that children need to play out their emotions, and that play could be used as a defence mechanism.

The purpose of friendship at this age seems to be to help the child to understand objects and relationships. Children can explore many objects by themselves, but some objects (such as a see-saw) take two people. Games such as 'Mummies and Daddies' and 'Doctors and Nurses' may help them to understand adult relationships. Another possibility is that children are beginning to test themselves against others and establish their place in a group. Some children are assertive and may dominate weaker children.

Middle childhood and 'friends'

By four or five years old children have developed a sense of gender and their friendships are more likely to be with another boy or girl. They often play in a 'sex appropriate' way with 'sex appropriate' toys. At first children like their friend because the friend does things for the child.

The only major requirement for making a friend seems to be that the children must see enough of each other. Differences such as physical attractiveness, religion, skin colour, race, class, and status aren't noticed by young children unless emphasised by adults. They simply share play activities thought to be 'appropriate' to their sex. These relationships are rather longer lasting than earlier ones and some friendships formed now can last throughout childhood and beyond.

For further information on friendships see Chapter Eleven on schooling.

As children start school and learn that they must cooperate friendships become more equal. Each partner begins to help the other. They usually play on the same side in school games, join the same team, won't play without the other, etc. They work in pairs and learn from each other too.

Exercise

1 What does Piaget mean by 'conservation?'

2 What does Piaget mean by 'egocentric thought'?

3 Give some reasons why pre-school children make friends.

4 What did Freud mean by defence mechanisms? How might play be used as a defence mechanism?

5 Give some reasons why middle-school children make friends.

Try to find out what you and your friends' favourite pastimes were when you were around five years old. (You might ask your parents.) Compare them to the favourite pastimes of members of the opposite sex.

Sex differences in young children's play

From the time they are three most children know which sex they are, and that the other sex is different from them in some way. They also seem to prefer the company of members of their own sex. Boys usually choose the more adventurous, noisy active toys and activities such as the climbing frames and construction sets. Girls often play with quieter toys and activities, like 'the shop', the Wendy house, painting, and sewing. Boys tend to be more independent than girls

For further explanations of these early sex differences in behaviour, see Chapter Fifteen.

too. They play further away from the teacher, and are less likely to ask for help than girls. The two sexes don't mix very well. Some teachers have tried to encourage boys and girls to mix, and play each other's games, but the children themselves have resisted. By the time the children start school the two sexes are very firmly divided, and any child of one sex who seems to want to play with toys of a child of the opposite sex will soon be discouraged.

◄
Noisy boys and quiet girls?

Play seems to be a very complex phenomenon, and a lot harder to define than you may have thought. It will mean different things to different children at different ages. What we can say is what play is not. It is not 'simply to move around in a lively manner', neither is it 'activity with no other end than enjoyment', and it is not 'something which has no serious point to it'.

Some psychologists would talk about the serious business of play. What do you think they mean by this?

3 Play in severely maladjusted children

There are a number of ways in which children's development can go wrong. Severe maladjustment may be the result of genetic disorders. Autism and Down's Syndrome are examples of genetically inherited conditions. Or maladjusted behaviour may be due to a problem during pregnancy, birth or socialisation. For example, a child who isn't allowed to mix with other children because his over-protective mother thinks he is fragile or delicate may remain emotionally dependent on his mother. Other children may have some particular learning difficulties which may stop their play being as normal as that of other children.

Children with symptoms of mental retardation have been extensively studied in America by **Ann Brown** and **Joseph Campione**. Their observations of the cognitive skills of such children have important implications for how these children play. Remember that Piaget claimed that children's play contributes to their cognitive development too.

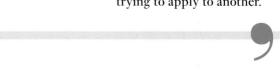

Brown and Campione's Studies

Conclusions	Implications
1 Retarded children think more slowly than other children. They do not immediately see connections between things that other children might.	1 Board games such as Snakes and Ladders, Ludo, and Junior Scrabble may not be so easily understood by children who are slow to learn.
2 They have slower reaction times.	2 Games like table tennis, cricket, football, etc., will be more difficult for children who take longer to react.
3 They need to hear detailed instructions several times before they begin to understand what any game is about.	3 Any game which involves rules which are very complicated may never be fully understood.
4 They cannot apply the knowledge and skills they have acquired from one situation to another one.	4 Skills which apply to one kind of activity may not immediately be seen by the child as relevant or worth trying to apply to another.

Many seriously maladjusted children can, and do, learn. It's just that the learning of most skills will take longer, and will need far more practice and help from others.

Play in one example of maladjusted children

So far we have been looking at the patterns of play usually found among children in societies like our own. But even in our societies not all children will play in the ways we've described. Some children will suffer mental or physical handicaps, or will be emotionally or socially maladjusted. One of the most extreme and tragic forms of maladjustment in childhood is **autism**.

Review
The nature of play

Play can mean hard work, as well as passing time, as children acquire the cognitive and social skills which they will need later. They learn about what objects are for, and what they can do with them, about other people, and about themselves. This takes place gradually as children stop their solitary play, go through parallel play, and start becoming sociable. Sex differences in play can be seen in many playgroup and nursery school children. Not all children are lucky enough to enjoy this normal development, and for some – such as severely maladjusted children – play may be very restricted.

Autistic children are severely emotionally withdrawn. They seem preoccupied by their thoughts and feelings, and barely notice other people. Their play will usually involve a small number of objects such as a toy, an item of clothing, or a blanket. They will want to keep it close to them. They will often repeat the same movement over and over again. For example an autistic child might sit on a chair and rock backwards or forwards for hours on end. Or he or she may turn a toy round and round in his or her hands for hours. One movement that is even more distressing is when an autistic child bangs his or her head against a wall for hours.

Autistic children strongly resist any change in their environment. Often they will not go out, and will not explore any new objects, which a non-autistic child would. They do not usually talk, and if they do it's rarely more than a simple two-word sentence. They often avoid looking at other people. These things mean that social exchanges during play are usually impossible.

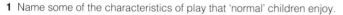

Play

1 Name some of the characteristics of play that 'normal' children enjoy.

2 Looking back to the list of pastimes that Sue and John could remember enjoying from their childhood. Which of these could severely autistic children enjoy?

3 Outline some of the differences in the play of 'normal' and 'maladjusted' children.

4 Piaget's view of play

Several psychologists have studied children's play. One influential theory which looks at the role of play in cognition comes from Jean Piaget. Piaget claimed that a child's cognition develops through four main stages. During each stage the child is mastering certain ways of thinking which are more advanced than those in the previous stage. For the first few years children are fairly egocentric in their thinking. They improve their abilities to assimilate and accommodate new information as their schemas expand. Sometime around their seventh birthday children learn to decentre.

According to Piaget, cognitive, and possibly intellectual, development would benefit greatly from play. Piaget believed that there would be different kinds of play activities among children in each stage. For example, the child's first tasks are to learn movement and interaction with the immediate environment. Piaget identified three types of play: play in the sensory motor stage; play in the pre-operations stage; and play in the concrete operations stage.

Play in the sensory motor stage

During the first two years, play allows children to explore and manipulate their environment, mainly to see how they can master it. Early play consists of repeating actions that give babies pleasure. Some of this play will be quite solitary, some will involve 'give-and-take' and 'exchange' games with adults. During the first few months the child learns hand-to-eye coordination, what can be reached, grasped, picked up, etc. By 18 months most children can walk and control their movements quite well. They will also be able to use some words, and understand a lot more. They will be learning something new about their environment and the people in it practically every day. Piaget said these first two years were for **mastery** or **practice** play.

Play in the pre-operations stage

The changeover from playing alone during the **mastery play** stage to playing with other people is gradual. At first children may use other people (rather as objects) in their early games. By the end of this stage other people are important partners in play. By about two years of age a child can let one object stand for (or **symbolise**) something else. A box can be a car, a stick can be a pencil, a doll can make someone who has it into a parent, etc. Children often play 'pretend' games when they make believe they are someone else. For example, wearing a box on one's head might make a boy into a policeman. He sees how other people respond to the role he is playing, and this helps him to 'try out what it feels like' to be someone else. Sometimes children invent an imaginary friend, who has a name, who sits by them at mealtimes, and who even shares their food! Piaget called the kind of play that goes on in this stage **symbolic**, or **make-believe** play. Children in this stage must be encouraged to think and do things for themselves. They can be helped to find the right way of doing things, but they learn best when they learn for themselves.

> What does Piaget mean by 'schemas', 'assimilation', and 'accommodation', 'egocentric', and 'decentre'? If you're not certain, go back now and read Chapter Eight on cognitive development again.

> Symbols are things which stand for other things.

Background reading – An example of symbolic play

A psychologist could investigate whether children use play to settle any emotional difficulties they feel. A five-year-old girl could be told that she has to do something which she doesn't want to. She must, of course, obey. This creates an 'emotional crisis' which she must overcome. Here's an example.

It's lunch time and Kerry's mother has called her in to wash her hands. Kerry was happily playing an elaborate game with her friends and she didn't really want to stop. Having hurriedly washed her hands Kerry sat down and ate some of her soup. After a few mouthfuls she said she had finished, and could she go outside to play with her friends again. Kerry's mother said 'no', she could not go out until she'd eaten all her soup. Kerry finished the soup very reluctantly. An hour or so later Kerry might be observed with her doll. She might play the part of an adult who was making the doll finish all her food. This symbolic play may be helping Kerry to understand what happened to her, and how to deal with these feelings.

Play in the concrete operations stage

Singing nursery rhymes like *Ring-a-ring-a-roses* and dancing around in a circle is useful for developing motor coordination, for being sociable, and for having fun. By the time children reach the concrete operations stage, from around seven years, they are capable of far more advanced activities than these. Children who can decentre can take other people's feelings and needs into account. They make up their own rules about things which might seem like a good idea to them. They learn about rules which are imposed on them by others. They become more sociable and cooperative. As they learn to use rules of logic and reasoning, they can understand the point of playing games with rules that affect themselves and the other players. They learn about sharing and about rights and responsibilities. Piaget calls this kind of play **play with rules**.

Background reading – An example of play with rules

By eight or nine years of age, children learn that team games, such as rounders, netball, football, and cricket, and board games, such as Monopoly, Junior Scrabble, and Ludo, are played according to set rules.

Piaget's three stages in young children's play activities

Age	Stage of intellectual development	Name of type of play	Main features
0–2	Sensory motor	Mastery or practice play	Play lets children explore and manipulate their environment, mainly to see how they can affect it. They must master the skills of muscle and limb control, so they can attract the attention of their caregiver.
2–7	Pre-operational	Symbolic or make-believe play	Children's play reflects their increasing experiences and imagination. Children pretend to be someone else, imitating their behaviour, and seeing how others respond. They are also learning how to communicate symbolically through language.

7+	Concrete operations	Play with rules	Children learn about rules which are imposed on them by others. They are now becoming sociable, and, as they learn to use rules of logic and reasoning, they can understand the sense of playing games with rules that affect themselves and the other players. They learn about give and take, and about their, and other people's, rights and responsibilities.

Expanding schemas through play

A report of an observation in a local playgroup

Sheila is four years and three months old. She is playing in the sandpit. Other children are also playing in the sandpit, but they all seem to be in their own little worlds. Sheila is trying to build a sandcastle. She has a bucket which she half fills with sand. When she turns it over the sand just falls into a little heap. She tries this several times and the same thing keeps happening. She doesn't seem to be very pleased with it. Mrs Hawkes notices that Sheila is beginning to become frustrated, and is about to give up, so she goes over to help. She doesn't, however, make a sandcastle for Sheila. She tries to explain that the bucket needs to be full, and she shows Sheila what she means. She shows Sheila how to turn the bucket over quickly. I didn't think Sheila understood what Mrs Hawkes was saying, but when Mrs Hawkes left, giving Sheila the empty bucket, Sheila filled it to the top, turned it over very firmly, patted the bottom of the bucket, and she made a sandcastle. She seemed very pleased, for a moment. She looked at it, touched it, walked round to the other side of it and looked and touched some more. She seemed totally fascinated by it. I thought she was going to play with it but she didn't. She looked at it, smiled, and slowly and deliberately knocked it over.

1 What is the name of the technique used for collecting these data?

2 What is the sample size?

3 Why didn't Mrs Hawkes simply help Sheila to build her sandcastle?

4 What do you think the phrase 'they all seem to be in their own little world' in the third sentence means?

5 How would a Piagetian psychologist explain Sheila's behaviour when she made her sandcastle?

6 What is associative play?

7 How could the reliability of these observations be checked?

Review
Piaget's view of play

Play seems to reinforce the cognitive experiences the child is having. Mastering early sensory motor coordination may help children with symbolisation which will encourage imagination. Imagination and symbolisation encourage cooperation, and cooperative play may provide help towards decentring. At each stage, imagination should be encouraged by parents, teachers, and other adults. Toys and games should develop problem-solving skills, muscle development, hand-to-eye coordination, etc. Play helps assimilation and accommodation best when children respond to some demand made by their environment (e.g. parental rules). Play is essentially active.

11

Going to School

There are several types of pre-school childcare, as we saw in Chapter Four. Some, such as playgroup and nursery school, may involve opportunities for children to learn from the materials and experiences provided. These experiences will be social as well as cognitive since some of the children will be mixing with others for the first time.

Piaget said that for their first few years, children's thinking is quite egocentric. They can't see the benefits of cooperation and sharing since they are only concerned with their own needs and wants. However, more recent researchers such as **Martin Hughes** and **Olivera Petrovich** have challenged Piaget's claims. They have shown that children of four, or even younger, are capable of benefiting from social experiences.

Piaget's theory has been adapted to promote ways of dealing with children in the primary and junior school. The work of B. F. Skinner has been adapted so as to explain some teaching and learning experiences in the secondary school.

In this chapter we will be reviewing:

1 whether there are any benefits of attending playgroup or nursery school;
2 what changes occur when children first attend school;
3 the school as a cultural and social experience;
4 the role of friends in schooling;
5 Piaget and discovery learning;
6 Skinner and programmed learning.

1 Will playgroup and nursery school experiences help development?

As we said in Chapter Four, playgroups are run for younger children, usually by some of the mothers. Nursery schools take older children and are usually run by qualified staff. The kinds of activities that we would expect to see at each may be slightly different. At playgroup and nursery school, children can come together to play with different toys, in different ways, alongside different children. Some activities will be clearly organised and will have to work to some kind of a timetable. Others can be less restricted,

Background reading – Playdough

Playdough is used in many playgroups and nurseries now. It can be bought commercially, but isn't difficult to make. Mix a cupful of flour, half a cupful of salt, and a cupful of water together in a saucepan. Stir in a tablespoonful of cooking oil and two tablespoonfuls of cream of tartar and some food colouring, and warm the pan over a low heat. Stir the mixture until it lifts away from the sides of the pan. Let it cool, and it makes a cheap, harmless, and creative plaything.

and the children can be encouraged to express their ideas more freely. Some materials will be more useful for this than others. Playdough, water, sand, and paint are some of the more expressive materials.

What children do with their play objects changes as they pass from playgroup and through nursery school. These changes may reflect changes in their cognitive development. For example young children start by exploring and experimenting with playdough. They want to know what they can do with it. As they grow they seem to enjoy the sensations that playing with playdoughs can give. They derive pleasure from seeing and feeling it change shape. The next stage is to make the playdough into something (perhaps by accident at first). It might be a dog, or a house. Finally they realise that the shape that they have made is a model of what they are calling it, that is, it's a dog-shaped lump of playdough, not a real dog.

Water contains just about all the elements from which children can build up their experiences. It has form which can be moved around, can be contained in differently shaped containers, can be coloured, made into bubbles, can be 'got into', floated on, and even drunk. It can be silent, or make noises, it can be poured, spilled, mopped up, wrung out, and thrown away. Water has many qualities that can stretch young imaginations.

There have been a number of studies of children's play. In general the research hasn't come to any really firm conclusions. Since we don't really know what the purposes of play are, we can't really know if it is going to do anything useful for cognitive or social development. It certainly is not possible to separate the benefits of these early experiences. Improving sociability, practising skills, and developing cognitively are closely interlinked.

Children's play

Imagine that two psychologists made a half-hour videotape of the play of five boys and five girls between three and five years old at playgroup. They also filmed five nine-year-old boys and five nine-year-old girls. They wanted to see if there were any sex differences in the sociability of the two sexes. They averaged how many minutes each group spent, during the half hour, in the following activities:

Number of minutes spent in three activities

		BOYS		GIRLS	
Age		3–5	9	3–5	9
Playing alone		19	2	16	1
Playing alongside other children		8	2	7	1
Playing with other children		3	26	7	28

1 What was the total sample size used in this study?

2 What was the hypothesis being studied here?

3 What type of play was most common for the playgroup children?

4 Which group spent the longest amount of time playing together?

5 Outline the way children's play changes from around the age of seven, according to Piaget.

End of topic test on play

1 Draw three columns with the headings 'Mastery play', 'Symbolic play', and 'Play with rules'. In each column write some examples of the kind of things you would see if observing a child in each of the three stages.

2 Explain how Piaget's view of play fits in with his general theory of cognition.

3 What are solitary play, parallel play, associative play, and cooperative play? Give an example of each type of play.

4 How does the play of maladjusted children differ from the play of 'normal' children?

5 Why do some psychologists refer to 'the serious business' of play?

John Shea observed some three- and four-year-old children during their first 10 weeks at a nursery school. He defined five dimensions of sociability. These were, aggression, rough-and-tumble play, how far a child was from any other child, how far any child was from the teacher, and how often each child spoke to or played with another person.

Some of the children began by attending only two days a week. Some attended three days a week, whilst others attended all five days a week. Over the 10 weeks just about all of the children went through the same kind of behaviour pattern. They all started off by staying near to the teacher, and were wary of each other. Some children were occasionally physically and verbally aggressive towards the others. This usually resulted from disagreements over toys. As the weeks went by this behaviour changed. The children were more content to play further away from the teacher, and nearer to each other. They were less aggressive too.

The children who went to school for five days a week became more sociable more quickly. Those attending for two days a week took the longest to become more sociable.

A study emphasising the social benefits of early schooling

1 What do you think the hypothesis of John Shea's research was?

2 What research method was used?

3 Outline Shea's conclusion.

4 What do the terms 'social development' and 'cognitive development' mean?

Review
Play and schooling

As children grow their play activities will change. They will use the same materials, but in different ways, probably reflecting changes in their cognitive development.

Kathy Sylva, Carolyn Roy, and **Marjorie Painter** conducted some research for the Oxfordshire Pre-school Project. They wanted to see what play activities would be most useful for developing a young child's cognitive development. They conducted naturalistic observations of 120 children aged between three and five, and made detailed recordings of what each child was doing, whether this was solitary play or involved others, whether it included talking and listening, what materials were used, whether the child appeared to be deeply involved in trying to solve something or was just passing the time. They evaluated each activity for the contribution it made to social and intellectual development. Kathy Sylva and her colleagues concentrated on what they called **complex play** which involved the children in some thoughts and actions that stretched them. This is different from **simple play** which merely passes some time.

Kathy Sylva's study suggests that children benefit from a balance between doing things in their own way (**free play**), and being organised, for example, to listen to a story (**structured play**). This balance can be achieved by well-run playgroups. Children learn from things which have a specific end: for example, completing a Lego house, making something with plasticine, or solving a jigsaw. Playgroup children work well in pairs as children learn much from each other. A variety of adults should be encouraged to be involved with the children, since children seem to learn best when adults are providing models, and suggesting alternative ways of doing things when children become stuck and are about to give up. Overall they found that playgroups could be of great benefit to stimulating cognitive development.

At playgroups and nursery schools, children are able to experience a wider range of toys and materials than they might find at home.

Play activities

1 How might materials like playdough and water be used at playgroup to help children's cognitive development?

2 Name some materials or activities that could stimulate playgroup children's social development.

3 What types of play activities may be most likely to stimulate cognitive development?

4 What types of play activities are least likely to be stimulating for cognitive development?

5 What advice would you give to the organiser of a new playgroup?

2 Going to school

Children who have been lucky enough to have attended playgroups will become used to the idea of going out to play and learn in the company of other children. They should be more aware of others, and able to cooperate more than children who didn't go to playgroup. All children must start going to some kind of school from the age of around five in Britain. When children first go to school several very important aspects of their lives change. There is a physical change – they leave home for several hours each day, and go to a new place, they must find their way around and learn the routines of the school day. Even those who attended playgroup will have new routines to learn. Social aspects of their lives change too – they will be mixing with new people, adults and children. Ideally, they will overcome these changes to their routines in the first few weeks. Another major change comes later. It involves mental changes to do with learning. Before starting school children learn things through play, by imitating others, by modelling, by reinforcement, by trial and error, by accident, and occasionally by being taught. At school the emphasis is going to be on *being taught*. They will *be taught* new skills like simple arithmetic, reading, and writing.

When children start school, sometime after their fourth birthday, they have to make some important adjustments to their world. They must adjust physically, socially, and in how they learn.

Some children make the transition from home to school without difficulty. They seem to enjoy the challenges, and benefit from the experiences. For other children the change does not go smoothly. Some of the reasons for this can be explained by their early socialisation. Those who have been encouraged to be independent, active and curious are more likely to do well in school than those who have not. Psychologists, sociologists and others have researched many of the factors that affect children starting school. They include how old the child is, and what the child's personality is like, how the parents have prepared the child for the challenge of school, what teaching materials are used in the school, what the teachers, expect of the child, what the child thinks of the teachers, and what subject is being learned.

All children do not have the same expectations of school. Do you know how you responded to school during your first year or so?

3 Some social and cultural issues affecting schooling in Britain

When children first go to school

The child's first class will probably contain 20 or more children. Each is an individual with individual needs and abilities. At home each child will probably have been treated as an individual. A child who was curious about something there always had someone around to ask. If it was asked a question it could just shout the answer back. Many researchers, including Freud, Skinner and Bandura, have all claimed that children acquire at least some of their attitudes and behaviour from their parents. Either by identification, reinforcement, or modelling, children become like their parents in many respects. They will also speak the same language as their parents. Some parents will have prepared their children for school by telling them to enjoy it, and to be active and ask questions. Other parents will tell their children that they must be quiet and good, or they'll be in trouble. Some of the children will be inquisitive and interested in what's going on, others will be quiet and shy.

What the first school offers the child

A single teacher can't teach 20 or more individual five-year-olds. If many of them are asking questions at the same time, trying to play with things, and getting in each other's way, then there would be a lot of noise, very little actual learning, and an unsafe classroom. There must be some organisation. There must be rules which will govern the children's behaviour. For example, teachers usually insist that children put their hands up if they know the answer to a question. They must not speak out, as they might have done at home. Otherwise some children will dominate and others will be left out. One of the most important things the school first offers the child is discipline. According to Piaget children who can't yet decentre will accept rules which are imposed on them by others.

What teachers expect of children

The teacher will define what is meant by success in school. A successful girl will be one who accepts the teacher's authority, who is polite and well mannered, who does as she is told, and who learns the material expected of her. An unsuccessful child will be one who is reluctant to conform, whose individuality is interpreted as silliness or rebelliousness, and who doesn't fit in with what a teacher defines as a good pupil. A number of studies have shown that teachers respond differently towards children whom they have interpreted as able, compared to those interpreted as less able. They smile more, are friendlier, use a lower tone of voice, and give more opportunities to do well to good pupils. When a child whom a teacher has defined as low ability doesn't answer correctly the teacher will probably ask another child. When a higher-ability child answers incorrectly the teacher may provide some more clues and encourage the child to try again.

Children must conform to the teacher's rules. Some will find this easier to do than others. Those who conform may be regarded more favourably than those who do not.

Teachers form opinions about which children are 'better' than others, and they may not always respond to each child in an identical way.

Going to school

1 Name some of the ways in which pre-school children learn.

2 Name some of the changes that will occur in children's lives when they start to go to school.

3 What sorts of thing can parents do to help their children start school?

Background reading – Teachers' expectations and pupils' performance

In the mid-1960s, Lenore Jacobson and Robert Rosenthal conducted a now famous study on teacher–child interaction in a Californian elementary school. They told the teachers about a new kind of intelligence test which wouldn't just measure intelligence, but would actually predict it. Knowing what a child's intelligence was going to be could be of enormous benefit to teachers. The pupils were given the tests, and, based on the results of these, each teacher was told that five of the children in their class would become 'rapid bloomers'. Jacobson and Rosenthal claimed that the teachers would expect these children to make good progress in school. Rosenthal and Jacobson returned eight months later and retested all the pupils, and, indeed, many of their predictions were proved correct. Not only had most of the rapid bloomers make significant gains in their IQ scores, but their record cards showed that the teachers thought they had made very good progress in, for example, reading skills.

In fact the rapid bloomers were simply a 20 per cent random sample that Jacobson and Rosenthal had taken from each class register. Jacobson and Rosenthal claimed that the improvement in these children's performance in school must be explained by the only real difference that existed between them and the other children, that is, their teachers expected more of them than of the others.

Some concerns have been expressed about this study. For example, some of the teachers claimed that they couldn't remember who the 'bloomers' were, so couldn't have treated them differently. The study still suggests that teachers do have considerable influence over some aspects of their pupils' progress.

How do teachers define success

Children's social class may be one factor in explaining their attitudes to schooling. What attitudes did your parents take to your schooling?

Schools have been defined as middle-class institutions. To put it very simply, the middle classes are typically people who work in office-type jobs. Teachers, insurance agents, doctors and bank managers are all members of the middle classes. Lorry-drivers, plumbers, gardeners, and electricians are described as belonging to the working class. Sociologists have claimed that typical middle-class people have different attitudes and beliefs compared to typical working-class people. For example, typical middle-class parents are more likely to see the benefits of a good education for their children. They take more interest in their child's progress at school, and help more with homework, etc. Typical working-class people are more likely to see education as useful for learning basic skills, but leaving school at 16 and getting a job is considered to be more important.

Middle-class teachers, it was argued, have more in common with middle-class pupils, and are more likely to define them as good. Many of the books, films, visits and other educational materials which are used in schools tend to have more in common with middle-class backgrounds than with working-class or many ethnic minority backgrounds. Working-class children, and children from many ethnic minority backgrounds, may not share the teachers' ideas about the importance of high achievement in school. They are more likely to be defined as *poor achievers*.

Why do some children do better than others in school?

Teachers may not necessarily be aware that they are favouring some children over others. Did any of your teachers seem to have any 'teacher's pet'?

Once defined as someone who should do well, or someone who will not make much progress, a child may be treated accordingly by the teacher. If teachers have low expectations of children's abilities they are less likely to push them. Where teachers have high expectations the children are more likely to do well. Many sociological studies have linked teachers' expectations to the social class of the child. The researchers are not suggesting that teachers deliberately favour some children and discriminate against others. It's just that teachers seem to treat some children differently, often without having any idea that they are doing so.

A study of teacher–child interaction

Here are some extracts from an observational study of two children, Robert and Jamie, made by Roy Nash in Edinburgh, Scotland, in 1971. Each is a ten-minute observation of a fairly typical primary school day. Nash is making the point that it's not necessarily the child's background that teachers use to make their judgements, but rather their early perceptions of the child's abilities and personality.

A: Robert 'Most of the class are doing project work. Three boys still seem to be doing English. This means they haven't finished quickly enough. Teacher looks over to them. "Robert, you could be doing an excellent drawing for me, but you're so slow with your English." Robert looks glum. He puts down his pencil. It looks like he's finished at last – or given up. He goes to teacher who is telling Albert what a "lovely wee fire" he has painted. She sees Robert standing a little behind her, not drawing attention to himself. "Ah, now you can help me here," she says. She leads him over to the model tray. "We're going to have the mountains either side, and that's going to be a wee pass. Are you very good at making mountain shapes?" Robert looks doubtfully at the heap of papier-mâché. "No?" asks teacher. "Well I'll get someone else to do them then." She tells him to do a picture instead. Robert goes back to his desk. He looks about, sees that he hasn't got any paper to do his picture on, and decides to finish his English. A couple of minutes pass. "Anyone still doing English?" calls teacher. Robert raises his hand. "Oh, come on Robert," she says.'

1 What is Robert doing when nearly everyone else is drawing or painting?

2 Most of the children would find drawing and painting more interesting. What did Robert do to try to get something more interesting to do?

3 What was the teacher's response to Robert over the model mountains. How would you explain her behaviour?

4 What does the teacher tell Robert to do, and what is his response?

5 The observer concluded that Robert isn't very happy at school. What evidence for this is there in the passage?

B: Jamie 'Jamie is waiting in the queue at teacher's desk. He talks to Iain. Teacher takes his book. "Right," she says. Then, "Some of you are not using very sharp pencils. I can hardly read it." Quickly she corrects his work. "Jamie, there you are." Jamie takes his book. . . . One of the boys in the queue asks him a question, and Jamie pauses for a moment to talk to him. Teacher asks who is talking? "I just can't concentrate with this noise, whoever it is", she says. There are about 20 children now around teacher's desk. The noise grows louder again. Teacher warns the class. "Shirley, I don't want that shrieking," she adds. Jamie works hard for three to four minutes . . . (teacher) gives instructions about the project she wants them to do. "Everybody is going to write diaries of a western pioneer family." . . . She looks around to see who has finished their English. "Right," she says, "Jamie, you pick your wagon." Jamie grins and stands up, and makes a great play of picking his friends who move over to his desk.'

1 How does the teacher respond when Jamie's pencil is blunt, and when he is talking?

2 How does she respond when Shirley is talking?

3 Why is Jamie allowed to 'pick his wagon' and what does he feel about it?

Having decided what a child is like the teacher treats the child accordingly. The teacher (in the exercise extracts above) is quite unaware that she is treating the two children differently. As Roy Nash says, 'it is possible to see that the teacher regards Jamie in more favourable terms than Robert. Jamie she sees as forthcoming, easy-going, industrious, confident, interested, quiet, boisterous, and bright. By contrast Robert is seen as a worrier, talkative, and tending to be emotionally disturbed, lazy, lacking confidence, shy, and with a low IQ.' (What evidence can you find for the teacher regarding Jamie as forthcoming, easy-going, industrious, confident, interested, quiet, boisterous, and bright?)

Psychological contributions to ideas about schooling

We have discussed many of the special terms that Piaget and Skinner used in previous chapters. If you're not sure about any of them refer to the relevant chapter.

While others have been interested in issues concerning the school as a social and cultural environment, the main areas of research in psychology have concentrated on answering the question 'How do children learn?' If we knew the answer to this then teachers could use their time more efficiently, children could learn more easily, and potential learning problems could be reduced. One major contribution has come from Jean Piaget and others who see learning as one part of a general development of cognition. The main application of this approach has been to primary schooling. The other major contribution is made by learning theorists like B. F. Skinner, who say learning is the result of reinforcement. These ideas have been more widely applied to the secondary school.

4 The role of friends in schooling

Egocentric children can't take other children's needs into account. They use their friends for their own benefit.

Peers are equals who see each other frequently, have similar ideas about what sort of behaviour is right for them, and who often have similar aims or goals to achieve.

As children start school and learn that they must cooperate, friendships become more equal. Each partner begins to help the other. Previously children liked their friend for what their friend could do for them. Now children can benefit from giving and helping, sharing and cooperating.

Peers can have two effects on individual children. First, they may be seen as rivals and barriers to the child's own success. Being egocentric a child might believe that only one or two children can 'come top', or gain all the teacher's attention and praise. The more children there are, the less likely any one child is to succeed. This could be a negative influence causing jealousy and hostility. The child who does best might be disliked or even mistreated. Calling a bright girl a teacher's pet or abusing her in other ways may make her less keen to do well in future.

On the other hand, according to Bandura, children can learn much by modelling themselves on others. A successful peer may become a powerful model too. Seeing someone else do well and gain some benefit might encourage the others to do well too. Although peers can be important models, it is important not to over emphasize their role. Children don't always do what their friends are doing!

Children form themselves into gangs or close-knit groups. Being a member of one group or another is especially important to many children. Each group develops its own norms of behaviour, of dress, etc., and its own values of attitude to work, to authority, etc. Group members will go to great lengths to ensure that they stay in the group and avoid the risk of being rejected. So a group that is 'pro-school' will encourage its members to work hard and achieve success. An 'anti-school' group will resist authority and penalise any member that might appear to do well.

Can you remember?

1 Can you remember any of your friends from primary or junior school?
2 Were you ever a member of a 'gang' or 'group'?
3 Were there any members of the opposite sex in your group? If so, what proportion?
4 Did you, or anyone you can remember, act against the norms of the group? What happened?

5 Discovery learning

Piaget was interested in the way children think. He was interested in the following questions. Why did the sample of children for an intelligence test he was working on consistently give the same wrong answers? Where did children's natural curiosity come from? Why will a seven-year-old keep on making the same mistake without realising it? Why can't a child realise that Michael being taller than Sean, and Sean being taller than Lorraine, means that Michael has to be taller than Lorraine too? How can we discover what children think about, and how do the ways they think differ from the ways adults think?

Piaget was fascinated by biology, and speculated about human brain structures. He thought there must be some biological structures in the brain which expand as children grow and gather more experience. These **schemas**, as he called them, develop through a fixed sequence of stages as children find out about their world. Piaget saw the way these schemas develop changing at about two and then at seven years of age. After seven, the child's thinking starts being **operational**, that is, the child is able to accept adult rules of logic. Before seven a child's thinking has quite a different logic.

Moving from pre-operational to operational thought from around six to eight years of age probably marks the greatest change in a child's cognitive development.

Piaget and learning

1 Write a brief summary of what Piaget meant by 'schema' and 'operations'.

2 How do children up to the age of about seven learn, according to Piaget?

3 What did Piaget mean by 'symbolic play'?

Discovery learning

Piaget didn't make specific recommendations for what should happen in school, but it isn't difficult to apply some of his conclusions to education. His approach is generally referred to as **discovery learning**. He insisted that children learn by acting on things, by using things in all sorts of new and different ways. As we said before, children are naturally curious and are well motivated to discover things

Why do you think some supporters of Piaget might think 'nursery school *teacher*' wouldn't be a very accurate description?

for themselves. Children ask all kinds of questions which seem quite sensible to them. They arrange and play with their toys in all sorts of ways which parents might not begin to understand. Since children actually enjoy learning, nursery school teachers have an excellent opportunity to help them.

The role of the primary teacher in discovery learning

First, teaching should not emphasise the passing on of knowledge. There'll be enough time for that later, when the child is able to think more widely. Since children are naturally curious, and they learn by manipulating objects and materials, teachers should provide them with new things to master when they seem to have learned as much as they can from the existing materials. The materials should be provided in the amounts that children can manage. Discovery learning is a very active process and children must be given all the stimulation they can act upon. This does not mean that the child is to be pushed. According to Piaget, schemas will develop as the child masters and accommodates the skills involved. Children need time to practise and shouldn't be hurried.

Second, children can learn from each other, so they may be seated in pairs, or even small groups for some activities. Some activities need more than one child, and children often imitate each other's speech and behaviour, especially if they see their partner receiving some benefit. Cooperation and learning to share are important skills which can only be learned from others.

Third, the teacher must be aware of which stage of development each child is in, and know what skills each child has acquired, and will be preparing to acquire. The materials and resources provided should be designed to help the children achieve mastery of the tasks of that stage. This is generally known as **the readiness approach**, and does not try to force children to learn. Development will only occur when the children are ready for it. As children near the end of one stage teachers should prepare them to achieve the skills of the next stage. The changeover (called **stage shift**), when it comes, should be smooth. For example after the age of six or seven children will be starting to think operationally. One aspect of this is the ability to conserve number. The teacher might provide things which can be counted, moved or put together to help prepare the child for conservation of number.

Teachers should show children that there are other, possibly better, ways of achieving something when the methods they are using cannot possibly succeed. When a child has achieved the concrete operation stage, skills like doing arithmetic, using actual objects such as beads, must be taught.

If these are the roles of the teacher, then the role of the child is actively and enthusiastically to explore, manipulate, play, and develop techniques for solving problems. Children should respond to their own curiosity which is stimulated by the things in the school. Most of all they have to find out for themselves.

Background reading – Cognition and the under sevens

Here are some of the differences between pre-operational and operational thought.

1 Children below about seven years of age cannot think about numbers and space in the same ways that adults do. They think that things always are what they look like, for example, if we show a pre-operational child 10 model farmyard animals which are spread out, and 10 which are bunched together, they will say that there are more animals in the first group than in the other group. Tall, thin containers look as though they hold more liquid than shorter, fatter containers. However other experiments suggest that children under seven can think in these ways, and their major problem may lie in their use of language. Bryant and others suggest that children have difficulty in expressing ideas about, for example, more or less. However they can be taught to think in these ways, and carefully designed experiments will show that they do have the ability to conserve. For example, McGarrigle and Donaldson's use of naughty teddy, allowed over 60 per cent of their sample of four- to six-year-olds to demonstrate their ability to conserve number. Hughes found that younger children could decentre too.

2 Piaget has also shown that young children cannot understand time, movement, and speed, for example, age is confused with size – bigger things must be older. A car about to overtake another will be described as going slower since the car in front is thought of as being the faster car!

3 Nor do children understand space. Squares, triangles, and circles will all be copied as much the same shape. In children's paintings some rules that they have learned will be applied rigidly, i.e. trees grow at 90 degrees to the ground, so even if the painting shows a hill, the trees will still be at 90 degrees to the ground!

Children seem to start with the basic elements of understanding and gradually add to them until they grasp the whole idea. Piaget says that these schemas are formed and developed through manipulation, i.e. through the child's handling materials like paper, water, sand or plasticine. They must discover for themselves, by trial and error, such things as 'what goes with what', 'what happens if . . . ?', and 'how does that work?' This process of discovery is essentially active. The children must actively participate, using their sense organs to the full. Mastery and symbolic play will help develop schemas of how to deal with things.

Comments on discovery learning

Good points

1 Piaget's theory of how cognition develops in children was based on many years of patient investigation, and is a breakthrough in the way we think about children's intelligence. It provides us with a series of ages around when children's style of thinking changes from pre-operational to operational.

2 **Discovery** learning provides a logical and practical guide to what children in various stages of development should be able to understand. Parents and teachers can put Piaget's theory to practical use in the way they deal with children.

3 Discovery learning provides a model for the approach of teachers in the first school in terms of what signs to look out for that a child's thinking is changing.

Comments

1 The idea that children's style of thinking changes at around seven years of age could be regarded as a major breakthrough in our understanding. Other researchers have cast doubt on some of Piaget's methods, and therefore on any conclusions derived from them. Children are capable of thinking in more advanced ways before the age of seven than Piaget believed.

2 Children aren't all the same, and any rigidly applied theory will be inappropriate for some of them. General guidelines can be useful, specific dos and don'ts are less so.

3 Being ready to help children pass through the various stages of cognitive development would be helpful if we knew precisely what children in each stage were capable of, and exactly when each child was passing through it. We are unlikely ever to have such information.

Review
Discovery learning

Piaget claims that cognitive development, learning, and intelligence are all closely related. When we are young they will be affected by how we act on, and with, objects and people around us. Children below about 10 years learn best when they learn for themselves. When they are cognitively ready they will start to learn about things like time, space, number, length, mass and volume. Discovery learning suggests that teachers employ the 'readiness approach' to help children pass through the various stages of cognitive development.

The readiness approach

Daljit was six and a half years old when she asked her teacher, 'When is Christmas?' It was October, so the teacher explained that it was in eight weeks' time. Daljit thought for a moment and said 'there are seven days in a week.' Her teacher said there were, and asked the girl when a day started. Daljit replied, 'when I get up.' During the next week Daljit asked several questions about time. She wondered why we start school at nine o'clock. She knew why we went home at three, it was to have something to eat! She asked why her teacher looked at her watch. Daljit's teacher started to bring the large cardboard clock out of the cupboard and put it near to Daljit. Daljit seemed interested in numbers, and in time. Daljit's teacher started to show her how to tell the time.

1 The teacher's behaviour here is an example of the readiness approach. Explain what this means.

2 Why did Piaget think that it wouldn't be possible to teach a younger child how to tell the time?

3 Outline how discovery learning fits in with Piaget's views about cognitive development.

4 Outline the roles of the teacher and the child in discovery learning.

5 Give one example of how you could use discovery learning if you were helping at a junior school. Mention some of the materials you would use, and say what you think the child will learn from them.

6 Programmed learning

As we saw in Chapter Six, Skinner was not very interested in the possible existence of biological structures (in this case schemas). He didn't think scientific psychology should be too concerned with things which can't be shown to exist. His careful scientific measurement of how reinforcement and punishment can bring about learning was very different from Piaget's view. Skinner said that learning is the result of living in a particular environment and behaving in particular ways. Any behaviour which is reinforced will be repeated, behaviour which isn't reinforced will be extinguished. This is the principle on which the whole of operant conditioning is based.

Skinner showed that even quite complicated behaviour could be **shaped**. **Behaviour shaping** refers to the way in which behaviourists try to change certain behaviour. It was discussed in Chapter Seven. In school the thing to be learned is mainly the contents of our lessons. Maths, English, history, geography, and the other lessons, all consist of information that children need to know. Skinner developed a method which would present the information which had to be learned in each lesson, give the children a chance to learn it, test their knowledge, and offer a reinforcement for a correct answer. This has become known as **programmed learning** and many attempts were made to use it during the 1950s and 1960s.

Programmed learning involves individual learners, either with their own text, worksheets, teaching machines, or with their own computer terminal or similar machine. Several different types of program have been developed but they all follow much the same general procedure.

The topic to be learned is stated, and all the items which are relevant to it are broken down into their smallest parts. Each part is arranged logically in order, usually in a series of frames. The learner

Do you think there are some things which may be very difficult to study scientifically? For example, do you think scientific psychologists could study love?

reads each frame in turn. At the end of each one there will be some question to answer, or perhaps some problem to solve. When the information on the frame is learned, and the correct response is given, the learner will be given immediate feedback, stating if the given answers are right or wrong. Skinner said that telling learners that they have the right answers is the positive reinforcement which will encourage them to try to answer the next frames correctly. The frames form a logical sequence and when each has been mastered, so the overall lesson will have been learned.

Skinner's original version was the linear program. A fairly small amount of information was given, and was followed by a question that would be almost impossible to answer incorrectly. The correct answer was given immediately after the response anyway. Skinner thought it was important that the children should make as few errors as possible because an error might accidently become reinforced and learned. The reinforcement would be the children's success in operating the machines, and knowledge of their results as they followed the lesson, although the occasional 'well done' could appear after the answer. If the learners achieved about 80 per cent or more correct answers they would be allowed to go on to the next lesson. If they achieved less than this, then they would have to go through the present one again. The reason for this is that each lesson to be learned depends to some extent on knowing the previous lesson. Those who score less than about 80 per cent probably won't know the information well enough for them to be able to base the next learning required by the next frame on it.

Programmed learning 1

The Linear Program
FRAME 12
The most powerful way to reinforce a learner is after every correct response. This is called 'continuous reinforcement'.

   Reinforcing a learner after every correct response is called

_____ .

continuous reinforcement – If this is what you wrote, well done.

FRAME 13
However it isn't necessary to reinforce continuously. We could use a schedule of reinforcement whereby all children are reinforced sometimes when they give the correct answer.

   A 'schedule of reinforcement' is when all children are reinforced _____ when they give the correct answer.

   sometimes

FRAME 14
A positive reinforcer will be anything the learner finds pleasing. Just knowing that the correct response has been given may be sufficient positive reinforcement. This is especially true with older learners.

   Anything the learner finds pleasing will be a _____
   positive reinforcer

The small amount of information that Skinner's frames gave, and the type of questions asked, didn't really let students think about what they were learning. They just responded, rather like a robot. Many subjects at school require students to think, and to use their knowledge. They must apply the principles which they have learned for one situation to any other which is similar to it. Learning is more to do with application of principles than regurgitating knowledge.

A development of Skinner's linear program was made by **Crowder** to overcome this criticism. It was called the *intrinsic* or *branching* program. This is more complex, but also more flexible, and resembles more closely how a real teacher behaves. The learner is given a fair amount of information in the frame. Where Skinner gave learners a couple of sentences, Crowder gave them a paragraph or two. They were then asked a question and given a number of possible answers from which to select the correct one. This is more like a multiple choice exercise. Unlike Skinner, Crowder allows for the possibility that students will make some mistakes. When learners make a mistake they will receive more information which should help them make the correct choice.

Programmed learning 2

The Branching Program

FRAME 27 (the question)
The most powerful way to reinforce a learner is after every correct response. This is called 'continuous reinforcement'. Do you think that teachers continuously reinforce every correct response in every child?

   YOUR ANSWER _____

FRAME 27 (the response) Very unlikely indeed.
If you said something similar to 'very unlikely', go on to **FRAME 28**.
Otherwise go to **FRAME 99**.

FRAME 99
If you thought it might be possible to reinforce every correct response you may have been thinking that there was only one child per teacher. In most classrooms there are many children, and teachers can't pay equal attention to all of them all the time. Go back to **FRAME 27** and try again.

FRAME 28 (the question)
Positive reinforcement will be anything the learner finds pleasing. Just knowing that the correct response has been given may be sufficient positive reinforcement. This is especially true with older learners. Children may need something more concrete, such as sweets or stars.
Which of the following would be positively reinforcing for a 10-year-old:
(a) a sweet, (b) a gold star, (c) being smacked, (d) being made to stand in the corner.
   YOUR ANSWER _____

FRAME 28 (the response) (a) and (b) are the most likely to reinforce 10-year-olds.
If you agree, go on to **FRAME 29**.
Otherwise go to **FRAME 100**.

FRAME 100
If we punish a 10-year-old we are showing the child that we disapprove of whatever she or he was doing, but it doesn't provide any positive information about what the child should do. Positive reinforcement should increase the likelihood of something happening, not decrease the likelihood of something else happening. Go to **FRAME 28**

Many criticisms have been made of the branching program. Most are the same as would be made of any multiple choice test, i.e. they encourage guessing rather than trying to work out the right answer. Very little of real life consists of multiple choice situations, so to use this as a learning device is a long way removed from reality. It reduces the activity of the student, leaving her or him rather passively awaiting information, rather than, as Piaget insists, taking an active part in learning. This leads to a general criticism of programmed learning. It doesn't explain how children *learn* at all. It explains how they may be *taught*. All it says about learning is that it is a change in behaviour that comes about through some previously reinforced response. Some critics argue that this claim is simply untrue.

A comparison of linear and branching programs

	Linear program	Branching program
Theorist who developed the approach	Skinner	Crowder
Amount of information in each frame	little information in short frames	fair amount – quite long frames
Any extra information?	not available	plenty available
How difficult to complete	easy	rather harder
Likelihood of giving wrong answer	unlikely	much easier to go wrong

There are other variations on the linear and branching programs.

Comments on Programmed Learning

Advantages

1 Both the teacher and the learner know exactly what is expected from the lesson. It has been carefully planned and the objectives to be achieved are clearly stated.

2 The learner learns through doing, i.e. she or he takes an active part in problem solving and achieving the set goals. We usually learn best when we actually have to do something, rather than just hearing someone else telling us about it.

3 The learner can proceed at his or her own pace. Some people naturally work faster than others. Some people will absorb some things quickly and other things less quickly.

Disadvantages

1 Programmed learning isn't of much use for teaching subjects like art or music appreciation, literature, or anything which involves essay writing, i.e. where the learners have to think for themselves. Therefore it tends to be used in remedial teaching, and lower-school teaching. The GCSE tests what you can do, and what you understand, not just what you know. Programmed learning isn't very useful for teaching these skills.

2 Not all subjects can be learned through doing. Programmed learning only puts across the specific subject that the program is about. It can't broaden experience as classroom teachers can.

3 Computers, language laboratories, and teaching machines can be very expensive to buy, maintain, and run. The programs take a great deal of time and effort to prepare. They must be thoroughly checked, and this can make them very expensive. Having different children at different stages in their learning can be wasteful of the resources.

4 The teacher can monitor each individual learner's progress. If someone runs into problems in understanding a particular frame or topic, the teacher will be there to explain it to the individual. One-to-one teaching is often more effective than group teaching because the teacher can respond specifically to the particular, individual problems.

4 Teachers can't watch all the children at once. Those children who have finished and are waiting for the teacher could become bored and tire of the teaching machine, the subject, and even school itself.

5 Programmed learning can be useful for those subjects which can be broken down into small elements that could fit into a frame. The basics of foreign languages, for example, can be taught in this way. Larger schools and colleges have their own language laboratory where this sort of thing goes on. Simple mathematics can also be taught in small steps that fit into frames. Some basic remedial teaching of reading has also used programmed instructions.

5 The program is fixed and inflexible. It can't be changed or modified in any way. If the learner doesn't understand something the program can't offer other examples in the way that human teachers can. This is particularly important in remedial teaching.

Two ways of teaching maths

Two parallel classes in a large school were chosen to take part in research into various ways of teaching maths. It was judged that both classes contained children of equal ability. One class was taught in the usual way, with teachers explaining, and getting children to do examples, and correcting any mistakes as they occurred. They were called the *traditional group*. The other group learned from a computer program that had been written specifically for teaching maths at this level. They were called the *programmed group*. At the end of the course the two groups were tested to see how well they had understood the topic. Here are the percentage raw scores for each group:

Traditional group: 67, 49, 45, 72, 39, 76, 51, 34, 82, 43, 62, 84

Programmed group: 65, 71, 77, 56, 44, 56, 88, 72, 66, 71, 72, 84

1 Why was it necessary that each class should contain children of equal ability?

2 Find the mean score of the two groups and state which of the two teaching styles appears to have been most successful.

3 Describe what is meant by programmed learning.

4 What theory is it based on?

5 Discuss the strengths and weaknesses of programmed learning.

6 How might programmed learning be used in a classroom to teach reading or mathematics?

How do discovery learning and programmed learning compare?

Both Skinner and Crowder's approaches are radically different from Piaget's. Piaget's cognitive development theory aims at explaining the stages of development that children's abilities for mental processing pass through. Hence sensory-motor stage children can only think in certain ways, pre-operational children can only manage certain ideas, etc. Skinner's behaviourism argues that children are basically little adults, and the reason why they aren't able to understand certain things, like conversation, is that they haven't learned enough about those things yet. Piaget claims they will find things out for themselves when they are ready. Skinner's approach suggests that children will generally learn things, if reinforced in some way for doing so. Piaget's approach has been thought to be more relevant to primary school children, Skinner's has been applied more in the secondary school. If Piaget is right then learning in childhood will happen when the child is ready, willing, and able to learn. If Skinner is right then children will learn something when they are taught it. Now that every primary school has access to at least one computer, and some good educational software is being produced, perhaps younger children may benefit from some kind of programmed learning.

A Summary of the main differences between discovery and programmed learning

Discovery learning

1 Piaget believed that children find out for themselves.

2 Piaget's approach seems more appropriate to the nursery school. Teachers should provide a safe, stimulating environment for children to learn in.

Programmed learning

1 Supporters of programmed learning expect children to sit in front of machines and receive knowledge.

2 Programmed learning seems more applicable to the secondary school.

Review

Programmed learning

Skinner showed that animals would learn fairly complicated behaviour if the task could be broken down into its smallest parts, which were arranged in order, and if each successive part of the skill is reinforced as it is learned. He applied the same principles to children's learning in school. A frame of information could be, for example, a simple question. A correct answer to the question would prompt immediate feedback and immediate reinforcement.

3 Teaching should be relaxed, informal, and encouraging.

4 Piaget believed children will motivate themselves to learn since they are naturally curious.

5 Children will learn when they are ready and able to do so.

3 Teachers should provide the programs and monitor the progress.

4 Teaching must get across a fixed set of knowledge.

5 Skinner and Crowder believe all learning needs some kind of reinforcement, such as knowledge of progress.

Children will·learn what the program reinforces them for learning.

The Nature of Intelligence

In Chapter Eight we saw that Piaget argued that we acquire our knowledge through interacting with our environment. However this doesn't mean that if everyone had the same environment they would end up with the same knowledge. Some people are more likely to learn more things, and learn them more quickly, from the same environment, than others. Take two four-year-olds in the playgroup. Rachel is curious and interested in the sand and water, in the dolls and skipping ropes, and in the puzzles and books, and becomes involved with them and uses them inventively. Mary is more likely to be found banging a drum, on the rocking horse, or messing around with the paints. It seems that the activities Rachel chooses are more likely to encourage imagination and intellect than Mary's choices. Even if both girls played with the same things, they could still benefit in different ways. If Rachel benefits more, could we describe her as being 'more intelligent' than Mary?

In this chapter we will be looking at early and modern ideas about intelligence and intelligence testing.

1 'What is intelligence?' and 'What is intelligence testing?'
2 How have intelligence testing and IQ developed?
3 What are the differences in 'intelligence' between boys and girls?
4 How are intelligence tests used in school, and what are their limitations?
5 How does the nature–nurture debate apply to intelligence?

1 Defining intelligence

Intelligence has been one of the most thoroughly researched areas in psychology during the last 100 years, but we still can neither define it precisely nor measure it accurately. To put it simply, intelligence is that marvellous skill that humans (and, to lesser extents, some other animals) use to allow them to *adapt to their environment*, and *adapt their environment to them*. When humans first covered themselves with animal skins to keep warm in the cold climate, they were adapting themselves to their environment. When they first planted seeds for food crops, instead of relying on food they had hunted or gathered, they were adapting their environment to themselves.

Review
What is intelligence?

It is almost impossible to give a simple definition of intelligence because it consists of so many different skills. However, a stimulating environment seems to be involved in developing it.

Defining intelligence

1 Write what you think the definition of intelligence is, if possible compare it to someone else's definition.

2 Look 'intelligence' up in a dictionary and see how close your definition came.

3 If you have more than one dictionary look it up in the others and see if each definition (a) has something in common with the others, and (b) has things which others don't.

There has always been disagreement among psychologists about precisely what intelligence is, where it comes from, and if it can (and should) be measured. The *Penguin Dictionary of Psychology* concludes that 'intelligence will be what it has always been, "the ability to profit from experience", and . . . what it has become, "that which intelligence tests measure".'

Developing intelligence

Explain, with examples, what is meant by this quote from the Comment box below, *Some factors in developing intelligence.* 'Another important factor (in developing intelligence) will be the parent–child relationship, for example, how much each parent talks to the child, how much interest generally the parents take in the child.'

Comment box – Some factors in developing intelligence

1 One important factor is the ability to use language. Children can interpret and react to their world much more quickly and effectively when they can ask questions, understand answers, and obey instructions or advice. Someone telling a child, 'don't go near the fire' and explaining why not, is better for learning than trial and error! From language comes one of the major sources of our superiority over other animals: our ability to reason.

2 Ideally we need well-developed sense organs to provide a variety of information. Serious defects in one sense can be overcome (e.g. what a blind person cannot take in through sight may be compensated for by taking information in through well-developed hearing and sensitive touch). Serious defects in two or three senses may limit intellectual potential.

3 A healthy nervous system and the ability to control our muscles and limbs may help us explore our environment, and this may contribute to intellectual development. A fully functioning body isn't essential at all, however. Many highly intellectual people are physically handicapped in some way, including some eminent writers and academics.

4 Intellectual development may also depend on the richness of the learning environment – i.e. the opportunities available at home and school for stimulation from things like educational toys, materials like paint and plasticine to manipulate and experiment with, exciting and enthusiastic schools, good books, and so on. Evidence suggests that children who do not have these things may not develop intellectually as well as others.

5 Another important factor will be the parent–child relationship, for example, how much each parent talks to the child, how much interest generally the parents take in the child.

2 Intelligence testing

How can we measure intellectual development? The area of psychology which deals with the testing of human abilities is called **psychometrics**. We must say, straight away, that some psychologists do not believe that trying to 'test' someone's intelligence is worthwhile. Piaget, for example, totally rejected the idea of 'intelligence testing' since he did not believe that 'intelligence' is a 'thing' which can be tested and measured.

Many modern psychologists are suspicious of intelligence tests, since they do not believe that intelligence is a thing which can be measured.

How does intelligence develop?

So far we've mentioned several factors which are involved in intelligence. Write down as many as you can. Look back if you can't remember them all.

Intelligence tests involve someone sitting down for some time working through a series of questions. They need subjects who can stay alert for some time, who understand language, can read and write, and who can follow instructions. Babies and young children can't do these things, and so aren't given intelligence tests as such. Instead their progress is measured on what are called **developmental scales**.

Developmental scales

These are a range of tests and procedures which try to measure the progress of infants and pre-school children towards passing certain developmental milestones. They involve getting children to do something and rating their performance, or getting them to talk and answer questions, and measuring their verbal skills. For example, as a six-month-old infant can sit up without support, any six-month-old who can't do this will be 'behind'. The score a child makes on a developmental scale is called a **development quotient**, or **DQ**.

Developmental scales are used to judge a child's progress in acquiring physical, social, and intellectual skills.

Some examples of developmental scales

1 The Gesell Developmental Scales
This was the first organised attempt to describe children's performance in the areas of motor skills, adaptive behaviour (i.e. coordination, alertness, problem solving), language development, and personal-social development. During the 1920s and 1930s **Arnold Gesell** and his colleagues observed hundreds of children in order to establish **age norms** of what average children were achieving at given ages. There are two sets of scales, one for infants, another for pre-school children. Gesell's scales are simple descriptions and do not allow us to make predictions. Nor do they suggest anything about the origin of intelligence or the factors which affect it.

2 The Bayley Scales of Infant Development

Nancy Bayley's scales are probably the most widely used now, particularly in America. They consist of three types of test aimed at measuring infants from two months to 30 months of age.

(a) There is a **mental scale** which measures things like aspects of perception, learning ability, following direction, searching for a missing toy, memory, and simple problem solving.

(b) The **motor scale** measures coordination skills such as are used in sitting, walking, manipulating objects, throwing a ball or climbing stairs.

(c) The **infant behaviour record** rates social and personality development, persistence, attention span, etc.

3 McCarthy Scales of Children's Abilities

These are aimed at children between two-and-a-half and eight-and-a-half years old. There are 18 tests which rate children on scales for verbal skills, perceptual skills, mathematical skills, memory skills, and general cognitive skills. Cognitive skills are usually taken as a measure of intellectual development.

4 Wechsler Scales

David Wechsler has devised a whole series of intelligence tests which are very widely used today. The Wechsler Adult Intelligence Scale (WAIS) was modified for use with six- to 16-year-olds as the **Wechsler Intelligence Scale for Children (WISC)**. The **Wechsler Preschool and Primary Scale of Intelligence (WPPSI)** is for children below six years. The Wechsler Scales give two scores, one for **verbal ability** and the other for **non-verbal performance**, and they do correlate positively with educational performance generally.

Evaluation of developmental scales

Correlation is a way of assessing whether changes in one thing occur at the same time or same rate as changes in another. A positive correlation would mean they do. Generally, children with high or low DQs do not go on to have similarly high or low IQ scores.

There isn't a very positive correlation between children's scores on many developmental scales (their DQ), and their scores on intelligence tests, or their achievements at school, or any other way of measuring their intellectual skills. This has led to considerable criticism of the usefulness of developmental scales. However, yet again, this illustrates the problem of drawing conclusions from correlations. The reason why the correlation isn't strong is probably because developmental scales and intelligence tests aren't measuring the same sorts of abilities. Developmental scales for infants and children measure motor skills, memory, perception, social and personal development, etc. Intelligence tests try to measure more abstract things like verbal reasoning, seeing relationships in time and space, choosing and applying appropriate principles to solving abstract problems, etc. We shouldn't necessarily expect there to be any correlation between them.

Developmental scales are useful for diagnosing any particular areas of difficulty a child is having at the time, rather than any kind of prediction for future intelligence. Developmental problems, such as backwardness in motor development or difficulties with perception or with the manipulation of objects, may be caused by physical, neurological problems which will need to be dealt with by doctors or therapists. Further, children do not develop at the same rate. A child might be advanced in motor skills, but be retarded in language skills. Some of the tests on the Bayley Scales have been found to be accurate predictors of future language performance.

Administering developmental scales is expensive because they take time and skill to do. Therefore only children who are thought to have something wrong with them are given the tests. Many American and British institutions which deal with children have some screening procedures which may be administered by nursing staff.

Review

Developmental scales

Intelligence tests are used on those children who are old enough to understand what is expected of them by the test. Developmental scales are used with younger children to judge whether certain aspects of their development are proceeding normally. They can provide useful indicators of any areas in which children are not making good progress.

Developmental scales

1 What's the difference between positive correlation and negative correlation?

2 What are developmental scales used for, and why?

3 Say, in your own words, why scores gained on developmental scales may not be good predictors of scores on intelligence tests.

Intelligence tests

The term intelligence test is really very misleading since intelligence is not one single thing which can be measured. Instead, an intelligence test is simply a test of a sample of abilities. Many tests exist. Some are individual tests (where one person is tested by one tester). Others are group tests (where larger numbers of people can all be tested by one tester at the same time). Which type to use depends largely on what the results are to be used for. To survey the progress of all children in a class requires one kind, to evaluate the extent of brain damage in a particular patient requires another.

The first intelligence test was designed by **Alfred Binet** in Paris in 1905. The French government had asked Binet to devise a way to identify below-average ability French school children. It was thought that having low-ability children in a class might hold the average and bright children back. These below-average children could be sent to special schools.

Binet believed that mental ability matured as the body matured, so he spent many hours conducting naturalistic observation and experimentation to find out what children of various age groups could do. He produced a long list of skills which most five-year-olds had mastered, another list of the typical abilities of six-year-olds, another for seven-year-olds, etc. These skills included things like reasoning and deduction. Binet's tests do not attempt to measure the whole of a child's intelligence, just some aspects of it. Binet never claimed that

The first intelligence test was used to measure French schoolchildren, but was developed for use elsewhere.

his test could assess general intelligence, or that they could be used as general tests for all children. They were simply a practical way of discovering children who had some learning problems in some particular skills such as arithmetic, or language.

Other researchers either overlooked these reservations, or tried to overcome them. Binet's original test was modified at Stanford University in America for use with American school children. The Stanford Binet test gave an individual score for each child. It soon became popular and has been revised many times since it was invented and is still used today. It consists of a series of subtests which are arranged from easiest (for youngest children) to hardest (for older children). There are subtests for every half-year from two to five-and-a-half, then for each year from six to 14, and then there are four adult levels. The idea is that an average person of a given age could pass all the tests for those younger and the same age, but none of the tests for someone older. For example, an average 13-year-old could pass all the tests which are meant for 12- and 13-year-olds, but could not pass any of the tests for 14-year-olds.

Of course some children would be able to pass some of the older children's tests, while others couldn't pass all of the tests for their own age group. Binet used a simple formula to give each child a score. He distinguished **chronological age (CA)**, which is actual age in years and months, from **mental age (MA)**, which is worked out from the number of correct answers given to the subtests.

Intelligence tests often assess someone's mental age (or MA). This is compared to their actual, or chronological age (or CA).

Example 1: If a five-year-old girl (CA = 5) could do all the tests of a typical five-year-old, she would have an MA of 5. This would make her perfectly average. If she could do all the tests of a five-year-old, and all those for a five-and-a-half-year-old as well, she would have an MA of 5.5. She would be well above average.

Intelligence and IQ

A German psychologist called William Stern invented the concept of the **intelligence quotient (IQ)**. He found that dividing one's actual age into one's mental age would give a figure which could be used to express one's intelligence. So the formula mental age/chronological age $\times$ 100 = IQ was invented.

Example 2: Someone who was four years old, but had a mental age of four and a half would have an IQ worked out as 4.5 (MA)/4 (CA) = 1.125. However, 1.125 isn't a very attractive way of communicating a measurement of someone's intelligence, so two further steps were taken. The number could be expressed more simply by rounding it to two decimal places, for example 1.13, and it would look much neater if we lost the decimal point, so Stern multiplied it by 100. This produced an IQ of 113. Stern expressed Binet's findings as the formula MA/CA $\times$ 100 = IQ.

Review
The Intelligence Quotient

Someone's IQ is discovered by dividing their mental age by their age in years and months, rounding it to two decimal places, and multiplying it by 100. It is expressed by the formula IQ=MA/CA $\times$ 100.

Example 3: A 17-year-old who can answer all the tests for someone of 17, but none of the tests for anyone over 17 will have an IQ of 17/17 × 100 = 100. The average IQ score is 100.

Example 4: A child of five with a mental age of 5.5 would have an IQ of 5.5/5 × 100 = 110.

Recent evidence suggests that the average IQ has increased since Binet's time, by about 13 points. As people's diet, housing, and experience of life has improved, so has the average IQ.

IQ

1 What is the difference between mental age and chronological age?

2 Briefly describe how an IQ score is calculated.

3 What would be the IQ for a seven-year-old who could do the tests for six-year-olds, but none of the tests for older children?

4 Find the IQ for a six-year-old who can do all the tests for a six-year-olds and below but no others.

5 What is the IQ of a four-year-old who could do all the tests for a five-year-old?

These IQ scores do not show the amount of anything which someone has. Someone with an IQ of 125 doesn't have 125 units of intelligence. They are simply a way of indicating someone's average stage of mental development, as measured by the particular test.

The normal distribution

If we were to take a massive population – for example, the 1,000 million people who live in India – and we measured how tall every one of them was, we'd find that a few are very short, and about the same number are extremely tall. Some would be smallish, and about the same amount would be tall. The vast majority would, of course, be of average height. There is a statistical device called **the curve of normal distribution** which allows us to predict more or less what percentage of the population will be of any particular height. Binet assumed that there would be roughly equal numbers of very intelligent people and very dull people, the same number of fairly bright and fairly dull people. He thought intelligence would also follow the curve of normal distribution.

Normal distribution

Look at the background reading on page 204 and then answer these questions.

1 What percentage of people would have IQ scores within 15 points either way of the average score?

2 How might the government benefit from being able to predict how many children are likely to be educationally subnormal, or extremely intelligent?

Background reading – The normal distribution for IQ scores

If we plotted the normal distribution curve on a graph it would look something like this diagram. This is called the bell-shaped curve or the **curve of normal distribution.**

If we could apply the curve of normal distribution to intelligence, then 68 per cent of people would score in the IQ range of 85 to 115; 95 per cent of people score between 70 and 130; 99.7 per cent fall between 55 and 145, whilst only 0.3 per cent would have IQ scores at the two extremes. To put it another way, three children in every 2000 would have IQs below 55, and another three would be geniuses with IQs over 145.

However, the idea of normal distribution is only a statistical model. It is unlikely to exist with such accuracy in real life.

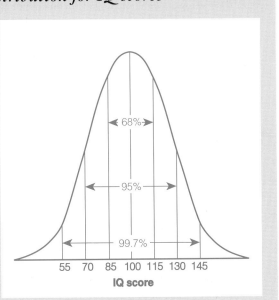

3 Gender and IQ scores

Children's IQ scores and their progress in school are positively correlated. However, being very intelligent is not the only explanation for why some children achieve more than others. Another explanation is that some children are well motivated and others are given low expectation of achieving much. An intelligent child who does not expect to do well in school may actually achieve less than a child who isn't as bright, but who believes she or he can do well. Some research indicates that, as children pass through their schooling, girls increasingly underestimate their abilities, and boys increasingly overestimate theirs.

Although there are no differences in the average IQ score for boys and girls, there are some slight differences in particular skills. None of the differences is very marked, and there are many exceptions to them. Some do not appear until the teenage years. Up to about the age of six girls are slightly ahead in basic arithmetic, although boys take over some time after that age. Girls develop language skills slightly ahead of boys, on average, and stay slightly ahead. By the time they reach adolescence boys are slightly better at artistic abilities, such as thinking about abstract shapes, whereas girls are slightly better at verbal reasoning, such as solving word puzzles. There are two possible reasons for these slight differences.

First, it is possible that there are differences in the ways in which boys' and girls' brains are organised. This reflects the nature side of the nature–nurture debate. The language centres may be slightly

There are slight differences in the skills which boys and girls score more on. The differences are not great. The explanation for why boys and girls achieve differently may be because parents expect them to be good at different things.

more efficiently organised in females, whereas the parts of the brain concerned with processing numbers may be better in boys. This explanation seems fairly unlikely however, because the overall differences are small, and there is tremendous variation between individuals.

Second, boys may be socialised into thinking in terms of science, mechanics, and things which involve numbers. This reflects the nurture view. Girls may be encouraged to be more talkative, more sociable and cooperative, and generally to use language more.

The importance of parental expectations and roles on children's achievement has been studied by **Jacquelynne Parsons**. Parsons asked some American parents of secondary-school-age children for their attitudes to various school subjects. Most of the parents said that they thought maths and science subjects were more important for boys than for girls. They also said that they thought that maths was easier and more enjoyable for boys than for girls. Parsons found that the children's expectations of their abilities were in line with their parents' expectations. Girls who had similar abilities and scores in maths compared with boys, said that they didn't think they had the same potential or aptitude for the subject as the boys claimed they had. When girls did well at maths their parents said that it was because they had worked very hard at maths. When boys did well their parents said that they had ability. Such attitudes were bound to influence the children's perceptions of their ability.

Review
Gender differences in intelligence

There are very small differences in some intellectual skills between boys and girls. If an intelligence test is being given which has items which emphasise a skill that one sex has more than the other, then it may be necessary to have slightly different marking systems for each sex's scores. Parsons suggests that parental influences affect children's performance and that boys are encouraged to do well in those subjects which will be better rewarded.

4 Intelligence tests in school

Binet's original instructions were to design a test that would sort children into the most appropriate school for them. IQ tests are still used for this purpose today, particularly in America. Before school starts children may be given some kind of diagnostic test if there are any doubts about their ability. IQ tests may be given to school children who seem to be too intelligent for the work that their peers are doing, or to those who can't keep up for some reason. In either case children's score may be one of (many) factors which are considered when deciding whether they should be moved to another class or another school. In Britain's comprehensive school system we tend to use tests only for diagnostic purposes.

The value of intelligence testing

What do IQ tests measure?
We've said that it is extremely difficult to define intelligence so psychologists often assume that it means 'that which intelligence tests measure', e.g. logical problem solving, numerical ability, verbal reasoning, ability to understand time and space, etc. Many psychologists now prefer the term 'intelligent behaviour'. At least this can be measured to some extent.

Intelligence tests do not measure the whole range of abilities that people have – merely a sample of them. Here are a few examples of some of the skills which modern IQ tests do measure. (The answers are at the end of this chapter.)

1 Seeing relationships between series of things: for example, what is the next letter in the sequence A D G J, or in the sequence Q P M L I?

2 Seeing what pairs of words have in common: for example, *wood* and *coal*, *apple* and *peach*, *ship* and *car*.

3 Unscrambling sentences: for example 'school back we Monday it's so go tomorrow to'.

4 Vocabulary: for example find a word which means the same as stake and mail.

5 Which is the odd one out: tootap, prinut, tintek, otrrac?

6 Unscrambling words. Which of these towns is not in England? grothnib, yuqtora, drifcaf, hercest, sheeldiff?

Other skills which are tested include memory span, number ability, copying shapes, finishing sentences, pointing out illogicalities, following a maze, doing a jigsaw, assembling coloured blocks in a particular pattern, etc.

It is important to remember, however, that all that IQ tests really measure is our ability to deal with items in the particular test.

Are intelligence tests accurate?

To be accepted as accurate IQ tests must be **standardised measures of psychological functioning**. This rather grand phrase means that each item on the test has been given to many hundreds of people (called the **standardisation sample**), who have been chosen to form a representative cross-section of the population (men, women, white, non-white, rich, poor, old, middle-aged, and young). If the standardisation procedure is accurate, then an average person of any given age should make an average IQ score of 100. (Or perhaps 113 now.)

IQ tests must be **reliable**, and **valid** (see Chapter Seventeen for definitions and explanations of these terms), and questions must be clear and easy to understand so that there's no confusion amongst the people taking the test as to what they mean.

Regrettably some tests fail in one or more of these areas, and none is completely accurate. They give an indication of a general level of ability.

What are the main criticisms of IQ tests?

1 To use an intelligence test assumes that there are some particular abilities which make up intelligence, and which we know about and can measure. Not everyone agrees.

2 According to Binet, children's intelligence is fixed at birth and intelligence would be distributed normally throughout the population. Many psychologists dispute both assumptions.

3 IQ tests do not measure all the skills we may have. One child may be especially good at verbal reasoning and vocabulary, and less good at numeracy (ability with numbers). Another may have good numeracy, but not be so good with language. If the test has lots of questions which involve verbal reasoning then the first child will have an

advantage. To give one IQ score is, therefore, misleading. (Many autistic people have some exceptional abilities – for example in painting and music.) The belief that intelligence consists of many abilities has led psychologists to devise many tests of specific ability, such as aptitude tests for things like mechanical ability and musical capabilities.

4 IQ does not remain constant over time. The reasons for this are that our abilities vary according to the environment we grow up in, and an individual would take different tests which measure different skills. There is no reason to imagine that your average score for one set of skills when you are six years old should be the same as your score for some different skills when you are 20 years old.

5 If intelligence were something we were born with, which couldn't change, and if IQ tests were accurate, then it wouldn't be possible to be trained to pass an IQ test (e.g. the old 11-plus exam, which was used to help decide whether children should go to grammar schools or secondary moderns). Many primary school children were taught how to tackle the 11-plus. IQ tests try to measure some of the skills someone has, but don't indicate anything about where such skills come from.

6 The relationship between the examiner and the child might well affect the child's performance. The examiner may not always appear to be friendly and sensitive to the child.

7 The mood the child is in, whether or not it feels that it wants to cooperate, etc., can be particularly important with younger children. Just because a child doesn't do something correctly in an artificial test, it doesn't mean she or he can't do it correctly.

8 IQ tests do not always work satisfactorily with people from different cultures. Different people speak different languages, have different norms and values, have different early experiences, and have different expectations. The tests may be biased in favour of children who have the same sorts of background as the people who set the test. In Europe and America this tends to be white, middle-class people.

9 IQ tests are not accurate!

Review
Evaluation of intelligence testing

At best IQ tests can only measure a range of abilities. At worst all they may measure is how good someone is at doing IQ tests! They are sometimes unreliable measures too. Many factors can influence a child's performance on an IQ test, quite apart from his or her intelligence. They are still sometimes useful for measuring general ability or for showing up areas of particular need. However they do also run the risk of having someone labelled as intelligent, or below average, etc., and such labels may be hard to break away from.

Evaluation of intelligence testing

1 What is an IQ test?

2 What do IQ tests measure?

3 When applied to intelligence testing, what do the terms 'reliability', 'validity', and 'standardisation' mean?

4 Outline the main uses of IQ tests in schools.

5 Outline the argument against the use of IQ tests in schools.

6 Suggest two possible explanations why girls tend to do slightly better than boys on tests of verbal fluency.

The nature side of the nature–nurture debate claims that intelligence is genetically inherited. The nurture side claims it is largely the result of the amount of stimulation in the environment in which someone grows up.

5 Is intelligence genetically inherited or acquired socially?

Although we can't measure intelligence very accurately, no one would deny that some children seem more able to do certain things than others. We've all heard people say that one child seems very bright while another is rather slow. An important question is: how do these differences between children happen? There are two obvious possibilities. Intelligence could be acquired genetically, and therefore would be fixed at birth. If so, there's nothing much we can do to alter it. Alternatively, it could be acquired socially. If so, then changing the amount of stimulation children have would alter their intellectual abilities.

Nature–nurture

Some psychologists, who believe that intelligence is socially acquired, are asked to advise a school for children with IQs of less than 70. Many of the children there have learning difficulties with basic skills like simple arithmetic.

1 What is the average IQ score?

2 What sort of recommendations might the psychologists make in this situation?

We will review the arguments for the nature and nurture cases here.

The case for heredity

Heredity refers to the passing of genetic material from parents to children.

This argument can be traced back to Charles Darwin. Darwin was a famous nineteenth-century biologist who found a mass of evidence to support his view that all species living on the earth, including human beings, would have to evolve in order to survive. Those species which could not evolve would die out. He thought that most of the differences between most members of a species were the result of differences in their genotypes, and this would include the differences in intelligence between people. Here is some of the evidence for the case for heredity and nature.

1 Many human characteristics are fixed at conception

At conception in humans a male sperm fertilises a female ovum. The resulting egg contains 23 chromosomes from the sperm, and 23 chromosomes from the ovum. Each chromosome consists of thousands of genes, each of which carries some information about how parts of the body will be formed. There are genes for the colour of our eyes, hair, and skin, for our sex, eventual height, shape, and for what we will look like. The mix of the parents' genes determines a number of things about the individual, long before it is born. Intelligence may be one of the things determined by our genes. During pregnancy, however, some things could happen to the mother which might also affect the child's intelligence. For example, taking certain drugs, suffering from particular diseases, or having some kinds of accident, could all affect how the foetus develops.

2 Selective breeding

Racehorse breeders try to put their best mares and stallions together so that their foals might inherit their parents' speed. Most animal breeders try to mate their adult animals so that their offspring will possess the characteristics which the breeders want to emphasise. We hear people say that a child has her mother's eyes or his father's chin. But these are physical characteristics. Can we breed other characteristics selectively too? Can we breed intelligent animals to see if their offspring are more intelligent?

Intelligence may be one of the human characteristics which we acquire as a result of genetic transmission from our parents. It may develop as the foetus develops. A foetus is a developing baby between the third month of pregnancy and birth.

In the late 1950s two researchers called **Cooper** and **Zubeck** took a sample of rats, and put each in turn into a maze. They counted the number of mistakes each made, and timed how long it took them to complete the maze. Those who made the fewest mistakes were called the 'maze bright' group, and were only allowed to breed with each other. Those rats who made most mistakes were called the 'maze dull' group, and they were only allowed to breed with each other. After a few generations the descendants of the 'maze bright' group were much better at running mazes than their ancestors were. The descendants of the 'maze dull' group were much worse than their ancestors at running mazes. Different temperaments (fearfulness, aggression, sociability, etc.) have also been selectively bred in animals.

There are two problems in using selective breeding as evidence for the nature case. First, we can't really know what intelligence means in animals. It certainly can't be compared to human intelligence. Second, interbreeding in humans seems more likely to produce a child with some disability than to produce a genius.

3 Identical twin studies

For every 1000 babies born, about 12 will be twins. There are two types of twins, identical and fraternal. **Fraternal twins** occur when two male sperms fertilise two female ova at the same time. A fertilised cell is called a zygote, and fraternal twins are called **dizygotic twins (DZ** for short). Two babies develop in the womb. The only other thing they have in common is that they are born at about the same time. They are just like ordinary brothers and sisters. **Identical twins** occur when, for some unknown reason, the single zygote divides into two virtually identical halves. They each have the same chromosomes carrying the same genes. Because they come from a single zygote they are called **monozygotic twins (MZ** for short). MZ twins must have just about identical genotypes. If intelligence is the result of our genotypes, then MZ's must have just about identical intelligence.

It would obviously be immoral and probably impractical to breed human beings selectively. Selectively breeding physical characteristics like speed of running or the length of an animal's tail is not the same as trying to breed mental characteristics like intelligence.

Probably the best way to discover the effects of the environment, and of genetic inheritance, is to study the IQs of four groups of people. Two groups need the same heredity and different environments, the other two need the same environments and different heredity. If the IQs of the people who share the same environment are similar, then we could say that intelligence is largely determined by the environment. If those with identical heredities have similar IQs, then intelligence is mainly genetically acquired.

Genetic inheritance

1 What do MZ twins have in common?

2 What do DZ twins have in common?

3 To be absolutely sure of the influence of heredity and environment we would need the following four samples:

MZ twins		DZ twins	
Reared together	**Reared apart**	**Reared together**	**Reared apart**
same heredity,	same heredity,	same	different
same	different	environment,	environment,
environment	environments	different	different
		heredity	heredity

Explain why testing the IQs of these samples should help us to solve the 'nature–nurture' debate on intelligence.

It isn't difficult to find people who have grown up in the same environment. Most twins do, to a large extent. Finding people with identical genotypes (i.e. identical twins) isn't so easy. A small number of identical twins who have been brought up separately have been found. They have been studied in three main surveys. All three found a high correlation between each member of the pair of twins' IQ score. This supports the idea that intelligence is innate. We will return to this idea later.

Not everyone agrees that the similarities in monozygotic twins, whether reared separately or together, is evidence that intelligence is a result of heredity. **Leon Kamin** has summarised the evidence against this view. He says that probably the most widely quoted of the studies which found a high positive correlation between the IQs of MZs reared apart was conducted by Cyril Burt. Burt's work has been questioned, and although no proof exists that his research was flawed, he has been accused of inventing some of his data. Kamin suggests that we should ignore this study. He also claims that those who were separated were often reared in very similar homes, and treated in similar ways. They may have been reared separately, but they weren't reared differently. For example, two thirds of the twins in the Shields study were actually raised by the same family, one twin by its mother, the other by her mother, sister, etc. Most were treated similarly, attended the same school, and saw a great deal of each other.

If we found that monozygotic twins who were reared apart had similar IQs this might prove that intelligence is inherited. The studies that have been conducted on family members do find that identical twins, with similar genotypes, have similar IQ scores.

Another problem Kamin identified is with the nature of the IQ tests the twins were given. In each of the studies the twins were given different IQ tests, some of which were not properly standardised for the group taking the test. For example, most of the twins in Newman's study (1937) were female (as were the majority in each of the studies quoted). Newman used the Stanford Binet test (1916), which hadn't been properly standardised for adults, or for females.

A final problem concerns the unrepresentative nature of the twins studied. Most had answered advertisements in the media asking for twins who had been reared separately to contact the researchers. Each sample was therefore self-selected. Self-selected samples are unlikely to be typical.

Studies which have found that identical twins do have remarkably similar IQs are not scientifically acceptable. Their authenticity, validity, or use of statistics have all been found to be suspect.

The case for the environment

The case for the environment appears to be rather stronger than the case for genetics. Animals and children whose environments have been changed and whose IQ has changed, provide support for the argument that environment factors affect intelligence.

1 Impoverishment and enrichment studies

If intelligence is the result of the environment, then someone brought up in an **impoverished** (unstimulating) environment would not be capable of very intelligent behaviour. Enriching (improving) the environment should lead to an increase in their intellectual skills.

Although psychologists cannot deliberately impoverish children's environments (for the same reasons that we discussed earlier when looking at maternal privation), the same restrictions do not apply to animals. However there are some problems with applying findings from studies of animals to human intelligence. Here are two of the main problems. First, what exactly do we mean by intelligent behaviour in animals? Second, can we generalise from the behaviour of animals to the mental functioning of people?

It is possible to alter animals' behaviour by interfering with their environments. Giving them practice with some materials will improve their performance. But an animal's responses to some test situations does not tell us about the origins of human intelligence.

Impoverishment

Write a paragraph reviewing the main reasons why we cannot conduct research into the effects of privation and impoverishment on children.

Studying animals isn't really of much use in untangling the role of nature or nurture in intellectual development in humans without facing all sorts of practical, moral, and ethical problems. We can't deliberately manipulate children's environments. We could see if there are any differences in intelligence scores between children raised in deprived environments (e.g. children in orphanages where there are few facilities) with those in enriched environments (e.g.

children in orphanages where there are many facilities). This would be a natural experiment. If the average IQ score for children in well-staffed and well-equipped orphanages were greater than that of children in poor orphanages, then it may be that the environment affects the intellect.

This still wouldn't prove that environment has a greater effect on us than heredity, because we could not match the children in the different institutions for the key variables like age, intelligence, health, etc. If those children in the better-equipped orphanage did turn out to be more intelligent than the others, they might have been more intelligent to begin with. A number of such studies have been conducted however, all finding much the same results, that environment has a major effect on intellectual growth.

2 Orphanage studies

Until 1956, the adoption of foundlings (illegitimate children) or those whose mothers could not cope was not legal in the Lebanon. In 1955, just before adoption was legalised, **Wayne Dennis** measured the intelligence (DQ and IQ as appropriate) of a group of children in the deprived environment of a Lebanese orphanage. Their average score was 53. (NB   the 'average' DQ and IQ score is 100.) Dennis also measured the IQ of some teenagers who had been in the institution for some years, and found that they too had IQs well below average. An impoverished environment did correlate with poor intellectual and social development in the children, i.e. those children raised in the least well-equipped orphanages had the lowest DQs and IQs.

After 1956 many of the children were adopted, some by American couples. Fifteen years later Dennis traced and retested the children. Almost all the children showed an increase in their scores. Those who were the youngest when they were adopted showed the greatest increase. Dennis suggests that the Lebanese children who were adopted by two years of age caught up with normally reared children. If adopted after two years of age their intelligence stayed behind by the number of years spent in the orphanage after the age of two. A child adopted at five, for example, would remain around three years behind in its intellectual development. Dennis suggests that around two years might mark the end of the sensitive period for intellectual development for these children. He says, 'there is a period near the second birthday which is critical with respect to complete recovery from the effects of . . . deprivation upon intelligence. Those adopted before age two recover completely . . . among those adopted later there is a marked persistence of retardation.'

In his study Wayne Dennis found some correlations between the amount of stimulation in children's environment and their intellectual development. But remember, positive correlation does not prove cause.

If impoverished environments hold back child development, then enriched environments should encourage it. Dennis provided increased stimulation for some orphanage children – giving them more to play with, things to watch, etc. He found that the extent to which the child progressed was determined by its state of maturation

– more stimulation would not improve motor or intellectual skills unless the child was maturationally ready.

A second major series of studies of children whose environments have changed was conducted by Harold Skeels and his colleagues. Most showed a corresponding change in their intelligence. In a 21-year longitudinal study of two groups of children, **Skeels and Dye** found that those who lived in the most stimulating environments increased their DQ and IQ scores over those who did not. Skeels knew about two children in a state orphanage in America who were so backward it was decided to put them in a special institution for backward children. One had an IQ of 35, the other's IQ was 46. A few months later they were retested, and now showed dramatic increases to 87 and 77 IQ points respectively. It seemed that the other children in the institution, and the staff, 'mothered' them and gave them lots of stimulation and attention. Within two years both children were fostered, having IQs which were just below average. This observation suggests that intelligence can be influenced by the amount of stimulation a child's environment contains.

Skeels and Dye decided to test this more thoroughly. They found the DQs of 25 nineteen-month-old orphans in a rather deprived and overcrowded orphanage where there was little to do or see. Thirteen of them had such low DQs that they were considered unadoptable. They were then moved to an orphanage for slightly subnormal older girls who cared for the children for much of the time, acting as substitute mothers. Eighteen months later the babies' DQs had risen on average by 28 points, from around 60 to nearly 90.

The 12 babies who remained in the first orphanage acted as a kind of control group. They lost up to 26 DQ points. Their DQs were now the same as the first group before they were moved – around 60. Two and a half years later the differences were still there, and when Skeels tested them again when the two groups were 21 years old those from the 'better' environment were still ahead.

3 Operation Headstart

During the 1950s and 1960s in America, many children were leaving school with very little education and no qualifications. Many came from the ethnic minorities and the poorer home backgrounds. The fact that they were unqualified, together with the general shortage of decent jobs for unskilled people, meant that many were living on welfare benefits, and some were turning to crime.

Oscar Lewis suggested that their lack of success in education was due to the fact that many lived in deprived neighbourhoods which did not have the usual facilities like libraries, parks, theatres, etc. These children often spoke their own native language at home, so their American English was poor. Lewis concluded that their culture was deprived when compared to that of normal American children. This deprived or impoverished culture would hold those groups of children back in later life, which would be bad for them, and quite

Improving children's environments does lead to an improvement in their intellectual responses, so environmental factors must be important.

Skeels and Dye's studies seem to support the nurture side of the nature–nurture debate. But it is important to point out that IQ tests are notoriously unreliable and DQ tests for very young children aren't necessarily testing intelligence.

Do you remember Jarmila Koluchova's report of the MZ twin Czechoslovakian boys who'd been kept isolated from 18 months to seven years old? Their DQs were very low when they were found, but by their middle teens their IQ scores were 100 and 101.

Oscar Lewis was a social anthropologist. An anthropologist studies the relationships that exist between different groups of people in a culture.

possibly bad for America as a whole since they would end up in the dead-end jobs, or on welfare, or in prison!

In response to this, and as a part of a much wider government policy to combat poverty called the *War On Poverty*, the government made a massive attempt at enrichment, to improve the culture of these children. It spent 17 billion dollars on a series of programmes of compensatory education for disadvantaged children. Some of the programmes emphasised social development, some emphasised cognitive development. The general aim was that 100 000 deprived children would receive some pre-school remedial education. One of the best-known programmes of compensatory education was **Operation Headstart** which started in the summer of 1965.

The people running the many Headstart programmes often had different ideas about what the children needed. Some of the centres were very education centred, with children being taught discipline as well as basic skills. Others were more child centred, trying to help children be more sociable, cooperative, or confident. Most of the children in Headstart and similar programmes would go on visits to parks, and have people come into their neighbourhoods, even into their homes and teach them about road safety and where to play. They had extra teaching in English and maths, they received free medical and dental checkups, and generally were encouraged to absorb the competitive atmosphere that dominates American schools. In this way, it was argued, they would be academically as prepared for junior school as their native American classmates, and they would

Most of the children in the American Operation Headstart programmes came from poor homes which lacked many of the basic necessities. Their diet was often inadequate too. Project Headstart was based on the idea that their culture wasn't as good as the native American culture, and the project proposed to make them more like normal Americans.

Background reading – Operation Headstart

The number of children who could benefit from Headstart was about five times greater than the government had realised, and the first year's cost came to 96 billion dollars. In all about half a million people were involved in Headstart at over 4,700 centres. There were 100 000 doctors, dentists, and teachers for a start!

Over the next few years the numbers increased still further. There were 200 000 more children in the scheme by 1967.

By the late 1960s doubt was being cast on the success of Headstart. A study in 1969 found no differences in the educational performance of children who'd been through Headstart compared to those who hadn't. Funding for the scheme was not increased further, and the number of people involved started to fall. Some psychologists started to reject the idea that intelligence can be altered by changing environmental factors, and that it was, as Binet said, fixed at birth.

Over 9 million children have now been through Headstart, and although there are still more poor people now in America than ever before, it seems that Headstart does have some long-term benefits that couldn't have been realised in 1969. In one study it was found that Headstart children were less likely to appear in the crime statistics, more likely to finish college, less likely to become pregnant before marriage, less likely to need to live on welfare benefits, etc. It was estimated that if all these things are costed, for every thousand dollars spent on pre-school provision, the community saves four thousand dollars later on not having to pay welfare benefits, and not needing so many police officers, jails, etc.

be able to join in the games, the competitions, the individual achievements, etc., too.

Most of the children benefited from their early enrichment. However, once they were in school many of the Headstart children started to fall behind their better-off classmates. Many coped better than they may have done before, at least for the first few years of schooling, but very few actually improved very much by the end of it. By nine or 10 years of age, the vast majority had slipped behind their better-off American counterparts.

So why didn't more of the children who went through these compensatory education programmes improve in their schooling? Perhaps, the influence of the home and family as the children grew was greater than the influence of spending a few hours a day in the programme when they were young. Those Headstart programmes that involved parents did seem to be more successful than others. Enrichment only seems to have any real chance of success when all the areas of one's life are affected, for example when a child is removed from one institution, such as a poor orphanage, and reared by loving parents. A few extra hours of enrichment could not begin to outweigh the disadvantages of being brought up in a poor, deprived environment.

Some critics argued that Operation Headstart probably failed to produce many lasting effects because children's intelligence is determined at birth. It's more likely that Headstart wasn't the success that many hoped it would be because the children spent most of their time in the home environment that lacked the kind of intellectual stimulation they needed.

4 Twin studies

It is common to find similarities among identical twins. To have so many similarities seems to demand that genetic preprogramming

Background reading – Studies of twins separated at birth

Scientists at Minnesota University, USA, have been studying monozygotic twins for 15 years. Many striking similarities have been found among the 20 or so twin pairs so far studied. Here is the case of some twin boys – adopted separately within two months of birth. Both married a girl called Linda, divorced her and married a girl called Betty. One twin named his first son James Alan. The other named his Alan James. Both children had owned a dog named Toy. Both had worked in the same type of job. Both spend their holidays at the same place. Both chain smoke the same cigarettes. Both have had vasectomies. Both have had two heart attacks. Both have had haemorrhoids. Both have basement workshops and do woodwork. Both had the same favourite subject at school. Both have white benches built around the trunk of a tree in their gardens, etc., etc.

Other twins show striking similarities. A British pair bought the same type, make and colour of diary for the same year – even filled out the same pages! Another pair had both fallen down stairs in the same year and injured their ankles. Two others both tinted their greying hair the same shade of auburn, both enjoy the same two authors, both fell down stairs at the same age, both met their future husbands at town hall dances, both laugh compulsively, both suffered miscarriages with their first babies, then gave birth to two boys followed by a girl, both hated maths and games at school, both had been Girl Guides, both loved ballroom dancing. When they met for the first time since they were adopted, they turned up wearing identical dresses. But have such notable similarities anything to do with intelligence?

Twins may be socialised to emphasise their similarities. They may learn to accept and expect that they are similar, and must remain so. They share the same environment even more so than normal brothers and sisters.

It is obviously true that we inherit certain potentials for developing intellectually from our parents. It is also true that whatever potentials we possess will not develop unless they are stimulated by factors in the environment.

does have a role to play in understanding some human behaviour. However many of these similarities could be explained by coincidence, and most have little to do with intelligence.

And what about all the differences between the twins that we aren't told about? Perhaps one twin was a deeply religious person and the other was an atheist. Perhaps one twin always started the day with a large glass of carrot juice and the other twin hated carrot juice. We are only told about the startling similarities, which imply that there must be something mysterious about them.

Peter Wilson has gathered and analysed the available information on twin studies (published in his book *Twins* in 1981). He is not convinced by the genetic nature of the similarities. He suggests that mothers treat identical twins in very similar ways, doing the same things with both of them, dressing them in similar clothes, and emphasising all the similarities between them. Once established, this early bond may be hard to break. The individuals are treated as a unit and similarities in their behaviour, tastes, expectations, etc., may well stem from this. The twins may become dependent on each other, and their socialisation will not be ordinary.

Twin studies

1 Does the fact that some identical twins have a number of similarities mean that their intelligence will also be similar?

2 Some similarities can be explained by statistical coincidence. What does this mean?

Conclusion

Trying to untangle whether human intelligence is the result of genetic or environmental factors is (a) impossible, and (b) a complete waste of time. There's little doubt that both environment (nurture) and heredity (nature) are involved. One useful explanation of the origin of intelligence sees our genetic inheritance as a rubber band. People who could be intelligent have long rubber bands, less bright people have shorter bands. The environment which we grow up in decides whether our band is stretched.

The rubber band hypothesis

This graph shows the effects of environment on genetic potential. The length of the rubber band represents the potential for intellectual development which is fixed at birth. The amount of stimulation in someone's environment will determine how intelligent they actually become.

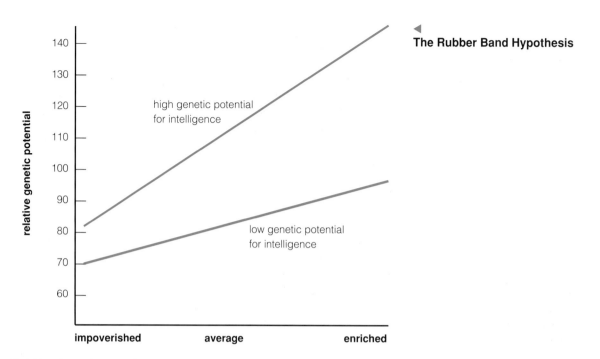

The Rubber Band Hypothesis

Enriching the environment for someone with a low genetic potential could lead to an increase of something like 30 IQ points. Someone with a higher genetic potential may be able to improve by up to 60 IQ points.

1 What is the average IQ score?

2 Can someone with a low genetic potential ever achieve a higher IQ than someone with a higher genetic potential?

3 What sort of things provide 'enrichment'?

4 Outline Skeel's findings from the 25 orphanage children he studied.

In view of these findings, some people have wondered whether we could create a perfect environment, and teach all parents to use ideal child-rearing methods, so that every child would develop its full potential for intelligence, being cooperative and caring and all the other human qualities that many parents find desirable. Unfortunately this isn't realistic, for the simple reason that we all have different genotypes, and different things stimulate different people in different ways.

Answers to the intelligence test items on page 206

Answer	Explanation
1 M	A [B C] D [E F] G [H I] J [K L] = M
H	H I J K L M N O P Q are from the alphabet. Reading backwards we have Q P, missing the next two gives us M L, missing the next two gives us I and H.

2 *Wood* becomes *coal* if left long enough under pressure.

Apple and *peach* are both edible fruits.
Ship and *car* are both forms of transport.
3 It's Monday tomorrow so we go back to school.
4 Post means the same as stake and mail.
5 Kitten   tootap = potato
               prinut = turnip
               tintek = kitten
               otrrac = carrot
6 Cardiff (isn't in England)
               grothnib = Brighton
               yuqtora = Torquay
               drifcaf = Cardiff
               hercest = Chester
               sheeldiff = Sheffield

Background reading – Statistical coincidence?

There are about 5500 million people on earth. Many of them are bound to have some similar characteristics. There are 14 900 000 000 000 000 trees. Many of these will be similar, yet we are not surprised at this. There are estimated to be about 3 000 000 000 000 000 000 000 000 000 000 000 000 000 000 000 000 000 000 000 000 000 000 000 000 000 000 000 000 000 living things on this planet. Similarities and coincidences should occur. The chances of winning the football pools are 1 in 22 000 000, but every week some people win and we are not surprised at this. You have a very much greater chance of being struck by lightning than of winning the pools, which is only 1 in 2 million!

Visual Perception

13

Perception is the general name given to the process of taking in and using information. It includes the following:

- activity in all our senses which detect stimuli in our environment;
- converting physical energy such as light into mental energy, such as nervous activity;
- interpreting information for meaning by consulting memory;
- attending to some information and filtering out other information;
- making sense and becoming aware of information, i.e. achieving cognition;
- having thoughts and feelings about information;
- enabling a possible range of responses to information received.

Of all the perceptual senses sight is probably the most frequently used and possibly provides most of the information that we take in. The human sense of vision is highly evolved. There are about 120 million light-sensitive cells called rods and 6 million cells called cones on the retina of each of your eyes. Simply put, rods respond to lower light levels (and result in our impression of black and white), while cones respond to daylight. There are three types of cone, each responding to different wavelengths of light that give us our impression of colour.

In addition to the highly developed rods and cones there are several other layers of cells on the retina. Information travels from the eye along nervous pathways called the optic nerves. These nerves relay with other senses, particularly hearing. They pass through several organs where information of various types is decoded or added until the information that they carry is finally interpreted as *sight* in the visual cortex at the rear of the brain.

As human visual perception is so highly developed and virtually instantaneous, it has been thought that some human visual skills are probably innate. You may remember that Robert Fantz, Genevieve Carpenter and others (see Chapter Two) have investigated the human baby's preferences for human sights and sounds.

Vision includes a number of abilities such as the ability to recognise shapes (pattern perception), the knowledge that things don't change their size or colour just because they appear to be larger or darker (size and colour constancy), and to judge distance (distance or depth perception). There are three possible explanations for the

The nature–nurture debate has been raised over some aspects of human visual development. Visual perception means making sense of information received through our eyes.

The sense of vision is highly developed in humans and involves several parts of the brain. It allows us to see and to act upon what we see very quickly indeed.

origin of these and other skills. They may be there from birth (and therefore *innate*), they may be genetically transmitted but only appear when the baby is maturationally ready (innate), or they may be learned.

In this chapter we will examine the evidence that:

1 some perceptual skills are innate;
2 some perceptual skills are learned;
3 some perceptual skills are best understood by combining the two explanations.

1 The nature view – perception is innate

Form perception

Do infants perceive objects as wholes? Do they have any preference for looking at one shape or texture rather than another? The main work in this area has been conducted by **Robert Fantz**, beginning in the 1960s. He started with some chicks which he hatched in total darkness. Since chicks will peck at grain soon after birth, and before they could have learned that grain is their food, it is conceivable that they have an instinctive knowledge of what their food looks like. So Fantz gave them eight different-shaped objects and recorded the number of times they pecked at each of them. The objects were different shapes, from a small ball-shaped object, similar to a grain, to pyramid-shaped objects. The chicks pecked 10 times more at the round objects than the ones which didn't look anything like grains. Fantz concluded that chicks innately recognise round shapes and objects with three dimensions. This supports the nature view that shape recognition in chicks is innate.

As chicks rely much more on instinct and are much more mobile than human infants, it is plausible that the ability to recognise food might be genetically inherited. Like following the first thing they see, knowing what food looks like should have considerable **survival value**.

The question which arises from this research by Fantz concerns whether human infants have any kind of recognition for things which could have survival value for them? Fantz tested some human infants. He suggested that he could decide whether babies liked looking at one thing or another by observing their eye movements, facial expressions, and body movements. If they stared and looked happy when shown one object, and looked away and became restless when shown another, then they must be able to perceive the form of these objects, and to prefer one to another.

To test this he designed some experimental apparatus called **the looking chamber**. It consisted of a cot above which various objects could be suspended, and a viewing hole through which the baby's face and eyes could be observed. Objects were to be presented in pairs and the infant's reaction to each object in the pair was

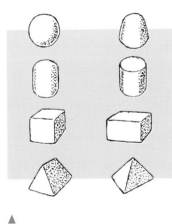

Fantz's chicken food

Fantz showed that chicks can instinctively recognise food-shaped objects. Why might this have survival value? Is there any reason to suspect that anything similar might exist in humans?

measured. Fantz tested 30 infants at weekly intervals, from when they were one week old, to when they were 15 weeks old. He showed them a number of shapes and patterns such as a bull's-eye pattern, stripes of various textures, a cross, a chessboard design, plain triangles, and plain squares. Fantz found that even the youngest infants generally preferred the more complex shapes, such as the bull's-eye and the chessboard. This suggests that some degree of form perception may well be innate.

Fantz claimed to have shown that babies can perceive form or pattern from one week of age and that they can see objects of increasing complexity over the first six months. Next he investigated whether babies have a preference for the human face, as opposed to other shapes. (You may remember from Chapter Two that Ahrens had suggested that they did.)

Fantz's looking chamber experiments suggested that young babies do seem to prefer looking at complex, round shapes. These might appear to be 'face-shaped' to the child.

Form perception

1 How did Fantz measure the babies' ability to recognise and show if they preferred any particular patterns?

2 What sample size was used in this experiment?

3 What IVs are used here?

4 What is the DV and how is it measured?

5 What does Fantz conclude about the origin of form perception?

6 Can you think of any potentially confounding variables in either the patterns presented, or the way in which they are presented?

7 Outline some of the main difficulties in using babies as subjects in experiments such as this.

Fantz had three pictures which he could show to babies in the looking chamber. The first was a face with black features painted on a pink background. The next was the same as the first but the features were all jumbled up, and the third was a pink face shape without any features, except the top part was black (to resemble hair).

Fantz sampled 49 infants, from just four days old up to six months old. He showed them the three faces in every possible combination. Most of the infants ignored the face without features. The six-month-olds barely glanced at it. The children up to about three and a half months of age seemed interested in the 'scrambled' face. However, the infants all seemed slightly more interested in the picture that most resembled a real face. The differences weren't great, but enough for Fantz to conclude that babies do have an innate awareness of, and preference for, the human face. This claim aroused considerable interest among psychologists who claimed that babies have innate capacities to recognise, and therefore attach to, their caregivers.

Criticism: The difference between the babies' reactions to the face and scrambled face was not very great, and other researchers have used Fantz's methods and repeated his experiments, but either have not obtained the same results, or have explained them in other ways. For example, some found that very young babies had no preference for one picture over any other, and any who did were simply preferring symmetrical patterns to jumbled ones.

Older babies did seem to prefer the face shapes, but they could by then have learned to associate the human face with food and comfort. Anyway the pictures which Fantz showed to the babies were rather unrealistic, two-dimensional drawings of faces coloured pink and black. They didn't really look like human faces at all.

Perhaps the reason for the error in Fantz's early work was his method – just because a baby looks at one shape more than another doesn't have to mean that baby prefers one over another.

Review
Pattern perception

Fantz claimed to have shown that very young babies can only perceive a certain level of detail, but that this increases over the first months. He claimed that they have an innate preference for looking at the human face, but this claim has not been confirmed.

Pattern perception

1 Summarise Fantz's experiment to demonstrate infants' abilities to recognise certain shapes.

2 Summarise the main criticisms of the basis for these claims.

The visual cliff
▼

Gibson and Walk's visual cliff experiment has shown that depth perception is innate in some animals. Does knowing this help us to resolve the nature–nurture dispute in humans? Explain your answer.

Depth, distance and direction perception

If humans do have some innate preference for looking at round, face-like shapes, do they have any other innate visual skills? The ability to perceive depth has been demonstrated in a number of newborn animals. The classic experiment in depth perception was conducted by **Eleanor Gibson** and **Richard Walk** in 1960.

Gibson and Walk constructed some apparatus known as the visual cliff which consisted of a glass shelf which had a shallow side and a deep side. Checked cloth could be seen just under the glass on the shallow side, and at some depth on the deep side. Some newborn animals were placed on the shelf, and Gibson and Walk noted whether they would wander all over it, or would prefer either side. Most of them would not walk over the deep side. Even one-day-old chicks never strayed on to the deep side. Lambs and kids placed on the deep side refused to stand, and kittens either froze or circled backwards aimlessly. Rats base their depth perception more on touch, by using their whiskers rather than on vision. They wandered across either side. But when their whiskers were trimmed, and they were forced to use vision, they then wouldn't move on to the deep side. This seems to confirm the view that animals have innate depth perception.

Gibson and Walk also put some human infants on the visual cliff apparatus. Thirty-six infants between six and 14 months of age were studied. They were placed on a ledge in between the shallow and deep sides. Their mothers called them alternately from one side, then from the other side. Nine infants refused to move at all, but of the 27 infants who did, 24 would only crawl to their mothers over the shallow side, and only three would crawl over the deep side. Some crawled away from their mothers when called from the deep side, others just cried

Background reading – How do we perceive depth?

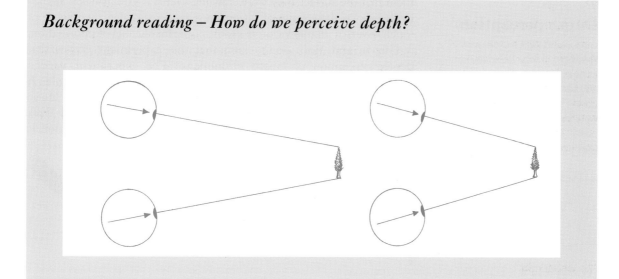

Our eyes are set about 6 cm apart. The picture we receive from each of them is slightly different. This is called retinal disparity. You can see this by looking at something quite close to you first with one eye, then with the other. If you look at something from a distance then the pictures are very similar. The part of our brain which is mainly responsible for interpreting what we see (the visual cortex) compares the pictures it receives from each of our eyes, and judges how similar the pictures are. The more similar the picture is, the further away the object we are looking at must be.

Information from the muscles which move the eyeball is also sent to the brain, for example, if an object is close to us, our eyes turn slightly inwards. If it is more than about 50 metres away, they look straight ahead. This turning of the eyeball is called convergence, and it can also give us clues about how near the object we are looking at is. See the diagram above.

Our eyes and ears have one ability that our other senses do not. They exchange informa-

tion with each other, so if the thing we are looking at makes any sound, that sound could help us judge its distance from us.

There are a number of clues in the environment which may help us to perceive depth. Gibson and Walk suggest that motion parallax is one. This refers to the way in which nearer objects seem to move more quickly than distant objects. When driving at night the moon doesn't seem to move at all, but the houses at the side of the road whizz by. If your brain is sent messages that some object hardly seems to move, while it knows that you are moving, then it may reason that the object is some distance away.

Other clues to depth include relative size. If you see a horse and a double-decker bus in the distance, and they look the same size, the horse must be closer to you. You know that horses are smaller than buses. Interposition is where one object blocks the view of another. It must be nearer. Shadowing provides another clue. If one object casts its shadow on to another while the light is coming from the observer's position, then it must be in front.

because they couldn't reach their mothers. Some of the infants fell on to the glass on the deep side, and started to crawl towards their mothers, until they looked down. Once they saw the checked cloth at some distance below them they became very distressed. Before looking down these babies were presumably using their sense of touch, which told them that the surface they were crawling over was safe. As soon as they looked down their sense of vision must have overruled their sense of touch. Even in infants vision is a most powerful channel of information.

Gibson and Walk don't claim that this experiment proves that depth perception is innate in humans. The experiment needed infants who could crawl, so they had to be about six months old. A great deal of learning takes place during the first six months of life so the babies could have learned depth perception. Gibson and Walk did say that the results support their view that depth perception is innate in animals.

Review

Depth perception

Gibson and Walk's experiment showed that very young animals appear to have innately acquired abilities to judge depth. The human babies they used on the visual cliff were six months old however, and during that time they could have learned about depth and distance.

Depth perception

1 What was the sample size for children?

2 What was the purpose behind the visual cliff experiment?

3 What was the DV in this experiment?

4 What evidence is there in the passage to suggest that perception may be innate in animals?

5 Explain why these findings may not be used to solve the nature–nurture debate on depth perception in humans.

Cues to perceiving depth

Summarise the evidence which has been used to show that depth perception is innate?

Distance and direction

Tom Bower has investigated babies' abilities to judge distance and direction. Doctors use babies' defensive reactions to test whether babies are blind. An object is moved towards an infant's face. If the infants are blind, there will be no reaction. If, however, they can see the approaching object, they will try to move out of the path of the object. The infants will also lift their hands as if to protect their faces. It is possible that the infants are responding to the rush of air towards their faces as the object approaches. To test this more thoroughly Bower arranged an experiment with three experimental conditions.

Condition 1

A cube is moved towards the baby's face at the same time the air around it is displaced. This produced the classic 'defensive' response.

Condition 2

The air was displaced, but there was no object. The babies made no attempt to protect themselves.

Condition 3

The object was moved towards the baby, but the air was not displaced. (The baby saw a film of the travelling object.) This produced no reaction at all.

Babies can tell the direction of an approaching object well. They become disturbed if objects appear to be heading straight for their faces, but do not show concern when the same object would miss them, even by just an inch or two! The defensive reaction is also probably innate. This would make sense since it could have considerable survival value.

These experiments also illustrate some of the limitations of the baby's visual system. It can take in a great deal of information, but cannot process that information as quickly as an adult, for example, in the 'defensive reaction' experiment, if the object was heading for the baby at any great speed, then it didn't respond at all. The information would probably have been sent to the brain, but the brain isn't mature and well organised enough to respond very quickly.

Size constancy

An orange held only half a metre from your eyes will cast quite a large image on your retinas. The same orange held two metres away will cast a much smaller one. Even so, we know that it is still the same orange, not a satsuma which has suddenly appeared! This is known as **size constancy**. There are other visual constancies, of course. You know that something doesn't change its shape just because you see it from different angles. You know the colour of your front-room curtains, whether you're passing them on a sunny day, or returning home in the middle of the night. They may appear to be different colours, but you know that they are not.

In 1966 Tom Bower conducted an experiment to investigate whether size constancy was innate or learned. A supporter of the nurture side would argue that young infants would not show size constancy because they would not have had time to learn it. A nativist would argue that infants would show size constancy because it is an innate ability.

Don't confuse **nativist** (a supporter of the nature side of the nature–nurture argument) with a **naturist** (someone who enjoys nudism).

Bower used a sample of babies of just a few weeks old. One at a time, the babies were placed on a table in a comfortable cot from which they could see a screen. Behind the screen was a 30 cm cube. This was placed about one metre away from the babies.

When the screen was moved and the babies saw the cube they were reinforced. Bower used operant conditioning to teach the

Bower's experiment

children that if they turned their heads to one side when they saw the cube (or when they became bored of looking at the cube) they would be rewarded by their mothers' playing 'peek-a-boo' and tickling. (See Chapter Six for an explanation of reinforcement.) After several trials the babies were conditioned to turn their heads towards their mothers when they saw the 30 cm cube.

Now the 30 cm cube was moved back to three metres from the babies, and the number of head turns was counted. It was still the same cube.

In the third condition, the original cube was removed and one three times as big was put one metre from the child. Bower knew that a cube three times as big (90 cm) set three times as far away (three metres) would cast the same size image on the retina as the original cube. So in the fourth condition the larger cube was placed three metres from the babies. If the babies perceived this new cube to be the same as the original cube, they should turn their heads for their reward.

The four experimental conditions therefore are:
1 a 30 cm cube at one metre;
2 a 30 cm cube at three metres;
3 a 90 cm cube at one metre;
4 a 90 cm cube at three metres.

In each experimental condition the number of times the children turn their heads for a reward was then used as a measure of how similar the infants thought each cube was to the one they were conditioned to look at.

If babies are born with size constancy they should respond most to conditions 1 and 2, as these use the original cube. They should respond rather less to conditions 3 and 4. If they have to learn size constancy then they should respond most to condition 1, then to the one that cast the same size retinal image (condition 4), and then to conditions 3 and 2.

Here is a table of Bower's results:

Experimental condition	Number of correct responses
1 30 cm at one metre	98
2 30 cm at three metres	58
3 90 cm at one metre	54
4 90 cm at three metres	22

These results seem more to support the nativist view – that babies are born with size constancy. As the baby could recognise the original size cube at different distances it also suggests that depth perception (or a form of it) is innate.

Bower's experiments

1 Summarise the conclusions from Bower's 'distance and direction' experiment.

2 What would Tom Bower's hypothesis for this experiment have been?

3 What would Tom Bower's hypothesis for the size-constancy experiment have been?

4 Explain the method Bower used to teach the babies to turn their heads.

5 Explain the nurturist prediction (given above) for the DV.

6 Explain what the results actually show.

Review
Size constancy
Tom Bower used very young infants to show that they seemed able to judge size, shape, and distance. This is further confirmation that these sorts of visual skills are innate.

2 The nurture view – the case for learning

If perception had to be learned, then people who had been unable to see, and who then had their sight restored, would take some time to learn to recognise all the things that normally sighted people take for granted. For example, a sighted person may have the various constancies we described earlier, whereas people who have their sight restored through surgery, may not. However, just because adults can learn visual skills, such as judging distance, this doesn't mean that babies have to learn them.

If visual skills in humans have to be learned, then humans should be able to learn to change their behaviour if their visual experiences are changed. The following experiments suggest that this is the case.

Stratton (1897) wore a lens over one eye, which turned his view of the world (through the eye) upside down. He kept the lens on for eight days. He covered the other eye with a patch, forcing him to look through the lens. By the fifth day he was able to walk around without bumping into things. While he was moving around everything looked normal, but as soon as he stopped, and concentrated on an object, it appeared to be upside down.

J. and J. K. Peterson (1938) used inverting lenses on both eyes of a sample of people, and found similar results to Stratton. Eight months later they retested their subjects and found that they adapted to their upside down world more quickly than before. They soon returned to behaviour they had learned during the first trials. So humans can learn to adapt – but maybe not fully. In the Petersons' experiment, even after two weeks, not all of the subjects had fully adapted to their new world.

Kohler (1962) wore a variety of lenses which distorted vision in a number of different ways. Some had different-coloured lenses, some turned the line of sight slightly to the left or right, etc. After a few hours of wearing each of his distorting lenses he was able to adjust to cope with his changed visual experiences.

There are some criticisms of these **readjustment** studies. Human beings do seem able to make some adaptation to changes to their visual experiences. However, these adaptations may not be visual adaptations at all. They may be simply learning what to do to compensate for the visual distortion. For example, seeing something

Several experiments have shown that humans can make an adaptation to an altered experience, but the adaptation may not be visual. The subjects may well have learned to cope with an altered visual experience.

Review
The nurture view

Studies showing that humans can adjust to a perceptually distorted world provide further evidence of just how well integrated various aspects of the human sensory system are. We can adapt our behaviour to suit the distorted world. However, adapting our behaviour is not the same as adapting our vision. Even if adults could learn to make visual adaptations to distorted visual perceptions, that doesn't mean that babies have to learn to adapt to a normal visual world.

which you know is set off to the left by a few degrees will not stop you learning to point at it accurately. It may not be new visual learning, however, it may be simply adapting your behaviour. Some of our senses, such as our sense of balance and the senses which respond to muscle and limb movements, are generally described as our body sense, or **proprioception**. Proprioception adapts to altered vision. When the Petersons' subjects learned to move around they were adjusting to an upside down world, not seeing one which was the correct way up.

3 Combining the two views – the need for genetics and learning

So far we've seen evidence which seems to support *either* the nature view *or* the nurture view. Few psychologists now would disagree with the idea that visual perception relies on both genetics and learning. For the first few months of life a baby's visual system isn't fully developed. The nerves carrying information about what the infant is looking at, in the visual areas of the brain, aren't as well insulated as they will become. This results in interference (like a radio that isn't quite tuned properly). Some of the signals are lost, others get confused. As the baby's visual system matures so the baby's ability to see and perceive will improve.

Despite these limitations babies can see fairly well right from birth. We can do tests to measure how far a baby can see, and even what sorts of things it can see. This supports the nature argument. We cannot know what it makes of the things it sees. Genevieve Carpenter showed that by two weeks of age babies may recognise their mother, and will expect her face to move and change expression. Other research suggests that babies of just 36 hours will recognise and imitate certain facial expressions under certain conditions. It is clear, therefore, early experience is necessary for the infant to make sense of what it can see.

Other evidence for the need for both innate factors and experience comes from studies of animals who have been deprived of various kinds of visual experience.

Deprivation studies with animals
A. N. Reisen (1950) deprived one male and one female chimpanzee of sight for their first 16 months of life, except for some short (45 second) periods each day when they were fed. When exposed to light at 16 months they showed the following reactions: their pupils weren't as open as those of normally reared monkeys, they were frightened by sudden intense light, they did not blink when sudden or threatening movements were made towards their faces, and they showed no interest in their toys unless they touched them with some part of their bodies.

One chimp then had longer periods in the light until it was 21 months old. It developed normal sight. It could recognise objects, had good hand-to-eye coordination, etc. The other chimp was kept in darkness until 33 months. When exposed to normal light it behaved in the same way as it had earlier. Its abilities improved slightly over the next few weeks, then declined.

It seems that chimps (and presumably other animals) need light during the first year or so, for their eyes to develop normally. If this is correct, then it would be necessary to rear subjects who can see light, but not see objects. Reisen reared another chimpanzee who was made to wear a translucent mask which allowed one and a half hours of diffused, unpatterned light to enter the eye each day. (Like looking through greaseproof paper.) The mask was removed at seven months. This chimp also did not develop normal sight.

However Reisen's experiments were often carried out on very few subjects (and sometimes only one) and so we must be cautious about any generalisations we make from them. Some of Reisen's operationalised experimental procedures can be questioned, for example, the chimps reared in darkness had 45 seconds a day (feeding time) of light. Maybe this was enough to allow the development of some visual abilities.

Colin Blakemore and **Grahame Cooper** (1966) reared kittens in large drums which were painted on the inside. One drum had vertical black and white stripes, while the other drum had horizontal black and white stripes. The kittens could only see vertical or horizontal black and white stripes. The critical period for kittens developing visual skills was thought to be from three to 15 weeks of life. Their visual abilities were tested from when they were five months old. At first they did not recognise anything with edges that were different from the ones they had grown up with. Those brought up to see only vertical lines weren't supposed to be able to see horizontal lines. They bumped into anything which had no vertical lines, such as a pencil waved horizontally across their path. This does not mean that responses to lines are purely environmental. It could be that the cat's ability to respond to vertical lines and horizontal lines is there at birth, but the cells which respond to horizontal lines may not have developed. There is a problem with the design of this experiment. No doubt many of the playful kittens would have rolled around and moved their heads to different angles, during the time they were allowed to see the stripes. The result is that they would be seeing stripes at different angles. Some independent judges couldn't tell which of the kittens had been raised among vertical stripes, and which among horizontal stripes.

Richard Held and **Alan Hein** (1965) designed some apparatus to overcome the problem of the cat's movement. They wanted to see if the cats' bodies, particularly their paws, affected visual development in kittens. Their apparatus, called **the kitten carousel**, gave two kittens the same amount of the same type of visual experience. They were linked together by a series of pulleys and strings. The kitten carousels were placed inside drums with vertical or horizontal stripes.

Reisen's results suggest that patterns are needed as well as light for normal visual development. In other words environment (nurture) is necessary for the development of normal visual perception.

Blakemore and Cooper suggested that the visual system needs a variety of shapes and patterns to stimulate it. Their experimental subjects could have received such stimulation.

The kitten carousel

Held and Hein's kitten carousel experiment still does not prove the nature–nurture debate either way. Their results were not entirely conclusive, and we can never know exactly what the animals could perceive.

One kitten (called the active kitten) could move around inside a drum and its actions were transmitted to the other kitten (called the passive kitten) through the pulleys. The kittens were given three hours' exposure to light on the apparatus every day for several weeks. When tested for paw-to-eye coordination it was found that the active kittens were far superior. For example, after 30 hours' exposure all the active kittens could put their paws where they wanted. None of the passive kittens could. Experience in the environment seems necessary for normal development.

There is a problem with these kinds of experiment. We cannot say that deprived animals do not perceive, only that they do not act as if they perceive. We have studied their behavioural responses to various forms of deprivation, but haven't begun to study their visual experiences.

Conclusion

A newborn's skills such as depth perception, size constancy, and pattern recognition are impressive. Most of the research seems to support the '**nature modified by nurture**' view that most psychologists hold today. We are not so interested nowadays in what skill is innate or learned. Instead we are more interested in what skills babies can have, and how we can encourage our children to use their skills to their greatest advantage.

Humans are born with a number of skills that will develop if their environment allows them to develop. Babies have other skills that we can only guess at. Even very young babies will imitate their mother's facial expressions. But when mother sticks her tongue out, and baby imitates, how can it possibly know what part of the mother's face is being funny? How does the baby know that the thing which is sticking out is a tongue, and how could it know that the thing in its mouth, which it has never seen, is also a tongue? Why should the baby want to imitate its mother anyway? Why does the baby want to be sociable? Perhaps that's innate too. Many researchers suggest that it is.

Is perception innate or learned?

1 Summarise the evidence for each side of the nature–nurture debate on size constancy.

2 Describe some of the evidence from studies of animals which suggests that the environment may be necessary for the development of visual perception.

3 Describe three different techniques that have been used to study the perceptual skills of babies or young children.

Review
Combining the two views

Several animal studies have shown that parts of the visual system need a variety of changing visual experiences, together with interaction with the environment, in order to mature. Both nature and nurture are needed for the full range of visual skills to be developed.

14

The Development of Language and Communication

We've all heard dogs barking, cats meowing, birds singing, and cows mooing. Compare these sounds to what you would hear in any park or school playground where children are playing. What do you imagine that the animals are trying to communicate? What are some of the things that the children may be communicating?

Write a two-sentence definition of 'language'. Then look it up and see how close you were.

Try to answer these questions yourself, and then try them on your family and friends. Make a note of whether or not they could answer all the questions.
Are the hand signs that deaf people make to each other language?
Is there any such thing as body language?
Are the flags that ships fly signalling distress language?
Is Morse Code language?
Are the ways in which we talk to computers language?
Can animals such as dolphins use language?
Is it possible to say at what age babies stop babbling and start using language?

All spoken languages consist of **phonemes**, which are the basic sounds, and **morphemes**, which are groups of phonemes which have some meaning in the particular language.

The study of the origins and development of language is called **linguistics**. Until quite recently it was not really considered to be a part of psychology at all. Those who supported the nature side of the nature–nurture debate would claim that language was an ability that humans developed when they were maturationally ready. It was used for communication, and had little to do with topics concerning the human mind and human behaviour which psychologists were interested in. However, Piaget and others have emphasised the importance of the contribution that children make to their own socialisation. Children should be actively involved in exploring and discovering things for themselves. The ability to ask, to find out, and to share knowledge will help children to expand their understanding. During the first two years of children's lives they will become mobile, and so be able to explore actively, and they will learn to talk. These achievements will transform seemingly rather helpless infants into sociable and inquisitive human beings. Largely because of the work of researchers such as Jean Piaget, and B. F. Skinner the study of language is now seen as an important part of psychology.

In this chapter we will be interested in the following questions.

1 What exactly are language and communication?
2 How do psychologists study them?
3 What are the 'stages' of language development in children?
4 What are the main theories to explain language?
5 Can only humans use language, or can any animals be taught to communicate?

1 What is language?

Let's start with a definition. To put it simply, language is an organised system of symbols which humans use to communicate. These symbols can be spoken, signed (so-called sign language used by people who are deaf and without speech), or written down (such as handwriting, printing, or braille). Spoken language is made up of basic sounds, called **phonemes**, which are combined to form more complex sounds with meaning, called **morphemes**. For example, 'st' and 'op' are phonemes; 'stop' is a morpheme.

Communication is rather easier to understand. It is the transmission of something (usually some message or some meaning), from one place to another. The meaning of the communication may be vague, or precise.

Our ability to use language is one of the main things which separates us from the rest of the animal kingdom. As far as we know, humans are the only species which have the ability to use *language*. Various animals have been studied to see if they use anything like a language system. Many animal species *communicate* with each other. If one zebra senses a predator it will start to run. This is taken by the rest of the herd to be a sign to run too. The first animal is *communicating* with the others, it isn't talking to them. When the honey bee performs its figure of eight dance back in the colony it will rattle its wings together in a way which communicates to the others that a useful source of pollen is to be found in a particular direction. Dolphins appear to have some high-pitched sounds which they use to communicate simple messages to other dolphins. Each species seems to be equipped with just as much ability to communicate as it needs in order to thrive in its environment. Humans live in very complex environments, and have very complex relationships with each other. Perhaps we are the only species which needs such a sophisticated communication system as language.

What do the following communications mean, and how exact is their meaning?
The red flag flying at the seaside
A green traffic light
The thumbs-up sign
A dog barking at another dog
A 'No Smoking' sign in a classroom
A 'Keep off the Grass' sign in the park
A 'Danger Keep Away' sign on an electricity generator

What is language?

Write a paragraph beginning 'The difference between language and communication is . . .'

2 How do psychologists study language development?

During the nineteenth century some people started to take an interest in how language develops. They listened carefully to growing children's speech, and kept careful diaries of what they said. Piaget used the **diary method** a great deal for studying the cognitive development of his own three children in the 1920s and early 1930s.

The diary method does have some advantages. It is longitudinal, often lasting for the first five or six years of children's lives. It is conducted by someone who knows the children well, who knows what they mean by whatever strange thing they are actually saying. The children will behave normally with someone they know, and the recording is a complete record since it can include every day in their lives. But it also has some severe disadvantages too. The record may be patchy, not covering all of the children's speech, and a study of one or two or three children cannot be representative of all children. Most of the diary keepers were well educated and so provided rather better models for their children to learn from than might many parents from the poorer groups in society. Parents may not be the most reliable people to study their own children, and while they are writing down what the children

The earliest method for studying children's speech was by keeping detailed diaries. This method does give a longitudinal record, but generalisations made from the small and biased samples used may not be very helpful.

The tape recorder allowed more scientific analysis of more children, but can only record what children say, which isn't always what they mean.

have said, many other words and sentences may be missed.

During the 1950s and 1960s tape recorders became more widely available and affordable. The **tape-recording method** allowed several children of the same age to be recorded, and an average made of their abilities. The children could be visited every week or fortnight, and everything they said, for example during one hour, could be recorded. What was being measured was how far the children had advanced along the road to achieving 'adult-type' speech. Sometimes children were brought into the laboratory so that situational variables like distractions (toys, sounds, smells, etc.) could be controlled. But children may not respond naturally in a strange laboratory, as they would in their normal environment. Even in their home, when an unfamiliar researcher is present children may not respond normally. Remember stranger fear?

Speaking can be an efficient way of communicating ideas. However, it's not the only means of communication that we have. When you say you are cold that's a very simple way of communicating what you are feeling. But we use much more than just speech to communicate. If you are turning blue or shivering you probably do not need to say anything at all. If an eighteen-month-old girl tries to reach for a beaker, her mother will probably understand that she wants a drink. If the toddler screws her face up having taken the first sip, then she doesn't need to say that the drink doesn't taste very pleasant. We all use **non-verbal cues** such as facial expressions, body position, gestures, etc., to aid communication. (Non-verbal means without speaking, and a cue is something that prompts someone into doing something.)

Sometimes we can communicate effectively by shrugging our shoulders or raising our eyebrows, and we haven't used any words at all! We can only really know what children are communicating if we can see what non-verbal cues they are giving us. Hence **videotaping** is now widely used. Each film can be analysed by several researchers. Filming a whole scene will allow researchers to analyse both the verbal, and the non-verbal components of communication. However, it can be fairly time-consuming, and expensive.

Listening to, and analysing, children's normal speech is not the only means of studying linguistic development. Psycholinguists have devised a number of **psychometric** tests (such as *comprehension* tests) which ask children to choose from a number of pictures or objects the one that the researcher is naming. Unfortunately young children can only pay attention to a very few pictures or objects at any one time. Another type of test discovers children's knowledge of the rules of grammar such as plurals, tenses, etc.

Review
Methods of studying speech

As in many areas of science, the way we study something is largely determined by the technology we have to study it. Charles Darwin and Jean Piaget used diaries to record their children's development because that was what they saw as the best method available to them. The tape recorder was widely used in the 1960s, as it became available. The video and some deliberate tests are the main techniques used now.

The problem with studying language

All these methods share the same problem. They all involve small sample sizes. Why is this a problem when researching the age at which children acquire certain language skills etc?

3 The main stages of language development

For something to occur in stages, there must be a period of time when some activity is occurring, which gives way to another period when some different activity occurs. According to Freud our personality develops through four main stages, each dominated by some unconscious urges concentrating on an erogenous zone. Piaget claimed that cognition also develops through four stages. Each of the stages he identified is dominated by a different type of thinking. Here we are suggesting that language develops in stages too. You may remember that not everyone accepts that human abilities develop in stages at all. Behaviourists such as Skinner, for example, argue that our various abilities simply *unfold* as we gain experience and receive various reinforcers.

Children all over the world are thought to follow the same sequence in acquiring language. We will describe it as consisting of three broad stages, the pre-linguistic stage, the stage of first words, and the stage of first sentences.

The pre-linguistic stage – from 0 to 12 months

Using the voice requires quite a complicated arrangement of skills. We must control our breathing, face muscles, tongue muscles, have ideas about what we want to say, etc. It will take babies a few months to acquire these things. However, that doesn't mean that neonates have no knowledge of language and communication. **William Condon** and **Lewis Sander** showed that by just a few hours after birth babies seem able to distinguish speech from other sounds, and they may even have a genetically acquired preference for listening to human speech. Studies of brainwave activity in babies suggest that the human voice stimulates the language centres in the left hemisphere of the brain, while music sounds stimulate areas in the right hemisphere, just as happens in adults. So babies are probably able to *discriminate* (tell the difference between) the human voice and other sounds, although that doesn't necessarily mean that they would know what they are listening to. Heredity and maturation dominate the first months.

Between two and six months babies start **babbling**, that is making sounds that are similar to human speech, but not just the sounds that the babies will have heard around them. They are not simply imitating what they have heard. Some of the sounds that babies make do not occur in the language which their parents use, and which they will have heard around them. For example, British-born babies will make sounds that only occur in Japanese or Chinese. They have never heard these sounds before. Babbling is probably a genetically acquired response, but it can have some communication value, and can be modified by social learning.

The first few months of life are dominated by infants' **heredity** and need for **maturation**. What does each of these terms mean?

Most babies start babbling by about six months of age. All over the world babies are likely to babble just about all the sounds which exist in any language.

During the first year of pre-speech the infant is maturing and developing some of the ideas which it may want to communicate in language later.

Even though babies can't talk, this doesn't mean they can't communicate. Several studies of parent–child interaction claim that communication is an important part of their interaction.

A great deal of evidence now exists to show that babies benefit from social interaction. We know that children in the deprived orphanages – studied by people like Wayne Dennis and Howard Skeels – (see Chapter Twelve) had poor language development. We also know that infants seem to enjoy human companionship. Dan Stern has shown that babies of just a few months old move their bodies in **interactional synchrony** with human speech. Infants must wait a few months before they are maturationally ready to start making speechlike sounds, and before they are able to start learning their particular language. These first months of life are known as the period of **pre-speech**.

Colwyn Trevarthen and **Martin Richards** filmed five babies, once a week, from birth to six months of age. The babies sometimes had toys hanging in front of them, or were with their mothers. The mothers were asked to chat with their babies. Trevarthen and Richards wanted to know if there would be any differences between each baby's behaviour towards the toy and towards the mother. They noticed that from about six weeks old the babies' behaviour changed when their mothers were present. The babies moved their hands differently, the expressions on their faces changed, and the tone of their voices altered. They moved their lips as if trying to speak, and took turns at 'speaking' with their mothers. Trevarthen calls this elaborate activity pre-speech. This encouraged their mothers to respond, and so the conversation went on.

The early, innate responses, like babbling and hand movements, were modified by interaction with the mother. Such social relationships may modify other innate tendencies too.

Reciprocity

1 What are Trevarthen and Richards looking for in this observational study?

2 What is the sample size, and what are the independent variables?

3 What dependent variables were being measured?

4 What is meant by pre-speech?

After six months babbling increases, reaching its peak at around 10 months. **Jerome Bruner** filmed the interaction between some mothers and their babies, and noticed that communication is an essential feature of their play. Before about nine months children will be quite passive in games like give and take. Mother does all the giving of an object, such as a toy, the baby reaches out and takes it. From about nine months the infant becomes more active, and will offer the toy to the mother. By 12 months mothers and babies are equal in the amount of giving and taking they do. Bruner suggests that games such as these give children ideas about taking turns which they will practise later with language.

By 10 months many babies are stringing sounds together such as 'popopopa', 'babababa', and 'dididi'. It may be that parents reward their children when they make English-type sounds and don't reward them when they don't. The child may associate the making of some sounds with the warmth and comfort shown by the parents. This is mainly the explanation which behaviourists such as B. F. Skinner would support. It may explain how children acquire some aspects of speech. The babbling sounds that are most often rewarded (or reinforced) will be those which sound most like human speech. At the same time babies' vocal organs and nervous system are maturing, and they may begin to enjoy imitating sounds they hear around them. (NB: Daniel Stern has shown that babies are very sociable almost right from birth.)

Quite a lot of language skill is acquired through imitation (e.g. when talking to a man, infants' voices are usually a little louder than when talking to a woman!). They must have heard that men speak louder than women, so perhaps they are imitating what they think is the right way to speak. Babbling also seems to reinforce itself. Babies may well enjoy hearing their own noises! Profoundly deaf babies start to babble at about the same time as hearing babies, but stop after a few months. This may be because they can't hear themselves, and so can't reinforce themselves.

One explanation of how babbles become words emphasises the importance of selective reinforcement. Those sounds which are selected to be reinforced are likely to be used by the child, while those which are not are less likely to be repeated.

The pre-linguistic stage

Construct a two-column table with the heading *The pre-linguistic stage*. Head one column *Up to six months*, and the other one *Six months to one year*. Write three of the baby's main skills in each column.

Review
The first twelve months

The first few months are dominated by the biological needs of getting used to life. There's a great deal for an infant to learn, such as how to use various muscles and limbs. Babbling starts as a biologically inherited activity which probably isn't intended to convey any meaning, although it may be shaped later into having some meaning for itself and its caregivers. Caregiver–child interaction may prepare the child for important aspects of language, for example, taking turns.

The first words – from 1 to 2 years

Babbling is mainly for amusement and doesn't appear to communicate anything very much. From about 10 to 12 months two important changes occur. First, the infants are mature enough to have control over their vocal chords, tongue, breathing, etc., which they need for speech. And second, the cognitive structures in the infants' brains are mature enough to accept that sounds they hear or make can stand for something they know about. So when a mother makes a sound like 'BALL' she actually means the thing the infant rolls along the ground.

Here are some examples of first words from the vocabulary of one child of 12 months:

Word	Refers to
kaa	mother, juice, bottle, or milk
gaga	no
papa	doll, rattle, buggy, blanket

These sounds can be thought of as one-word sentences or

Most children start to use their first words from around their first birthdays. The first words they learn will be for people or things which they are most familiar with.

holophrases. (This period is sometimes called the holophrastic stage.)

The first words children learn are for things which are most familiar to them, 'mam', 'dada', 'milk', 'juice', 'doggie', 'bath', etc. All children, no matter which language they're learning, seem to have one thing in common – they all make pronunciation mistakes.

Inevitably when we first learn anything we will make some mistakes. The most common mistakes babies make are in trying to make the word sound correct so that other people can understand what the child is saying and apply the word to the correct thing which it describes.

Mistakes with pronouncing words

When babies first learn to talk they often double their syllables. 'Baba', 'mama', 'dada' are all quite common words for a child of 18 months. The reason for this might be that children cannot hear adults saying the words 'baby', 'mummy', or 'daddy' very clearly. Another reason is that some adults seem to want to teach children the wrong word. Adults may well say 'moomoo' when the child sees a cow, and the child will be taught this wrong word. Second, some sounds are quite simply easier to make than others. Babies will use words that have sounds which they have mastered, and will avoid using words which are difficult to say. These first words are often ordinary words reduced to their simplest sounds. For example since 's' is a difficult sound to make, 'smack' becomes 'mack', and 'spoon' becomes 'poon'. Some children will continue to simplify difficult words until they are four or five years old. And of course some sounds are simply more enjoyable than others for children to make. Sounds which vibrate the vocal chords such as b, d, and g, are often substituted for the less pleasant p, t, and k. So 'pie' becomes 'bie' and 'toe' becomes 'doe'.

Mistakes with applying words

Babies frequently **overextend** the meaning of the words they use. Having learned the word dog and associated it with the family's pet labrador, they will then apply the word to anything which has some similarities to a dog, for example, four legs and a tail. So horses will be called dogs, as will cows and sheep. Just because children describe oranges, plums, and tomatoes as apples this doesn't mean that they don't know exactly what an apple is. They just don't know the words plum, tomato, etc., and apple is the nearest to them that they do know.

Here are some examples of overextension from one child's vocabulary:

Word	First applied to	Later applied to
da	father	all men, boys, some women.
baw	ball	toys, most fruit, stones.
mil	milk	all drinks, bathwater, urine, the sea, a goldfish

Babies also **underextend** some words. Having learned that a dog is an animal, for example, the child believes that all animals must

Babies often make mistakes in pronunciation and in applying the words they know correctly to the objects or events they describe.

have the same characteristics as a dog, for example, four legs, etc. Fish and birds clearly can't be animals! Having learned that grass grows in the child's garden, the child will **underextend** the word so that grass can't grow in the park too.

Early errors

Write a paragraph summarising the main errors that children make in their early speech.

Background reading – Why do children make mistakes?

Eve Clarke proposes the **semantic features hypothesis.** (Semantic loosely refers to the meaning something has.) She says that the child identifies one or two of the main features of an object, for example, its shape, colour, smell, sound, weight, etc. So 'da' first applies to father, and father is tall and moves, talks, etc. Height and movement are two semantic features of things called 'da'. Therefore all tall things will be 'da', particularly if they are people. As children grow they become capable of using more features to define a word.

Katherine Nelson proposed the **functional similarities hypothesis.** (Functional refers to what something does.) She says that a child learns what someone called 'da' does. Anyone else who does the same thing will be 'da'.

Richard Prawat and **Susan Wildfong** conducted an experiment to test these alternative hypotheses. A group of three- and four-year-olds were shown some familiar objects like cups, which were being used in unusual ways, for example, having cereal poured into them. If the semantic features hypothesis is correct then the children will still call them cups, because they look like cups. If the functional similarities hypothesis is correct they will call them bowls, because that's what they are being used for. The results seem to confirm Eve Clarke's semantic features hypothesis. Other research conducted on two-year-olds supports this hypothesis.

Children learn what words mean long before they can use the words themselves. If asked, many nine-month-old infants could point to daddy, the milk, the clock, etc., long before they could say any of those words. Learning to talk will take some time. From the day they start to learn about language, children build up two kinds of vocabulary – an **active vocabulary**, which consists of the words they can use, and a **passive vocabulary**, which consists of the words they know but can't use. From the time children use their first words they take another three or four months to learn to use another 10 words. After this the rate of learning speeds up very greatly. By around two years many children have a vocabulary of about 50 words, although it's impossible to say exactly just how large an average child's active vocabulary is. Different studies give different averages and not all children develop language at the same time. It's not uncommon for children of 14 and 16 months not to have said their first word. On the other hand some children speak their first word at seven or eight months.

Even before babies can use words themselves, they have some understanding of what some words mean. They have both active and passive vocabularies.

Learning the first words marks a great achievement in communication. Children can make requests, state their preferences and dislikes, etc. But single words do not allow complicated ideas to be expressed. Try explaining the following observation by using a few single words: 'A red-haired boy was being chased down the road, in his pyjamas and bedroom slippers, by an angry policeman. He tripped on a loose kerbstone and fell into a large, green furniture van that was parked in the road.' The best a child could do might be 'Boy, run, hit, fell.'

The first words

1 Define an *active vocabulary* and a *passive vocabulary*?

2 Make a list of the things children who knows some words can do which will help them to become more sociable and independent.

The first sentences appear between 18 and 24 months in most children. They have to learn how to make the word sounds, what they mean, and what order to put them in. These things are to do with grammar.

The first sentences – from round 2 years onwards

From around 18 months to two years children start to combine their words into simple two-word sentences. They tend to leave out some words which do not necessarily add anything to the meaning of the sentence. The result is called **telegraphic speech**. They also start to use **grammar**. Grammar is the rules of a language. It includes things like putting the words in a sentence in the correct order so that they mean what the child wants them to mean. It includes the correct use of tenses, meanings of words, sound of words, etc.

Grammar

Spot as many of the grammatical errors as you can in this passage from a nine-year-old speaker.
'One day I was playing in the grounds an' I seen a mice. I frightened of mices so I run to find Michael. He's older 'n me an' he catched the mice . . . the mouse. My dog would eat them if I fetched her but she had to go away for a blind dog. She'd eat.'

To begin with, children's speech has a limited number of themes. These include action, possession, place, etc. Some adult conversation is still dominated by these themes!

Children's first speech has several main themes. They talk about actions such as what has happened to what – 'me hit ball', 'me fall', 'car go bang'. They seem preoccupied by *possessions* and who owns what – 'my teddy', 'daddy pen', 'mummy car'. They are also concerned with the *place* of things – 'cup in box' 'car in garage', 'mummy outside'. They also learn about *repetition* – 'more milk', 'go again'. They *label* things – 'that teddy', 'this one', 'this car'. They learn about *nonexistence* – 'beads all gone', 'no more apples', 'all gone now'. Some are able to express their feelings, and to say what they want and do not want.

This list represents what just about all two- and three-year-old children can do, regardless of which language they are learning. Perhaps we are all born with the same basic mental structures for such things as action, possession, location, repetition, naming things, and non-existence. Or perhaps these are 'going on' around the child so it is most likely to be aware of them. The earliest recorded two-word sentences have been spoken by a child of 10 months, the average age is about 18 months, but it's not uncommon for children of 24 months not to have spoken a two-word sentence.

Background reading – Grammar

Here are some examples of the use of grammar. **Word order:** No one is certain why babies seem to use two of the basic rules of grammar as soon as they start to join words together. They rarely make mistakes, unlike when they are learning pronunciation. First, they seem to know that the subject of a sentence usually appears before the word which describes what it is doing. For example a baby will say 'I go', and is unlikely to say 'go I'. Second, babies correctly put words which describe before a thing they are describing, for example 'big lorry' is rarely said as 'lorry big'. It may be that they have heard adults using these rules in their own speech.

Adding morphemes: As we said earlier, morphemes are the smallest parts of language which convey some meaning. Children start to learn that adding an 's' makes a word into a plural, so 'dog' becomes 'dogs'. Also 'ed' makes it past tense so they learn 'dream' becomes 'dreamed'. Some common mistakes are 'runned', 'sleeped', 'eated', 'tooked', etc.

Semantics: Semantics refers to the meaning of words. A two-year-old with a vocabulary of 50 words or so may not be able to say that 'Alexandra has fallen off her tricycle.' 'Alex fall' or 'Fall bike' may be the nearest that can be managed. By three or four years of age children use three- and four-word sentences ('Don't want hot milk' and questions like 'Where's daddy gone?'). These are examples of telegraphic speech (the small connecting words are left out).

Cross-cultural studies

Let's imagine that some psychologist was interested in whether children in other cultures spoke their first words and sentences at the same ages as they do in Europe. Imagine she puts adverts in three national daily newspapers in three countries, asking for mothers to fill in a questionnaire. She may have received 250 replies from mothers from one society, 150 from another, and 100 from the third. The following table summarises her findings.

	First words Age (in months)		First sentence Age (in months)	
	Mean	Median	Mean	Median
First society	13	14	22	23
Second society	9	9	18	19
Third society	11	10	20	22

1 Define a mean and a median? (If you don't know, look at page 320.)

2 What was the total sample size?

3 How was the sample drawn, and what were the dangers in using this method?

4 Which society has children who are quickest to start learning language?

5 What is a cross-cultural study?

6 What are the major drawbacks of cross-cultural research? (If you don't know, look at page 292.)

7 Write one or two sentences about whether you think the results obtained from this survey would support the original hypothesis, giving your reasons.

Roger Brown's study

Longitudinal studies follow a (usually small) group of subjects for various periods of their lives (See page 292.)

An American researcher, Roger Brown, has conducted a very detailed 10-year, longitudinal, naturalistic observation study (published in 1973) of the speech of three children he called Adam, Eve, and Sarah. One of the things he was interested to find was the way in which children acquire 14 of the most commonly used morphemes, as this would give an indication of the kinds of grammar they are capable of using and understanding as they grow. He tape-recorded each of the children talking, for an average of one hour per week, until each was five years old. Here is an extract from Adam's first session (when he was 27 months old.)

Adam	Mother
See truck Mommy	Did you see the truck?
See truck	
No I see truck	No, you didn't see it?
	There goes one.
There go one	Yes, there goes one.
See a truck,	
See a truck Mommy	
See truck	
Put truck Mommy	Put the truck where?
Put truck window	I think that one's too large to go in the window.

This example points out some features that are common to conversations between children and their parents at this age. For example, the subject is immediate, that is, they are talking about real things that are happening now. The mother's sentences are short and contain simple words. She uses grammatically correct replies, and Adam repeats a shortened version of what he has heard.

Adam says 'See truck' after his mother said 'Did you see the truck?' Later he says 'There go one' in response to his mother's 'There goes one'. Children leave out the least important words. Brown calls this shortened version 'telegraphic speech' (since it's what people did when they sent telegrams). Here are some examples from Roger Brown's study. The responses of three children of different ages are shown here. Each child is repeating a 'model' sentence.

Sentence	Child's age (in months)		
	25.5	30	35.5
I showed you the book	I show book	Show you the book	CORRECT
I will read the book	Read book	I read the book	CORRECT
Do I like to read books?	To read book?	I read books	CORRECT

The third sentence is rather more difficult for a child to understand than the first two. Can you see why?

This table illustrates the rapid progress children make between about two and three years of age. The 25.5-month-old child seems to use telegraphic speech for the simpler sentences and misses larger parts of the more difficult sentence. By three years of age even this difficult sentence can be imitated correctly.

Telegraphic speech

1 Write these sentences in telegraphic speech: 'I've fallen off the swing and hurt my knee.' 'Shall we go for a walk?' 'Let Daddy sit there.' 'How long is the train?' 'Didn't you have some milk yesterday?'

2 How would you describe the main differences between these sentences spoken by Eve:

At 18 months	At 27 months
More grapefruit	I got a pencil 'n' write.
Mommy soup	Don't stand on my ice cubes.
No mommy read	I put them in the refrigerator to freeze.
Write a paper	An' I want to take off my hat.

Being able to move around on their own feet, to use their hands to pick things up and explore them, and to use their language to ask questions, make statements, etc. transform the potential for development.

The explanation why children repeat certain words and not others might be because the adult puts more stress on the more important words than on the less important ones. Roger Brown calls the less important words **functor words**. They may not always add much to the basic meaning of a sentence, but are used to make the sentence grammatically correct. The message 'No, and you may not go to the swimming-baths either' contains the functor words 'No, and, you, may, to, the', and 'either'. The way that adults put stress on certain parts of a word may also explain why children repeat parts of a word when the whole word is too difficult for them to say. For example 'Mummy's computer' may become 'Mummy's puter', and 'Daddy's harmonica' may become 'Daddy's monica'.

Brown also noted that parents often imitate their children's speech. They usually expanded the child's statement. For example Adam's mother says 'Yes, there goes one' when Adam had said 'There go one'. The adult's replies provide models for the child to expand his understanding of language. Although the age at which Adam, Eve, and Sarah mastered the rules of grammar varied, each child mastered them in exactly the same sequence. This led Brown to suggest that language develops in five stages.

Children's intellects can grow very quickly. Can you think of an example of such a study?

Roger Brown's five stages of language acquisition

Stage One: Simple two- or three-word sentences which describe actions ('hit ball') or possessions ('my ball'). Brown describes these sentences as telegraphic speech. Children miss out the unimportant words, probably because they can't remember every word. Instead they repeat the words which have had more stress put on them.

Stage Two: Language becomes more complicated as children learn the names for objects and events ('that a pencil'), and they start using word endings ('Adam walking', 'Eve sleeped').

Stage Three: They start asking questions beginning with what, why, who and where, and questions like 'Does Eve like juice?'

Stage Four: What used to be two short sentences – 'Who's that?', and 'Singing song?' – are now joined to become 'Who's that singing that song?'

Stage Five: Children can now join more complicated sentences together ('I ran and I kicked the ball'), and they can deal with sentences containing two subjects ('Michael and John are eating apples'). They are now ready for school, which relies very much on a child's ability to understand and use language.

What Brown is suggesting is that children learn about the rules of grammar by concentrating on one or two ideas at a time. They begin with words about action, then possession, etc. When they have expanded their basic ideas (or **sensory motor schemas**, as Piaget called them) for one thing, then they go on to the next. By the time children reach school they have usually mastered enough rules of grammar (called **syntax**) to be able to communicate quite well, although they continue to play with language in things like silly jokes which involve a play on words, nursery rhymes, riddles, etc.

Review
The first sentences

From around 12 months children are expanding their idea that some sounds that they hear can have some meaning. By 24 months they've learned that these bits of meaning can be strung together in a particular order, and the meaning can be expanded or made more precise.

Brown's study

1 Describe the method that Roger Brown used to study his sample of children. What is the main advantage of this method in studying children's language development?

2 Divide this sentence into telegraphic speech and functor words: 'David will be going to London on Thursday.' Does the telegraphic sentence make sense? Do the functor words make sense?

3 What response is a child expecting when asking the following question? 'Adam and Eve and pinch me went down to the river to bathe, Adam and Eve were drowned, who was the only one saved?'

A summary of the development of language

By around three to six months babies start to 'babble'. They make all the sounds that appear in any language in the world.

By 10 to 12 months they are making their first 'words'.

By 18 months children probably have a vocabulary of about 50 words although they still spend a large amount of time 'babbling'.

By 24 months not only has the number of words increased, but children are putting two words together to make simple sentences such as 'take cup', 'see car', etc. Not only can children name an increasing number of objects and actions, they can also interact with other people.

By 30 months babbling will have mostly disappeared, and children spend time extending their vocabulary. Several new words may be learned each day. Two, three, four and even five words are strung together in a 'sentence', for example, 'no coat, too hot'. Whilst the communication may not be grammatically correct, it is a powerful and adequate system of communicating feelings, needs, and opinions. Further, although their ability to respond may be limited, children of 30 months can understand a great deal of what is said by other people.

By three years old children may have a vocabulary of about 1,000 words, and about three-quarters of their utterances are understood, even by strangers.

It was thought that these first few years are crucially important for learning language. During their first two years of life many human babies make two enormous advances. First, they start to communicate through language, and second they start to be able to move around their environment on their own, by crawling then walking. Both of these skills occur when the child is mature enough, and they tend to occur together. However, as we saw earlier, the maturation process varies for each skill. It is not uncommon to find a one-year-old who talks constantly, but makes little effort to walk, or an 18-month-old who rushes around everywhere, but who rarely speaks. Further it is wrong to think that these early years are so crucial. A number of studies have shown that children who have learned no language at all during their early years can still learn it perfectly well later.

A child's communication

Here is a description of conversation between a young mother and her 27-month-old daughter which a student tape-recorded recently. The daughter was helping her mother to fill some small fruit pies that she was making.

Daughter	Mother
Me do Mummy.	
Me do.	Do you want to fill a pie?
Me want fill.	Don't drop any off the spoon will you?
	15 second pause
	Be careful, you're tipping the spoon.
Some of the apple filling must have fallen on the floor.	
	Sounding a bit annoyed:
	Look what you've done. You've dropped apple all over the floor. Fetch me the cloth, oh never mind, I'll do it.

In English we use the past and present tense, we can make things plural, we can describe the location of something, etc. Some of these skills are harder to grasp than others. Roger Brown and others have shown that there is a fixed order in which children acquire these rules of grammar.

Sounding unhappy:
I clean. I clean Mummy.
The apple don't mind.

1 Give an example of telegraphic speech from the passage.

2 Name some functor words which are used by the mother but not by the child.

3 What is animism? Give an example of it from the passage. (If you can't remember what animism is, turn to page 136.)

---

4 The main theories of language development

Language is learned

In 1957 B. F. Skinner outlined the **operant conditioning** approach. He said that any speech-like sounds that babies babble will be reinforced and become learned words. Sounds which go unreinforced will extinguish. After these words are learned the parent stops reinforcing them when they are spoken by the child. To be reinforced now, the child must produce strings of words. This is a fairly simple *behaviour-shaping* explanation. Skinner totally rejects any reference to any mental structures (such as inherited aspects of language or *schemas*). Instead he says the child learns to name objects and ask questions. With these two abilities the child's vocabulary will be expanded by selective reinforcement.

A major criticism is that this may explain how children learn single words, i.e. how their vocabulary grows, but doesn't begin to explain how children manage to combine all the words they have learned into so many original sentences. If we had to learn everything we communicate by reinforcement it would take several lifetimes, and we would still be very poor communicators. Another criticism stems from research which has shown that parents do not generally reinforce their children's speech. If children say something which is wrong, or a lie, or something which is hurtful, their parents are likely to correct it. They are less likely to correct simple grammatical faults. If Skinner's explanation were true then children would learn to tell the truth, and not to be hurtful, using bad grammar! This simply is not true.

Language is innate

A few years after Skinner's theory appeared, an American theorist called **Noam Chomsky** proposed that we are biologically programmed for language. He totally rejects Skinner's view, and is dissatisfied with the vagueness of Piaget's. Chomsky says that we are born with all the things we need to produce language, i.e. parts of the left hemisphere of the brain, where language centres are located, and the speech-producing apparatus in the throat and mouth. We will also be able to control our breathing, which is also necessary for speech. Chomsky calls these things which human beings inherit our **Language Acquisition Device (LAD)**. Unlike any other animal we are also born with the potential to understand the structure (grammar) of any language, and the vocabulary and grammar of the particular language we use.

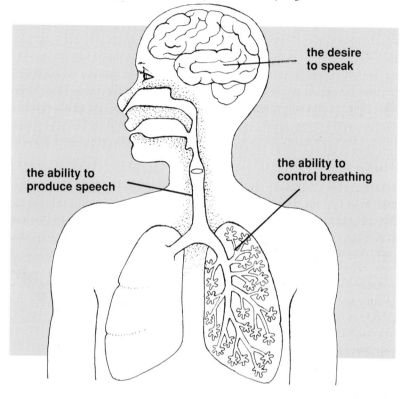

the desire to speak

the ability to produce speech

the ability to control breathing

◀
Producing language

Chomsky's theory does explain why children make some mistakes in the way they join parts of words together. The morpheme 'ed' means to make something into the past, as in 'walked', 'picked', and 'painted'. The LAD is said to apply such rules of grammar as 'how to make a past tense', which it has learned, to new words, which it is learning. Hence a child may say 'drinked', 'goed', 'runned', 'felled', or 'eated'. Chomsky claims that LAD contains the skill of being able to distinguish 'surface structure' (the actual words and grammar used) from 'deep structure' (the knowledge of underlying meaning, of what the child is meaning and trying to communicate).

A problem with this explanation is that if language acquisition is innate, surely it would develop soon after we were mature enough to control our voices, sometime around our first birthday. Why does language need to take even a few years to develop? And why do children make so many mistakes, like over- and underextension? And why are there such wide individual variations between children?

Piaget's view

For the last 20 years or so it has been recognised that to use adult speech as the measure of how good a child's speech is may be quite wrong. Piaget has shown us that children's thought processes are not the same as those of an adult. They don't use the same logic, and aren't able to use the same problem-solving behaviour. According to Piaget, symbolisation is the process of learning the right words to describe the schemas which the children are developing through their manipulation of objects in their environment. (NB schemas develop first, the right words for them appear second.) Such schemas as 'milk', 'walk', 'mine', and 'cuddle' are well known to children before they have any idea what the correct word for them is, or even that there exists any word for them, or what 'words' are at all. Knowing the right word allows children to communicate better and helps imagination to grow, thus allowing more schemas, and the words to describe them, to be learned.

So the role of language is to allow the correct word to be used for a schema which will help to clarify and reinforce it in the child's mind, and help to refine it. For example, 'hot' and 'cold' are useful words, but the schemas hot and cold can be considerably refined by 'below freezing', 'freezing', 'very cold', 'bitterly cold', 'tepid', 'warmish', 'very warm', 'boiling', etc.

Review
Theories of language

Piaget explains language development as a factor contributing to cognition. The main explanations of how we acquire language come from learning theory, which says that selective reinforcement of some sounds rather than others is the main reason, while Chomsky argues that certain key features such as deep structure are innate.

The theories of language acquisition

1 Write the title *The origins of language* on a new sheet of paper. Divide the page into two columns. Head one column *NATIVIST VIEW*, and the other column *NURTURIST VIEW*. Give a brief description (with examples) of each argument.

2 Briefly contrast Skinner and Chomsky's explanations for the origin of language.

3 Piaget used the clinical interview as one of his major methods for investigating children's thinking. In view of what he says about the relationship between language and cognition can you suggest a problem he will have?

---

5 Can animals be taught to use language?

Until the influence of biologists such as Darwin started to spread, most people in the West were taught that human beings were created by God, in His own image. We were special, and had been given many special gifts by God, such as the ability to think and communicate. Darwin's suggestion that human beings were merely descended from the animal kingdom caused a furious outcry against him from some sections of the Christian Church. If we were descended from the apes, then might they share any of our special gifts?

Several attempts have been made to teach non-human primates to communicate with humans. If humans use spoken language, and if humans descended from the apes, then might there be some apes who are able to speak? The few attempts to teach monkeys and chimps to speak which have been made were complete failures. During the 1930s the **Kelloggs** tried to teach a chimp to speak. They raised Gua from when he was about ten months old with their own son, Donald. They tried to teach Gua everything they taught Donald. By the time Donald was 16 months Gua knew the meaning of 95 words, but couldn't speak any of them. (A chimp's larynx is quite different from a human's. Chimps can eat, drink, and breathe all at the same time. They probably could not produce speech sounds.) The Kelloggs' experiment was abandoned because of the possible dangers to Donald from the rapidly maturing and playful chimp. During the 1960s and 1970s attention turned to see if some animals can learn to communicate in other ways. Several attempts have been made to teach chimpanzees to communicate.

One of the best known was a study by **Allen and Beatrix Gardner**. They tried to teach a female chimpanzee called Washoe to use **American Sign Language** (ASL or sometimes called AmeSLan). To avoid confusing the animal they never spoke in front of her. They helped her by showing her how to shape her hands, and they rewarded her with tickles when she made the sign correctly. She was 10 months old when they started teaching her. By 18 months she knew four signs, by 30 months she used 30 signs, and by 60 months she used 160 signs. Here are the first signs that she learned, in the order in which she learned them: 'come-gimme', 'more', 'up', 'sweet', 'go', 'hear-listen', 'tickle', etc. She used signs in the same way that children produce words, always knowing more signs than she could use, using one sign, then, later, combining two or three signs. The order in which Washoe learned and used signs was rather similar to the way children learn language, from holophrases to telegraphic speech.

The Gardners claimed that Washoe wasn't simply conditioned to give responses when stimulated. It was possible to hold a simple conversation with her. One exchange went:

Human: 'What's that?'
Washoe: 'Bed.'
Human: 'Whose?'
Washoe: 'Mine.'
Human: 'What colour is it?'
Washoe: 'Red.'

Washoe sometimes began a conversation too. She asked for things, and could describe them. She seemed to understand some of the basics of language. However she never learned very much grammar and couldn't use different tenses. She made very few original statements, although when she saw an aeroplane (she knew the sign plane), she pointed to it and said 'You me ride plane'. And the first time she saw a duck (which she didn't know the sign for) she combined the two signs 'water' and 'bird'. However most of her utterances were rather simple responses to rather simple questions, and some of her signs didn't make much sense at all. Washoe's language never progressed beyond what might be expected of a two- to three-year-old human.

When Washoe was physically mature the Gardners returned her to a zoo where one of her trainers worked with a group of chimps. She was seen trying to teach some of the infants ASL. Washoe often 'talked to herself' in ASL too.

Washoe learns ASL ▶

Washoe the chimp

1 What increase had taken place in Washoe's vocabulary between 10 and 60 months?

2 What is the name of the method used in this study?

3 Name two limitations of this method as used by psychologists.

4 Why didn't the Gardners let Washoe hear them talk?

Ann and David Premack used operant conditioning to teach a six-year-old chimp called Sarah that red plastic shapes could stand for particular objects or descriptions, for example, there were shapes that stood for 'Sarah', 'apple', 'chocolate', 'is', '?', 'give', 'take', 'no', 'yellow', 'brown', etc. She also had shapes for the names of her trainers. By arranging them in order on a board she could construct 'sentences'. Sarah lived in a laboratory and was trained for an hour each day, using operant-conditioning techniques.

Over a 30-month period Sarah learned meanings for hundreds of shapes, and did learn to construct fairly complicated answers to specific questions. Her training did not allow her to 'play' with the symbols she was learning, nor to communicate freely with her trainers. However what Sarah has learned are some specific skills for a particular form of communication. This isn't really the same as learning or using language. 'Real' language involves asking questions, making statements, giving instructions, making requests, etc. Sarah couldn't do any of these things.

Duane Rumbaugh taught a two-year-old chimp called Lana to press various symbols which were put on to keys on a computer-assisted machine. Pressing the keys would cause lighted symbols corresponding to them to appear on the machine. If she could construct the symbols to make a reasonable 'sentence' the machine would provide what she requested. For example if she wanted some apple she would have to press 'please', 'give', 'Lana', 'some', 'apple'. She learned that particular symbols stood for things such as 'open a window', and 'give Lana some banana'. Lana learned over 100 symbols, and could press them in appropriate ways to communicate. She certainly appeared to know the difference between 'Tim groom Lana', and 'Lana groom Tim'!

Again, however, this isn't really language as we know it. Lana has simply learned to associate some specific symbols with some particular reinforcers, although she has also learned something about the order in which the symbols have to be arranged.

Methods of studying chimps' communication

Outline the methods which have been used to teach animals to communicate.

Conclusion – Chatty chimps or conditioned chimps?

These studies show that chimps can communicate, to some extent, but not that they can use language. Forty years ago no one imagined that a chimp could learn any ASL, and if they learned the signs they wouldn't be able to use them appropriately, but Washoe did. She made lots of mistakes, she never learned about past and future, and she could understand more signs than she could use herself. But some psychologists are more sceptical of the claims that such chimps are using language. **Herbert Terrace** started as a believer in the idea that chimps did have some idea about communicating in ideas which are similar to those used by humans. He taught a chimp (called Nim Chimpsky – a play on the name of Noam Chomsky) to use sign language, but later realised that the animal wasn't using its signs in an inventive or original way at all. It seemed that the chimp was simply making some signs as a response to the signs he had made. This is simple operant conditioning. He reviewed the reports and films of the other studies like these of Washoe, Lana, and Sarah, and concluded that none of these chimps used language at all. What they did was to give some operantly learned response to a stimulus from their trainers, presumably expecting some reward.

Nativists (like Chomsky) argue that humans are alone in having a capacity to use language, since we alone have the biological structures (the Language Acquisition Device) which are needed. **David Premack** argues that animals can use language, and the only reason why they don't learn very much is because they don't have the intelligence, not because they lack any LAD. **Francine Patterson** and some deaf assistants taught a gorilla named Koko to use ASL, using a similar approach to the Gardners. Gorillas are much bigger than chimps, and were not thought to be as intelligent as chimps. Within 29 months Koko learned to use over 200 signs, and she combined them in original and creative ways. Patterson claims that Terrace is quite wrong in his interpretation of animals' communication. She said that Koko talks to herself a great deal, using her signs, and has even scored around normal on a non-verbal intelligence test for four- to five-year-old humans! Perhaps the most convincing evidence for a chimp understanding English comes from **Sue Savage Rumbaugh** and a chimp called Kanzi. He appears to understand some spoken commands and communicates well with a large number of symbols. Savage Rumbaugh insists Kanzi, and chimps generally, can understand language, although others are still sceptical.

Review
Animal language

Whilst it might be a pleasant thought that one day we could talk to the animals it's extremely unlikely ever to come about. Most do not have the ability to produce the kind of phonemes that humans would understand, even if they had anything which they wanted to say. Attempts to teach animals to communicate have been made. How successful they have been seems to depend on who is interpreting their findings. Nativists say that only humans can use language, nurturists say that other primates may be able to, although few possess very much intelligence or learning capacity.

Teaching animals to use language

1 Why didn't these researchers try to teach the animals to speak?

2 What are the main criticisms of the claims that animals can be taught to use language?

15

Acquiring Gender Roles

Once children start using language the amount they can take in increases greatly. They can ask questions and understand the answers. Piaget has shown how important **symbolisation** is to cognitive development. One of the many important things children must learn during their first few years is what sex they are. This knowledge is called **sex identity**. At first they aren't sure whether the sex they are is permanent or will change, and they judge what sex other people are largely by their appearance. It takes time for children to learn their sex identity. During the first few years children also learn that boys and girls are expected to behave in different ways. Boys are often encouraged to be active and independent. Girls may be encouraged to be quieter and more caring. Learning to behave in the way which is considered appropriate for their sex involves learning their **gender identity**. Sex identity and gender identity are both aspects of cognition, they are bits of knowledge that children have acquired. **Gender role** refers to the actual behaviour that each person has. A male may perform his gender

Background reading – Some questions developmental psychologists ask

Around what age do children acquire their sex identity? When do they realise that they are going to stay that sex all their lives? When do they become aware of the 'appropriate' behaviour for boys and girls? When do they acquire their gender identity and when do their gender roles start developing? Are the differences in the way the two sexes behave genetically transmitted or socially learned? Do children in all societies show the same pattern of development?

The results of their studies indicate that most children begin to acquire their sex identity from around 18 months. By about two years they begin to identify what sex other children are, although they're not too sure of their own gender identity until somewhere between two

and a half and three years. Piaget, and others, have shown that children's ideas about objects are dominated by what the objects look like. The same principle applies to deciding what sex someone is. If you show a two-and-a-half-year-old child a picture of another child, and ask it whether the picture is of a boy or a girl, it will look at the hair, and what the child in the picture is wearing. Although a three-year-old may know that she is a little girl, she doesn't really know what that means. A five-year-old girl may still think that she can become a daddy if she changes her appearance to look like a daddy. Children begin to conserve their sex from around seven. This is about the same time that Piaget thought that they were beginning to conserve other things too.

We inherit our sex, we learn our gender. What kind of toys would you give (a) your son, and (b) your daughter?

Name some of the things that Piaget says we learn to conserve from around seven years of age. What are the major changes in the way children think, that Piaget claimed occurred from around seven years? Does the way children learn that their sex does not change, confirm or contradict Piaget's claims?

role in a very macho way, or may be something of a wimp. A female may behave in a very feminine way, or may be quite a tomboy.

For the last couple of centuries gender roles in Western societies have been fairly clear. Boys were supposed to be strong, brave and masculine, girls were supposed to be weak, passive, and feminine. The subjects children took at school reflected this too. Boys did the more technical subjects, while girls often did the more domestic subjects. These gender roles were seen in the media too.

How do we acquire our gender roles?

Our sex is determined by the chromosomes we inherit from our parents. Those who support the nature side of the nature–nurture debate will argue that the behaviour that goes with being male or female is also explained by biological forces. Those who support the nurture side will say that each society expects males and females to behave in certain ways. They claim that we acquire our gender roles by observation, modelling, and being reinforced for behaving accordingly.

Gender roles? ▶

Theories emphasising biological forces look for experimental evidence, mainly from animal studies, that links certain kinds of male hormones with certain kinds of behaviour. For example, research has shown that some adolescent boys who are highly aggressive also have higher levels of **androgens**, the male sex hormones. Girls with large amounts of male hormones also tend to be aggressive and tomboyish.

Contrasting with this view is the view of the social learning theorists, who have shown that genetic forces can be overcome by social ones. Aggression in children, for example, can be reduced by using a combination of reinforcements and punishments. Freud's psychoanalytic theory attempts to combine both biological and social forces, while Lawrence Kohlberg suggests a cognitive explanation for learning gender identity.

So, in this chapter we will study:

1 Biological explanations.
2 Social learning theory.
3 Freud's psychoanalytic approach.
4 Kohlberg's cognitive theory.

Sex and gender identity

1 What is meant by 'sex identity'?

2 What is meant by 'gender identity'?

3 What are 'gender roles'?

1 Biological theories of gender roles

John Bowlby argued that some differences in the attitudes and behaviour of males and females are genetically transmitted instincts. Since babies need to form attachment bonds with their mothers (or mother substitutes) then, Bowlby argued, mothers must have maternal instincts to form bonds with their babies. According to Bowlby, these maternal instincts will show themselves some time after puberty. A young girl will spend time with, and become like, her mother because she has certain maternal instincts. This explanation is not widely believed now. Males and females may well have different levels of hormones in their bodies, and these hormones may be linked to certain kinds of behaviour, but this does not mean that socialisation cannot overcome biological urges. For example, many women nowadays are deliberately choosing not to have children, for various reasons.

Review
Sex and gender

Those biologists and psychologists who emphasise the role of instincts and genetic inheritance explain gender-role behaviour in terms of chromosomes and hormones. Social learning theorists maintain that whatever our genetic inheritance, it can be overcome by social pressures. Traditional Freudian psychoanalysis sees gender roles emerging as a result of identification. Cognitive theorists emphasise the process by which children acquire their ideas about their sex.

Bowlby claims that the role of caregiver is simply something which girls are born with.

Background reading – The major hormones in physical and sexual development

Hormone	Gland	Effects
Many growth hormones	Pituitary	This 'master' gland affects the rate of maturation, controls the activity of some other glands, stimulates sexual development such as ovulation and milk production in females, and sperm production in males.
Thyroxin	Thyroid	Metabolism, brain development, and aspects of physical growth are stimulated by thyroxin.
Adrenalin	Adrenal	Adrenalin has many uses in the body, including changes at puberty, some sexual effects, and general levels of arousal.
Androgens (boys)	Testes	The androgens influence general male characteristics, for example, body shape, muscle growth, voice change at puberty, body hair, levels of aggression, body fat.
Oestrogens (girls)	Ovaries	The oestrogens affect female sexual characteristics such as body fat, breast development and menstruation.

There are obviously biological differences between males and females. For example, each sex is the result of different combinations of chromosomes (males having XY and females XX combinations). As a result of this, the hormonal balance of members of each sex is different, and their sexual and reproductive organs are different. These biological differences explain someone's sex, but do not explain their gender role. If gender role differences were genetically transmitted then we would expect that any differences in the behaviour of males and females would begin to appear soon after birth. Also each person's sex-related behaviour would be determined by the levels of sex hormones. This should also be true of the higher non-human primates, such as gorillas, chimps, and monkeys. And people in all societies would have similar sex-related behaviour. We will examine each of these points in turn.

Early differences in male and female behaviour

Male babies are generally bigger and heavier than female babies. They often sleep less, cry more, and are generally more active. They are usually more irritable, and are harder to comfort than females too. Female babies tend to be rather hardier than boys. They are often talking before the average males, and usually reach physical maturity more quickly too. Observing these differences might make us think that male and female babies are genetically programmed to follow the roles that will be expected of them later.

Comment: Social learning theorists do not dispute that there are these early differences between males and females. However, they do say that social factors will also be important. Perhaps parents are more likely to play rough-and-tumble games with their boys, and be more quiet and cuddling with their daughters. It might be that daughters are spoken to more often, and so pick up language sooner than boys. We will return to these ideas shortly.

The effects of hormones
Certain glands in our body produce hormones which change the state of some other organs. The main female hormones are called **oestrogens**, the male hormones are called **androgens**.

Experiments with animals

Many of the body's glands and organs need to send messages to other glands and organs. They do this by making chemical substances called hormones. These hormones are carried around our bodies by our blood. Males and females have different amounts of various hormones.

Some research on lower-order animals, such as rhesus monkeys, has shown that their behaviour is greatly influenced by their levels of sex hormones. For example, W. C. Young injected a pregnant monkey, whose foetus was genetically female, with a course of testosterone (an androgen). Every day from the 42nd to the 122nd day of her pregnancy she received the male hormone injection. When the infant monkey was born, it was genetically female, and had female sex organs. It also had a well-developed set of male sex organs. It behaved in the same assertive ways that male rhesus monkeys behave, joining in rough-and-tumble games, and challenging other males to fight for a higher status in the group. When sexually mature, it even tried to mount a female monkey for mating. Other experiments have shown that monkeys injected with testosterone between birth and puberty developed similar assertive behaviour. Other lower-order animals will behave as though they were of the opposite sex when their hormone levels are altered. When females have male hormones they become more assertive and behave more like males. When male hamsters were prevented from producing testosterone they behaved as though they were females.

Comment: Numerous experiments have shown that altering the balance of various hormones will change the gender-role behaviour of various animals. We must be careful not to generalise these findings to human beings, who are much more aware of the effects of their behaviour, and much better able to control it.

Research with humans

Some of the main research in the areas of hormonal effects on human gender roles has been collected by **John Money** and his colleagues. They noted the cases of a number of mothers who had been given a drug during pregnancy which would help prevent miscarriage. The drug contained androgens which affected the development of the sex organs of some of their foetuses. At birth the female babies looked as though they had male sex organs. They were diagnosed as having **androgenital syndrome (AGS)**, and they needed surgery to restore their sex organs to normal. Money followed some of these cases, and found that many of the girls became unusually tomboyish. They dressed and played like boys, and preferred the company of boys to girls. A career took priority over having a family. Those who eventually did have children were quite satisfactory mothers, so their early experiences didn't affect their maternal behaviour.

Comment: It seems from this evidence that a girl's behaviour, attitudes and interests are affected if her mother received a male sex hormone during pregnancy. However, parental influences may well play a part. Even if hormone balances and gender-role behaviour are related, it still doesn't prove that all gender-role behaviour is caused by hormone levels.

Do children everywhere acquire the same kind of behaviour?

If such male characteristics as aggression were biologically determined, then they would appear when children reached about the same age, in all cultures. Some research has shown that aggression in males does begin at around two years of age in many cultures. Males continue to be more aggressive. This has been explained by the fact that they have higher testosterone levels than females.

Comment: Hormone levels not only cause changes to occur,

Biological theories of gender role

Those who emphasise the biological influences on gender-role behaviour show how the levels of various hormones correlate with typically male, or typically female behaviour. There is some evidence to suggest that males are more likely to be aggressive than females. There are few, if any, others aspects of behaviour which exist in the majority of cultures which are exclusively male or female.

but can themselves be changed by the experiences we have. It is possible that boys are reinforced for behaving aggressively, and this makes them produce more testosterone. Apart from aggression, there is no other behaviour which occurs consistently between the sexes in many cultures. Margaret Mead's studies will show this most clearly later in this chapter.

Biological explanations for gender-role differences

1 Mention some of the physical differences between male and female infants.

2 What are some of the main functions of oestrogens and androgens?

3 According to the research on humans and animals, what effects do hormones have on behaviour?

---

2 Social learning theories of gender roles

Social learning theorists do not accept that chromosomes and hormones determine much of our behaviour, and even offer an alternative explanation for aggression being largely a male characteristic. They see the environment, the socialisation process, modelling, reinforcement and punishment, and social customs, as being just as important. Attitudes and customs change, and the behaviour that we expect from males and females will also change. In our own society, for example, there has been a dramatic change in the roles of men and women during this century. Women were regarded by most men as being inferior in just about every important way. Today, women are being accepted increasingly as men's equals.

A baby's sex is determined at the moment that the father's sperm fertilises the mother's egg. By six weeks of age babies with male chromosomes will start to develop the tissue which will become testes. Parents aren't usually aware of the sex of their child until moments after the birth. From that time onwards just about every aspect of the way the child is treated will be influenced by its sex. Parents have usually already decided on its name 'if it's a girl' or 'if it's a boy'. The child will be spoken to differently, dressed differently, handled differently, have different things expected of it, will be encouraged to do different things and act in different ways, and be expected to regard members of the opposite sex in certain ways too. Unfortunately, the tradition in the past was to see males and male things and interests as superior, and to see females and female things as inferior.

Social learning theorists argue that children learn the behaviour which their society expects of people of their sex in two ways. Children are either deliberately taught what is appropriate, or they see it for themselves and imitate it. Either way, many parents encourage their children to behave appropriately and reinforce them when they do. Here we will review some of the evidence for social learning theorists' claims.

Western society and a child's sex

1 Sort this list into girls' toys, boys' toys, or toys for both sexes.
   doll, ball, drum, chemistry set, pram, nurses outfit, toy shop, gun, skates, skipping-rope, sports equipment, cuddly toys, bicycle construction sets.

2 Here is a list of nicknames that parents have called their children. Which sex would each apply to?
   darling, tiger, boxer, beauty, pretty little thing, tough guy, matey, angel, daddy's favourite, cowboy.
   Add any nicknames which you know of to your lists. Do the lists suggest any differences between what parents will expect of male or female children?

3 Mention one way in which male and female babies are dressed differently.

4 What sorts of thing do you suppose a parent might say to comfort a daughter who has hurt herself? Might the parent say anything different to a son when he hurts himself?

5 In view of your answers to the above questions, describe any differences between the ways the two sexes are being treated.

6 If a girl behaves like a boy she may be described as a tomboy. What would you call a boy who behaves like a girl? Which of the two do you consider to be an insult?

▲
Cross-sex behaviour

Goldberg and **Lewis** sampled 32 girls and 32 boys. When the children were six months old they were observed with their mothers, and the mothers were asked various questions about how they treated their children. The researchers built up a picture of what each mother thought were normal or appropriate ways to treat their sons or daughters. When the babies were 13 months old they were brought to a special playroom, one at a time, with their mother. The room contained nine toys, some of the toys could be used in an active way, others were more likely to be used passively, by sitting quietly and loving the toy. More active toys include balls and drums, and such things which involve movement or noise. Goldberg and Lewis also provided some non-toys which could be explored and investigated, for example a door knob and latch. At 13 months children will usually become distressed if separated from their mother (NB separation distress was discussed in Chapter Three), so the mother started by sitting with her child on her lap, in one corner of the room. When the child settled she would put it down on the floor. By 13 months, children are usually fairly mobile toddlers, and,

What kinds of thing are boys between two and four years rewarded for? What kind of behaviour are girls of this age rewarded for?

as long as they know mother is near by, they are usually happy to explore. For 15 minutes the child and mother were observed. The mother received no instructions, but acted normally with her child. Again, Goldberg and Lewis observed their behaviour, and compared it to their earlier observations, and the answers the mothers had given to their questions about how they treated their babies. At the end of this series of 15-minute observations of the mothers and babies the researchers noted some distinct differences in the way the boys and girls were acting. Here is a summary:

	Reaction to play	**Reaction to mother**
Girls	Tended to prefer the passive toys such as those which could be explored from a position near to mother. Girls generally played with the cuddly toys, using fine movements of their limbs including stroking and caressing.	They usually explored quite briefly, returning to be near their mothers quite quickly, bringing their toy with them. They seemed more dependent on their mothers, wanting their help, or them to share their experiences with the mother. They talked to their mothers and touched them quite a lot too.
Boys	Preferred bigger and noisier toys, or those which could be investigated further, such as the door latch. Their movements were generally less fine than the girls. For example, they enjoyed banging things.	They were more likely to play away from their mothers, and didn't seek their help or comfort, or sharing their experiences with their mothers very much. They seemed generally more independent, active, and energetic.

We have a picture of the girls being fairly dependent on their mothers, and the boys being fairly independent. Remember these children aren't much over one year old. Goldberg and Lewis decided to intervene in these observations. In another play session they waited until all the children were separated from their mothers, and arranged for a mesh fence to form a barrier between the children and their mothers. The mothers weren't to go to retrieve their infants immediately. The infants' behaviour was observed. Here is a summary:

Girls   The usual reaction was to look at the mother and try to approach her by going to the centre of the barrier. After a few moments looking through the barrier the girls lowered their heads and started to cry. If they weren't retrieved very soon their cries would increase in intensity.

Boys Most attempted to explore the barrier. Having failed to find a way through the barrier where they were when they first noticed it, they would move along it until they reached the point where it joined the wall, and continue to try to find a way through.

Taking the evidence from the interviews at six months, and observation and experiment at 13 months, Goldberg and Lewis were able to draw some conclusions to explain the differences in the two sexes' dependency on their mothers. At six months (and presumably before and after it) girls and boys were being treated quite differently, and different expectations were being made of them. They were reinforced for different sorts of behaviour too. Girls were more likely to be breast fed than boys. They were handled more than boys too, that is, they were more likely to be picked up and cuddled, and the length of time when they were being held was longer than for boys. When the parents spoke to their girls they used a softer tone of voice. The boys were treated and spoken to more robustly. Goldberg and Lewis suggest that some of the differences in the children's behaviour at 13 months would have resulted from the differences in the ways they had been treated during their first year of life. By the age of one year or so, gender roles are already being learned.

Beverly Fagot sampled 24 families, each with a child between 20 and 24 months old. Fagot visited each family's home five times, observing the parents and child playing together for an hour each time. She recorded the kinds of behaviour which the parents encouraged, and discouraged. She found that the parents were very deliberately 'shaping' the child's behaviour, according to its sex. Here is a summary of some of the behaviour she saw.

Girls were encouraged to:
ask for help when it was needed, follow and stay near to a parent, dance, take an interest in girls' clothes for dressing up, play with dolls.

Girls were discouraged from:
running around, jumping, climbing and generally being too active, being aggressive, playing rough games, manipulating and exploring objects.

Boys were encouraged to:
play and explore toys such as trucks, building blocks, and things which encouraged strength and muscle building.

Boys were discouraged from:
playing with dolls, asking for assistance, and anything the parents though was feminine.

Parents didn't encourage and discourage their children equally though. Boys were more actively discouraged from playing feminine roles than girls were for playing masculine roles.

An example of gender-role socialisation

1 What sample size was taken in this study?

2 What name is given to this method of investigation?

3 Define the term socialisation.

4 Can you think of any reasons why the parents would discourage their boy children from playing feminine roles more than they discouraged their girls from playing masculine roles?

5 Summarise Goldberg and Lewis's conclusions about gender roles.

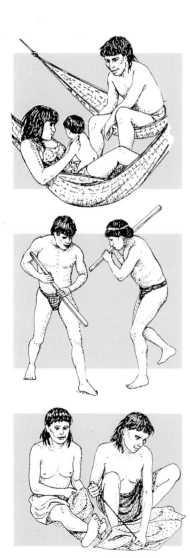

▲
Margaret Mead's study

Margaret Mead's studies of sex and temperament

As we said earlier, if gender roles were controlled by our genetic inheritance, then boys and girls all over the world would behave in very similar ways.

Some of the earliest studies of child-rearing styles in other cultures were conducted by anthropologists such as Margaret Mead. During the 1920s and 1930s Mead studied several tribes in some Pacific islands such as Samoa and New Guinea. She claimed to have found considerable differences in gender role behaviour in each culture. Mead's work suggests that sex and gender roles are the result of how people are brought up in their culture, not a result of their genetic inheritance. Here is a brief description of three tribes she studied.

The Arapesh Indians

This tribe (between 8000 and 9000 of them) lived in the mountains. They were poor, gentle, humble, caring and cooperative. Both men and women were unaggressive and maternal. Husbands and wives shared everything, including pregnancy! The man lay next to his wife as she went through labour, and they both 'had the baby'. They both shared child care, and they raised their children to be like themselves. Acts of aggression were extremely rare. For example, rape was unknown, and sexual matters were treated with gentleness and consideration. The Arapesh lived mild, happy, and respectful lives. Gold was discovered in a part of their land, and Western influences changed much of their lives.

The Mundugumor tribe

This tribe (about 1000 of them) was quite the opposite. Until their lands were taken under the protection of New Guinea it was claimed that children of 10 and 11 had been cannibals. Both adults and children were aggressive, quarrelsome, and arrogant. The adults were suspicious of people in the other villages, and when they weren't actually fighting, or making alliances and truces, they were spying on each other. Children were not regarded as being very important to the Mundugumor. The father and his daughters tended to form one group who seemed to compete with the mother and her sons. Consequently pregnancy was not greatly welcomed by either parent in case the child was of its own sex, and would therefore join forces with the other parent. Wives were just as aggressive as their husbands, and were not thought to be inferior to them, just not quite as strong. Parents tended to ignore their children, and the children learned that they had to fight to obtain anything they wanted.

The Tchambuli tribe

This tribe (of about 500 people) had quite distinct ways of rearing boy and girl children. Their gender roles were the opposite of what used to be the Western pattern. In Mead's words 'The women are industrious makers of mats, baskets, rain capes, and mosquito baskets; the men spent most of their time carving, painting, and preparing elaborate theatrical displays.' They socialised their boys to be artistic and sentimental, while the girls were taught to be competitive. Both sexes were reared by the women, and the boys weren't allowed to join male adult company until they were teenagers.

They were cosseted by the women and never learned to be competitive. Women took care of all the tribe's trade and commerce. They were efficient. They worked together in an easy, friendly way. They supported the community, and took the lead in sexual matters. The men concerned themselves with gossip, art, looking pretty, and arranging ceremonies. Their lives revolved largely around the women.

Margaret Mead's studies

1 According to John Bowlby, children need a close, loving relationship with their mother if affectionless psychopathy is to be avoided. What evidence can you find in Mead's work to support or contradict his view?

2 What evidence is there in Margaret Mead's studies that gender roles are socially learned, not biologically acquired?

Differences in gender roles

	Boys	**Girls**
Traditional view of the West	Active, competitive, independent	Passive, cooperative caring
Arapesh tribe	Unaggressive, caring and cooperative	Unaggressive, caring and cooperative
Mundugumor tribe	Aggressive, impatient and irritable	Aggressive, impatient and irritable
Tchambuli	Artistic and gentle	Competitive and assertive

1 In which of the tribes are there differences in the ways boys and girls are raised?

2 What is a 'cross-cultural study'?

3 Describe one problem that people doing cross-cultural research face, which wouldn't be encountered when studying a single culture.

4 Does the evidence in this table support or contradict the view that gender roles are genetically inherited? Explain your answer.

Comment: If such strong differences as these exist between tribes, social learning must play an important part in learning gender roles, even if there are genetic or hormonal differences between the sexes. However, Mead's work has been criticised quite extensively for some shortcomings there may have been in some of the research, so we cannot be certain that all of the differences she noted did actually exist.

Peer-group pressure on gender-role behaviour

Peer groups are groups of equals. A nursery school child's peer group will be other children in the nursery. The children will usually all have the same status and influence.

Teachers and parents are important models for children's behaviour, as children see a great deal of them, and because they have the power to reinforce some behaviour and punish other behaviour. But can peers affect a child's behaviour since they have the same status as the child? The evidence from many studies suggests that peer-group pressure can affect children's behaviour, including their 'gender role' behaviour. **Michael Lamb** studied a number of three- to five-year-olds, of both sexes, playing with various toys. There were toys that are usually played with more by one sex than by the other, and toys that both sexes could play with. When they played with the toys in a sex-appropriate way, the games were quite inventive and involved everyone. For example, a group of boys who were all playing climbing, or building games were deeply involved in what they were doing. This involvement in the game seemed to reinforce the children's wish to play it again. But if one child started to play in a way usually associated with the opposite sex, then they would be interrupted and criticised. If one of the boys picked up a doll the other boys were very critical.

When a child's peers became critical, the child soon stopped playing in the 'wrong' sort of way, and rejoined the group of its own sex. Lamb noticed that the child was usually back with its same sex peers within one minute of picking up the wrong sex's toy! Clearly children as young as three have a good idea about what is 'correct' behaviour for their sex and what is 'wrong' behaviour. They are also keen to make sure that none of the members of the group behaves 'incorrectly'.

Comment: Piaget claimed that children under seven years old believe that rules must be obeyed at all costs. They make each other conform because they fear the punishment that they'll receive if one of their group is behaving 'wrongly'. Beverly Fagot's study shows that some parents do socialise their children into how they should behave. Social learning theorists say that children have learned the correct behaviour and reinforce each other for maintaining it.

Cross-sex sanctions

Social learning theorists say that children learn by modelling, as well as being taught what they should do. If this is so then the ideas they learn from the media will be important.

The effects of the media on gender roles

In Britain and many other countries, children's books, stories, films, and television all used to present a very similar picture of the roles of boys and girls. They were stereotypes.

Early media – Nursery rhymes

1 Each of the following nursery rhymes could give children some ideas about what girls are like. What are these ideas?

Complete these rhymes:
   Polly put the kettle on . . .
   Mary had a little lamb . . .
   Mary, Mary, quite contrary . . .
   Little Miss Muffet . . .

2 What impressions might little boys learn about what boys are like from the following rhymes?

Complete these rhymes:
   Little Jack Horner . . .
   The Queen of Hearts she baked some tarts . . .

In children's media, boys were often shown as the central characters. They were brave and inquisitive and had 'adventures'. Or they were sneaky and cunning little horrors! Adult males were always brave and took care of people who were weaker than themselves (usually women!). Males usually took the lead in emergencies. They made the important decisions. Any suggestions from females were usually overruled. Girls were often seen as either helping the boys, or being a nuisance. They were usually seen as being impractical, indecisive, and dependent on the males. Stories in girls' comics showed them being interested in looking after animals, or in pony clubs or ballet classes. Not many of them had adventures which involved being active and brave.

Comment: If young children are constantly exposed to these sorts of stereotypes, they will draw some impressions of the sort of behaviour expected of males and females. These effects are found among some adults too (particularly those who haven't reached the higher levels of cognitive development and moral reasoning outlined by people like Piaget and Kohlberg). No doubt the success of films and TV programmes starring the strong, decisive male can be explained by males identifying with the characters portrayed. (We will examine the relationship between the media and aggression later.)

Imagine you were going to have a debate about what sort of behaviour should be encouraged and discouraged in your local playgroup. What do you see as the arguments for and against allowing peer groups to influence their members to hold these sexual stereotypes of what boys and girls should be like? (Stereotypes are fairly rigid and very simple over-generalisations about certain groups of people. They are usually far from the truth. We may categorise the Scots as mean, and the Welsh as always singing. A stereotype that some Americans might have of a typical Englishman is someone who is quiet, reserved, and goes to work in a pin-striped suit, bowler hat, and carrying an umbrella and a brief case. How many people do you know who are like this?)

Think of some popular children's TV drama series. What sort of things do the males do? What sort of roles do females play?

Changing socialisation

Earlier we mentioned **John Money's** work on children whose sexual development was disturbed in some way. He studied some children whose **androgenital syndrome** was not identified until some months or years after birth. Money found that if the mistake was realised and corrected (with surgery, and teaching the child to have a new gender) before the child was about 18 months old, the child could adapt behaviour and gender identity without serious consequences. If the mistake wasn't discovered until the child was three years or more, then it would be extremely difficult to re-educate the child. Social learning theorists argue that children have learned their gender identity by then and that it will be difficult to change.

Money and his colleagues reported the case of a girl who had been identified as a boy at birth. 'He' was three and a half years old when the mistake was realised. The decision had to be made whether the child was to continue as a boy, or whether the parents should try to change the child's gender identity to that of a girl. It was decided to continue as a boy, and the child had some surgery and hormone treatment. The child continued to behave like a boy. He preferred male company until adolescence, and then took an active interest in girls. Money suggests that there is a critical period of between 18 months and three years for developing a gender identity.

Perhaps the most convincing case which supports the social learning theory was also reported by John Money. It concerned a seven-month-old identical twin who had his penis badly damaged when a faulty device was used for circumcision. It was decided that the injured twin would have treatment to make him into a female, and at 17 months the child had surgery. Meanwhile the child's parents worked hard on giving 'her' a new gender. The child accepted the new role without any great problems, and by five years old she clearly preferred feminine things. Unlike her brother she enjoyed having her face wiped by her mother since she disliked being dirty. She liked pretty clothes. She moved gently and carefully, and spoke softly. She was neat and tidy, and enjoyed having her hair set into new styles.

This illustrates that someone whose genotype is female can behave like a male if he or she has medical treatment and is treated like a male.

Comment: This evidence confirms the idea that children acquire their gender roles. Remember, these were identical twins, and therefore had identical genotypes. They both had the same biological forces acting upon them, at least until the hormone treatment started at 17 months, but they soon had very different gender roles. These differences resulted from the combination of hormones and socialisation.

3 Psychoanalytic theory of gender roles

Freud's theory argues for both genetic and social forces in acquiring knowledge about gender. According to Freud the libido is an instinctive drive which will determine the amount of energy we put into being the sex we are. Our libido is supposed to be genetically inherited from our parents. However, we also take on their attitudes to gender roles when we identify with them during the phallic stage of development. According to Freud a boy will identify with his father in order to reduce his fear that his father might castrate him because of his feelings for his mother. If his father is a good model of what a male should be like, the boy will develop confidence in his own masculinity. If his father is weak, or is frequently absent, the child will be unsure about what his masculinity should be.

Freud pursued no equivalent of castration complex in girls. They identify with their mothers, and so develop their ideas about femininity, because they want to be like their mothers so that their fathers will love them. Their fathers also pay them more attention when they are being feminine.

Comment: As we have said before, there is no evidence for the existence of any Oedipal or Electra Complexes. Castration complex and penis envy assume that children from three years of age know much about the sex organs of their parents, and each other. Recent research shows that even five-year-olds don't really know the anatomical differences between male and female sex organs.

4 Kohlberg's cognitive development theory of gender roles

As we have seen, social learning and psychoanalytic theories assume that children acquire their gender roles from observing the behaviour and attitudes of both sexes, imitating members of their own sex, and being selectively reinforced and punished for appropriate and inappropriate behaviour. Kohlberg disagrees. He says that children acquire their gender role in the same way as they acquire other cognitive skills. Acquiring gender roles occurs in three stages.

Basic gender identity
Children have some **basic gender identity** from around three years of age. They know what sex they are, although they do not know that this will be fixed for life, nor do they have much idea what it means to be a girl or a boy. Their knowledge of gender at this stage is confined to the name of the sex they are, some of the main features of what members of each sex look like, and some of the differences in their expected behaviour. A child will know that she is a girl, and therefore has something in common with other girls. Knowing this will encourage her to play with other girls. Playing with other girls helps the development of the schema for girls.

Gender stability
After a time (and the development of further ideas about sex-linked

Review
Social learning theories of gender roles

Social learning theorists believe children learn their gender roles through a combination of being taught by their parents, and observing important models around them. Mead's studies of some tribes shows the influence of socialisation and observation, with each tribe expecting quite different behaviour from their males and females. The media are also influential in providing role models. John Money's research has shown that social factors and hormone treatments can help children to change sex.

Review
Freud's psychoanalytic approach

A central feature of Freud's theory is the relationship that exists between a child and its parents between about three and six years of age. The child will learn its gender roles by identifying with its same-sex parent. There is very little evidence to support some of the concepts that Freud uses in this explanation.

behaviour), children realise that gender is fixed, and will not change with age. This is called **gender stability**. For example the child now knows that she will grow up to be a woman, like mummy. The gradual movement to this stage was probably helped by observing other boys and girls and men and women, and asking questions about the roles of the two sexes. Gender stability is also being achieved through mixing with other members of the same sex. However children sometimes make mistakes since they are still judging things by their appearance. For example a long-haired male may easily be mistaken for a female, whilst short-haired women wearing trousers may sometimes be described as men. Children may also think that a member of one sex might actually become a member of the other.

Gender consistency

According to Kohlberg the need to develop the schemas for what being a girl or being a boy means will cause each child to mix with, imitate, and identify with other members of their sex. By the time children reach six or seven years of age they will be realising that gender is fixed, and cannot change, regardless of how people appear or behave. They have now achieved **gender consistency**, that is, they have learned to **conserve** gender identity.

These are the three stages in Kohlberg's cognitive theory of gender. The major difference between Kohlberg's cognitive theory and the others is that where social learning and psychoanalytic theories see learning about one's gender being the *result* of imitation and identification, Kohlberg sees it being the *cause* of imitation and identification.

Comment: Other studies have also found that children's gender concept develops gradually, through the stages that Kohlberg identified. However Kohlberg's idea that children start developing their gender concepts from about three is not supported by other studies. Even younger children appear to prefer same-sex toys and activities, long before they take notice of same-sex peers.

Review
Kohlberg's cognitive theory

Kohlberg claims that conservation of gender can only occur when the child is mature enough. Just as he or she will need to manipulate various objects in order to learn their properties, so the child will learn the properties of being his or her sex by mixing with other members of it.

Psychoanalytic and cognitive theories of gender

Answer the following questions for   **Freud**   **Kohlberg**

1 At what age do children start to acquire their gender concepts?

2 Where do children's gender concepts originate?

3 What 'stages of development' are involved in acquiring gender concepts?

Comments on theories of gender roles

Main Points	Comments
Biological theory There are sex differences which are the result of conception, and of hormone balances during maturation. Biological forces do act on us as we are 'human animals'.	Gender roles vary between people, between cultures, and between members of the same sex in any one culture. If biological factors explained gender behaviour such wide variations would not exist.
Social learning theory Even very young children act according to how they are expected to act. Their behaviour can be conditioned in quite informal ways, by other children, as well as by adults.	Although the behaviour which is generally associated with boys and girls may vary according to their socialisation, the extent or depth of it may be explained by hormone levels.
Psychoanalytic theory Freud saw a child's knowledge of its gender roles being acquired through the process of identification with its same sex parent as a part of resolving the Oedipus Complex. This was a radically different way of looking at gender-role acquisition.	There is no evidence to support the existence of the Oedipus Complex, and gender socialisation and gender roles are learned by children who do not have a same-sex parent with whom to identify.
Kohlberg's cognitive view Kohlberg sees gender socialisation occurring in stages, as cognitive development occurs. If cognition does develop in ways like those suggested by Piaget and Kohlberg then it seems logical that other aspects of knowledge, like gender, would too.	Not everyone agrees that (a) any aspects of development, including cognition, occurs in stages, and (b) that the distinctions between the stages that Kohlberg identifies are distinct enough to be of any value in understanding gender role socialisation.

16

Aggression in Children

Another important issue in child psychology concerns aggression in childhood. Children's sex is *biologically determined*, as we saw in Chapter Fifteen, but they *learn* the roles which society expects of them as boys or girls. Will the level of aggressive behaviour children use also reflect their learning? All children are occasionally aggressive, and some are more aggressive than others. Watch any group of children in a park or playground and you'll easily spot the aggressive ones. For a start, they're usually boys!

Aggression is another of those words that we use, and know more or less what we mean by it. Yet defining it isn't nearly as easy as you might think.

Aggression

1 Define aggression.

2 Name three ways in which three- and four-year-olds might be aggressive.

3 Name three reasons which might make teenagers behave aggressively.

4 Do things MAKE us behave aggressively? Explain your answer.

There are a number of definitions of aggression, most include some idea of harming someone or something. The least harmful kind of aggression may be simply calling someone a name. This is usually intended to be psychologically upsetting. Physical aggression may be more serious. Either way it is generally antisocial and undesirable. However if you are being attacked you may use aggression to defend yourself. Defensive behaviour isn't generally seen as antisocial or undesirable. Aggression clearly isn't a straightforward term to define!

Psychologists tend to use a number of distinctions. There is **hostile aggression**, which is simply intended to hurt someone or damage something. It can be verbal, or physical, or both. **Instrumental aggression** covers behaviour which uses aggression in order to achieve a particular end, including self-defence. This kind of aggression isn't necessarily a bad thing. Many parents and teachers teach their children to stand up for themselves to some extent. A related

A useful distinction is to separate hostile aggression, which is deliberate behaviour intended to harm someone else, from instrumental aggression, where the aggression is incidental.

term which is much easier to define is **violence**. This involves the deliberate use of physical force against someone or something. Violence is the most extreme type of aggression in humans, and has been most widely studied.

Background reading – The pattern of aggressive behaviour

Usually children start being physically aggressive, towards things rather than people, from around two to four years of age. After four many children are more likely to use verbal rather than physical aggression. This is intended to hurt someone's feelings. From about six or seven many children channel their energies more into competition and sport. Outbursts of aggression are increasingly likely to be controlled as the child grows.

In this chapter we will be looking at the following areas.
1 The evidence for a biological basis for aggression.
2 Studies showing the social influences on aggression.
3 The sense in combining biological and social learning explanations.
4 Do the media affect children's behaviour?

Even very small children sometimes show instrumental aggression, usually towards things or people that are stopping them from doing or having something they want. Their aggression may not be intended to hurt anyone else. Piaget would say that they are thinking egocentrically. Two-year-old toddlers sometimes hit or kick another child. Perhaps the other child won't take turns with the toys, and the aggressive child may be using aggression to try to make the other child play properly.

Some children soon learn hostile aggression. They start to tease and call names, and they learn that hostility can be used deliberately to harm others. Social and developmental psychologists have studied the origins of aggression and have found links with both biology and the environment. Those supporting the view that aggression is caused by biological forces show how changing hormone and metabolic levels will alter aggressive behaviour, and have conducted animal experiments to discover which hormones are involved. Social learning theorists have shown that genetic forces can be overcome by social ones. Aggression in children, for example, can be reduced by using a combination of reinforcements and punishments.

We shall look at each of these explanations for aggressive behaviour in children.

Think of some actual examples of violence, hostile aggression and instrumental aggression which you might see in a playground of six- to eight-year-olds. What sort of thing might have set this behaviour off? Which sex is most likely to be involved in being aggressive, and being violent?

Very young children use instrumental aggression as they try to organise their world. Piaget says that they are totally egocentric, so wouldn't necessarily see their behaviour as intentional aggression. By three or four they may be learning to be hostile.

Types of aggression

1 Give two examples of hostile aggression, showing clearly that you know what the term means.

2 Give two examples of instrumental aggression, showing what the term means.

Instrumental and hostile aggression ▶

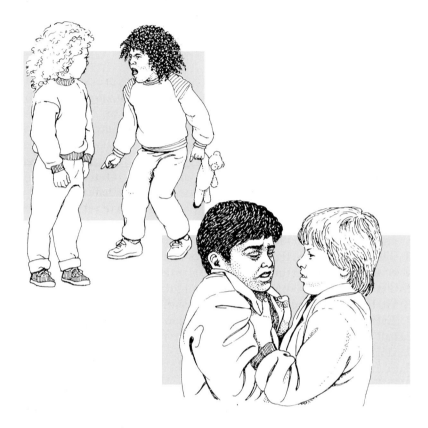

1 Biological explanations of aggression

People have used aggression of one kind or another since humans first appeared on the Earth. This has encouraged some people to think that aggression must be part of our biological make-up. There is considerable evidence that aggression is, at least partly, genetically transmitted. It can be seen in animals and humans, at quite young ages, and it has been shown to be affected by hormone levels. (Look in Chapter Fourteen for a discussion of hormones.)

Evidence to support the biological explanation comes from those theories which see instinctive forces governing aspects of behaviour, and from experiments using animal subjects. The main theories which concentrate on biological factors are Freud's psychoanalytic theory, and Lorenz's ethological theory.

Sigmund Freud's psychoanalytic theory (see also Chapter Nine) This argues that people are born with aggressive impulses (including the death instinct). These urges are thought to be a part of the id. They are irrational and demanding. They try to make the child expose itself to danger, and this conflicts with the life preservation instincts within the libido. From when the child is about three years old, these aggressive instincts must be kept under control by the superego. If the child has not been socialised to think that aggression is wrong, its superego may not be strong enough to resist the aggressive instincts, and they might break through into consciousness as aggression. Unpleasant feelings which have been repressed into the the unconscious mind may also be released through aggression. Freud called this release of repressed feelings **catharsis**. According to Freud, humankind will always be aggressive. Wars will always break out since we have instinctive urges which will occasionally break through into consciousness. Freud did think that aggressive urges could be channelled into aggressive sports, work, other aspects of one's own life, or even to watching others behave aggressively. As we shall see, numerous studies have shown that the opposite of Freud's claim is true!

Comment: This early psychodynamic theory seemed to provide answers which appeared to fit the facts. For example some studies have shown that some people who commit acts of excessive violence were very strictly brought up, and never allowed to express themselves freely. Their repressed feelings may break through into an act of violence. Freud's work also claimed to be scientific. However there's little scientific evidence to support concepts like catharsis and superego.

Konrad Lorenz's ethological theory

This suggested that we have evolved an instinct or innate drive to be violent. His definition of aggression is 'the fighting instinct in beast and man which is directed against members of the same species'. We would have needed to be aggressive in order to catch and kill animals for food, to defend ourselves against attackers, etc. The urge is usually stronger in the male than in the female because the male in most (but by no means all) animal species does most of the hunting of prey, defending himself and his territory, and challenging other males. Even today the urge to be aggressive will build up until it has to be released. Sometimes something will simply set the aggression off (we may call it 'the final straw'), although sometimes aggression occurs for no apparent reason. According to Lorenz our instinctive energy 'boils over' and we behave aggressively.

Comment: Instinctive behaviour may well be the result of evolution and adaptation, and aggression may be an instinctive response in some circumstances. However most animals rarely use aggression against their own species, and most only really use it for catching food or in some mating rituals. Humans are not slaves to their biology. We can control our urges. People in different cultures do not show the same levels of aggression. Mead reported that many of the Arapesh Indians had virtually none, while the Mundugumor were constantly aggressive.

Catharsis refers to releasing our repressed anxieties, memories, feelings, etc., from the unconscious into the conscious. Here they can be dealt with. Freud thought that watching someone behave aggressively will reduce our aggressive feelings. Do you think this is true?

The superego is a major factor in controlling human aggression, according to Freud. Where does the superego come from, and what are its two parts?

Have you ever had one of those weeks where everything seems to go wrong? You become more angry with each disappointment until, in the end, you do something that we might call aggressive. Lorenz thought we have an instinctive urge to be aggressive when tensions mount up.

Biological theories of aggression

1 Briefly describe Freud's explanation for the origin of aggression in humans.

2 What did Freud mean by catharsis?

3 Summarise Lorenz's explanation for aggression. Why may it not help us to understand aggression in humans?

Experimental evidence which supports biological explanations

Apart from these theories we do have experimental evidence that biological factors influence aggressive behaviour. We will mention two areas of study: hormone influences and brain centres.

The effect of hormones

In the last chapter we mentioned an experiment by W. C. Young who gave a pregnant monkey a large amount of the male hormone testosterone, whilst its baby was developing in its womb. When it was born the female infant monkey behaved in a much more assertive way. It joined in rough-and-tumble games, and challenged the males for a higher status in the group. Other experiments have shown that monkeys injected with testosterone between birth and puberty developed similar assertive behaviour.

The aggression centre in the brain

There is a part of the brain (called the limbic system) which is closely concerned with aggression. Laboratory experiments with numerous animals show that aggressive responses can be deliberately triggered by electrical or chemical stimulation of this part of the brain. Animals as large as bulls have been stopped from charging by certain kinds of electrical stimulation of the aggression centre in their brains.

Experiments on various animals have shown there to be some particular brain centres which are involved in aggression.

Through selective breeding, laboratory researchers have produced rats and cats that are extremely placid. However, even they will strike out at, and pounce on, things around them when their aggression centres are stimulated electrically.

It has also been found that those people with brain disorders involving the part of the human brain which controls aggression are more likely to be aggressive than others.

Comment: These experiments and observations support the idea that biological forces are involved in aggression. However, much of the research used rats and cats, and other manageable animals. Their brain structures and functions aren't the same as those of a human. The equivalent part of the human brain (the limbic system) is closely connected with cognitive centres, so we are aware of many more factors in the situation than laboratory animals are. There are other brain centres which can overrule any aggression centre.

The organisation of the human brain is rather different from that of other animals. We can take many more features of a situation into account before deciding whether and how to respond.

If aggression were biologically determined in humans, then it would appear at about the same age in all cultures. Research has shown that aggression in males does begin at around two years of age in the cultures studied. Males continue to be more aggressive. This has been explained by the fact that they have higher testosterone levels than do females. But not all males within one society are equally aggressive, and some males are aggressive sometimes and not at other times. It seems unlikely that biological factors alone could explain such variations.

Biological explanations for differences in aggression

1 Name the three parts of personality in Freudian psychoanalysis.

2 What is the major criticism of Freud's explanation of the origins of aggression?

3 Why would humans have evolved aggressive drives, according to Lorenz?

4 Briefly state what hormones are.

2 Social learning explanations for aggression

Animal behaviour generally relies more on instincts than human behaviour does. Therefore animals may not need to learn about aggression. Humans do not have the same instincts, or, if we do, we can control them. The rules we apply in deciding whether to be aggressive are mostly socially learned. We learn how to be aggressive, who to be aggressive towards, when to show, and when not to show, aggression, etc. People from some cultures show less aggression than others. The most aggressive Arapesh child may have been less aggressive than the average American or British child. Arapesh children must either have learned to control their urges, or to control the behaviour that the urges give rise to.

There are hypotheses, and studies of children in families, which show that at least some aspects of aggression can be explained by social influences.

Social learning theorists such as Bandura, Walters, Ross and Mischel say we learn about aggression through a mixture of tuition, observation, imitation, modelling, reinforcement, and punishment. Bandura and his colleagues have conducted many experiments to show the effect of observation and modelling on many aspects of behaviour, including aggression. When a sample of pre-school children saw an adult behaving aggressively towards the Bobo doll, they were more aggressive towards it. Bandura and Walters also asked a group of nursery school children to call their dolls bad and wicked. They gave them small presents as reinforcements. A control group was reinforced for not verbally abusing their dolls. The two groups were then observed playing with various toys. Not only were the children who were reinforced for verbally abusing their dolls more verbally abusive towards other toys, they were more aggressive in

Review
Biological theories of aggression

Freudian references to the death wish breaking through into consciousness can't easily be checked. Lorenz suggests that some kind of aggression is an 'innate drive' which we have acquired through evolution. There is some experimental support for the biological explanation from animal studies, but we must not generalise laboratory research on the behaviour of lower-order animals to humans.

Since humans have great powers of cognition it seems likely that we may learn that we can use aggression quite deliberately, or we may learn that we can choose not to respond aggressively.

other ways too. They were more likely to hit, kick, or throw their toys down. It seems that reinforcing aggressive behaviour increases the likelihood of a child's being more aggressive in the future. Observation, imitation, and reward are apparently powerful influences on the likelihood of children behaving aggressively.

Frustration and aggression

The frustration–aggression hypothesis was the result of an early attempt to apply the principles of behaviourism to biological claims about the origins of aggression. Under what sorts of circumstances are you less likely to be aggressive? HINT Think of practical things like who, when, where first! Then try mood.

One early attempt to explain aggression in learning theory terms saw aggression always being caused by frustration, and frustration always leading to aggression. This is known as the **frustration–aggression hypothesis**. One psychologist deliberately frustrated some preschool children by giving them difficult tasks to do before a play session with their dolls. They were observed to be much more aggressive than a control group who hadn't been frustrated. However, not all aggression is the result of frustration. People who deliberately go looking for fights do not behave aggressively because they've been frustrated. A modification of this hypothesis says that frustration can lead to anger, and anger can lead to aggression. This is true, but not all aggression is the result of anger either, nor does everyone behave aggressively when they are angry.

Comment: No doubt each of these explanations has something to offer. As children we've probably all observed and imitated some behaviour. If our parents approved we were probably rewarded, if they didn't we were probably punished. No doubt we've all turned to aggression because we've been frustrated in some way when we were young. However these theories do not explain the causes of aggression, but rather the factors which contribute to some aggression in some people at some time.

Studies of aggression and the family

The family is usually the first, most important, and most long-term influence on the child. It is usually an intimate grouping, and parents can provide love and security models for children to imitate, and a range of discipline. Its influences on most aspects of the development of the child are likely to be great.

The ways in which parents bring up their children can differ greatly. Some parents are very firm and strict. (They may be called **authoritarian**.) They make firm rules and only reward their children when they think it appropriate. Other parents are easygoing. (They may be called **permissive**.) They let their children do very much as they like. Yet others are fair and just, but at the same time firm. (They may be called **authoritative**, or **democratic** parents.) These different ways of bringing up children are called **child-rearing styles**.

Here are some studies which have shown the effects of different 'child-rearing styles' on children's aggression.

The studies on child-rearing styles reflect the importance of parental models. What do these studies suggest is the most sensible way to use punishment?

Mother's consistency

John and Elizabeth Newson studied levels of aggression and mothers' attitudes to it in 700 four-year-old children in Nottingham (1968).

They found that 61 per cent of the mothers told their children to 'hit back' if someone showed aggression towards them. At the same time the children were discouraged from showing aggression towards their parents! These mothers tended to come from the lowest social classes and tended to be less well educated and poorer. Telling four-year-old children to behave in one way in one situation and another way in another situation will make it difficult for them to understand what they should and should not do. Young children need a more consistent message if they are to learn appropriate behaviour

Sex differences
Most people accept, almost without a second thought, that boys are more aggressive than girls. **Mary Rothart** and **Eleanor Maccoby** analysed tape recordings of parents and children interacting normally. They found that daughters were told off far more for acts of aggression than were sons. The mothers seemed to expect their sons to be aggressive, but not their daughters. Numerous such studies suggest that the reason for the differences in levels of aggression between the sexes is much more to do with how the two sexes are treated than it is to do with biology.

Female offenders

Here is an extract from an article by F. Heidensohn. Read it and answer the questions at the end.

'If we were to try to show a portrait of the "typical" female offender . . . she would be a young girl, a first offender charged with shoplifting, and her likely destiny would be a caution or a non-custodial sentence (that is, not being sent to prison or remand centre, etc.). There are, of course, small groups of women who deviate from this: the regular drunk with a string of convictions, or the prostitute regularly fined for soliciting, as well as a sprinkling of women convicted of serious crimes such as murder, and offences associated with terrorism.'

1 What is being suggested is the typical first offence for young girls?

2 What is likely to happen to the typical female offender if she is caught?

3 Does the typical female offence involve any aggression?

4 What evidence is there in the passage that females are less likely to be involved in aggression?

Parental discipline
One of the most famous studies of aggressive behaviour in children was conducted in the 1950s by **Robert Sears, Eleanor Maccoby,** and **Harry Levin.** They interviewed 379 American mothers of five-year-olds to study the relationship between the two variables, **child-rearing style**, and **parents' reports** of their children's aggressive behaviour (i.e. the researchers asked parents what kind of things they punished their children for). They found the following relationships.

Permissive parents used very little discipline, and were very inconsistent in the way they used punishment. They allowed their children to do almost anything they wanted to. They said things like 'anything for a quiet life', and 'boys will be boys' as simple excuses for their own failure to discipline their children. Occasionally they used quite severe punishments. The children of these parents were highly aggressive. Since their parents 'gave in' to the children's demands, so the children learned that being aggressive and making demands was the way to obtain what they wanted.

Sears *et al.* identified a group of parents who seemed just the opposite. They used excessive discipline, and punished their children for relatively minor faults. Their children were almost as aggressive as those of the permissive parents. These children would feel frustrated at their treatment, and since their parents modelled aggressive behaviour towards their children, the children learned that aggression was an appropriate way to achieve what they wanted.

A third group of parents seemed to take a more reasonable attitude towards discipline and punishment. They used measured discipline and punished their children's occasional bouts of aggression (without punishing them unduly). They explained to their children what was expected of them, and explained why they expected their children's cooperation. Their children were more in control, and were least aggressive.

Six years later Sears revisited the children (now 12 years old). The children of permissive parents continued to be aggressive whilst the children whose parents punished them excessively had become less aggressive than they had been, but they had also become more anxious and nervous. The children of the disciplined group still showed the least aggression.

Parental conditioning
Diana Baumrind has also studied the relationship between parental child-rearing styles and children's behaviour. Her sample comprised 134 preschoolers and their parents. Each child's behaviour at home, and in nursery school, was observed and rated for sociability, independence, self-reliance, self-control, achievement, etc. Their parents' behaviour towards the children was found to fall into one of three broad categories.

There were authoritarian parents who made rules which children were expected to obey. If the children obeyed they were sometimes rewarded. If they did not obey they were punished. Authoritarian parents were very strict.

The second group was made up of authoritative parents who were firm, but fair. The children were encouraged to be independent, but the parents made it clear what standards of behaviour they accepted, and what they did not. They were consistent in the way they imposed discipline on the children if their behaviour fell below the standards set.

The third group was made up of permissive parents who did not use sensible discipline at all, or they used discipline inconsistently.

Baumrind found that the permissive parents had children with very low social skills and poor cognition. The children of the authoritarian parents were almost as poorly socially and cognitively developed. The children of the authoritative parents were most highly socially and cognitively developed.

In the last 50 years there has been a movement away from punishment-centred childcare in Britain and America (although there are signs that it may re-emerge, as some parents are being encouraged to believe that they should be more strict with their children).

Learning from our parents

1 What three groups of parental child-rearing style did Sears *et al.* identify?

2 How would social learning theorists explain the effects of child-rearing styles?

3 Here is an extract from Diana Baumrind's description of the authoritative parent:
   'The authoritative parent . . . attempts to direct the child's activities, but in a rational . . . manner. She encourages verbal "give and take", and shares with the child, the reasoning behind her policy. . . . She balances her own special rights as an adult [against] the child's individual interest.'
   Rewrite this extract in your own words.

4 Here is an extract from Diana Baumrind's description of the permissive parent:
   'The permissive parents attempt to behave in a nonpunitive, acceptant, and affirmative manner towards the child's impulses, desires, and actions. She consults with him about policy decisions, and gives explanations for family rules. She makes few demands . . . [and] presents herself as a resource for him to use as he wishes, not as an active agent responsible for altering . . . his behaviour.'
   Rewrite this extract in your own words.

5 Describe the major differences which Baumrind found between authoritative and permissive parents.

Review
Parental influences

Children learn many of their attitudes and behaviour from their parents. Parents who are over-strict, or too easygoing, may have children who are less able to control themselves and their demands, less self-reliant and independent, and generally less mature.

A study of the role of the peer group in aggression

Gerald Patterson and his colleagues found that one child's behaviour can act as a model and reinforcer for another child's behaviour. If four-year-old Christopher hits four-year-old Susan, who then 'gives in' and cries, her submissive behaviour will give some satisfaction to Christopher. Satisfaction is a reinforcer which will increase the likelihood of Christopher hitting a third child. Also, by showing other children that she 'gives in', Susan is likely to be attacked even more. If, on the other hand, Susan fought back when Christopher hit her, then Christopher is more likely to back off and find someone else to hit. The problem is that 'victims' who find that fighting back can be rewarding may well become aggressors themselves who then go on to attack other children.

To summarise Gerald Patterson's conclusions:
● If Child A (aggressor) attacks Child B (victim) and Child B gives

Patterson's study emphasises the importance of conditioning in explaining how children use aggression. It doesn't explain why they use it.

in, Child A may be reinforced by Child B's response and attack another child.

- If Child A (aggressor) attacks Child B (victim) and Child B retaliates, Child B may be reinforced by Child A's response and may attack another child.

Patterson also noticed that no one child was always the attacker, but that the 'attacker' one week tended to be the victim the next. It seems that children do influence each other's aggression.

Review
Social learning theory of aggression

Social learning theorists stress that children observe and imitate behaviour that they see around them. If adequate reinforcements or punishments are applied, children's aggression can be controlled. Bandura and Walters have shown that children may generalise and increase their aggressive responses after reinforcement. Other studies have shown the importance of both parents and peers as models for their children's behaviour.

Social learning

1 Why do humans rely less on instinct than other animals?

2 How does the 'frustration–aggression' hypothesis explain aggression?

3 What did Bandura and Walters conclude about aggression in preschool children from their study?

4 Why will it be difficult for some children to learn about aggression according to the Newsons?

5 Summarise the conclusions of Sears, Maccoby, and Levin's study.

6 Outline the findings of one psychological study of the role of the peer group on aggression in children.

3 Putting the theories together

Both biological and social learning theories are correct as far as they go. They both explain aspects of aggression. Neither can fully explain why some people are aggressive. Rather than seeing them as separate, opposing explanations we might understand more about aggression if we combine them.

Psychoanalysis and Lorenz's ethological theories see the urge for aggression building up slowly until it finally breaks out. Something might finally trigger the aggression, or someone might just start being aggressive for no apparent reason. The frustration–aggression hypothesis sees some frustrations causing the aggressive drive to build up, until it is finally released. It isn't always possible to release the aggression when and where it is being caused.

Releasing aggression

Stacey is seven years old and lives with her mother, father, and their cat. Stacey's father comes home from work one Thursday evening, and doesn't give her the sweets he normally brings on a Thursday. Stacey had been looking forward to her sweets all day. Her father just dropped his tool bag in the hall and went straight into the kitchen. Stacey heard him complaining to her mother about a customer for whom he'd done some electrical work. The customer had phoned his boss and complained about the mess that had been left. He'd tried to explain that he'd left the apprentice to clear up when he went off to the next job, but his boss wouldn't listen and blamed him. He'd moaned about his boss several times before. Stacey's mother hadn't had a very good day either. Several clients of the advertising agency where she worked had cancelled their contracts that day, and she was worried about how she could find new ones. When she tried to tell her husband he kept on moaning about his own problems.

Meanwhile Stacey was becoming rather annoyed and bored playing with her ball. She had been patient long enough. She wanted her sweets, so she opened the kitchen door and went into the kitchen. Her father was sitting at the table and her mother was trying to struggle past him to the fridge. Stacey was right in the way. Her mother shouted at her to get out of the way and pushed her back through the door. Stacey was furious. She saw the cat sitting in the hall, and threw her ball at it.

1 Why had his boss made Stacey's father angry?

2 Why didn't he do something about these feelings in front of his boss?

3 What did he do instead?

4 How might some social learning theorists explain the unfortunate cat's involvement in the drama?

Unlike some animals, humans have the ability to control their anger and frustration. Many people can reason, even when they are angry, that it would not be wise to be aggressive in some situations, for example, when talking to one's boss, teacher, or a police officer. They can release their anger in more socially acceptable ways. Knowing what makes us aggressive, and when and what to do about it, is a result of social learning. We are probably all born with different amounts of the things which will produce aggression, and we each learn whether, when, how, and where to release aggression.

Review
Biological and learning theories of aggression

Rather than trying to explain aggression as being the result of either biological or social forces it might be more useful to see how they act together to produce levels of aggression in children. Each child may be born with the potential to behave in aggressive ways, but the levels of aggression they actually show are largely explained by social influences.

❛ *Comments on the main theories of aggression*

Claim	Comment
Biological explanations	
1 Humans are animals and some of our moods, attitudes, and behaviour will be affected by hormone levels and other internal biological forces.	1 Humans also have higher brain centres which can control our behaviour according to our perceptions, previous experiences, etc.
2 Aggression has been shown to be linked to instincts and to other biological events in numerous animal experiments.	2 Human behaviour is not so governed by instincts as the behaviour of other animals is. We have consciousness which other animals do not.

3 Aggressive behaviour may sometimes have survival value, and the basis of survival value may be partly instinctive.

Social learning theories

1 Because human beings have consciousness they develop an awareness of themselves. Part of what we know about ourselves comes from seeing how others treat us. Our behaviour is constantly changing to adapt to changing circumstances around us. If others behave aggressively towards us, we may learn that aggressive behaviour is an appropriate response.

2 Some groups of people, and even some entire cultures, are more aggressive than others. It is unlikely that they all have aggressive genotypes or instincts. It is more likely that they have learned their aggression as they grew up.

3 Many consciously worked out strategies which avoid aggression may have even better survival value. Aggression only has survival value if the aggressor wins!

1 Some people are more likely to resort to aggression than others in certain circumstances. If they are generally more aggressive it may be because they have higher aggression-related hormone levels.

2 People in different cultures have different diets, different climates, different experiences, etc. Over a period of time these differences could well affect their genotypes. Some research has suggested that people who eat meat may be generally more aggressive than those who do not. (This assertion is far from proven!)

4 The relationship between aggression and the media

During the last 30 years or so there has been an increase in the amount of violence in our society. There has also been an increase in the number of people who watch television, an increase in the number of hours of television broadcast and watched, and an increase in the amount of violence shown on it. Put simply, a correlation could be found between the amount of violence shown on television, and the amount of violence in society. This alone does not prove that one variable causes the other, but it has led a large number of people to assume that it does, and to blame television for the violence.

There are essentially two arguments here. One says that the media

Watching television

is a powerful influence on young minds, and should be regulated in some way. The other says that there are many influences on young minds, and television may be one, but restricting it will not make a great difference to general standards of behaviour. Psychologists are involved in this debate.

An outline of the first case

Albert Bandura, and other social learning theorists, have shown that children imitate some models more than others. Those who appear to be powerful and have higher status are more likely to be imitated. Children may find models in their comics, story books, and, particularly, television. Many television programmes contain acts of violence performed by powerful or attractive models. We've probably all seen children playing at being 'Superman', 'Batman', or 'He-Man'. In America children between about three or four years of age until about puberty watch between three and four hours of television a day. In Britain we watch slightly less television, although the figures are still very high. After puberty, television watching may decline, as children become interested in other things like hobbies, sport, and games. If social learning theorists are correct then television can have a very powerful influence on young minds.

If you believe that the media is corrupting young minds, and making society less stable, then you will want to see some regulation. Applied psychologists suggest that older children and adults are not so easily influenced, and that regulating the media will have little benefit to general standards of behaviour.

An outline of the second case

However television isn't the only, or even the major influence. What children see in their everyday lives is likely to have more effect than what they view during a few hours of television. Michael Rutter has pointed to the influence of home conditions on children's behaviour. In homes where there is generally contentment, children are more likely to become well adjusted. In homes where there is parental conflict the child is more likely to feel anxious, and this anxiety may contribute to children's antisocial behaviour. If children are exposed to many hours of television, when other people aren't with them, then its influence may well be stronger, but we must not blame television for the way some families 'look after' their children. Add to this the poor living conditions, the shortage of money, the boredom, and the lack of hope which some children and young people endure, and we have a recipe for potential antisocial behaviour. Several crimes have been committed by teenagers who admitted that their general poverty and lack of prospects led them to break the law. They claimed rarely to have watched television, and couldn't afford to go to the cinema.

Children do not spend all their time watching television. Popular indoors pursuits amongst seven- to 10-year-olds apart from TV are drawing and painting, model making, sewing and knitting, making scrapbooks, looking at books and comics, and collecting things. Can you think of any games that children play which might involve aggression? Do both sexes play these games equally?

A third possibility

Supporters of the biological explanation might say that children whose hormones and chemicals make them more aggressive are more likely to want to watch programmes containing aggression. This case cannot be proved since it is impossible to measure exactly how much of these chemicals and hormones individuals have.

A large part of the rest of this chapter is devoted to examining the first two claims.

Human behaviour is the result of the interaction of many complex influences, including association, reinforcement, punishment, modelling, cognition, moral development, motivation, and others. Television is only one influence on these.

Psychological theory and the influence of the media

1 Summarise social learning theory's explanation for some learning during childhood.

2 Outline one piece of experimental research conducted in social learning theory.

3 Outline how social learning theorists would explain the influence of television.

4 List some other explanations why some children behave aggressively.

What do children watch on television?

Make a list of television programmes that children might watch, which contain acts of violence.

She-Ra, He-Man, Bugs Bunny and Tom and Jerry and many other children's cartoons rely on aggression or violence for part of their stories.. Daleks and other enemies of Doctor Who often threatened to exterminate anyone who stood in their way too. Batman and Robin had to sock, pow, and zap their way out of many difficult situations. Children have been seen behaving quite aggressively after watching such programmes.

Children do appear to enjoy exciting, colourful, and even 'scary' images, and they do watch many hours of programmes containing such scenes throughout childhood. These programmes also often contain acts of violence.

Children do not only watch children's television. Many eight- and nine-year-olds also watch quite a few adult programmes. When asked what programmes they prefer, children say they like situation comedies. Even some situation comedies include verbal abuse and sarcasm. The other kind of programmes they enjoy contain excitement. Fast-action sequences, like car chases, and scenes involving spectacular special effects, are also popular. Programmes including these features also often include scenes of aggression.

Review
Aggression and the media

Many children watch a lot of television. Some children's programmes contain aggressive acts. Social learning theorists say that children may learn to be aggressive by watching these programmes, and the British government is pressuring the broadcasters to reduce the amount of violence they show. Others believe that there are many important influences on children's behaviour, and television needn't be a major one.

Younger children's viewing is usually restricted to early evening prime-time television. It is estimated that about 80 per cent of all prime-time television programmes in America contain at least one scene of violence. On average there are 7.5 acts of violence an hour during prime time. There are about seven acts of violence during the same time on British TV. (This is hardly surprising since one-third of all programmes broadcast in Britain are American imports!) Two American psychologists estimated that average 16-year-old American children will have spent more hours watching TV than they have in school, and they will have witnessed over 13 000 killings on TV. The question has to be asked, does seeing all this violence on TV encourage children to become more aggressive? We would like to think that parents and teachers try to teach children self-control, and not to behave aggressively without good reason. There are two points here. Does watching aggression and violence on television reduce any inhibitions children might feel about being aggressive, and does watching violence make children less sensitive to its effects on the victim?

The effects of television aggression and children

There are two main ways in which we can find out whether watching violence makes children more aggressive. These are before and after experiments (laboratory or field experiments) and correlational studies.

Experimental data

One method of discovering the effects of TV on levels of aggression in children is to measure their general levels of aggression, then show them some violent TV programmes for a few weeks, then measure their behaviour again. (This is what we mean by before and after.) Many hundreds of experiments along these lines have been conducted (mostly in America). The majority of them show that watching violence on TV does increase the number of aggressive acts amongst children. Even if they are given an opportunity to help or hinder another child, those who'd seen violent TV preferred to hinder or hurt the other child. Some experiments have shown children models who were being helpful and caring. Helpful, cooperative, and caring behaviour is called **prosocial behaviour**. This prosocial behaviour has also been modelled. However several of these experiments can be criticised for being rather 'artificial', and other research has given contradictory results.

The American government have commissioned many experiments to test the relationship between the media and people's behaviour.

One notable experiment was conducted by **Aletha Stein** and **Lynette Friedrich** in 1972. They chose to study the effects of anti-social and prosocial models on very young children. This immediately poses a problem. What programme could they show to the children which would be sufficiently interesting for the children to want to watch, and sufficiently aggressive for the researchers to know that the children were behaving more aggressively after seeing it? At the same time the programme must not be so unpleasant as to offend any of the parents of the children. Stein and Friedrich settled for Superman and Batman cartoons.

In the first part of the experiment Stein and Friedrich observed 92 preschool children over a three-week period to discover exactly how often each of them behaved aggressively. By taking an average of the number of aggressive acts which each child performed during one hour, they established a baseline of aggression which could be used for comparison purposes later.

In the second part of the experiment the children were randomly assigned to three experimental conditions. Each experimental group would inevitably contain some children who had been observed to be generally quite aggressive, some who appeared moderately aggressive, and some who hadn't seemed aggressive at all. For the next month these three groups of nursery school children were shown one television programme each day, as a part of their day's activities.

Children in one group were shown one Superman or one Batman cartoon, which contained a number of aggressive acts. Children in

Modelling television

Stein and Friedrich found that these preschool children did behave more aggressively when they saw aggression. Look at the models the children in this group actually saw. Do you think copying these characters necessarily means behaving aggressively? Explain your answer.

another group saw one prosocial programme (an American show called Mr Rogers' Neighborhood). Children in the third group watched neutral programmes about circuses and farm animals.

After a month of watching their television programmes the third part of the experiment began. This was the postviewing period. The children's play was observed for two weeks to see if their behaviour had changed in any way.

Stein and Friedrich found that those children who had seen the programmes containing aggression did behave more aggressively than either of the other two groups. Those children in this group who had appeared to be the most aggressive before the start of the month's viewing had the largest increase in their aggressive behaviour. Even those who were fairly timid at the beginning behaved more aggressively having watched Batman and Superman programmes for a month. This finding suggests that television can have a bad effect on the behaviour of very young children. However the group who watched the prosocial programmes increased their cooperation. They were even more caring and cooperative than before. The third, control group showed no change.

As with all research on young children's play, we have to be careful about what we define as aggression, and what the child might think of as aggression. Adults can distinguish **hostile** from **instrumental** aggression, and we might observe a child behaving in a way which we would define as hostile. The child may not see it as aggression at all. When we watch Batman sock and pow his way through the criminals, we would describe that as aggressive. Can we be sure that three- to five-year-olds would also see it as aggression? The children who behaved aggressively towards the Bobo doll after seeing an adult be rewarded for such behaviour may not have been modelling aggression, but rather what they saw to be appropriate behaviour. When children play out what it feels like to be Batman they may not be modelling aggression at all.

Stein and Friedrich's study

1 What is a before and after study?

2 Why did Aletha Stein and Lynette Friedrich establish 'a baseline of aggression' for each child before starting their experiment?

3 What sample size was used in Stein and Friedrich's experiment?

4 What does 'the children were then randomly assigned to three experimental conditions' mean?

5 What independent and dependent measures are being taken here?

6 Do Stein and Friedrich's conclusions support or reject Bandura's explanation for children's learning? Explain your answer.

7 'TV viewing is bad for young children.' Does the evidence so far support or reject this claim?

Stein and Friedrich claimed that 'These [aggressive or prosocial] effects occurred . . . in a naturalistic setting . . . that was removed in both time and place from the viewing experience. They occurred with a small amount of exposure . . . and they endured during the postviewing period.' Not everyone agrees that the setting was so natural.

Feshbach and Singer conducted what they claimed was a naturalistic study of two groups of boys living either in private homes for underprivileged children or in boarding schools. The boys ranged in age between nine and 15 years, and their television viewing was controlled by the staff. One group was allowed to watch comedy shows, variety shows, and almost any show which didn't contain acts of violence. The other boys were allowed to watch quite a number of shows containing scenes of violence. The behaviour of both groups was easily observed. It soon became clear that the opposite of what one might have predicted was happening. The boys who weren't allowed to watch any violent television were more likely to become angry and lose their temper, and became involved in more arguments and fights, than the other boys. The boys who watched the violent programmes actually became less aggressive and those boys who had previously been quite aggressive became very much less so.

These findings seem to contradict other research, such as Stein and Friedrich's. Feshbach and Singer are not suggesting that the way to reduce aggressive behaviour is to make children watch violence. They suggest that one possible reason for their findings is that theirs was a 'real life' study, that is, the boys in the two groups were allowed to talk to each other, and each would have known that the other group were seeing different things on the television. Those who weren't allowed to watch any violence may have felt cheated, or that they were being treated unfairly. These feelings may have led to increased frustration, anger, and aggression. The boys who watched the aggressive programmes may have felt that they were being given a privilege, and this might have reduced their aggressive behaviour.

One of the differences between this study and others, like Stein and Friedrich's, is that whilst Stein and Friedrich studied young children who were very impressionable, Feshbach and Singer studied adolescents, who were much more in control of their behaviour. They know whether they are acting aggressively or not. Older children won't simply 'observe and imitate' in the way that young ones might. Their 'cognitive centres' in their brains are sufficiently well developed to know what they are doing, and what it means.

Correlational Research

Evidence exists that those children who watch a great amount of violence on television behave most aggressively themselves. For example, **L. D. Eron** and some colleagues drew a sample of over 800 male and female eight- and nine-year-olds. They needed to establish a baseline of aggression for each child, so they observed each child,

Feshbach and Singer's study claims to be more natural than many others. They found that older children will resort to aggression for social reasons which have nothing to do with the amount of violence seen on television. However no one is claiming that all violence is caused by violent television, only that some might be.

Review
Experimental data on aggression

Many experiments, such as Stein and Friedrich's, have found that deliberately exposing young children to aggression leads them to behave more aggressively. Perhaps they think that this is the appropriate way to behave. However, Feshbach and Singer say that the case isn't proven since most of the experiments are artificial. Their study was conducted in 'real life' and found that adolescent boys are less influenced by what they watch on television than by other things which they know are happening to them.

Eron found a positive correlation between the amount of violence watched on television, and the level of aggression in a large sample of children's behaviour.

There are actually four correlations in Eron's study. One is between watching violence on television and violent behaviour in eight- and nine-year-olds. Another is between watching violence on television and violent behaviour in adolescents. A third one is between watching violence as a child, and watching it as an adolescent. And the fourth is between behaving aggressively as a child, and behaving aggressively as an adolescent.

Social learning theorists would say that girls are not usually reinforced for being aggressive, and so are less likely to behave aggressively, regardless of television viewing. Also there are fewer female aggression models to imitate. Supporters of the biological explanation would say that males are genetically more likely to behave aggressively and would watch programmes containing aggression.

Review
Correlational data on aggression

Eron's study found positive correlations between the amount of television violence watched by young boys, and how aggressive they were as young adults. There are other factors involved in why certain boys tend to watch certain TV shows, so we may not say that watching aggression on television causes aggressive behaviour.

and they asked other people about whether the child was aggressive. They then found out when he or she watched TV, and what kind of programmes they enjoyed. They found a positive correlation between the amount of violence watched on television, and the amount of violence that children used in their everyday behaviour.

Frustration and aggression

1 How old were the boys in Feshbach and Singer's study?

2 What was the main difference in the viewing between the two groups in the study?

3 Summarise Feshbach and Singer's suggestion why one group was less aggressive than the other.

4 How would supporters of the frustration–aggression hypothesis explain Feshbach and Singer's findings?

5 How might Freud explain why the boys who watched the violent programmes became less violent? (HINT catharsis)

6 How would supporters of the biological explanation for aggression explain that those who watch violent television programmes tend to behave more aggressively?

7 If each of the groups in Stein and Friedrich's experiment contained children with equal amounts of biological aggression, would their findings support or contradict the biological explanations?

Ten years later Eron followed up half the sample. (The rest weren't available for various reasons.) Again how aggressively each individual behaved was measured. They were given a test which measured their tendencies towards delinquency, and their friends and people who knew them were asked questions about how aggressive the adolescents were. The adolescents' favourite television programmes were also noted. Again there was a positive correlation between watching scenes of violence on TV and behaving aggressively, that is, those who watched the most violent television programmes behaved most aggressively. Eron also found a high positive correlation between the amount of television violence watched at around eight or nine years of age and the amount of aggression shown by the child 10 years later at 18 or 19. Those who didn't watch many programmes containing violence at eight or nine weren't very aggressive when they were adolescents.

All of these findings were only true for boys though. Girls did not behave particularly aggressively, whatever programmes they watched.

Television as a prosocial informer

So far we've stressed the potentially harmful effects of TV programmes. But TV can have good effects too. Some TV programmes are prosocial, and do try to encourage children to be constructive, imaginative, and cooperative. Some, such as the annual Blue Peter appeal, encourage sharing and helping too. Experiments show that after watching these programmes children do behave more caringly. Stein and Friedrich's prosocial experimental group did behave more co-operatively. This seems to confirm the social learning theory explanation. However, adults also often encourage prosocial attitudes and behaviour, so the child's cognitive awareness is increased. Knowing that what it is doing is approved of may explain some of its good behaviour, rather than simply learning by modelling on someone else. Biological theorists do not claim that there are hormones which promote prosocial behaviour, nor is there likely to be a 'prosocial area' in our brain.

The uses of television

1 Give three examples of antisocial behaviour, and three examples of prosocial behaviour.

2 What was Feshbach and Singer's sample size?

3 What is a positive correlation?

7 What correlations did Feshbach and Singer's study provide?

Television can be used to inform, to educate, and to model desirable behaviour. Some argue that television should be used to teach 'desirable' behaviour, others believe television should not be used to model either kind of behaviour. What do you think?

Review
Television and socialisation

Television can have prosocial as well as antisocial consequences. It can be a major influence on those young and impressionable minds who see a lot of it. Whether the influence is for good or bad depends on what is watched. Television mustn't be blamed for all aggression in children. The real life models they have and the expectations these models have of them could be far more influential.

Background reading – Should TV be used to socialise children at all?

British people spend more time watching TV than other Europeans. Almost half watch 20 hours or more per week. Many of these are children. Some people argue that TV is a very powerful conditioner and that it should never be used deliberately to change a child's behaviour, even if it was trying to make the child more co-operative and caring. The reply to this is perfectly simple. Television is being used (unintentionally of course) to a very consider-able extent already, to give children the idea that the world is a violent place, and that to be aggressive is normal. For example a housemaid in California was just in time to see a seven-year-old child emptying some ground glass into his family's food after seeing someone do it on television!

If the television is already being used in this conditioning way, then many people claim that it should be used to encourage prosocial, rather than antisocial, behaviour.

Conclusion

In conclusion we can say that a great deal of evidence supports the view that television can influence our behaviour. However, the evidence often appears contradictory or inconclusive. A number of other variables are involved, which aren't always taken into account. For example:

What exactly is the definition of violence as used in research? Would an incident lasting five seconds of a cowboy punching a card-playing cheat in a Western bar be classed as an act of violence, in the same way as a five-minute massacre of dozens of the enemy in a war film?

Must the violence be actual, or will imagined violence have the same effect? (Imagined violence isn't actually shown, the audience is led to believe that it has happened.)

Can children discriminate real from fantasy violence? Does watching news stories from war zones showing the effects of shelling and bombing on people have the same effect as watching the Daleks destroy their enemies?

Are children more likely to model on human characters than on fantasy models? Children are much less likely to pretend to be either Tom or Jerry than they are to be Superman.

Will young people become bored, and therefore less likely to be influenced by violence in the media if they watch many hours of televised violence? In the early 1970s each tragic killing in Northern Ireland made front-page news. Violence in Northern Ireland doesn't have the same impact in the rest of Britain now.

The age of the child is important. Very young children may not be sufficiently aware of the impact of their behaviour, and may not be 'learning to be aggressive' when they imitate various models.

There are many variables which will need to be examined before we can say for certain exactly what effect being exposed to all sorts of images in the media will have on children and young people. For the time being it would be wrong to blame television alone for influencing children to be aggressive. When parents physically punish a child they are modelling the use of aggression to get their own way. Research suggests that children who are given aggressive toys like guns and knives are also likely to behave more aggressively than children who have neutral toys. Television is just one source of information, both pro- and antisocial.

A knowledge test on aggression

1 What is aggression?

2 What do Freud and Lorenz's explanations have in common?

3 Summarise Bandura and Walters' conclusions from their experiment involving reinforcing preschool children for being verbally abusive to their dolls.

4 Outline any sex differences which psychologists have found in aggressive behaviour.

5 How do supporters of the biological theory explain sex differences in aggression?

6 How do social learning theorists explain sex differences in aggression?

7 Outline Stein and Friedrich's conclusions?

8 Outline Feshbach and Singer's conclusions.

9 Outline Eron's conclusions.

10 Why can't we blame violence on television for violence in children?

17

How Psychologists Study Children

Psychologists use both informal and formal methods to study children. **Informal methods** include talking to parents and children, watching children's behaviour, reading what people have written about children, and what children have written about themselves. These informal methods are useful for gathering some basic ideas about childhood. They may be a starting point from which researchers can do further research. **Formal methods** are more scientific; they include making detailed observations of specific aspects of children's behaviour, conducting experiments, preparing case studies, etc.

Find an account of some research on children in a newspaper or magazine. If you can't find one, choose one from a psychology book. Which method has been used to gather the information?

1 Three types of research study

Cross-sectional studies

Cross-sectional studies try to produce findings which are true of all members of a particular group. For instance, studies of children's attitudes towards aggression, right and wrong, or opposite sex would require psychologists to find groups of children, at various ages, whose attitudes and behaviour are *representative* of all children at each age. Any conclusions which can be drawn from these **cross-sectional** studies can then be applied to all other children. The

Cross-sectional studies take representatives from the whole group, and study them, using whatever methods are most appropriate. Conclusions from cross-sectional studies may then be applied to all other members of the group.

◄
Cross-sectional studies

problem here is whether we can be quite sure that those children who were studied actually were representative of all children. Studying the attitudes towards various activities at school of 50 children between the ages of five and six may not provide conclusions that are true of all five- to six-year-olds. One way round this is to take quite a large number of representatives, because the more children that are studied, the higher the probability that they will be representative. If psychologists can be sure that the people studied are typical of all the people in their group, then it is possible to study only a fairly small number of them, and still have acceptable results.

Longitudinal studies

Alternatively psychologists may be interested in how people change as they grow older, or if they change when they move to different environments. For this they use **longitudinal studies**. For example, we could take a group of two- to three-year-olds who have spent all their lives in an orphanage. They are all studied at one time, then they are studied again later, and possibly again later still, for example when they are each 7, 14, 21, and 28 years old. This sort of study is useful for seeing how ideas develop and behaviour changes as people grow, or as their environment changes.

▶
Longitudinal studies

Cross-cultural studies

Cross-cultural studies show the effects of different child-rearing styles on how children develop. Remember Margaret Mead's work in Chapter 15?

There is a tendency in psychology to concentrate on studies which have been conducted in Europe and America, since these are relatively easy to acquire and understand. Many are written in English and researchers can visit and talk to each other. Funds for such research may be more available in the West. All this is a problem, however, because we may be finding things which are actually true only of American, British, or European children. We must, therefore, also study children in other cultures, and for this we have **cross-cultural studies**. Cross-cultural studies are studies of some aspect of development, such as how males and females are expected to behave, in different cultures. They show up any similarities and differences in development. For example, psychologists could find that children everywhere start to talk at about the same age, yet the age at which they learn to read may vary.

There are a number of problems with cross-cultural studies. They can be expensive and time-consuming. They also rely on the observers' interpretations of what they see. For example, an observer may interpret how children from a particular culture solve a puzzle. In our culture we may think that doing things quickly shows intelligence. If the children were very slow in solving the particular task, the observer might conclude that the children of this culture weren't very intelligent. The culture being studied simply may *not* see speed as important. It could be that there isn't any equivalent phrase for 'quickly' in the culture's language. The conclusions from studies conducted on some children in one country at a particular time may not be true of all children everywhere. Also few cultures remain completely unchanged between each generation. The children of each generation know many different things compared with the children of previous generations.

Types of research

1 Briefly, explain what is meant by the following terms: cross-sectional study, longitudinal study, and cross-cultural study.

2 Here are some examples of research projects. Which of these three types of study was used?
(a) Research into the age at which babies in African tribes and in British towns form their first emotional bonds with their mothers. (Mary Ainsworth)
(b) Research into the emotional stability of adults who were given lots of extra attention as pre-school children.
(c) Research into the attitudes of five-, 10-, and 15-year-olds today towards television.
(d) Research into the effects on children, and the development of their adult personalities, of receiving various amounts of punishment for different things.
(e) Research into the different ways in which different societies rear their children. (Margaret Mead)
(f) Research into British children's understanding of such social issues as looking after people with physical and mental handicaps, the elderly, poverty, and unemployment.

3 Why do psychologists conduct cross-cultural studies?

4 What sorts of things might psychologists learn from longitudinal studies conducted on children adopted from an orphanage? (William Goldfarb)

5 Outline the main advantage of doing a cross-sectional study.

Having decided whether our research is going to be cross-sectional, longitudinal, or cross-cultural in nature, we must now decide on which actual methods to use to gather the data.

Naturalistic observation

Naturalistic observation means studying subjects in their own environment. It is a useful and widely used method in child psychology. What sorts of things could you study using this method? What are the main advantages of using it? What are the main limitations of using it?

2 Some of the main methods psychologists use for collecting data

Naturalistic observation

This technique was invented by **ethologists**, who study animal behaviour in the wild. The subjects of the research are observed in their own environment, without the researcher interfering in any way. Watching children's play in school playgrounds, or in a special playroom through a one-way mirror, are good ways to discover how play changes as children grow. The observer won't try to record everything that happens but will be looking instead at particular aspects of children's behaviour such as helpfulness, independence, or aggression. With this naturalistic observation it is possible to see how particular behaviour occurs in various settings, for example, aggression when alone, aggression with others, or aggression at home.

There are a few problems with naturalistic observation as a method of gathering factual, scientific data. First, it isn't possible to record everything that one child does, much less if there are several children to be studied. Important things will always be missed. Second, the presence of an unfamiliar observer may alter children's behaviour. Nowadays a popular tool of naturalistic observers is the video camera, but some children may become shy when they see a camera, while others may want to show off. Either way, the behaviour may not be natural. Third, there is the possibility of **observer bias**. This means that observers might already have some ideas about why children behave in certain ways, and might interpret their observations to confirm their own existing ideas. Behaviour which doesn't support their beliefs might be ignored.

Case studies and clinical interviews

Case studies are detailed studies of the background of one person, or group of people. Studying the behaviour of members of one particular family, or the behaviour of one group of children with a particular disease, could each be a case study. Case studies are often used in clinical psychology where they concern someone who has a psychological problem or disorder such as extreme aggression, severe shyness, or childhood schizophrenia.

Apart from gathering medical records, school reports, and any other information which may be helpful in understanding someone's present state of mind, the usual technique for gathering personal and sensitive information for a case study is the **clinical interview**. During interview sessions researchers ask their subjects various questions relating to their problems. The answers are interpreted by the researchers to build up a picture of how their subjects see themselves, and other people and things in their lives.

There are four main problems in using case studies for collecting data about childhood development. First, young children cannot be given clinical interviews in the same way that adults can. Apart from any other reasons, children's particular problems may limit their understanding of the questions or their willingness or ability to answer them. Second, when case studies are built around adults' re-collection of their childhood, the clinical interview relies on their memories, which aren't always very accurate. Third, case studies often try to explain someone's present state of mind by examining past – and sometimes distant – experiences. Fourth, even if psychologists do find out the causes of one person's problems, these tell us nothing about what causes anyone else's problems.

Case studies provide detailed information about one individual, or a small group of people. They may give specific insights into their subjects' behaviour, but do not give general explanations for aspects of child development.

Surveys

Surveys consist of **questionnaires** and **interviews**. Answers may be written down or recorded for later analysis. Questions can be arranged in a strict order, or asked in the order the interviewer thinks most suitable. They can be open-ended, for example, 'What are your favourite pastimes?' Or they may be multiple choice, for example, 'How many cooked meals do you have each day: one, two, three, or more than three?'

Surveys are not widely used by child psychologists for several reasons. Children sometimes refuse to give answers, or they may give answers according to how they feel about the particular person asking the questions. Also, the researcher may assume that a question means one thing and the child may interpret it to mean something quite different! (What exactly is a 'cooked meal' anyway?) They are used to gather information from parents, although parents can't always be relied upon to remember how they brought up their children, or to tell the whole truth if asked. Michael Rutter's correlational study found that there was a higher incidence of delinquency among children who had grown up in unhappy or unstable homes.

Questionnaires and interviews are sometimes useful for obtaining some impressions, but contain too many problems to be of much use in child psychology.

Some methods for gathering data

1 Why do psychologists collect information?

2 So far we've mentioned observations, case studies, and surveys. Which method could be used to study the largest number of people at any one time, and which the least number?

3 Which method would be best for studying:
   (a) how babies play?
   (b) a mental patient's early childhood?
   (c) what people think of radio programmes for children?

Controlled experiments

Psychologists using most of the methods previously discussed do their best to observe and record children's behaviour but they do not generally interfere with it. Experiments, on the other hand, do interfere quite deliberately. They are carefully controlled situations, which allow psychologists to show that one thing *does* cause some change to occur in another. Anything which can change is called a **variable**. Intelligence, time of day, warmth, amount of noise, etc., are all common variables. For example, a psychologist could give some pre-school children special training in language skills (language skills are a variable) to see if they would make better progress in primary school than they might otherwise have made. Scientists try to control everything in the situation – for example, the amount of pre-school training given – and they keep careful notes of the children's progress. If children in the experiment receive different instructions, or have different things done to them, or go through the steps of the experiment in a different order, any of these things could explain some of the differences in their scores. Clearly all the children in the experiment must have **standardised** instructions and procedures.

The main difficulties of using experiments on children are that children don't always cooperate, they can't always understand what they are being asked to do, and they will not always behave naturally in an experiment.

Natural experiments

There are many aspects of human development that psychologists might like to know more about, but can't investigate by controlled experiments. For example, would severe punishment stop a child from doing a very dangerous thing like playing with fire? (In this case, the 'punishment' and the 'playing with fire' are both variables.) Where would we find a sufficient number of parents who would allow us to experiment on their children? How can we always be observing the child, in case it starts to play with fire? How could we deliberately allow children to take some matches, just so that we can punish them later? How could we ask someone to do the punishing? The problems are enormous. Another example follows:

Klaus and Kennel were interested in the effects of very early contact between mothers and their newborn infants. Their idea was that those mothers (and fathers) who had a large amount of close contact with their babies during the first hours and days after birth would build a stronger relationship with the child than those who did not have this early contact. Ideally the researchers might have wanted to take two similar maternity wards which took women from similar backgrounds, of similar age, etc. One ward could have its routine altered, so that the baby and parents would spend more time together, while, in the other, the infant and its parents would not spend a lot of time together. Unfortunately, hospitals are unlikely to change their routine completely,

Standardising the instructions and procedures of an experiment involves deciding exactly what the instructions and procedures should be for the group being studied. It wouldn't be reasonable, for example, to expect children to understand the same instructions as adults. Every subject must then have exactly the same instructions and procedures applied to it.

When it would be impossible to conduct a controlled experiment researchers may be able to do a natural experiment. They do not control the main features of different situations, differences in the features they are interested in (variables) already exist.

Can you think of some other differences in the two maternity hospitals that might upset the natural research on the effects of extra contact following birth, and the closeness of the parent–child bond later?

particularly in sensitive or potentially dangerous areas such as maternity or intensive care units, just to suit psychological research. However, there is a possible solution to these problems. Different hospitals have different routines and procedures (i.e. different variables), and it may well be possible to find one that only allows a few hours' contact, and another which allows several hours' contact. The researchers themselves cannot control the amount of early contact, differences in which already exist. Finding out, under these circumstances, whether differences in the amount of early contact does or does not lead to any differences later, would be called a natural experiment.

One further example of a natural experiment could involve some orphanages that are inadequately staffed and provide very few toys and games for the children, and others that are well staffed with plenty to stimulate the orphans. It should be possible to measure the intelligence of the children in the different orphanages to see if the amount of stimulation has any effect on their intelligence.

What are the main variables in the natural experiment on orphanage upbringing and that on intellectual development?

One problem with natural experiments is that human behaviour isn't usually the result of just one or two features in a situation, but can be affected by all sorts of others too. For example, the well-equipped orphanages may all be in countries where there is plenty to eat and drink, and where there are good medical facilities. The children in the deprived orphanages may be in poorer countries and may not have good physical health and conditions. These differences may also affect their intelligence. In a controlled experiment such differences could be taken into account. In a natural experiment it may be impossible to do so.

Correlation

It is not possible to study all human behaviour by the methods listed so far. For example, psychologists couldn't study the statements 'The more a father was abused when he was a child, the more likely he is to abuse his own children severely', or 'The younger children are when they are removed from their mothers and placed in deprived orphanages, the more disturbed their emotional development will be.' Each of these statements says that two aspects of behaviour are related. The first statement claims a relationship between the frequency with which a father was abused when he was younger and frequency of abuse of his own children. The second identifies the length of time spent in a deprived orphanage and the extent of emotional development. These variables could not deliberately be manipulated.

Correlation is a statistical technique for predicting the probability of things occurring together. It does not prove that one causes the other.

Instead, psychologists might find instances where one of these things already exists, and then count how many times the other occurs. For example, we could find some children who have spent time in a deprived orphanage, and we could test their development. Or we might check the medical records of people who abused their children, and see if they themselves had been abused. Statistical analysis of this information then gives a measure of the likelihood of the two things occurring together.

Correlation is a statistical technique for measuring the *extent to which* two or more things vary together. It cannot show that one thing causes the other. Correlational studies are widely used by developmental psychologists.

A summary of the main methods of data collection used in psychology

Type	Advantages	Disadvantages
Observations	No interference by researcher so behaviour should be natural.	Things can be missed or misinterpreted.
Case studies	Allows detailed analysis of particular problems.	No generalisations are possible.
Surveys	Large group provides lots of data.	Limited range of questions which can be asked. Can't rely on respondents to answer or tell the truth.
Experiments	Allow control of relevant variables and offer proof of one variable causing a change in another.	Artificial. People may not behave normally.
Natural experiments	Allow investigation of variables which could not be tested in other experiments.	Other variables, which may also be relevant, are unlikely to be controlled.
Correlational studies	Used (where experiments can't be) to show statistical relationships.	Cannot show cause.

Children's intelligence

Read this extract from an imaginary article on intellectual development. There will be questions relating to it throughout the rest of this section:

'Scientists in Britain and Germany have been studying how children of seven to 10 years of age solve problems. They have both reached much the same conclusions. The British group had noticed that between the ages of seven and ten the way children think about the appearance of things changes. A junior school in a prosperous part of London was used in the research. At the beginning of the summer term parents were asked if they would mind if their children were used in the research. Sixty-one of the children's parents agreed. One day was set aside for the tests and the children all gathered in the main hall where the tests were to be administered. The children were each shown five different objects such as plasticine, water, and rows of buttons, each of which could be changed in some way (e.g. the plasticine was rolled into different shapes, and the water poured into various-shaped jugs). The children were then asked questions about the objects. One question was 'Is there more plasticine in the sausage shape than there is when it is rolled into the ball shape?' Their replies were written down by the teachers. For example, 'Alan, aged eight years, two months, said that a piece of string curled up was shorter than the same piece when it was stretched out.' Later the psychologists analysed these reports and tried to find any differences between the older and younger children's replies. They concluded that younger children's ideas about objects are determined mostly by the way the objects look.

In Germany, 10 schools were chosen, representing both poor and prosperous areas, some from cities and some from rural areas. Fifty children were picked to represent each school. They were matched for non-verbal intelligence, sex, and personality. The parents were told to collect their children an hour later than normal as the research was to be conducted after classes over four days and as it was nearly Christmas they wouldn't want to be standing around in the cold. The researchers predicted that children from wealthier homes would be more advanced intellectually than children from poorer backgrounds. They decided that the ways children used various toys would be a good way of assessing their intellect, so they observed children playing with various educational toys, and recorded them on video. The children were then rated by the psychologists for imagination, co-operation, independence, and leadership qualities. They found that children from poorer areas used little imagination, and were rather unadventurous. They played with the toys in a repetitive way, frequently making – and repeating – the same mistakes. The children from the wealthier homes scored higher on all the tests, and would experiment with the toys and games to see what they could be made to do.'

1 At what time of year were the British and German children each studied?

2 Who recorded the British children's answers, and how was the German children's behaviour noted?

3 Outline the differences in the ways the British and German children were chosen.

4 How did the German researchers assess the children's intellect?

5 In each case, what were the scientists trying to discover?

6 In your own words summarise the conclusions of these studies.

Advantages and disadvantages of methods used in psychology

Fill in the gaps in the table:

A summary of the main methods of data collection used in psychology

Type	Advantages	Disadvantages
Observations		
Case studies		
Surveys		
Experiments		

Review
Methods used in psychological research

Whilst experiments allow control of all the variables, they are not the only technique psychologists use for data collection. Psychologists also use observations, case studies, natural experiments, and correlations. Each has its advantages and disadvantages.

Type	Advantages	Disadvantages
Natural experiments		
Correlational studies		

Stating questions for research

If you ask the question 'What is the best way to bring up children?', parents will give answers ranging from 'by using strict discipline and teaching respect' to 'encouraging them to go at their own pace, doing what they want to do'. The one thing most parents probably have in common is that they will each believe *their* way is the way of common sense. To find the correct answers to questions such as this scientists need to do research. Research involves looking for relationships between things. For example, 'Does having deaf parents affect a child's language development?', or 'Does being brought up by very strict parents make us frightened of other people?' Most psychologists try to be **objective**. This means basing one's statements only on the facts and not on opinions. To try to achieve this **objectivity**, many psychologists use scientific methods to investigate children's behaviour.

Not all of the methods we mentioned earlier will produce objective data. Science demands evidence that one thing causes another, or leads to a reduction in another. For example we hope that medical science has provided evidence that the tablets our doctors give us actually will reduce the pain we are in. Some psychologists conduct experiments to gather evidence about human behaviour. Unfortunately, not all sources of information in our society rely on evidence at all, and this can sometimes give a misleading picture of how some things may be related.

Psychologists generally prefer to gather objective data rather than rely on common-sense answers which may be contradictory.

Research

What's the difference between the ways in which some people explain behaviour, and the ways in which many psychologists try to?

All research starts with observation.

In all sciences the process of finding out involves a particular procedure called the scientific method. It starts with making some observations to gain an idea about what factors go together. For example if psychologists observed that 18-month-old boys were generally nosier and more adventurous than 18-month-old girls, then they would have a basis for doing some research. Or in the primary school a psychologist might observe that ignoring children who are attention-seeking seems to reduce their disruptive behaviour. If we were interested in doing some research in this area we would find out what other research has already been conducted by reading the books and journals where this sort of research is published. We may want to check on the reliability of some research that has already been conducted. Or we may want to do some original research, perhaps observing several primary-school classes to see how teachers treat attention-seeking children.

After reading and making observations, psychologists should have a clear idea what their research is going to be about, and should define their aims at this stage, before beginning the research. Otherwise they may stray off the point, and never know for certain if they have found anything! This statement of aims and basis for research is called a **hypothesis**. If we are going to investigate the hypothesis experimentally we call it the **experimental hypothesis**. Or, where the research does not take the form of an experiment, it may be called the **alternate hypothesis**.

Review
Doing research

Any subject that is to be accepted as a science must deal in facts rather than opinions. These facts must be collected and presented objectively.

Observation

What evidence is there in *Children's intelligence*, on pages 298–9, that the British researchers had made observations before doing their research?

Testing hypotheses

Hypotheses are statements that scientists wish to test. An example of a hypothesis is, 'A teacher ignoring children when they are seeking attention will reduce their attention-seeking behaviour.' In this situation, the teacher would control one thing (ignoring the children), and then see how the children respond (their behaviour). In this example, the experimental hypothesis is stating that the first variable (ignoring the children's attention-seeking behaviour) makes the children change the other variable (reducing the level of attention-seeking).

A hypothesis can be defined, therefore, as 'a suggested, testable statement of a relationship between two or more variables'. Any variable that the experimenter controls is called an **Independent Variable** (IV for short). Any variable in the subject's behaviour which alters as a result of the influence of the first variable, is called a **Dependent Variable** (DV).

When stating a hypothesis, researchers must define precisely what they mean by all the terms they use. For example, what exactly do we mean by attention-seeking behaviour? Children may be demonstrating attention-seeking behaviour by any of the following: being out of their seats for more than two minutes in every five, shouting, asking more than three questions in five minutes, or pulling at their teacher's clothes. The teacher will ignore children when they are doing any of these things. From another hypothesis, when we say

Review
Hypotheses and variables

A hypothesis is a statement which a researcher is going to test. It states that two variables are related in some way and therefore, if the researcher can alter one of them, this may cause the subject to alter the other. The researcher must control the independent variables; any changes in the subject's behaviour are called dependent variables.

babies need lots of love, what exactly do we mean by 'love'? And exactly how much is 'lots'? This procedure of defining all our terms is called **operationalising**.

Operationalising variables

1 Read this hypothesis and list the five terms to be operationalised:
'Rewarding children when they are behaving well, and ignoring them when they are being disruptive will make them behave better.'

2 Imagine you are going to test this hypothesis. Give your operational definition of each of the five terms in the hypothesis.

3 What operational measure of the children's intellect was taken by the German researchers in *Children's intelligence,* on pages 298–9?

Scientists must operationalise all their variables and procedures so that they can be held constant and applied to all the subjects. This helps to ensure that any differences in the subjects' behaviour is a result of the IVs.

Situational variables can be anything in the situation where the research is being conducted that might influence some of the subject's behaviour.

Other things in the situation can also affect a child's behaviour. For example, even though the teacher is ignoring the child, the other children are not. Their complaints may be just the kind of attention the child wants. Here the independent variable (the teacher ignoring a child's attention-seeking) will have little effect. Other things in the situation, apart from the teacher, are influencing the child's behaviour. They are called **situational variables.** The time of day, the temperature, and the amount of noise, are examples of common situational variables.

The individual children we study will be different from one another, too; for example, there will be differences in personality, intelligence, aggressiveness, sociability, etc. Each of these **subject variables** could alter the way each child behaves. If we find that a quiet, frightened child does stop seeking attention when ignored, this doesn't prove that ignoring all children's attention-seeking will reduce it. An aggressive, moody child may be more violently

---

Background reading – Some hypotheses with the IVs and DVs

Hypothesis	IV	DV
Giving babies lots of love teaches them trust	Amount of love given by the parents	Amount of trust shown by the baby
Talking to children increases their language skills	Amount of talking to child	Size of child's vocabulary
Encouraging children to make decisions helps to make them independent	Amount of encouragement given in decision-making	Amount of child's independent behaviour
Watching violence on TV makes children more violent	Number of violent TV programmes seen	Amount of violence shown by child

attention-seeking than a frightened, lonely, or bored child. It would be simple if every time we ignored an attention-seeking child it gradually behaved more normally. Worried parents of aggressive children would probably be delighted to know that all they need to do to stop their children's aggression is to ignore them when they are shouting and hitting. Unfortunately life isn't so simple! A teacher can't ignore an attention-seeking child who is about to pour the paint water all over another child, or one who is walking down the table through all the other children's art work. A parent can't ignore a child who is screaming at the top of her voice, or one who is kicking his younger sister! These wide differences in subject variables could make it difficult to predict general rules or conclusions from research on only a few subjects.

The most common subject variables in psychology are age, sex, intelligence, personality, upbringing, and previous experience.

Variables

An experimenter wanted to investigate the possibility that children would apply their knowledge of the Green Cross Code better if they were taught to sing its rules to themselves as they approach the kerb. She taught some children the song, and gave them praise and sweets when they could each sing it without mistakes. Later she observed them crossing the 'pretend street' she had made in the playground. They all sang the song, looked right and left, etc., and crossed very carefully.

1 What hypothesis is being tested here?

2 What variables is the experimenter controlling in this experiment? What is the name for the variables that experimenters control?

3 What is the name of the variables which may change as a result of those the experimenter is controlling?

4 Name two situational variables which were different for the British and German children in *Children's intelligence*, on pages 298–9.

5 What subject variables did each school's children have in common in the German study?

Experiment on observational learning

Read about this experiment and answer the questions at the end.

A psychologist wanted to show that children of three and four could be affected by behaviour they observed around them. She selected two groups of 10 children, matching them (as far as possible) for age, intelligence, and personality. Each group watched a different Punch and Judy show. Group A saw Mr Punch behaving very badly. He laughed when he saw another puppet fall over and wouldn't help it to stand up. In Group B's performance Mr Punch was upset when the other puppet fell, and went to help straight away.

The children were observed in their playgroups for the next week, and the psychologist counted the number of times each child went to help another child, or ignored another who was upset. The average scores for each child were:

	Offers of help	Times ignored
Group A	7	18
Group B	21	5

1 What is the IV?

2 What is the DV?

3 What is the hypothesis in this experiment?

4 What do you think the phrase 'matching them for age, intelligence, and personality' means?

5 Further analysis of the data revealed that Group A consisted of seven boys and three girls, and Group B contained six girls and four boys. In view of this can you suggest any other explanations for the differences between the two groups scores?

Children's intelligence (see pages 298–9)

1 What hypothesis is the British team testing in *Children's intelligence*?

2 Give an example of an independent variable used by the British group.

3 What measures of the dependent variable were taken by the German team?

Refuting hypotheses

A hypothesis which states something like 'ignoring an attention-seeking child, except when the child is behaving properly, will eliminate its attention-seeking behaviour' will probably never be found to be completely correct. There will always be some children who refuse to stay in their seats. In fact, few hypotheses in psychology (or many other areas of science) are ever found to be absolutely correct. Instead we have to find a way of measuring the extent to which a hypothesis is supported.

For example, imagine that a psychologist observed that rats twitch their whiskers as they approach food. She could conduct an experiment to teach 30 rats to associate a flash of light with food, so that they would twitch their whiskers when they saw the light. (This is Classical Conditioning.) Her hypothesis might be that flashing a light immediately before giving a rat its food will lead to the animal's twitching its whiskers when it sees the light. However, she could find that nine of them never learned the association, while 12 learned it quite quickly, and the rest sometimes twitched their whiskers, and sometimes did not. In this case, has she supported her hypothesis? Has her flashing a light immediately before giving a rat its food led to the animal twitching its whiskers when it sees the light? Not completely, because only some of the rats learned the association, but neither is the hypothesis completely wrong, because some of the rats did learn.

In testing any experimental hypothesis, there are only two possible explanations. Either any changes in our subjects' behaviour were caused by the experimenter's manipulating the independent variable, or they were not. In our example, those rats that twitched their whiskers when the light was flashed had either learned to associate the light with the food, or they had not. Researchers state these two possibilities thus:

1 Flashing a light before presenting food will not teach a rat to twitch its whiskers, and any such whisker-twitching that does occur happens by chance. This is called the **null hypothesis**.

2 Flashing a light before presenting food will teach a rat to twitch its whiskers. This is the **alternate hypothesis**.

What we need to decide is 'what is the probability that our results did occur by chance, and that the null hypothesis is correct?' If we can reject the null hypothesis we are able to accept the alternate hypothesis. Luckily there are a number of tests which estimate how likely it is that changes in the independent variable really are causing changes in the dependent variable, i.e. that flashing the light is really causing rats to twitch their whiskers.

Background reading

Here are some examples of alternate and null hypotheses:

Alternate hypothesis	**Null hypothesis**
Picking a baby up as soon as it starts crying will cause it to cry less.	Picking up a crying baby will not make it cry less: any reduction in crying that does occur happens by chance.
Talking to young children will produce an increase in their language skills.	Talking to young children will not produce an increase in their language skills: any increase that does occur happens by chance.
Encouraging children to make decisions helps them to become independent.	Encouraging children to make decisions will not help them to become more independent: any increase in their independence that does occur happens by chance.
Watching violence on television makes children behave more violently.	Watching violence on television does not make children behave more violently: any increase in their violence that does occur happens by chance.

The null hypothesis

1 What was the IV in our attention-seeking child experiment?

2 Name some DVs that we're going to be looking for from our attention-seeking child.

3 State the attention-seeking child hypothesis in its null form.

4 What do experimenters expect will happen to DVs when they control IVs?

5 State the British researchers' hypothesis in *Children's intelligence* in its null form (see pages 298–9).

Null hypotheses

Two psychologists noticed that older children tend to boss younger children around. They decided to try to use this to teach the older children about responsible behaviour. The older children joined in a role-playing game in which they had to look after a younger child. The rules of the game made it difficult for them not to. They were praised for behaving so responsibly by a teacher who was playing the role of mother. The children's parents were asked to look for any changes in the way older children behaved towards their younger brothers and sisters, and many parents reported that their children had become more responsible since the experiment.

1 What prompted these psychologists to begin this experiment?

2 Their hypothesis was that a child who is rewarded for behaving responsibly will be more likely to look after younger children. Why do scientists state experimental hypotheses?

3 Why do scientists state null hypotheses?

4 Name four of the main variables that experimenters control.

5 Why are 'operational definitions' used?

6 How many children altogether were studied in *Children's intelligence*, on pages 298–9?

7 Design a simple experiment to test the hypothesis that 'giving babies extra contact with their mothers just after birth makes the bond between them even stronger'. You have 10 mothers who are about to give birth who will cooperate. What two groups do you need? What IVs and DVs will you use? You can have one year to conduct your experiment.

Review
Stating topics for research

Psychologists often like to collect their data in an objective way, and this often means following the scientific method, that is, doing some observation, formulating a hypothesis and stating that hypothesis in its experimental and null forms. Every variable and every stage in our research must be carefully operationalised before the hypothesis can be tested.

Sampling

In order to conduct any research we need some children to study. The **subjects** (which can be abbreviated to **Ss**) which are to be studied are called a **sample**. If we were studying children in playgroups we could find the nearest playgroup to where we live, and study the children there. But this wouldn't be very satisfactory since they may not be representative of all playgroup children. There is, therefore, a procedure we must go through to draw our sample.

To obtain a **sample** researchers must first identify the **target population**. This is the group that the study is concerned with. For example, a study on the attitudes of college students towards smoking would have a **target population** of 'all college students'.

A target population is the group the research is aimed at, and a sample is the group of subjects (drawn from the target population) which will be studied.

Target populations

What is the target population in each of the following studies:

1 An experiment to try to teach chimps to use sign language (Gardner and Gardner).

2 An investigation into the moral development of pre-school children (Piaget and Kohlberg).

3 A study of the development of language skills in deaf children.

4 An experiment to investigate the effects of television on four- to six-year-olds.

5 Research into the causes of some children's fear of spiders.

The next decision is about how many Ss to study. This will be determined by four main factors.

First, it depends on how large the target population is. The target population of three- to five-year-olds in Britain contains hundreds of thousands of children. Psychologists studying this target population would need a large sample if it is to be truly representative. If the target population is much smaller (for example, three- to five-year-olds in day nurseries), the sample may be much smaller, and still be representative.

Second, we need to consider how many Ss are available to be studied. If a psychologist wants to study language development in deaf children, but only knows six deaf children, and doesn't know how to find any more, then she or he doesn't have much of a sample. The few studied may well not be representative of all deaf children.

Third, we will want enough Ss to make our sample representative of the target population. If a psychologist studied 10 mothers who took heroin twice a week or more during pregnancy, and found that eight of the mothers had babies who were mentally handicapped, would it be acceptable to deduce that heroin abuse during pregnancy causes mental handicap? A sample size of 10 is too small to base such a claim on. If 80 per cent of a sample of 1,000 heroin users had handicapped children, this would be far more acceptable evidence. Unfortunately, developmental psychologists rarely have the resources to have so many children in their samples.

Finally, we do not want so many Ss that the study will take too long (and cost too much!).

The size of the sample used by psychologists is always a compromise between these four factors.

Having decided on the size of the sample we must then choose a method of drawing it from the target population. There are many ways of drawing a sample, but first we need a list of them from which we can choose. This list is called a **sampling frame**.

Random sampling

Here every member of the target population has the same chance of appearing in the sample. Names could be picked out of a hat, each

Deciding how many Ss to study will always depend on the number there are to study, the number that will be needed to make the study representative, and the number which the researcher has resources to study.

Review
Samples

The Ss that scientists use in their research are drawn from the target population they are interested in studying. The most popular method of drawing a sample in psychology is probably through random sampling.

possible subject could draw straws, or the researcher could stick a pin in names in the phone book. One popular method is to give each member of the target population a number, then to take numbers from random number tables, which are simply lists of numbers that have no pattern and are in no particular order. Each member of the target population whose number was chosen would be sampled. An exact definition of a **random sample** is 'a sample where no member of the target population has any greater chance of being chosen than any other'.

Systematic sampling
Here a name is chosen at regular intervals (e.g. every fifth or seventh name) from a list of the target population. For example, if there are 50 families in your street, and you wanted a 20 per cent sample of them, you could choose every fifth family.

Quota or judgement sampling
A list is made of every variable which may have an effect on the research. For example, a study may be conducted on the psychology of being housebound. The main people who might be housebound are old people, ill people, and mothers of young children. If these three groups account for 20 per cent, 10 per cent and 60 per cent respectively of all housebound people, the sample would have to contain these three groups in these proportions. Gathering such a sample would be extremely time-consuming and difficult to do. This method is rarely used in psychology.

Self-selected samples
Here subjects choose themselves; for example, they might answer an advertisement in a paper, or reply to a postal questionnaire. Most people do not answer newspaper adverts, and the non-return rate for postal questionnaires is often around 70 per cent. Therefore, those people who do respond must be atypical, since most people do not respond, and so the sample will be **biased** (and not representative).

Imposing sampling
This is where the Ss aren't given the choice of whether or not they want to be a part of the research. Babies and children can't be consulted, although, of course, their parents can.

Opportunity sampling
This is where the researcher takes advantage of having some Ss available to include in the research. For example, students at colleges and universities are often used by their tutors to take part in the tutors' research.

Samples

Ten four-year-olds with a wide range of intelligence levels and different personalities were sampled. Ten four-year-old girls were found with abilities and personalities which were similar to the boys. They all came from three inner-city playgroups. They were given a choice of toys to play with. Most of the boys preferred the more active, noisy toys, like balls and drums. Most of the girls preferred sitting quietly playing with dolls and clothes.

1 The sample used here is not likely to be representative of the target population of four-year-old children. What evidence is there in the passage to support this?

2 What would psychologists be saying about the target population of four-year-old girls if they generalised the findings from this study?

3 Outline the main factors governing the size of the sample psychologists use.

4 Define the term 'random sample'. Begin: 'A random sample is one where no . . .'

5 How was the sample chosen by (a) the British team and (b) the German team, in *Children's intelligence* on pages 298–9?

6 Why are self-selected samples never representative?

3 Design of investigations

As we mentioned earlier, some researchers have hypothesised that giving newborn babies and their mothers extra time together, in the days following birth, would strengthen the mother–child relationship. An experiment could be devised which would give one group of mothers some extra contact with their babies, and another group would have a more usual amount of contact. The closeness of the mother–child relationship in the two groups could be measured over the next year or so. If the researchers are correct, then the mothers who had extra contact should have a closer relationship to their babies than the mothers who had the usual amount of contact.

This experiment had a fairly simple design and uses one **experimental group**, comprised of the mothers who have the extra contact, and a **control group**, comprised of mothers who have the usual number of hours of contact with their babies. Control groups are used so that comparisons may be made between the behaviour of their members, and the members of the experimental groups. If mothers in the experimental group have closer relationships with their babies than do mothers in the control group, then we could say that having extra contact does lead to closer relationships.

It's important that the Ss in each group are as similar as possible, otherwise any differences that are found to exist between them may be because the Ss in each group were different to begin with. Researchers have to decide how to divide their sample between the various experimental and control groups. There are three main choices: independent measures, repeated measures, and matched subjects.

In any research it is useful to have a group whose behaviour hasn't been manipulated by the researchers, to compare with the experimental group, whose behaviour has been manipulated. This is the 'control group'.

Independent measures (or independent groups)

This is probably the easiest method. The sample is divided randomly into the various conditions.

Unfortunately there are two possible dangers with this research design. First, if the research involves some kind of testing we must make sure that every subject in each experimental group receives exactly the same treatment as every other. They must hear the same instructions about how to complete the test, and each must go through the same procedures. We mentioned this earlier, it is called **standardisation**. Second, if we accidentally place in one condition children who all have in common something which is relevant to the experiment, and in the other place those who do not have the same thing in common, then whatever results we obtain won't be caused by our IV. If this occurs, we say the results have been **confounded**.

Background reading – An example of independent measures design

In an experiment to discover whether encouraging children to make decisions for themselves will help them become more independent, a psychologist randomly divides a group of five- and six-year-olds into two experimental groups and one control group. The children in the first experimental group will have teachers who try to make them think for themselves and stick with their decisions. The children in the second experimental group are always told what to do by their teachers. Those in the control group have their usual teaching which sometimes encourages independence and sometimes wants the children to obey rules. All the children will then complete a series of tests to measure their independence.

Confounding variables

Read the following imaginary research study and answer the questions that follow.

The parents of 30 seven-year-old children responded to an advertisement which researchers had placed in a local newspaper. The children were randomly divided into an experimental and a control group. Both groups were asked to remember all the objects in a large picture, which they saw for one minute. As soon as the picture was removed the experimental group were told an exciting story about some children, like themselves, who found some stolen property whilst playing. They told their parents and the police, and were given a day out at the zoo as a reward by the owner of the stolen valuables. The children seemed to find the story quite exciting. The control group were told a neutral story about the job of the Post Office. Few of them seemed particularly fascinated.

Half an hour after hearing the stories both groups of children were asked to recall as many of the objects in the picture as they could. The experimental group could remember half of them, the control group could remember about two-thirds.

1 What kind of sampling technique was used to draw this sample? What was the final sample size?

2 Which group could remember fewest objects, and which could remember most of them?

3 Explain why it is important that the Ss in each group are as similar to one another as possible.

4 What explanation could you offer for the findings of the research described above?

Review
Independent groups design

If there are several experimental conditions, the researcher must decide which subjects will go into which conditions. The easiest way is to divide them randomly, but if by any chance some of the Ss in any one condition have some significant variables in common, this could confound the research.

5 Why do scientists use control groups?

6 Find as many potentially confounding variables as you can in *Children's intelligence* on pages 298–9. Compare your list with other people's.

Background reading – An example of confounding variables

Remember, the independent variable is the one that the researcher manipulates. At the same time the researcher tries to hold all the others constant. If an independent variable creeps in, which the experimenter isn't controlling, this can confound the results. For example, do you remember the groups of children who saw Punch and Judy shows where Mr Punch behaved in different ways? Those who'd seen Mr Punch being aggressive tended to be more aggressive themselves. Those who'd seen Mr Punch being helpful became more helpful. But were these changes in the children's behaviour simply the result of having seen Mr Punch's behaviour? If Group A saw the Punch and Judy show last thing at night when they were tired (tiredness is a subject variable), while Group B saw it when they had just had a lesson about helping others and felt they wanted to be helpful (motivation is a subject variable), this might explain some of the differences in their scores. The experimenter isn't controlling these variables. If tiredness and motivation do have an effect on the results, they are called **confounding variables**. Obviously it's important that both groups saw Mr Punch under similar conditions and circumstances.

Repeated measures

In repeated measures design all the Ss are put into both control and experimental groups.

There are three distinct advantages to using this design, over independent groups design. First, there are far more scores than with independent groups. We have 20 scores from the easygoing playgroup described in the background reading on page 312, and 20 from the strict playgroup, making 40 scores in all. If we'd used independent groups and put half our sample in each nursery we would only have had 10 scores from each, making 20 in all. Second, it reduces the risk of confounding. Because each subject becomes a member of each group, we can't have any group containing different sorts of Ss. Third, it allows us to see if any of the conditions in the research are usually accompanied by any particular behaviour by the subjects.

One possible problem with repeated measures design is that the experiences the Ss have in one condition (e.g. the experience of being in the easygoing playgroup), might affect how they behave in the next one (e.g. how they behaved in the strict nursery). These are called **order effects** and could cause confounding.

There's a simple way to reduce this problem. Putting half the sample of children first into the strict playgroup and then into the easy-going one, and putting the other half into the easy-going one first, and the strict one later, should eliminate most order effects. The technique is called **counterbalancing**.

Review
Repeated measures design

Using repeated measures design lets us put all members of our sample through each condition in the research, thus giving us many more scores. There may be a need to counterbalance to avoid any order effects.

Repeated measures design

Make up a hypothesis for an experiment which could use repeated measures. (NB: Do not use one already mentioned.)

Matched subjects

In this design each experimental group of subjects must be as similar as possible to one another. The researcher decides which subject variables are important, finds pairs of Ss who are similar, and puts one from each pair into one group, and the partner from each into the other group.

There are enormous problems with this research design. How could we possibly know all the relevant variables in any research? How could we measure every one of them accurately? Where could we find a sample which has an equal distribution of variables? Consequently this technique is very rarely used.

Background reading – An example of repeated measures design

We want to discover if children prefer more strictly run playgroups to ones where they are more free to choose what to do. We could take 20 children, put them in an easygoing playgroup for a month and measure their levels of enjoyment. Then we could put them into a strictly run playgroup for a month, and see if there are any differences in their levels of enjoyment. So repeated measures means using the same subjects in each experimental condition.

Review

Matched subjects design

In matched Ss design all of the important variables are identified, and the same number of Ss with each of these variables are put into each experimental condition. It is extremely difficult to do, and this technique is not widely used.

Matched subjects design

1 What variables are being controlled in the experiment described in the *Research Report* in the background reading on page 315?

2 Can you think of any other variables that could affect the levels of aggression in children?

3 What might happen if the intelligence tests and personality inventories were not very accurate?

4 How easy do you think it would be to find 20 five-year-old boys and girls who would be so similar?

5 Which type of research design was used by the German team in *Children's intelligence* on pages 298–9?

6 Which was used by the British group?

Research design

Which of these hypotheses could be tested with (a) independent measures, (b) repeated measures, (c) matched Ss, or (d) couldn't be tested at all.

1 Seeing a film of someone behaving in a caring way makes children more caring.

2 Encouraging boys to be soft, emotional, and caring will make them grow up to be weak and effeminate.

3 Solvent abuse leads to brain damage.

4 Learning ability varies in line with the level of noise.

5 Chimps can be taught to use sign language.

6 Increasing physical punishment heightens aggressive behaviour in two- to five-year-olds.

7 Eight-week-old babies think that when something is hidden from them it no longer exists.

4 Ethics in research

Psychologists need to conduct research in order to test their hypotheses. It is important that they only use fair and reasonable tactics to do this. You may not be very happy if you had been used as a subject in some terrible experiment without your permission. If you were lied to and deliberately misled, you might be angry, or if you were tricked into doing something that you wouldn't normally do, you could feel bad about it afterwards. When the researchers finally reveal that it was just an experiment, you may want to know by what right they thought they could cheat and mislead you in this way.

Would it be any better or any worse if the researchers treated a young child in this way? Explain your answer.

Background reading

Is it ever acceptable for psychologists, who have no special rights, deliberately to use children in psychological research without their parents' knowledge or consent? Are there circumstances which might justify doing this, for example, if the parents were unknown or unavailable? Think of some examples from this book where children have been used in this way.

Ethics is concerned with those aspects of human behaviour which are regarded as 'acceptable' or 'unacceptable', 'good' or 'bad', 'right' or 'wrong'. Questions of ethics are particularly important when gathering data about human behaviour.

There are two ways in which psychological researchers need to watch for ethical problems. First, some of the methods which psychologists use to study children may be more likely to have ethical implications than others. Second, the way in which the methods are used might have ethical problems.

Most of the methods used in psychology do not have particular ethical problems. The more control the researcher has over the subjects' behaviour, the greater the possibility of ethical problems arising.

Likelihood of ethical implications

Least likely	More likely
Naturalistic observations	Experimental research
Case studies	Controlled observations
Surveys	
Correlational studies	

Ethical guidelines in conducting research

(a) Wherever possible we must tell the subjects that they are taking part in research. Where children are too young to understand, then their parents must be fully informed about what the research is about, what exactly the researchers want to do with the children, and what they anticipate might be the likely effects on the children.

Comment: The problem with telling the subjects exactly what is going on might be that they may not then behave normally, but rather try to fit in with what they think the researcher wants. But if the subjects aren't told that they are being studied, then the researcher is deliberately deceiving them. Is deceit acceptable?

(b) The needs of the subjects must always be put before the needs of the researcher and the subjects must never be exposed to physical danger or the threat of psychological distress. Parents who fear their children may suffer must be reassured that they can withdraw their children from the research at any time without having to give any explanations.

Comment: This makes it difficult to gather data on topics that might involve stress in children. For example, we should not deliberately cause anxiety in a child so as to test our hypothesis that anxiety leads to more bed-wetting.

There are several ethical issues to consider in the study of children. Researchers must be honest with their subjects (or their subjects' parents), the children's needs must always come first, and anything said or done must be treated in strictest confidence.

(c) Parents must be reassured that their children's contributions to the research will be treated in the strictest confidence. Subjects' identities must not be revealed, and their privacy not invaded.

Comment: This doesn't usually present difficulties during the data-gathering stage, but it does make it difficult for researchers to follow up the children later to research any long-term effects.

In most countries where psychological research is conducted there are departments or committees to check that any proposed research doesn't break major ethical guidelines. In Britain the British Psychological Society (BPS) has published guidelines stating what kind of research or activities are permissible and what are not. It is unlikely nowadays that very much psychological research involving children gives rise to ethical problems.

A summary of ethics in research

When we conduct research on children we must not lie or trick them or their parents into saying or doing anything. Everything must be explained in detail. The children's needs must always come first, even at the risk of having to abandon the research. They must be guaranteed confidentiality and their privacy must never be invaded unless they have been told exactly what the researcher wants to know, and given their permission for the researcher to talk to them.

Background reading – An example of matched Ss design

Extract from a Research Report

Hypothesis: to investigate the effects of watching violence on TV, and levels of aggression in five-year-old children.

    Sample: 20 boys and 20 girls.

    Research design used: matched Ss.

    Relevant variables: age, intelligence, personality, sex.

    Number of experimental groups: two.

Procedure: each five-year-old given personality inventories and standard intelligence tests. Each group given equal numbers of above-average, average, and below-average intelligence boys and girls, ensuring each group contained children with similar personality characteristics.

---

5 Data collection and interpretation

No matter which type of research we've used, or which methods we've employed, or how we've chosen and arranged our sample, we're going to produce quite a mass of information, most of it in the form of numbers. These numbers are called **raw data** because they haven't yet been 'treated' in any way. Usually the first thing to do is to arrange them in rank order, i.e. from the lowest score to the highest score. If the score relates to a particular subject we may want to keep some note of who achieved that score. We call the first subject S1, the second S2, etc.

For example, here are the raw scores (in percentages) for 10 students in a class test: S1=60, S2=75, S3=75, S4=55, S5=60, S6=65, S7=55, S8=75, S9=70, S10=60. The lowest score is 55 per cent, so this begins our list in rank order, followed by 60 per cent, and so on, thus:

    55%
    60%
    65% etc.

This goes on until all the scores have been listed. Next, we might want to know how many students gained each score, so we construct what is called a frequency count. For each student, a vertical line is drawn next to that student's corresponding score. So, to begin, S1's score is 60 per cent, so a line is drawn against that score, thus:

    55%
    60% |
    65% etc.

Continue this until all the students' scores have been recorded. Each time a score occurs again, another vertical line goes next to the last mark made against that score. (Note: if you reach a fifth mark against any one score, you would put a diagonal line through the previous four, like this: ⾞

If you did a frequency count for these scores it would look like this:

Score	Number of Ss achieving it
55%	II (i.e. two Ss achieved 55%)
60%	III
65%	I
70%	I
75%	III

N=10 (N stands for number of Ss)

Data can be summarised and presented in either pictures or numbers. We will look at each in turn.

Pictures

The main ways of displaying results in pictures are tables, graphs, bar charts, and pie charts.

Tables

Tables are the most basic way of presenting data. They can show data with great accuracy, up to many decimal places, as in the following example.

Vocabulary use by time of day in three two-year-old children

Here are the number of words spoken by three two-year-old children during a five-minute observation period just before lunch.

Here the same children are recorded in two conditions. Condition one was conducted before 10 a.m., and condition two was conducted after 7 p.m.

Subject	Words	Subject	Condition 1 before 10 a.m.	Condition 2 after 7 p.m.
S1	37	S1	27	40
S2	23	S2	35	35
S3	11	S3	10	7
(N=3)		(N=3)		

Tables must always be clearly titled and labelled so that people can see the results at a glance.

Vocabulary

1 At what time of day does S1 talk most?

2 Describe S2's speaking habits.

3 Which child is the most talkative?

4 Which child is the least talkative?

5 What do these tables tell you about the speaking habits of S1, S2, and S3?

IVs and DVs

Read this description of an experiment.

An experimenter wanted to see if newborn chicks could recognise their food by its shape. He took two groups of chicks. Some were one day old, the others were one week old. He gave each group four, small, differently shaped objects which they could peck at. One resembled grain; the others were cubes, cones, and pyramids. On average the one-day-old chicks pecked 9 times at the cubes, 12 times at the pyramids, 6 times at the cones, and 48 times at the food-shaped objects. The seven-day-old chicks pecked 4 times at the cones, 5 times at the pyramids, 7 times at the cubes, and 86 times at the food-shaped objects.

1 Complete this table to show these results:

A Table to show the pecking behaviour of newborn chicks towards different objects.

Age	'Food shapes'	Cubes	Cones	Pyramids
One day				
One week				

2 What were the IVs in this experiment?

3 How was the DV measured?

4 What conclusions would you draw from your table?

Graphs

Graphs are used to show trends in how some aspects of behaviour change over time, or as the subject's experience changes. Here is a learning curve (Thorndike) that shows how the number of items learned increase with time.

Lines drawn on graphs are called **data curves** (even if they are straight lines). It is possible to have overlapping lines on a graph, to show comparisons, e.g. number of acts of helping, over a four-week period, before and after seeing Mr Punch behaving caringly towards other puppets.

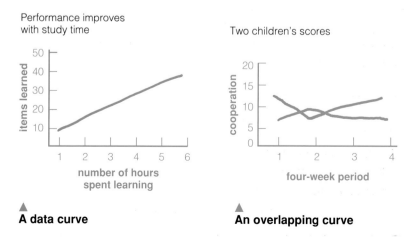

Performance improves with study time

Two children's scores

A data curve

An overlapping curve

Bar charts

Bar charts are used to show the frequency (or number of times) with which a particular score occurs. For example, three groups of children saw some adults behaving aggressively towards a large doll (Bandura). One group saw the adult behaving aggressively, and being congratulated for it, another group saw the aggressive adult, but there was no comment made by anyone else, and a third group saw the adult being punished for the aggression. The children were then given a large doll, and their behaviour towards it was recorded.

With bar charts the scores are always placed on the horizontal axis, and the frequency, or how often each score occurs, is placed on the vertical axis.

Histograms are a special type of bar chart. They are used when the area in each column is drawn in proportion to the number of cases that it represents. The horizontal scale may be divided into irregular bands, so that it is the area, and not the height, of each band that is important. They are more accurate than bar charts, and can be used instead of graphs.

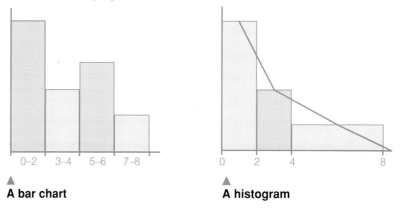

A bar chart   **A histogram**

Bar charts

Imagine that a journalist friend of yours is writing a report about a local school which is taking part in some research on intelligence testing. She asks if you'd help with the illustration, and you agree to construct a bar chart to display these IQ test scores.

Here are a few hints:
(a) count how many scores there are,
(b) find the lowest score,
(c) find the interval between the scores (what steps do they go up in?),
(d) make a list of all the scores from lowest to highest,
(e) find how many times each score occurs (e.g. how many Ss scored 120, how many scored 70, etc.) by using a frequency count,
(f) arrange these IQ scores in rank order along the bottom axis,
(g) plot the frequency for each score on the vertical axis. Do all this now.

S1 =140 S2 = 90 S3 = 80 S4 =100 S5 =110 S6 =120 S7 = 50 S8 = 70
S9 = 90 S10=120 S11= 90 S12=130 S13=100 S14=150 S15=110 S16= 60
S17=130 S18=100 S19=140 S20=100 S21=120 S22=110 S23= 60 S24=100
S25=130 S26=120 S27=110 S28= 90 S29= 80 S30=100 S31= 70 S32=110
S33= 80 S34= 80 S35= 70 S36= 90

If you've constructed the bar chart correctly, it should be perfectly symmetrical. (Symmetrical means equal on either side of the middle.)

Pie charts

A pie chart is a circle (which might resemble a pie!) divided into segments. Each segment represents a percentage of the whole. Pie charts give a very vivid impression of the share of something which the various groups have. They are useful if we know what all the factors or groups involved are, and if we know what the total amount is. We could use a pie chart to display what proportion of all families in Britain live in the various kinds of family organisations, for example, two-parent families, one-parent families, single people, etc. We can find the official statistics for the total number of families that there are in Britain, and we can list just about all the family arrangements that people can make. We couldn't use a pie chart if we didn't know the totals. For example, we can't know the total amount of aggression between children that occurs in primary schools, so we couldn't construct a pie chart to show what proportion of it involves kicking, hitting, spitting, throwing things, etc.

Households in Britain in 1985

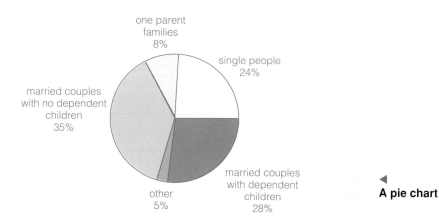

A pie chart

Which method to use?

The final decision of which method you use to display your results will be largely your own personal choice, bearing in mind some of the points we've been making here. Tables are able to show data most accurately. If precise figures are necessary then they may best be displayed as part of a table. Graphs are useful for showing the way behaviour changes over time, or with experience, or with age, etc.

Review
Displaying results in pictures

Psychologists use tables, graphs, histograms, and pie charts to display their results, although they will still need to write up their conclusions. Each method has its own advantages, but the choice of which to use rests finally with the particular researcher.

Review
Displaying results in numbers

The three ways of describing the 'middle' or 'typical' score in a group of scores are the mean, median, and mode. Each has its uses, although the mean is probably the most widely used.

They are good if a trend is being measured. They are also useful where two sets of scores can be overlapped. Pie charts are useful for showing percentages of the whole of something. If you happen to know what all the factors are, and what the whole is, pie charts can be very useful. Bar charts are useful for showing the frequency with which certain scores occur.

Numbers

Apart from showing their data in the form of pictures, psychologists often want to know what a typical, or average score is and there are a number of ways of finding this. They are called the **measures of central tendency**. It is also useful to know what the spread of scores is, between the lowest and highest scores. This is called the **range**.

The three measures of central tendency

The mean
The mean is found by adding all the scores together, and dividing the total by the number of scores. For example, five psychology students get the following percentages in their end-of-term test: 57, 63, 72, 77 and 86. Adding the scores together gives us 355, which, when divided by five (the number of scores) comes to 71. The mean is 71 per cent.

The median
All the scores are arranged in rank order, from lowest to highest, and the middle one is the median. Of the scores 57, 63, 72, 77, and 86, the median is 72. If there is an odd number of scores the median is easy to find. Count the number of scores, and find the one where there are as many scores below it as there are above it. It will be the median. If there is an even number of scores the median is the midpoint between the two central scores. Take the two in the centre, add them together, divide by 2, and there's the median. For example, in the scores 57, 63, 72, 77, 81, and 86, the median is the midpoint between 72 and 77, that is $72 + 77 = 149 \div 2 = 74.5$

The mode
The mode is simply the score that occurs most often. If we construct a frequency count it is the score that has most marks against it. The mode in the following scores is five, because there are more marks for five than for any of the other numbers.

1	I
2	I
3	II
4	III
5	IIII
6	II

Central tendency

1 Here are the results of both a control and an experimental group, in an experiment on reaction time and tiredness. The groups' reaction times were measured by their scores in three versions of a space invaders game. The experimental group was tested just before bedtime; the control group was tested at midday.

Experimental group scores: 17, 32, 34, 58, 69, 70, 98, 142
Control group scores: 61, 62, 64, 65, 66, 68, 69
(a) Find the mean average for each group.
(b) Can you think of any way in which this research could be confounded?

2 Find the median of the following two sets of scores:
(a) 78, 97, 102, 109, 131, 197, 201
(b) 9, 6, 0, 1, 14, 26, 2

3 Do a frequency count, then find the mode, of the following scores:
(a) 3, 3, 9, 1, 7, 6, 1, 0, 1, 0, 9, 8, 5, 8, 6, 3, 1, 2, 7, 2, 8, 3, 5, 9, 8, 3, 1, 3
(b) 17, 12, 19, 17, 15, 13, 14, 12, 11, 10, 19, 16, 18, 17, 14, 13, 12, 11, 15, 18, 10, 18, 17, 14, 18, 13, 11, 12, 14, 17, 18, 14, 10, 19, 17

The range

Sometimes, knowing the mean, median, or mode gives us only limited information about our data. Here are the percentage scores for ten psychology students in their class test: 45, 47, 47, 49, 49, 50, 52, 53, 53, and 55. The mean score is 50 per cent. It seems that everyone in the group is remembering about half of the work. The mean seems to give a reasonable indication of the progress of the whole class. In another class, the ten students scored 20, 21, 22, 32, 53, 60, 65, 70, 77, and 80 per cent. The mean average is still 50 per cent, but some children are obviously understanding a lot more than others. A teacher would treat these two classes quite differently. To clarify the mean score, therefore, we would calculate the difference between the highest and the lowest score. This is called the **range**, and is found simply by subtracting the lowest score from the highest score. In the scores 57, 63, 72, 77, 81, 86, the range would be $86 - 57 = 29$.

Displaying results in numbers

1 What is the range of the following scores?
27, 37, 42, 45, 51, 55, 70, 72, 83, 87, 98, 98.

2 Results (by percentage) for a group of boys and girls on a literacy test

Boys				**Girls**			
S1	58	S6	75	S1	86	S6	93
S2	61	S7	34	S2	72	S7	54
S3	54	S8	44	S3	53	S8	53
S4	47	S9	92	S4	68	S9	57
S5	76	S10	64	S5	83	S10	87

Boys (cont'd)				**Girls** (cont'd)			
S11	13	S16	75	S11	37	S16	79
S12	45	S17	35	S12	56	S17	35
S13	64	S18	43	S13	75	S18	75
S14	52	S19	37	S14	29	S19	79
S15	86	S20	42	S15	85	S20	78

(a)   What is the total sample size?
(b)   What is the range of scores for boys?
(c)   What is the mode of all the scores?
(d)   What is the mean score for boys?
(e)   What is the median score for girls?

One other type of result that we mentioned earlier comes from **correlation studies**.

Correlation studies

As we mentioned earlier, there are some areas of human life on which it isn't possible to conduct experiments, observations, case studies, surveys, or other kinds of research. Psychologists can't conduct research on things which might be dangerous, impractical, immoral, unethical, illegal, etc. Michael Rutter conducted a correlational study on early experiences and adolescent behaviour.

Testing hypotheses in psychology

Here are some hypotheses that couldn't be tested using the methods discussed so far:

(a) Removing a child from her or his mother and bringing her or him up in a deprived orphanage will limit emotional development.
(b) A father who was abused when he was a child is more likely to abuse his own children.
(c) Severe punishment stops bad behaviour in children.

1 Think of three examples of behaviour on which you couldn't conduct an experiment.

2 Write as many reasons as you can for why psychologists couldn't do such experiments. (HINT: Think of as many PRACTICAL problems as you can first.)

Developmental psychologists are often interested in things which go together. Some children suffer from high levels of anxiety, others have low levels of anxiety. Some children have more bed-wetting accidents than others. A psychologist may want to know whether there is a relationship between increasing levels of anxiety and the greater likelihood of bed-wetting. Others may want to know if there is a relationship between growing up in environments which have less and less stimulation, and lower and lower IQ scores.

This relationship between two or more variables is known as a **correlation**. Here is the procedure for finding the **correlation**: we will take the two variables 'number of years spent in a deprived orphanage', and 'level of intellectual development' (Dennis and Dennis). First, find a group of people who spent various periods of time in a deprived orphanage, the larger the group the better. Second, find an accurate and acceptable test for intellectual development. Third, give each person the test. Fourth, statistically analyse (correlate) each person's IQ score, and the number of years that person spent in the deprived orphanage. This correlation will produce a number which expresses the relationship between the two variables.

Correlation is represented by a number between –1 and +1. The greater the amounts of the two variables tending to occur together, the nearer the number will be to +1. Children's weight and height are **correlated**. That is, taller children tend to weigh more than shorter children. This is not always true however. Some tall children are quite light, and some shorter children are quite heavy. (The correlation for height and weight among British adult males is 0.47, and for females is 0.35 (Knight 1984).) We could test whether weight and height are positively correlated among children by measuring the weight and height of a large number (10,000 ought to be enough) of them. Correlating the scores for height with the scores for weight should produce a positive number. This is called a **positive correlation**.

If two variables such as 'how late children stay up every night' and 'the quality of the work they produce' were correlated, we'd probably find that children who don't often stay up too late generally produce better work, whereas those who consistently stay up late generally produce poorer work. If children who always go to bed very late always produce the poorest schoolwork, then the variables 'time of going to bed' and 'quality of schoolwork' would have a **perfect positive correlation**, represented by +1. This is rarely found in the real world, and certainly not in psychology. There will always be some people who seem able to stay up late and still produce good work.

Negative correlation occurs when an increase in the amount of one variable goes with a decrease in the amount of another. Increasing the amount of anxiety in children's lives may correlate with a reduction in their emotional development. A negative correlation of –1 means that when one variable is at its maximum, another one is at its minimum. The variables simply do not occur together.

A correlation of 0 means that there is no relationship between the variables. For example if someone correlated the variable 'number of six-year-olds who could solve a Piagetian conservation task' with the variable 'number of prosocial acts in six-year-olds', they would almost certainly find a correlation of 0.

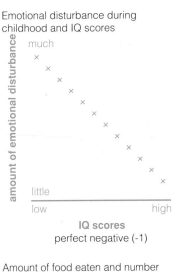

Emotional disturbance during childhood and IQ scores

amount of emotional disturbance

much

little

low   high

IQ scores
perfect negative (-1)

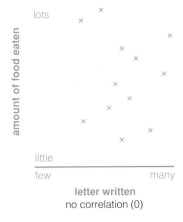

Amount of food eaten and number of letters written to friends

amount of food eaten

lots

little

few   many

letter written
no correlation (0)

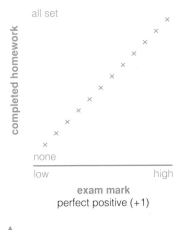

Amount of homework completed and exams passed

completed homework

all set

low   high

exam mark
perfect positive (+1)

▲
Three scattergrams

Scattergrams

Apart from expressing correlations as numbers, scientists also express them in pictures. The score each subject makes is plotted on a **scattergram**. The value of one variable is plotted on one axis (e.g. the number of years spent in an orphanage), and the value of the second variable (e.g. emotional stability) is plotted on the other.

Each × on the scattergram is the point where the pair of scores that each child made on the two dimensions named on the axes would cross. One of the children here spent three years in an orphanage and scored 50 per cent in the emotional stability test. Another child spent 11 years in the orphanage and only scored 10 per cent.

Three scattergrams to show correlations

The first **scattergram** shows an example of two variables which are perfectly negatively correlated. It shows the scores for the amount of emotional disturbance that 12 children suffered during their childhood, and their IQ scores as adults. The children who suffered the most disruption had the lowest IQ scores. So the greater the amount of the *emotional disturbance* variable, the less the amount of the IQ variable.

The second scattergram shows that the two variables 'amount eaten' and 'number of letters written' are not correlated at all. This is represented by a correlation of 0. Some of the subjects ate a lot, some ate a little. Some wrote many letters, some wrote few. The two variables are not statistically related.

The third scattergram shows that the two variables 'doing all of one's homework', and 'getting good results in tests' are perfectly positively correlated. The more homework each child did, the higher marks they achieved in exams.

There is something extremely important to be remembered about correlations. Correlations only show that two variables are statistically related. They do not prove that one variable causes the other. Another, third variable could cause them both. For example, the variable 'number of violent films watched' might correlate with 'amount of aggression shown by children'. A third variable which explains both these things, however, might be that the children's parents watch violent films and are aggressive. The children may be imitating their parents. Correlation can only describe a *statistical relationship* between two variables, it cannot explain how that relationship comes about. Psychologists often have to use correlational methods, so be careful that you do not confuse them with experiments. Of all the methods available to psychologists, experiments are the only ones that are sometimes able to show cause.

Correlation

1 Fill in five scores which might show the direction of the following scattergrams:
   (a) 'lots of stimulation' and 'extent of enquiring mind',
   (b) 'amount of darkness' and 'clarity of perception',
   (c) 'speed of running' and 'amount of children's musical knowledge'.

2 Complete this table by ticking the appropriate box to describe the correlation:

Type of correlation	Negative correlation	No correlation	Positive correlation
(a) 'lots of stimulation' and 'extent of enquiring mind'			
(b) 'amount of darkness' and 'clarity of perception'			
(c) 'speed of running' and 'amount of children's musical knowledge'.			

3 What two variables were the German researchers trying to correlate, in *Children's intelligence*? (see page 298)

Review
Correlation

Correlation is a statistical technique for measuring the extent to which two variables occur together. Positive correlation (up to +1) means that the more there is of one variable, the more there will be of another one. Negative correlation (down to –1) means that the greater amount that there is of one variable, the less there will be of another.

6 Some cautions in interpreting psychological research

We've looked at several of the main methods that psychologists use for gathering their information, and at the main ways in which they analyse and communicate it. By now you will have realised that none of the methods psychologists use for gathering information is perfect. There are three types of problem with their methods. The first consists of problems with subjects, the second involves problems with situations (and the researchers themselves), and the third concerns problems in drawing conclusions from the research.

Problems with subjects

These are to do with subject variables.
All children have different intellectual abilities, memory abilities, personalities, willingness to cooperate, desire to tell the truth, etc. Can we be sure that their participation is honest? The very fact that someone is being researched may alter their behaviour.

An extract from a fourteen-year-old girl's diary

MONDAY Five o'clock: Some lecturers from the university were visiting school today. They came into our class after lunch and asked if any of us fancied being in a psychology experiment. The guy who asked was really nice. I wanted to volunteer straight away, but Jane was shaking her head. At break she said she thought the lecturers were old and ugly. Everyone calls her boyfriend 'Gonzo', so what does she know? I managed to persuade her though; at least we'll be out of school for a day.

TUESDAY Just had tea: Jane said she'd changed her mind about doing the experiment. I had to promise her I'd go ice skating with her and Gonzo next week before she'd come. Ugh. I HATE ICE SKATING, and Gonzo is a creep.

WEDNESDAY 10 p.m.: Must get an early night tonight, I want to be fresh for the experiment in the morning. Jane's gone to the midweek disco. She's stupid because she won't be home 'till midnight.

THURSDAY Lunch time: Jane was really grumpy when I met her this morning. I wasn't going to let her spoil my day though. When we got to the psychology department the same guy who'd been at school met us. He explained that it was an experiment on 'perception'. We had to look through a hole into this machine which would flash three letters and a big number at us. Straight away we had to count backwards from the number we'd seen until he asked us what the letters had been. I thought it would be easy, but Jane needed it explaining again. This research must be really important, so I'm going to do my best this afternoon.

5 p.m.: Just got home. Had a great day. I got loads of my tests right. Hardly any of the others did though. Jane couldn't even count backwards half the time. Anyway, she split up with Gonzo last night so I don't have to go skating with them next week. BRILLIANT!

1 Write a paragraph which explains why this research may have been confounded. Include as many examples of confounding subject variables as you can find.

2 How was the sample of British children chosen in *Children's intelligence* on pages 298–9?

3 Do you think this produced a representative, typical cross-section of British seven- to 10-year-olds? Explain your answer.

4 Explain why the German sampling was better than the British attempt.

Problems with situations

These are to do with situational variables.

All the members of each experimental group must be tested under the same conditions and in the same situation as all the other members. If the weather is warmer, the place brighter, the other people friendlier, the time different, the background noise greater, etc., then these situational variables may affect the children's behaviour.

How Ss are used in the research can also alter their behaviour. Social psychologists have shown that people behave quite differently when they are being tested alone than they do when they are in groups. When in a group, people are more likely to agree with one another. People are less likely to say and do what they really think and feel if they know that other people are listening and watching.

One particular situational variable is the researchers themselves. Their behaviour towards the children may affect the children's behaviour. This is called *experimenter bias*, or *experimenter effects*. If an experimenter is in a bad temper, tired, or hungry, etc., and this shows in certain attitudes or behaviour, then this might affect how the children feel about doing the research.

Drawing conclusions from data

Before deciding finally to accept the findings of any particular research we might want to ask the following questions:

1 Was the sample representative of the population to which the results are to be generalised?

Review
Cautions

We can't always accept all of the findings from psychological research because subjects vary, situations vary, and there are problems with the way some research is designed.

2 Were the tests reliable? Research is described as reliable if it would show the same results if we repeated the test (using the same subjects) in the future.

3 Are the tests valid? (For example, does the research actually measure what it says it measures?) Many IQ tests, for example, are criticised for not measuring intelligence at all.

4 Many psychological studies can only show correlations between variables, but cannot say that one causes the other.

5 Scientists should never generalise from case studies, and it's never wise to apply to all members of any group the results of a study conducted on a small sample of it.

Problems with research

1 Write a paragraph which summarises the main problems people face when understanding the conclusions from psychological research.

2 The research described in *Children's intelligence* (on pages 298–9) is badly flawed. Outline as many of the differences between the British and German research as you can, and say why each makes the research unacceptable.

3 Write a report on the research described in *Children's intelligence* (on pages 298–9). Comment on as many of these things as possible:
   The type of research, the aim of the research, the methods used, the target population, the sample used, the procedures, the results, and the conclusions.

Background reading – Experimenter effects

An experiment by Rosenthal and Jacobson in Oak School, a Californian elementary school, showed how teachers affected the performance of some of their pupils. The teachers were told that the children were being given a new kind of intelligence test which could predict which pupils were about to improve very dramatically in their schoolwork. They didn't know that Jacobson and Rosenthal had randomly chosen 20 per cent of the children who would be high achievers. After a year those 20 per cent had developed considerably! Obviously the teachers must have behaved differently towards those children, although they were sure that they hadn't.

If you could secretly have observed this class during the year, what differences do you imagine you'd notice in the treatment of the 'bloomers' and the others?

Index